Beyond Zuccotti Park

FREEDOM OF ASSEMBLY AND
THE OCCUPATION OF PUBLIC SPACE

Edited by Ron Shiffman, Rick Bell,

Lance Jay Brown, and Lynne Elizabeth

with Anastassia Fisyak and Anusha Venkataraman

New Village Press • Oakland, CA

Published in the United States by
New Village Press
P.O. Box 3049
Oakland, CA 94609
(510) 420-1361
bookorders@newvillagepress.net
www.newvillagepress.net

New Village Press is a public-benefit, not-for-profit publishing venture of Architects/Designers/Planners for Social Responsibility.

In support of the Greenpress Initiative, New Village Press is committed to the preservation of endangered forests globally and advancing best practices within the book and paper industries. The printing papers used in this book are 100% recycled fiber, acid-free (Process Chlorine Free), and have been certified with the Forest Stewardship Council (FSC). Printed by Edwards Brothers Malloy of Ann Arbor.

Original paperback ISBN 978-1-61332-009-9
eBook ISBN 978-1-61332-011-2

Publication Date: September 2012

First Edition

Library of Congress Cataloging-in-Publication Data

Beyond Zuccotti Park : freedom of assembly and the occupation of public space / edited by Ron Shiffman... [et al.].
    p. cm.
  Includes index.
  ISBN 978-1-61332-009-9 (pbk. : alk. paper) — ISBN 978-1-61332-011-2 (ebook)
  1. Public spaces—Political aspects. 2. Assembly, Right of. 3. Civil rights. 4. Zoning, Exclusionary. I. Shiffman, Ron.
  HT153.B49 2012
  307.76—dc23 2012022472

Cover design by Lynne Elizabeth
Front and back cover photographs by Brennan Cavanaugh
Interior design and composition by Leigh McLellan Design

Beyond Zuccotti Park

i

Contents

Dedication   *ix*

Acknowledgments   *xi*

Foreword   *xiii*
Michael Kimmelman

Introduction   *xix*
Lance Jay Brown and Ron Shiffman

1 Occupy!

Occupying Public Space, 2011:
From Tahrir Square to Zuccotti Park   *3*
Karen A. Franck and Te-Sheng Huang

Occupy Wall Street, Social Movements,
and Contested Public Space   *21*
Benjamin Shepard

"A Stiff Clarifying Test Is in Order":
Occupy and Negotiating Rights in Public Space   *34*
Gregory Smithsimon

Being There   *49*
Wendy E. Brawer and Brennan S. Cavanaugh

Politics Out of Place: Occupy Wall Street
and the Rhetoric of "Filth"   61
  Julian Brash

To Occupy   67
  Saskia Sassen

The Office of the People   70
  Gan Golan

Some Unresolved Constitutional Questions   74
  Arthur Eisenberg

2 *Emplacing Equity and Social Justice*

Making Public, Beyond Public Space   89
  Jeffrey Hou

Freedom Corner: Reflections on a Public Space
for Dissent in a Fractured City   99
  Mindy Thompson Fullilove with Terri Baltimore

Occupying Dissent: A Conversation with Maya Wiley   112
  Ron Shiffman

Whose Voice: The Limited Participation
of People of Color in the Occupy Movement   125
  Roland V. Anglin

Emplacing Democratic Design   133
  Michael Rios

3 *Reimagining Public Space*

The Sidewalks of New York   143
  Michael Sorkin

Radical Imagination   146
  Caron Atlas

Room to Grow Something 156
Paula Z. Segal

Openhearted Cities 170
Lynne Elizabeth

Life and Death in Public Places 178
Nikki Stern

4 Public Space Over Time

The Grass Is Always Greener: A Brief History of Public
Space and Protest in New York City and London 187
Lisa Keller

The Romance of Public Space 197
Marshall Berman

Places that Matter: Zuccotti Park Before / After / Now 207
Alexander Cooper

Public Space and Its Disconnects 214
Rick Bell

Public Space Then and in the Future 236
Lance Jay Brown

Pushing Back Boundaries: How Social Movements
Are Redefining the Public Space 254
Sadra Shahab and Shirin Barghi

5 Responsive Change

5.1 Public Sector Agents of Change

Occupy and the Provision of Public Space:
The City's Responsibilities 265
Peter Marcuse

Is "Public Space" Possible? 271
David Burney

Making—and Governing—Places for Democracy   *277*
Brad Lander and Michael Freedman-Schnapp

Making Cities Work   *293*
Janette Sadik-Khan

5.2 *Designers and Developers as Agents of Change*

Blurring the Boundaries to Keep Public Space Public   *299*
Paul Broches

When Domestic Space Meets Civic Space:
A Case for Design Populism   *309*
Michael Pyatok

Shaping Public Space, Shaping Our City   *327*
Susan Chin

Public Space: Opening Streets and Sidewalks   *334*
Jonathan Marvel

Designed to Be Occupied   *339*
Signe Nielsen

POPS, Out of the Shadows: A Designer's Perspective   *351*
Thomas Balsley

Developing the Public Realm:
A Conversation with Jonathan Rose   *364*
Ron Shiffman

Programming Public Space:
A Conversation with Carlton Brown   *371*
Ron Shiffman with Anastassia Fisyak

A Call for Actions   *383*
Ron Shiffman and Jeffrey Hou

Contributors   *387*

Index   *397*

Dedication

We dedicate this book to our grandkids, their friends, and their generation. The actions we engage in today will build the foundation upon which they will be able to exercise their rights of assembly and free expression. Freedom of speech is more than being able to speak one's mind. If one is confined to only one way of thinking, then one's freedom of expression is limited; if one is denied access to education, then one's freedom of expression is limited; if one does not have exposure to the ideas of other social, economic, racial, and cultural groups, then one's freedom of expression is limited; if one is denied access to information and independent and accurate news coverage, then one's freedom of expression is limited. If we do not provide the real and virtual space for ideas to be debated, vetted, and questioned, we will be denying our children's children the rights we so dearly cherish.

This book is a tribute to those who summon us today to think about the spaces we have in our cities and in our lives and to discuss, formulate, and debate these thoughts. It goads us to rethink the policies that lead to the privatization of our politics, the privatization of our public places, and the privatization of our educational system. It inspires our planners, urban designers, and public policy makers to be creative and innovative. It stretches us to develop a new aesthetic derived from the way places we create function as well as the form that those places take. May this book begin the discourse and broaden the discussion on the important role of the public realm and how we can protect and enhance the liberties we value and so sincerely want to secure for our grandchildren—those born and those who are yet unnamed.

This book is for Jonah, Elijah, Jack, Mika, Erika, Sadie, Lucca, Marly, Sorella, Arissa, Zachary, Devin, Alexander, Jacob, and Hunter and to their generation of children throughout the world.

Acknowledgments

THIS BOOK IS the result of a co-operative effort of a great number of people whose common denominator is their commitment to the important role that public space, universal access, equity, and design can play to enhance democracy and promote freedom of expression. We would like to acknowledge the role of each of the essayists who contributed their time and ideas. Reading each of the contributor biographies is in and of itself an education in the role of place, design, and democracy.

Providing outstanding assistance to the editing team was Anastassia Fisyak, a Pratt graduate student who merged her past publishing experience with her commitment to First Amendment principles and urban planning. Anastassia was joined by Karen Kubey, who helped address some of the logistic needs of communicating with over three dozen authors. Anusha Venkatamaran, a talented Pratt alum, helped carry out some of the interviews and edit a few of the chapters that appear in this book. John Shapiro and Lacey Tauber of the Pratt Institute's Programs for Sustainable Planning and Development were supportive throughout. Dora Blount and Jessie Guiterrez worked with David Frisco to design and develop a video and other outreach material to assure that the message of this book will have a life in other media. Post-publication outreach efforts and the initial set of symposia that launched this entire effort owe their success to the work of the staff of the Center for Architecture in New York City, in particular, the work of Juliana Barton, Laura Trimble, and Rosamond Fletcher. Illya Azaroff, cochair of the Design for Risk and Reconstruction Committee, AIA New York Chapter, also joined in the design of post-publication activities.

A great thanks to Emily Sogner, Nina Mehta, Andrew Hiller, Jenn Nielsen, Liz Hynes, Ed Bear, Jordan Fletcher, and Matt Lepacek of May Day Radio; to Jessie Goldstein and the rest of the folks at Occuprint; and to Abigail Levine and everyone who generously agreed to work with the editors and authors of this book and to publicize the important role that space and place play in enhancing First Amendment rights. Special thanks to friends Roberta Gratz, Steven Goldsmith, Eve Baron, Eddie Bautista, Linda Cohen, Deborah Gans, Roger Katan, Tom Angotti, Elizabeth Yeampierre, Adam Friedman, Stuart Pertz, Daniel Goldstein, Shabnam Merchant, Chris Lazarus, Reverend Mutima Imani, the Honorable Letitia James, Congresswoman Nydia Velazquez, and the folks at FUREE who all helped in important ways. Much love and gratitude goes to Tom Bell who generously allowed the use of his photographs; to Fran Goldin, a community activist, who, along with Jane Jacobs, showed us the importance of understanding community and whose appearance at Zuccotti Park bridged generational divides and provided inspiration; to Elsie Richardson, who passed away before this book was completed, but who left her fingerprints all over this work; and to Irma Ostroff and Yvette Shiffman for lending their talents as in-house critics and providing the kind of welcome support that defies description.

Developmental editor for New Village Press Stefania De Petris deserves huge applause for her central role in shaping the manuscript. We wish to honor her acumen, focus, and kindness working with our contributors to bring out the best of each essay and keep the work as a whole on track. Line editor Laura Leone must be heartily thanked for her amazing concentration in correcting our language and punctuation and for her patience in placing late pictures. Much gratitude goes to the skill and giving spirit of graphic designer Leigh McLellan, and huzzahs go to Kayla Sussell for being a proofreading demon incarnate as an angel. Kudos go to indexer Sylvia Coates for shining despite impossible deadlines, and blessings go to the responsive and ever-reliable staff of printer Malloy Edwards, especially Bill Ralph and Stephanie Barker. Our appreciation extends to intern Ravi Venkatamaran, volunteer Kathleen Lanphier, assistant Emily Shurr, and adviser Laura Keresty for diligence in publicity.

We want to acknowledge the generous support of Ray Lifchez and the Nathan Cummings Foundation, and we send a heartfelt hurrah to supporter Amy Hagedorn, whose commitment to social, racial, economic, and environmental justice issues helped to launch this effort.

Foreword

Michael Kimmelman

THE OCCUPY WALL STREET move-
ment, with its encampments in Lower Manhattan, Washington, London, and many other cities around the world, proved that no matter how instrumental new media have become in spreading protest these days, nothing replaces people taking to the streets.

Anybody who can recall New York City on September 11, 2001 and during the days after will remember that hundreds of thousands of people went outside to gather in parks and squares and on the sidewalks. They didn't just retreat online. They sought out public spaces to be with each other. Our human instinct is to come together. People occupied those parks and squares and streets, hanging ribbons and photographs on fences, concocting makeshift memorials, gathering in clusters to talk and, in a sense, prove to each other that they belonged to a larger community, a greater city, that this community and this city endured, and that there was strength in numbers. They came together in public spaces to affirm solidarity in ways that online communication can't.

We tend to underestimate the political power of physical places. Then Tahrir Square comes along. Zuccotti Park, until the protests, was an obscure city-block-size downtown plaza with a few trees and concrete benches around the corner from Ground Zero and two blocks north of Wall Street on Broadway. A few hundred people with ponchos and sleeping bags put it on the map. Kent State, Tiananmen Square, the Berlin Wall: we use locales, edifices, architecture to house our memories and political energy. Politics troubles our consciences. But places haunt our imaginations, so we check in on Facebook and Twitter, but we make pilgrimages to Antietam, Auschwitz, and to the Acropolis, to gaze at rubble from the days of Pericles and Aristotle.

I thought of Aristotle, of all people, while I watched the Zuccotti Park demonstrators hold one of their general assemblies one day. In his *Politics*, Aristotle argued that the size of an ideal polis extended to the limits of a herald's cry. He believed that the human voice was directly linked to civic order. A healthy citizenry in a proper city required face-to-face conversation. It so happens that near the start of the protest, when the police banned megaphones at Zuccotti Park, they obliged demonstrators to come up with an alternative. "Mic checks" became the consensus mode of circulating announcements, spread through the crowd by people repeating, phrase by phrase, what a speaker had said to others around them, compelling everyone, as it were, to speak in one voice. It was like the old game of telephone, and painstakingly slow.

"But so is democracy," as Jay Gaussoin, a forty-six-year-old unemployed actor and carpenter who was among the protesters, put it to me. "We're so distracted these days, people have forgotten how to focus. But the 'mic check' demands not just that we listen to other people's opinions, but that we really hear what they're saying because we have to repeat their words exactly."

"It requires an architecture of consciousness," was Mr. Gaussoin's phrase.

What happens when privatization and the marketplace conflict with the public interest? How does a focus on the public good intersect with the preservation of democratic spaces and institutions? These were among the questions that the Occupy movement raised by virtue of occupying Zuccotti. But it wasn't just the simple act of occupation that elevated these questions beyond philosophy. It was the form that the occupation took. Much as it looked at first glance like a refugee camp, especially in the early morning, when the protesters were just emerging from their sleeping bags, Zuccotti Park became like a miniature polis, a little city in the making. That it happened also to be a private park is one of the most delicious and revealing subtexts of the story. Formerly called Liberty Park, the site was renamed in 2006 after John E. Zuccotti, chairman of Brookfield Office Properties, the park's owner. A zoning variance granted to Brookfield years ago requires that the park, unlike a public, city-owned one, remain open day and night, with few restrictions on its use.

This peculiarity of local zoning law—a loophole for such a park that private owners and public officials have hastily tried to close in the wake of

Zuccotti's occupation—turned an unexpected spotlight on the bankruptcy of so much of what, during the last couple of generations, has passed for public space in the United States. Most of it is token gestures by developers in return for erecting bigger, taller buildings. Think of the atrium of the I.B.M. tower on Madison Avenue and countless other places like it: "public" spaces that are not really public at all but quasi-public, policed by their landlords, who find a million excuses to limit their accessibility. Zuccotti, as an exception, revealed just how far we have allowed the ancient civic ideal of public space to drift from an arena of public expression and public assembly (Speakers' Corner in Hyde Park, say) to a commercial sop (the foyer of the Time Warner Center). City officials are forever closing streets and parks for celebratory events—parades and street fairs—but try getting a park or street closed for a political protest. This is partly because we don't really want these protests, not in our backyard anyway. Lisa Keller has pointed out that free speech in public space may be America's most undemocratic and rarely admitted NIMBY ("not in my backyard"). People want their streets and parks clean and quiet.

But what is the cost to the public good, to public discourse, and to civic freedom if the only way to spread one's message is to buy space? Occupy Wall Street, in part unintentionally, raised this question and others like it: where are the spaces in which we act as a community? Who governs them? Who decides on their design? Their use? And should we blur the controls, the boundaries, the authority, and the thresholds between public and private space, between streets and sidewalks?

One answer is that we need ambiguous spaces, multiuse spaces. Access to space breeds a feeling of ownership; ownership of empowerment, as Paul Broches has put it. But more than access, openness—or what Broches and others lately have taken to calling "sloppiness"—is the key to useful public space. From a design perspective, this means intentionally incomplete, and at least partly unplanned spaces that are completed in different ways by different users. But how do we create them?

Significantly, of course, the Occupy Wall Street protesters did not select the High Line or Times Square; they went to Zuccotti Park because all spaces are also symbolic. Zuccotti was up the street from Wall Street, in the shadow, the protesters believed, of corporate authority, and it was relatively compact. Occupiers across the country tended toward places like Zuccotti—places that could looked jammed and bustling with just a few hundred people, as opposed to, say, the Great Lawn, where the same size protest would have seemed insignificant. The comedy of Mitt Romney speaking before the Michigan caucus during the 2012 Republican nomination process in 65,000-seat Ford Field before an audience of 1,200 illustrated the point. The power of space extends to the ways space itself conspires to market a certain message, or subvert it.

As Jeffrey Hou notes, there are ultimately two kinds of public spaces: institutionalized spaces and "insurgent" spaces. Public space, Hou adds, must be "enacted" —occupied, used—for it to be truly public. It is this act of using it that makes it public, that makes it a real place. At the same time, any place can be occupied, taken over, despite the best attempts to design it so that protesters won't gather in it. A highway can be occupied if protesters really are willing to stop traffic. So can a bridge. The real question is not can a place be designed to prevent occupation but can a place be designed specifically for protest, or does the very designation of such a place as an official, sanctioned site for political action undercut its political and independent function? A healthy city has a robust diversity of public spaces: it needs destination places like Central Park, but these don't touch the daily life of most people the way neighborhood squares do. It happens that the grid that has defined and in many ways given birth to New York City's urban vitality had almost no squares or parks in its original plan, and generations of New Yorkers have had to carve them out of the grid, wrest them from its monotony. To the extent that the city has become more livable and humane in recent years, the improvement is attributable to the improved quality of the parks and the spread of public space along the waterfront and elsewhere. Public health and public space go hand in hand.

Living in Europe for several years, I often came across parks and squares, in Barcelona and Madrid, Athens and Milan, Paris and Rome, occupied by tent communities of protesters. Public protest and assembly were part of the Western European social compact that promised decent health care, housing, transportation, cultural programs, and schools in return for higher taxes. Maybe the difference in the United States, taxes aside, has something to do with our long-standing obsessions with automobiles and autonomy, with our predilection for isolationism, or with our preference for watching rather than participating. In Europe, the protests were about jobs, government rollbacks, and debt. As the euro crisis spread, they had increasingly to do with austerity measures, threatening the compact. That the message of the Zuccotti Park occupiers was fuzzy somewhat missed the point of the Occupy protest, I think. The encampment itself seemed to be the point to me.

"We come to get a sense of being part of a larger community," as Brian Pickett, a thirty-three-year-old adjunct professor of theater and speech at City University of New York and another of the protesters, put it to me. I found him during one afternoon sitting among the neat, tarpaulin-covered stacks of sleeping bags in a corner of the park. "It's important to see this in the context of alienation today. We do Facebook alone. But people are not alone here." And as a result, demonstrators also revealed themselves to each other. Egyptians described this phenomenon at Tahrir Square. Tea Partiers have talked about it, too. As with the post 9/11 gatherings, protesters don't just show the world a mass of people. They discover their own numbers—people with similar, if not identical, concerns. Imagine Zuccotti Park, one protester told me, as a Venn diagram of characters representing disparate political and economic disenchantments. The park was where their grievances overlap. It was literally common ground.

And it was obvious to me watching the crowd coalesce over several days that consensus emerged urbanistically, meaning that the demonstrators, who devised their own form of leaderless governance to keep the peace until the whole experiment fell apart, found unity in community. The governing process they chose was a bedrock message. It produced the outlines of a city, as I said. The protesters set up a kitchen for serving food; a legal desk and a sanitation department; a library of donated books; an area where the general assembly met; a medical station; a media center where people recharged their laptops using portable generators; and even a general store called the comfort center, stocked with donated clothing, bedding, toothpaste, and deodorant—like the food, all free for the taking.

That's where I found Sophie Theriault sorting through loads of newly arrived pants and shirts. A soft-spoken twenty-one-year-old organic farmer from Vermont, she had already spent many days and nights working as a volunteer. "We may not have all come here with the exact same issues in mind," she said, "but sharing this park day in and day out, night after night, becomes an opportunity for us to discover our mutual interests. We meet every night to talk about how to keep this place clean and sober, to keep it an emotionally, physically safe space for everyone. Consensus builds community."

Patrick Metzger, a twenty-three-year-old sound engineer and composer, echoed the thought: "From Web posts, you never get information about race, class, age—who people really are. Fox News talks about flakes and mobs. But you can see how complicated the mix really is: students and older people, parents with families, construction workers on their lunch break, unemployed Wall Street executives."

There were a few flakes, too, as at any political rally, and their numbers grew as did the agitators looking to undermine the occupation. But Mr. Metzger got it right. The protesters' diversity, at least for a while and during the day, was intrinsic to the protest's resilience. Not since 9/11 had so many people been asking, "Have you been there?" "Have you seen it?" about any place in Manhattan.

The occupation of the virtual world along with Zuccotti Park was, of course, what jointly propelled the Occupy Wall Street movement, and neither would have been so effective without the other. That said, on the ground was where the protesters built an architecture of consciousness.

Introduction

Lance Jay Brown and Ron Shiffman

ON SEPTEMBER 17, 2011, the tide of political thought in the United States changed dramatically. Our attention as a nation shifted from being consumed by fears of increasing fiscal deficits to profound discontent with policies that favored one economic class over another—the 1% over the 99%. A growing resentment over policies and actions that favored Wall Street over Main Street, lenders over homeowners and students, investors over workers, and polluters over the environment finally found its voice. Occupy Wall Street (OWS) became a household name, embraced by some, rejected by others, and perplexing to far more. Stories in the media emerged that focused on people, primarily young and idealistic, exercising their right to assemble, their right to petition their government. They occupied Zuccotti Park in New York, and others across the country occupied similar spaces. These "occupiers" were making their voices heard, and the substance of their message reframed the political discourse underway. Influenced by the events in Tunisia and in Tahrir Square in Egypt, and by the scores of encampments organized by the Spanish Indignants throughout Spain in May 2011, they sought not only to express their frustration but also to voice their aspirations. In many ways the "occupiers" echoed the revolutionary cry of the Arab Spring, and, perhaps without knowing it, they also reflected other events—the occupation of Rothschild Boulevard in Tel Aviv and scores of demonstrations in other cities that focused not on overthrowing a dictatorship but on making more perfect the promise of democracy and correcting the inequities and injustices that undermine social life. In many ways their actions were a harbinger of what was to take place in a multitude of places both known and unknown, in areas that were traditionally mainstream and conservative as well as those with a more progressive history. Even before OWS, in cities like Madison and other cities in Wisconsin and Ohio, workers had taken to the streets to fight back, and they had begun efforts to recall legislators and governors who were threatening to reduce wages and curtail the bargaining rights of teachers, municipal workers, and union members. Those protests had engaged in tactics ranging from electoral politics to mass rallies to the occupation of public places.

Plazas, squares, and piazzas are often a site of education, interaction, organizing, and action. However, the connective tissue of our communities—the sidewalks and the pathways—also function as places for encounters, communication, and action to take place. That was the case one November morning when two of us, walking in opposite directions, happened to meet on a sidewalk in Manhattan. This chance encounter sparked an intense exchange of views on the events occurring around us. The idea that New York City, in a country that professes to uphold democracy, should have so few, if any, public places for assembly was unacceptable. The fact that what precious public spaces exist are programmatically restricted, while others are privatized and subject to either convoluted regulations or the whims of their owners, was of great concern to us as well as to many of our fellow citizens. Together we decided to alter our intended paths and walked instead directly to the Center for Architecture (CFA) in New York City's Greenwich Village.

The Center sits across from a statue of populist New York City mayor Fiorello LaGuardia with his open arms outstretched. The statue reflects LaGuardia's commitment to the needs of poor and working people and his belief in the role that government could play in addressing those needs. Indeed, La Guardia by virtue of what he espoused and how he acted could be considered a permanent occupier, if only his actions and deeds were better known. La Guardia was a strong advocate of freedom of expression and the right to assemble, and as mayor he had ordered police to restrain themselves in the face of confrontation. What better place, we thought, to hold an open discussion about these issues. Rick Bell, director of the CFA, embraced our idea immediately, and we had a third partner plus a place to bring together a larger community to wrangle these issues. We also wanted to reach out beyond New York and arranged to have the event live streamed, in essence marrying the physical space and the virtual space to communicate the ideas and perspectives emanating from the forum. The collected work that follows builds upon the discussion begun that day.

Beyond Zuccotti Park is a metaphor designed to enable us to engage in a dialogue about enhancing our democracy. Ours is a pluralistic and diverse society often divided among ethnic, racial, religious, and class lines. What we have sought to do in the pages that follow is to weave a delicate balance between our individual liberties and our collective needs and to explore how we can collectively leaven our democracy with principles of social, political, and economic justice. In a pluralistic society democracy is and must be more than merely the rule of the majority. Majority rule must be enhanced by respect for and adherence to the diversity of needs and interests of all people and by the equal protection of their inalienable rights. In particular, given the peculiar spatial nature of recent protests around the world, we focus on the role that public space can play in attaining that objective.

The essays that follow create a kaleidoscope of the many ways in which public places allow us not only to express our needs but also to form what and who we are. These are spaces of social interaction that enable us to organize, learn, and share with one another; the spaces in which we can confront our fears and craft the political agendas that will enable us to be a better people. Access to those spaces is often in jeopardy and at times threatened by public and private policies. The contributors to this volume explore these threats from place to place, offering insights into useful agendas to govern our programs and policies and giving guidance to our advocacy.

Like our complex and pluralistic society, when taken together, the essays provide a diverse and emerging picture of the complex world we live in. They offer subtle and differing interpretations of comparable phenomena that yield a more important understanding of how we should or should not proceed. Our purpose is to unleash discourse about public space, to examine policies and codes of practice, and to engage decision makers, design practitioners, artists, activists, and citizens in enhancing public space for a multiplicity of roles—especially the roles it plays in strengthening our democracy.

The essays not only describe how public space facilitates civic engagement, but also how it can provide the opportunity for the content of that civic engagement to be jointly developed and refined—without ignoring the difficult question of who experiences the freedom to speak and who does not.

We do not focus here on the many diverse issues the Occupy movement has raised in this country and beyond, but rather on the physical arena Occupy actors and all citizens perform from. We focus on the right to social inclusion and the right to express one's grievances and to pursue one's aspirations—in essence, on the right to fully exercise one's democratic freedom.

We hope that this book can contribute to the continuation of a discussion that needs to take place and indeed has taken place in various forms across different times and places. This book is part of a greater advocacy effort to assure our constitutional rights to assemble and dissent in public space, a right that is foundational to the current Occupy movement and to the idea of a democratic country. It is a base upon which we can nurture our civic health and, in turn, assure an informed and enduring and just government by the people. In particular, our book and related civic discussion investigate the ways in which the design and use of public spaces not only serve civic engagement, but also provide vehicles to help develop and support what emerges from that engagement.

This book's publication date aligns with the 11th anniversary of the attack on the World Trade Center and the Pentagon and the downing of Flight 93. We have organized a series of post-publication discussions, exhibitions, and events that acknowledge and examine the lingering pain, concerns, and fear elicited by the WTC devastation and explore ways we can begin to build the public understanding that so many called for in the immediate aftermath. We are taking up those goals of listening and healing that were set aside during the past decade of war making—a decade that saw social and economic disparities intensify and our democratic institutions assaulted. This book is intended to further public exchange of views and contribute to efforts to redress the inequalities that divide us and rebuild faith in our democracy. May this book also stimulate readers to join with others in the places and spaces that they occupy to achieve the goals of a more just and equitable society.

———————————

Note: the opinions expressed in this volume are solely those of the individual contributing authors and are not necessarily shared by the other contributors, the editors, or the publisher.

1

Occupy!

Occupying Public Space, 2011

FROM TAHRIR SQUARE TO ZUCCOTTI PARK

Karen A. Franck and Te-Sheng Huang

OVER THE COURSE OF 2011, thousands of people in cities around the world occupied public space in political protest. In democratic societies and repressive authoritarian regimes alike, citizens made their concerns internationally known through their extended, joint physical presence in central urban squares and plazas. In some cases, the demands were specific, such as the resignation of President Hosni Mubarak in Egypt or the ouster of the monarchy in Bahrain; in Spain and particularly in the United States, the issues of concern were multiple and diverse. In nearly every case, local police or the military eventually forced the demonstrators to leave. In all cases, at least some violence occurred and demonstrators were injured; in the Middle East, demonstrators died. The occupying of public space in 2011 for political ends at the risk of arrest, injury, and worse, demonstrates how public space can still become "loose" (Franck and Stevens 2007) or "insurgent" (Hou 2010).

In this essay, we compare four urban spaces that were occupied in 2011: Tahrir Square in Cairo; Pearl Square in Manama, Bahrain; Plaça de Catalunya in Barcelona; and Zuccotti Park in New York City. We briefly look at their histories, their design features, and the activities they hosted in 2011. Then we take a more detailed look at the design and use of Zuccotti Park.[1] In all four cities, the intensive, creative use of urban public space as a tool

---

1. Information about the foreign cases is taken from published articles and online sources, an interview with a protestor from Tahrir Square, and Karen Franck's observations of Plaça Catalunya in late June 2011. For Zuccotti Park, online sources supplement the authors' own observations from September through November 2011.

3

Communicating and food distribution, Zuccotti Park, New York City. *Photos by Karen Franck (left) and Te-Sheng Huang (right)*

of political action was remarkable. While virtual communication via social media was essential to the planning and ongoing coordination of the demonstrations, the presence of significant numbers of demonstrators in a single physical space played an equally important role, particularly for reaching a much larger, international audience. While communicating to the public and to each other was essential, occupying public space over time also required that demonstrators organize the space and the provision of shelter, food, and security. As shown in the images of Zuccotti Park, communication and the tasks of daily life occurred side by side.

Four Occupied Spaces

Of the four public spaces described in this essay, Tahrir Square in the center of Cairo is the largest, functioning as a transit hub for metro, buses, and cars. A great many streets lead to the square from different parts of the city. Its form is loosely defined and comprises several different spaces, including a very busy traffic circle and a large construction site. Significant buildings—the headquarters of the Arab League and of Mubarak's National

Democratic Party, the Hilton, and the Omar Makram Mosque—border the space without enclosing it. A grassy plaza in front of the Egyptian Museum was once a popular meeting place but in the 1970s was enclosed with a construction fence as a means of subdividing the space and preventing assembly (Elsahed 2011).

Inspired by Hausmann's modernization of Paris, Khedive Ismail established the square as an open space in 1865 in his efforts to modernize Cairo (AlSayyad 2011). The square has long been the site of political protest: in 1919, Egyptians demonstrated against British rule and again in 1946 and

Pearl Square, Manama, Bahrain
Feb. 14 – Mar. 16, 2011

Plaça de Catalunya, Barcelona
May 15 – June 29, 2011

Zuccotti Park, New York City
Sep. 17 – Nov. 15, 2011

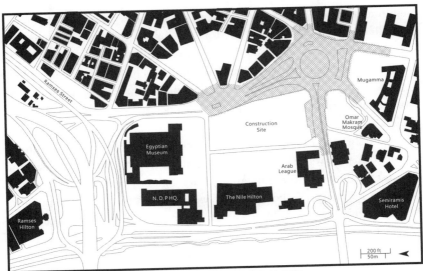

Tahrir Square, Cairo, Jan. 25 – Feb. 11, 2011

Occupied Public Space in Manama, Barcelona, New York City, and Cairo. *Courtesy of Google Maps, Google Earth, and Thompson 2011*

1951. Further demonstrations were held in 1977 against rising food prices, in 2001 in sympathy with the Palestinian Intifada, in 2001 against the US invasion of Iraq, and in 2006 in solidarity with Lebanon under attack from Israel. All these demonstrations involved significant risk, and many resulted in injuries and death; none lasted long (Taher 2012).

In January 2011, as many as three-hundred thousand demonstrators and possibly more gathered in the square on particular days and, despite the risks of injury and death, maintained their hold on the space. To protect themselves from anti-Mubarak forces, the occupiers barricaded streets to the square and operated checkpoints to review people's identification cards and to search for weapons. People waited in two lines to pass through these check points: women in one, to be searched by women, and men in the other, to be searched by men. After newcomers passed through the checkpoint on Ramses Street, occupiers warmly welcomed them with cheers and singing.[2] Since February 11, when Mubarak was ousted, the square has continued to be site of demonstrations.

In February 2011, Pearl Square, also called Pearl or Lulu Roundabout, was a grassy traffic circle accommodating four large roads in the heart of Manama, the capital of Bahrain, located close to the central market, the marina, and a large apartment complex. Its iconic status arose from the monument built on the traffic circle in 1982 to honor the first summit meeting of the Gulf Cooperation Council (GCC) to be held in Bahrain. The towering Pearl Monument was composed of six curved beams representing the six members of the council which held, at the top, a large cement pearl symbolizing Bahrain's history of pearl cultivation. At the base was a pool. The monument became a symbol of Bahrain, appearing on its half-dinar coins (Reisz 2011).

On February 14, Pearl Square, as one of Bahrain's largest and most symbolic spaces, was a good site for demonstrators to gather and demand the ouster of the country's monarchy. After a bloody crackdown by the city police on February 17, the protestors were allowed to return, staying until March 16 when Bahrain Defense forces along with military forces from the GCC and Saudi Arabia evacuated and bulldozed the encampment. On March 18, the monument was razed; then the traffic circle was removed and

---

2. Y. El Barry, in discussion with the authors, March 7, 2012.

replaced with traffic lights, eliminating any space for gathering that was free of cars. To remove any semantic association between the former square and the protest movement, the new space was renamed Al Farooq Junction. On February 14, 2012, security forces prevented marchers from returning to the junction, which remains cordoned off. Into 2012, subsequent protest marches have filled major streets in Bahrain but were prevented from reaching the new junction (AJE 2011; Mitchell 2011a).

Like Tahrir Square, Plaça de Catalunya functions as a traffic hub in the center of Barcelona, being the starting point for two of Barcelona's major streets (La Rambla and Passeig de Gracia) and hosting a great many bus lines and, below ground, four metro lines and one regional train station. Also like Tahrir, it was envisioned as part of an urban modernization plan in the mid-nineteenth century although it was not built until the twentieth century based on the design idea of Josep Puig I Cadafalch (Permanyer 2011).

Its design, however, is radically different from Tahrir's, being a clearly defined open space enclosed by streets and monumental buildings on all sides. These buildings include the department store El Corte Ingles, banks, hotels, and the historic Café Zurich. Unlike many European squares, the center of the plaza is open. Fountains and sculptures, mature trees, and some grassy areas are located around the periphery, leaving the central paved area empty, encircled by benches.

Starting on May 21, 2011, the plaza, along with public spaces in cities throughout Spain, became a site of a movement variously called Real Democracy NOW or the Indignants, which responded to problems of unemployment, increased costs of education, reductions in social benefits, and political corruption. Plaça de Catalunya is regularly used for political demonstrations (with permits), and is where thousands of fans of the Barca football team gather to celebrate victories. It was the expectation of such a celebration on May 28 that police gave as a justification for forcefully clearing the square of demonstrators on May 27, using rubber bullets and truncheons and injuring many. After the square had been cleaned, protestors returned and, with signs reading "No to violence," blocked access to many rowdy and often violent football fans (Tremlett 2011). Occupiers remained in the square until police moved them out in late June.

Of these four spaces of revolution, Zuccotti Park, the original site of the Occupy Wall Street movement, is the smallest and also the one where demonstrators raised the greatest variety of political, social, and economic issues. Located three blocks north of Wall Street, the park is bordered by four streets; the two largest are Broadway to the east and Trinity Place to the west. Zuccotti Park is also the only one of the four spaces described in this essay that is privately owned. U.S. Steel, the original owner of the building immediately to the north, built the park in 1968 in order to receive permission from the New York City Planning Department to add additional floors to the building beyond the existing height restriction (Kayden et al. 2000). The park, then called Liberty Plaza Park, was a popular pedestrian route between Wall Street and the World Trade Center, with people sitting there in warm weather (Kayden et al. 2000). After being covered in debris from the September 11, 2001 attack on the World Trade Center and then used as a storage area for heavy equipment during the recovery efforts, the park underwent an eight-million-dollar renovation in 2006 funded by Brookfield Properties, the current owner, and was renamed Zuccotti Park. Subsequently, the park was the site of several 9/11 anniversary ceremonies. It remains a popular route for pedestrians in Lower Manhattan and now, with many more people living in that part of town, it is also popular with families (LMCCC 2005).

From September 17, 2011 onward, the park served as a place of demonstration and encampment for Occupy Wall Street as well as a launching site for marches to Wall Street, City Hall Park, Foley Square, and Times Square. The park attracted hundreds of occupants who stayed the night and hundreds more who came during the day. Pedestrian traffic around the square continued to be heavy. As at Plaça de Catalunya, an officially stated need to clean the park (from Brookfield Properties) was the justification for the police's public announcement that the park would be evacuated on October 14. But under pressure from about twenty New York City council members and New York state senators, Brookfield cancelled the evacuation. Occupiers then agreed to keep the park clean and safe themselves (Moynihan and Buckley 2011). On November 15, at 1 a.m. with no warning, the police cleared all protestors in a very carefully planned raid under klieg lights, arresting some who resisted; the sanitation department collected anything left behind; and barricades were placed to limit access to the park (Baker and Goldstein 2011). The next day, a state supreme court judge upheld Brookfield's regulations against camping, setting up tents, and lying down (Baker and Goldstein 2011), discouraging any large-scale reoccupation of the park.

Manner of Occupying

The manner of occupying public space for political protest shows many similarities across the four cities. In all cases, except Zuccotti Park, the installation of a stage, microphones, and loudspeakers allowed for communicating to the large number of demonstrators within the space. Tahrir Square had two stages and a TV screen; Pearl Square occupiers had a satellite TV connection (AJE 2011; Fathi 2011; Mitchell 2011a; Yagopartal 2011). In New York, the demonstrators, following the police ban on loudspeakers or bullhorns, adopted their own mic-check system: the speaker paused after every few words, waiting as the crowd conveyed those words to others on the periphery, through successive waves of repetition.

Handmade signs and posters were evocative and plentiful. In Tahrir Square, the metal shutters of retail spaces became the canvases for a "gallery."[3] In Plaça de Catalunya, posters were hung on slack lines stretched across the square between trees; statues were decorated with words, clothing, and signs (Yagopartal 2011). In Zuccotti Park, demonstrators provided materials for people to make signs, which were then carried or held. The three legs of the red sculpture by Mark di Suvero were decorated with a few signs, but later, after a protester attempted to climb it, the sculpture was barricaded and remained untouched. On Trinity Place, the Seward Johnson sculpture was frequently decorated with signs and also a mask. Both Zuccotti Park and Plaça de Catalunya sported libraries and information desks (Yagopartal 2011).

Demonstrators' manner of living day and night in an outdoor public space showed similarities across the four spaces as well. Blue tents and tarpaulins were common everywhere, even after the city government banned "camping" in Zuccotti Park in October (the regulation was not enforced until November) (Kayden 2011). In Plaça de Catalunya, demonstrators stretched hammocks between the trees and built at least one tree house. Free food, donated by supporters, was available in all four spaces; in Zuccotti Park, people could also get free clothing and sleeping bags. Recycling was adopted there, in Tahrir Square, and possibly elsewhere, and demonstrators organized teams to clean the spaces. Zuccotti Park was the only occupied space without portable toilets on site, which the city also forbid, so until November 4, most

---

3. Y. El Barry, in discussion with the authors, March 7, 2012.

The J. Seward Johnson statue with mask, Zuccotti Park, New York City. *Photo by Karen Franck*

The Library, Zuccotti Park, New York City. *Photo by Karen Franck*

Camping at Zuccotti Park, New York City. *Photo by Te-Sheng Huang*

demonstrators relied on nearby restaurants. Then three portable toilets were donated to the protestors and installed at a private loading dock four blocks away (Shapiro 2011). In Tahrir and Pearl Squares, one could get a haircut and receive medical care in the nearby Omar Makram Mosque (Fathi 2011; Filiz 2011; Mitchell 2011b); in Zuccotti Park, a medical section was set up to provide first-aid and massages.

Despite the seriousness of the demonstrators' concerns and the risks to life and limb they faced, expressions of joy, pleasure, and humor were apparent in all cities. Singing, chanting, and playing instruments were common; a wedding took place in Tahrir Square; several demonstrators in New York donned masks and costumes to make their points (AJE 2011; Filiz 2011; Mitchell 2011b; Yagopartal 2011). People pursued daily routines, both mundane and spiritual. In Tahrir Square, some people jogged; in Plaça de Catalunya, demonstrators planted vegetables. In Zuccotti Park, large and small groups chanted and meditated; others did yoga.

In New York City and Barcelona, the occupied spaces were contiguous to the surrounding, heavily trafficked sidewalks. In New York, the activities of the demonstrators were immediately adjacent to the public sidewalks and often extended onto them. It was very easy for passersby to see what was

Painting in Zuccotti Park, New York City. *Photo by Karen Franck*

happening, to stop, to talk, to listen, and to enter the park and make their own signs. And they frequently did so. In Barcelona, such a close relationship between adjacent sidewalks and the occupied space was attenuated by the trees on the periphery of the plaza and by the demonstrators' concentration of activities within the center, but passersby and supporters could still easily enter the plaza without having to cross any streets. In Manama, to enter the occupied space one had to cross streets, and in Cairo, one had to pass though a security checkpoint. In both cities, the encampment spread beyond the boundaries of the square.

Evolution and Negotiation of an Occupation: Zuccotti Park

Since the park is a privately owned public space originally built in 1968 under New York City's Bonus Incentive Program, the current owner, Brookfield Properties, is required to make it accessible to the public twenty-four hours a day, seven days a week, and the police have no authority to remove people unless a law is broken (Kayden 2011). After the organizing group for Occupy Wall Street found that their first choice, One Chase Plaza, also a privately owned public space, was closed to passersby, they chose Zuccotti Park for its similar features: size, proximity to Wall Street, and the lack of an evening curfew common to city owned parks.

Up through early October, the park was sparsely populated, with plenty of room for people to move through on a designated path. Most speeches and visual communications to passersby were on the Broadway side; individual demonstrators stood along the sidewalk holding up signs, sometimes dressed in costume. Demonstrators also stood or sat on the granite walls that partly enclose the park on the north and south sides, particularly at the corners. Along all the sidewalks and inside the park, visitors and journalists, of all ages and from different countries, engaged in intense conversations with the demonstrators. In September and early October, ample amounts of cardboard, paint, and markers were available on the north and east sides, and all kinds of people, visitors included, made a great variety of signs and pictures. Eventually silk-screening and spray-painting equipment were used to print slogans and images of OWS on T-shirts to be sold to raise funds. After the middle of October, the sign painting area was replaced with tents, but the silk screening and spray painting continued.

Staffed information desks moved from one location to another, sometimes making use of the existing granite tables. The Information Center, always in the same location, was divided into "Information" and "Press." From September until late October, when they were removed by the fire department, six gas-fed generators powered laptop computers in the Information Center (Lemire and Boyle 2011). Next to the Information Center, a library section steadily grew in size and organization, as tables were added and books were arranged by subject matter. Meetings of the General Assembly and committees were held in different locations, including on the steps leading down from Broadway and in an enclosed, privately owned public space at 60 Wall Street (Gimein 2011).

At the beginning, people slept without shelter primarily in the western section of the park and daytime visitors would often see occupants lying on mattresses or napping during the daytime, possibly with a dog nestled next to them. Over time, as more people joined the encampment, personal

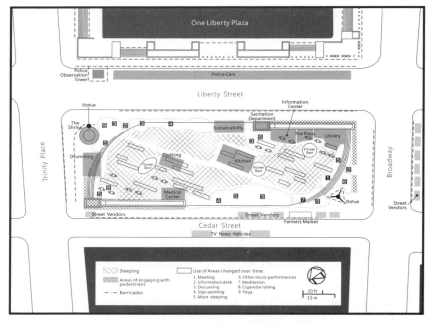

Use of Zuccotti Park, New York City, from September through November 2011. *Courtesy of Google Maps, Google Earth, Saget and Tse 2011, and Franck's and Huang's observations*

belongings in suitcases and knapsacks accumulated in great heaps, but a pathway through the park was kept open. In early October, tents began to appear and eventually, when most of the park was taken up with tents placed very close together, its appearance changed to that of a densely settled encampment, with a narrow, crowded pathway that became ever less welcoming and more difficult to maneuver through.

The kitchen area, consistently located in the center of the park, grew in size and became more sophisticated in its configuration as more tables, metal storage cabinets, and a canopy of tarpaulins were added. Donated food was offered at regular meal times to all who came (Gordinier 2011). A plastic container filled with gravel and topped with plants, demonstrating how gray water from the kitchen can be filtered and used to water plants, was originally placed next to the kitchen but was later moved to the sustainability area. Once a sanitation committee was organized, an area called the "Sanitation Department" with a recycling bin and cleaning materials was set up near the Information Center. After the fire department removed

Generating electricity at Zuccotti Park, New York City. *Photo by Te-Sheng Huang*

the generators, it was in this area that volunteers rode two stationary bicycles to generate electricity. Like the kitchen and library areas, the area for donated clothing grew in size and organization—from an assortment of boxes to clothes hanging on metal stands and arranged by type.

A rich variety of other activities contributed to the liveliness and intensity of life in the park. Early on, drummers gathered on top of the steps leading down to the sidewalk on the western edge of the park, which served as a kind of stage. However, the continuous drumming became a problem for residents in the neighborhood, and eventually, through negotiations with the local community board, the drumming was restricted to certain periods of the day, two times a day for two hours (Buckley 2011). It was also on the west

Drumming at Zuccotti Park, New York City. *Photo by Te-Sheng Huang*

side that an altar was established and became the site of yoga sessions. At different times, a guitar player, a baroque music ensemble, and a meditation group were observed on the far eastern edge of the park.

We, along with others, observed a growing difference between the two sides of the park: participants and activities more directly connected to OWS were located on the east side, while people more engaged in just enjoying the opportunities this occasion offered were on the west side (Packer 2011; Siegel 2011). Or, as one person walking by was heard to comment, "The punks are on this side, the political science majors are on the other side." As the park became more crowded with tents and belongings, and this difference in population and orientation became more apparent, we felt less comfortable entering the park. The atmosphere changed. It was not surprising to learn from news reports at the end of October that homeless people and recently released prisoners from Rikers Island had joined the encampment, finding there free food, clothing, shelter, and the lively company of others (Siegel 2011).

The New York City police kept careful watch over the park, lining the northern edge of the plaza with police cars and installing a watchtower at the corner of Liberty Street and Trinity Place. To keep people off the adjacent streets, police placed metal barricades along the street-edge of the sidewalk on the north and east sides of the park and later on the west side as well. Eventually, two sets of barricades were set up on the west side, along Trinity Place, creating an enclosed route for pedestrians who were sometimes urged by the police to "keep moving." Barricades also enclosed the linear plaza around One Liberty Plaza. From an observer's point of view, the number of police officers and police cars seemed excessive but not surprising given the police department's excessive use of force in previous demonstrations, including bicycle rides of Critical Mass and during the 2004 Republican Convention. The overriding concern appears to be the preservation of a high level of public order over all else, including the right to free speech.

Protestors' manner of occupying Zuccotti Park was eminently adaptive, responding quickly to particular site conditions (e.g., weather, increasing amounts of donated food and supplies, and increasing numbers of participants) and to outside constraints (e.g., the rule against loudspeakers or bull horns, the request from the community board to limit the drumming, and Brookfield's concern about sanitary conditions). From the beginning, it was a continuously *negotiated* use of public space, with the negotiations eventually extending to court cases contesting the enforcement of new regulations.

Dissent in Public Space

In all four cities, the spaces of dissent were simultaneously demonstration spaces, demonstration headquarters, and encampments. The occupying of a *physical* space gave these political movements international visibility through the transmission of detailed and evocative images in the media. At the same time, participants could hold planned and impromptu discussions of what to do next and how to do it. The role that public, physical space played in dissent around the world illustrates its continued, vital importance in the pursuit of democracy (Parkinson 2012). Notably, demonstrators made creative use of what features they found in the space. They also demonstrated organizational skill, and patience, in managing the activities within the space and communicating to the world, despite the difficulties and serious dangers they faced.

In New York City, demonstrators remained determined to maintain the nonhierarchical structure of OWS, to make decisions by consensus, and to remain inclusive of all comers even when the diversity of people living in the space created additional challenges. Occupying a public space over time allowed OWS demonstrators to enact, in public view, what they believe. They raised public awareness of issues of economic inequity making them a topic of public discourse, including during the 2011/2012 presidential campaign. Even though the movement became far less visible once OWS encampments were removed from public spaces in various cities throughout the country and so received far less attention from the media, the issue of economic inequity continued to be widely discussed (Schmidt 2012). OWS's use of public space is an example of the kind of disorder that Lynn Staeheli (2010) identifies as a powerful tool for airing conflict and fostering democracy.

The occupation of Zuccotti Park in fall 2011 also exemplifies a historically rooted and widespread phenomenon in the US: the management of public dissent through laws, regulations, city permits, police practices, and court cases (Mitchell and Staeheli 2005). Demonstrators were legally able to occupy the space because of existing regulations about its use. Eventually, new rules were adopted; those rules were upheld by a court decision, and the police were then able to move the protestors out. The new rules were again challenged in court in the winter of 2012. The tension between citizens' use of streets and squares to express dissent and authorities' exertion of control to maintain public order will continue—in public spaces and in courts of law in the US. If anything, Occupy Wall Street has reinvigorated this historical conflict.

References

Al Jazeera English (AJE). 2011. *Bahrain: Shouting in the Dark*. Al Jazeera documentary. http://www.youtube.com/watch?v=Lmg1N1AKfFc.

AlSayyad, N. 2011. "A history of Tahrir Square." Harvard University Press Blog, April 1. http://harvardpress.typepad.com/hup_publicity/2011/04/a-history -of-tahrir-square.html.

Baker, A., and J. Goldstein. 2011. "After an earlier misstep, a minutely planned raid." *New York Times*, November 15. http://www.nytimes.com/2011/11/16/ nyregion/police-clear-zuccotti-park-with-show-of-force-bright-lights-and -loudspeakers.html.

Buckley, C. 2011. "For annoyed neighbors, the beat drags on." *New York Times*, November 13. http://www.nytimes.com/2011/11/14/nyregion/for-neighbors -of-zuccotti-park-and-ground-zero-beat-drags-on.html.

Elshahed, M. 2011. "Tahrir Square: Social media, public space." *Places*, February 27. http://places.designobserver.com/feature/tahrir-square-social-media-public -space/25108/.

Fathi, Y. 2011. "In Egypt's Tahrir Square: Life is a battlefield." *Ahram Online*, February 8. http://english.ahram.org.eg/NewsContent/1/64/5187/Egypt/Politics-/ In-Egypts-Tahrir-Square-Life-is-a-battlefield.aspx.

Filiz. 2011. "Coming back to LIFE at Tahrir Square." *Medicine Words*, February 13. http://www.medicinewords.org/2011/02/13/coming-back-to-life-at-tahrir -square/.

Franck, K. A., and Q. Stevens, eds. 2007. *Loose Space: Possibility and Diversity in Urban Life*. New York: Routledge.

Gimein, M. 2011. "60 Wall Street: The real headquarter of OWS." *Business Week*, October 26. http://www.businessweek.com/finance/occupy-wall-street/ archives/2011/10/60_wall_street_the_real_headquarters_of_ows.html.

Gordinier, J. 2011. "Want to get fat on Wall Street? Try protesting." *New York Times*, October 11. http://www.nytimes.com/2011/10/12/dining/protesters-at-occupy -wall-street-eat-well.html?pagewanted=all.

Hou, J., ed. 2010. *Insurgent Public Space: Guerrilla Urbanism and the Remaking of Contemporary Cities.* New York: Routledge.

Kayden, J. S. 2011. "Meet me at the plaza." *New York Times*, October 19. http://www.nytimes.com/2011/10/20/opinion/zuccotti-park-and-the-private-plaza-problem.html?_r=1.

Kayden, J. S., New York City Department of City Planning, and Municipal Art Society of New York. 2000. *Privately Owned Public Space: The New York City Experience.* New York: John Wiley.

Lemire, J., and C. Boyle. 2011. "Firefighters, police raid Zuccotti Park for generators, gas canisters." *NY Daily News*, October 29. http://articles.nydailynews.com/2011-10-29/news/30337956_1_canisters-meeting-protest-generators.

Lower Manhattan Construction Command Center (LMCCC). 2005. "Liberty Plaza Park Turns Over a New Leaf." http://www.lowermanhattan.info/news/liberty_park_plaza_turns_38704.aspx.

Mitchell, T. 2011a. "Part 1: The roundabout clearance." Blog entry, December 4. http://tonydmitchell.wordpress.com/2011/12/04/hello-world/.

———. 2011b. "Part 3: Aftermath and social media." Blog entry, December 8. http://tonydmitchell.wordpress.com/2011/12/08/garhain-uprising-part-3-aftermath-and-social-media/.

Mitchell, D., and L. A. Staeheli. 2005. "Permitting protest: Parsing the fine geography of dissent in America." *International Journal of Urban and Regional Research* 29 (4): 796–813.

Moynihan, C., and C. Buckley. 2011. "Cleanup of Zuccotti Park is postponed." *New York Times*, October 14. http://cityroom.blogs.nytimes.com/2011/10/14/cleanup-of-zuccotti-park-cancelled/.

Moynihan, C. 2012a. "Barricades come down at Zuccotti Park." *New York Times*, January 11. http://cityroom.blogs.nytimes.com/2012/01/11/barricades-come-down-at-zuccotti-park/.

———. 2012b. "Zuccotti Park occupiers call arrests unjustified." *New York Times*, March 31.

Packer, G. 2011. "All the angry people." *The New Yorker*, December 5, http://www.newyorker.com/reporting/2011/12/05/111205fa_fact_packer

Parkinson, J. R. 2012. *Democracy & Public Space: The Physical Sites of Democratic Performance.* Oxford: Oxford University Press.

Permanyer, L. 2001. *Josep Puig I Cadafalch.* Barcelona: Ediciones Poligraf.

Reisz, T. 2011. "Bahrain: A roundabout way to signifying nothing." *Huffington Post*, April 5. http://www.huffingtonpost.com/todd-reisz/bahrain-roundabout_b_844276.html.

Saget, B., and A. Tse. 2011. "How Occupy Wall Street Turned Zuccotti Park into a Protest Camp." *New York Times*, October 5. http://www.nytimes.com/

interactive/2011/10/05/nyregion/how-occupy-wall-street-turned-zuccotti-park
-into-a-protest-camp.html.

Schmidt, M. S. 2012. "For occupy movement, a challenge to recapture momentum."
New York Times, April 1.

Siegel, H. 2011. "At Occupy Wall Street Central, a rift is growing between east and
west sides of the plaza." *NY Daily News*, October 30. http://www.nydailynews.
com/opinion/occupy-wall-street-central-a-rift-growing-east-west-sides-plaza
-article-1.969320.

Staeheli, L. A. 2010. "Political geography: democracy and the disorderly public."
Progress in Human Geography 34 (1): 67–78.

Schwartz, M. 2011. "Pre-occupied: The origins and future of Occupy Wall Street."
The New Yorker, November 28 http://www.newyorker.com/reporting/2011/11/
28/111128fa_fact_schwartz.

Shapiro, J. 2011. "Occupy Wall Street gets porta-potties." *DNAinfo*, November 4. http:
//www.dnainfo.com/20111104/downtown/occupy-wall-street-gets-portable
-toilets-following-community-complaints.

Taher, M. 2012. "Tahrir Square: Where people make history." *Ahram Online*, January
20. http://english.ahram.org.eg/NewsContent/1/64/32175/Egypt/Politics-/
Tahrir-Square-Where-people-make-history.aspx.

Tremlett, G. 2011. "Spanish police clash with protestors over cleanup." *The Guard-
ian*, May 27.

Yagopartal. 2011. "15M–Acampada BCB–Plaza Cataluña." YouTube video. http://
www.youtube.com/watch?v=4hxRzrO-V1E.

Occupy Wall Street, Social Movements, and Contested Public Space

Benjamin Shepard

ONE OF THE MOST remarkable aspects of the Occupy Wall Street movement (OWS) is its capacity to ground itself in a struggle for a public commons. For many involved, including myself, Zuccotti Park was our public commons, our agora, just as the gardens in Union Square have been for so many years in New York. "The agora was the center of athletic, artistic, spiritual, and political life of the city," notes OWS activist Morgan Jenness. Yet, today, many suffer from "agoraphobia… a fear of participating as a full citizen in the commons," she continues. OWS challenged this logic, grounding itself in the public commons from the movement's very first days.

First Days

In September 2011, I started receiving email messages about general assemblies for a plan to occupy the financial district in New York City. On Friday 16, 2011, activists held a general assembly, and a Critical Mass bike ride announced on Facebook: "Join NYC cyclists in support of the #OccupyWallStreet movement. Ride is open-ended and self-organizing, with a focus on downtown Manhattan. Be prepared to participate as long as you like." Bring: "Cargo bikes, sound bikes, walkie-talkies, chalk, flyers, and ideas for how we can support the occupation with scouting, food/water/supply transport, outreach and other actions." Activists from around the world were scheduled to meet the following day, September 17, 2011. That day, a group of idealistic street activists descended on Wall Street, the same week statistics came out pointing to an eighteen-year high in poverty levels. Dismayed with Obama, the GOP, Tea Partiers, a one-sided approach to serving the needs of bankers, and a lack of policy toward inequality, a new generation of activists turned back to the street to make their own solutions, creating a space—Liberty Park (known as Zuccotti Park), off Broadway at Liberty Street and Trinity Place below Trinity Church—where they would rally, cook, create art, and participate in an open-ended experiment in democracy.

On Saturday the 17th, the event included rallies, street actions, and general assemblies. No one really knew what to make of the action at the beginning. And few of the movement stars were involved. Youth had organized it, although looking around the people marching around the charging bull sculpture at Bowling Green Park on a Saturday afternoon I saw many of the usual suspects, police, a few supporters of Lyndon LaRouche, etc. Unable to camp in Bowling Green Park, these activists wandered over to Zuccotti Park with backpacks in hand. They held a general assembly and spent the night there. Many talked all night. The actions continued Sunday and so did the general assemblies. On Sunday night, my friend Marina Sitrin, author of *Horizontalism* (2006), sent out a dispatch:

> Thousands of people gathered on Wall Street yesterday. We marched, rallied, and then met in a park to form dozens of horizontal assemblies—some with over 100 people in each. At 7 p.m. there was a general assembly—with over 2,000 people—facilitated again with direct democracy. We used the "people's microphone" to communicate with one another.
>
> Then, hundreds stayed, sleeping in the park and organizing to take care of each other and make a democratic space. (There are food, bedding, health, legal, media, trash, security and art working groups.)
>
> This is New York City!
>
> As of Sunday night, it is still going on. Hundreds are still gathered in horizontal assemblies, hoping to keep the space occupied. I have not been this inspired in the United States in a very long time.
>
> Perhaps we are joining the world and waking up.

Throughout the weekend, Global Revolution media, a group of video activists, had been filming everything as it happened, live. That night, I turned to the live stream of the people's assembly along with some five thousand others from around the world. Members of the group discussed plans, logistics, and the connection between this movement and those of the Arab Spring. Many drew similar connections. For others, this was a continuation of actions taking place from Egypt to Wisconsin to Albany, where waves of protests had been challenging the politics of austerity. On May 12, 2011, activists from around the country had converged on Wall Street to protest budget austerity. With union people, students, teachers, and AIDS activists converging at Bowling Green at the lowermost tip of Manhattan. My friend Ron suggested this should be our Tahrir Square, four months before OWS.

On Monday, September 19, I rode down to the action once again, joining hundreds marching on Wall Street, where they were penned in between barricades. Others remained at Liberty Plaza where they painted cardboard signs about the economy and why they were there. "War is a racket," one read. Another highlighted the record-level inequalities in wealth seen in recent years: "The wealthiest 400 Americans own more than the poorest 60 percent (that's more than 18,000,000 people). Who do politicians really care about?" Talking with young activists, I saw a picture of a new generation ready to engage and create their own solutions, rather than wait for a leader or a politician. News reports from around the world were now covering the actions. Friends from California to Germany posted to Facebook that all eyes were on Wall Street.

On Monday morning, I ran into artist and squatter Seth Tobocman painting a cardboard box on the sidewalk in Zuccotti. We talked about the actions and commented that the city's reaction was different from the Giuliani approach, which would have involved more arrests faster.

On Tuesday, I rode down again. It was a colder, rainier morning, but it wasn't pouring. Still, summer was turning to fall and it was harder to sleep in the streets without some cover from the rain. I sat down to talk with a friend. As we talked, those who were camping brought out sandwiches, offering us a free bite of food. I was in awe that a sleeping encampment had lasted three nights. I hadn't seen this much camping since the Tompkins Square Park days in the late 1980s, when sleeping in the park was the city de facto housing policy. In the years since then, the homeless or those sleeping in the streets have become an emblem of poverty, a symbol to be pushed out of sight, out of New York's contested public spaces and into the city's new de facto housing: its jails. With Occupy, the criminalization of those sleeping in the streets and by extension poverty was brought out for full view.

A little after 10 a.m., the march on Wall Street ended and activists reconverged on the square, followed by a phalanx of police who appeared considerably less tolerant than the day before. A white shirt (a supervisory NYPD officer) pulled out a bullhorn and asked the group to put away their tents or they would be taken away. Within a few seconds, the police moved in, tearing away the tents and arresting those inside and those who got too close. A man who was sleeping in his tent fell, chipping his teeth. "Why are you doing this," someone asked. "I don't know," an officer confessed.

"Who are you protecting?" activists screamed. "I never had a reason to hate cops until this," vented Myles, a young activist who had slept there since Saturday. "Fourteen people have been arrested. Some were pulled away for chalking or getting in the way of the police, or wearing a mask. And we're just taking it," another man told me. "We need some solidarity." At this point, Vlad, an activist filming the live stream, stood up to remind the group about the need for nonviolence and solidarity.

General assemblies were scheduled for 3 and 7 p.m. that day. Walking away, I saw police lined around the square, some moving off and others moving in to keep an eye on the scene. Attrition appeared to be their strategy. Yet, more and more people would start to walk down to the space. In the coming weeks, no event arrests or cold weather would deter the burgeoning movement.

Over time, Brookfield Properties, which received millions in subsidies to create Zuccotti Park as a publically owned private space, would conjure excuses for evicting or restricting access to the park (Nyceve 2011). Yet, with each attempt to restrict access to the space for those involved in the Occupy movement, the park became more of an emblem of a problematic dynamic of late capitalism in which the rich enjoy privatizing profits and socializing losses. In this case, they were privatizing profits they made through the increased height and bulk of Liberty Plaza, the building adjacent to the park, which holds tenants (such as Goldman Sachs) in some of the most profitable real estate in the world. After all, the space was given for a concession. "It should be treated as a public space," notes Brooklyn College sociologist Greg Smithsimon, my coauthor of *The Beach Beneath the Streets: Contesting New York City's Public Spaces* (2011) and a contributor to this volume: "It is not the same as private space. They gave it to the public in exchange for very profitable zoning concessions, explicitly space, square footage. The building is more profitable because they gave the people that public space. It's a trade and the trade should be maintained." By successfully reclaiming the publically owned private space known as Zuccotti Park, OWS was using this space as it was intended by the New York City Planning Department.[1]

It was vital that OWS be able to occupy this particular space—within the financial district, in close proximity to Wall Street. In doing so, the movement was insisting that Wall Street itself is public space—that we have the same right to walk down it and walk past the Stock Exchange as we protest as any banker or broker does. This helped us to reimagine what the space could be—our own public commons, our own Tahrir Square.

Comrades from Cairo wrote an open letter of support to the OWS movement in which they commented on the possibilities of transforming space and by extension social relations:

> Discover new ways to use these spaces, discover new ways to hold on to them and never give them up again. Resist fiercely when you are under attack, but otherwise take pleasure in what you are doing, let it be easy, fun even. We are all watching one another now, and from Cairo we want to say that we are in solidarity with you, and we love you all for what you are doing.

Activists would sleep in Zuccotti Park for another two months. During that time, those in support of the 99% who've lost ground over the last three decades compared with the 1% who have gained[2] held rallies for health care and against police brutality; built solidarity with labor, immigrants, and AIDS activists; and shifted the national conversation. They targeted Goldman Sachs, the foreclosure crisis, and the need for public space where people can meet in the streets. And the dirty secret of income inequality in the US was exposed for all to see, and even possibly do something about. And gradually the world started to change.

---

1. It was what the city negotiated for the development of a park and in return waived building bulk and height requirements in 1968, prior to the zoning laws that allowed for bonus plazas. The NYC Planning Commission granted a "special permit" to the developers of 140 Broadway (who years later sold to Brookfield Properties) and waived bulk and height requirements for the building in return for a permanent open park to be built across the street that was to be open for 365 days per year.
2. For an overview of this dynamic, see Ratner 2012.

Evictions—November 15, 2011

We started hearing about the eviction plans late at night on Monday, the 14th. Walking back over the Brooklyn Bridge the next morning, I recalled my friend Seth's words from the first Tuesday of the occupation: "They keep you on a tight leash," he explained as he painted a sign. "They may give you a little room, but they keep the leash." I'd wondered when the other shoe was going to drop for two months now. It didn't happen that first Tuesday of the occupation, even after the police evicted people from their tents. It didn't happen the following Saturday, the 24th, when the police surrounded the square and then turned away once major media outlets arrived. And it didn't happen on October 14, when the city said they were coming in to clean the space and activists from faith to labor to health care organizations converged to sleep in solidarity with the burgeoning movement.

It happened instead on a Tuesday morning in mid-November shortly after midnight, when few were looking. Times Up!, the biking group I volunteer with, had finally finished getting fifteen bikes down to Zuccotti Park and attached bike-powered generators. Some of us had participated in the sustainability working group from the inception; others had worked with the performance guild, and others with the book project.[3] A group of us were sitting at ABC No Rio talking about Nabokov when calls started pouring in. "There is a huge buildup of police in East River Park," one caller declared. "It's a shift change. Call us when you get down there," another member of the group responded.

Riding downtown, we saw more police than usual on the streets. Riding past Maiden Lane, it seemed like hundreds of police were passing us by. By the time we got to Zuccotti Park, a little past midnight, there was no place to park our bikes. When I started to lock up my bike on Broadway, a policeman commented, "I wouldn't park it here. If you can't figure it out, use your eyes." I looked up and saw a policeman in riot gear with a baton in her hand. Worries about raids had come and gone for weeks. It was going to be tonight. Walking around the park, I could see police surrounding the space and turning on floodlights.

"Please get out of the park," police were advising everyone.

"Whose park? Our park?" some responded. Others started leaving.

---

3. See Writers for the 99% 2011.

Barricades spread everywhere. The police were now holding the streets around the park. By 1 a.m., no one else was allowed into the park. A wall of cops started pushing a group of us at Liberty and Broadway, a block away and out of eyesight. I knew the *New York Times* and some media people were inside. They'd gotten there before the raid. By 1:30 a.m., fire trucks were rushing down Broadway, their sirens blaring.

"When are you guys going to protect the people?" one man asked a policeman.

"Just doing their jobs ruining democracy," a photographer commented as the police pushed us up and away another block.

"Mic check—something horrible is happening here," another commented with the human mic.

Our bikes were parked down on Trinity Place near the Burger King across from the park. The police would not let us go back to retrieve them, so we walked past Ground Zero, across the highway, and back up to Trinity, or as close as we could get. The entrances were again blocked off. I talked with one man walking out from the space. He confirmed that the police had pepper sprayed those still inside the park and used sound rays to disorient them. They were now destroying the tents and reasserting control. There was no way to get my bike back.

"How long will it be before I can get my bike down there?"

"Maybe an hour, maybe all night."

"Whose streets? Our streets?" some screamed.

"We are the 99%!" another group chanted, as they blocked a van driving down Broadway.

The police spent the rest of the night trashing the People's Library, pushing people off the sidewalks, and violently arresting those who remained. When I left around 5 a.m., people were gathering downtown at Foley Square, planning their next move.

The next day, I rode by the space in the morning and everything was cleared out. The Times Up! bike-powered generators were gone. So much of the innovation was dispersed. Many from the OWS Homeless Youth Caucus had slept and ate there when other shelter spaces fell thin. And now a space that helped them feel powerful was gone. Back to the usual gaps in services, where were they going to sleep now? One of the things I loved about OWS was how it created spaces, however imperfect, for many. Yet, over and over the city take away these community spaces—whether they are community gardens or meeting places for Critical Mass bike rides. Over the next few months, the cat and mouse games between the movement and police would continue, with a seminal three-month anniversary action on Canal and 6th Streets on December 17, almost weekly rallies, pop-up occupations citywide, and a twenty-four-hour theatrical event called Occupy Broadway.

It is hard not to think about the Paris Commune of 1871 or the student protests of 1968 in moments such as this. The temporary autonomous zones rarely last long. Yet, after adrenaline fades and people go back to work, the question remains: Does everyday life remain the same? Or is it changed?

March Anniversaries

The six-month anniversary of the movement took place on a sunny day in mid-March 2012. After dancing and celebrating six months of peaceable assembly to petition the government for redress of grievances, members of the movement were told to leave Zuccotti Park around 11 p.m. on March 17. "We sat peacefully on the ground, arms linked, and the police picked us off like bits of trash, beating down people with batons, pushing us out of Liberty and barricading the park again," recalled OWS activist Monica Hunken. "But we are brave and enduring. There is a new joy, a sort of spring fever in the air. Get ready for Spring training!"

My friend L. A. Kauffman noted: "Last night at Zuccotti Park was a sweet, upbeat, street celebration…until the police attacked. I won't soon get over the fear and rage of watching Cecily Macmillan having a huge seizure while handcuffed, the terror of seeing her go completely limp and still on the cold pavement, while the police fumbled and dilly-dallied. Horrifying to see how little room for dissent there is in this collapsing country."

Times UP! had planned to meet at Zuccotti Park to ride over to Occupy the Empty Space, a movement theater event at Judson Memorial Church at 2:30 p.m. Yet, as soon as I got to Judson earlier in the day, I started getting phone calls that Zuccotti was completely gated off. My friend Erik and I rode over to Zuccotti. On our way, we visited the Statue of Liberty during Times Up! Peace Ride, wondering if Emma Lazarus's poem to those "yearning to breathe free" would be tolerated there today.

The park was gated up. We talked with a few activists taking part in the COOLS (Cultural Occupation of Liberty Square) session, a daily teach-in across from the park. The point was to get as many people as possible back into Zuccotti Park, where the movement began. This gesture was not as much about recreating anything from earlier in the fall as about keeping the conversation going, keeping the stories of resistance moving forward into different directions. To ground these conversations, we needed public spaces to remain open, specifically Liberty Square, serving as our commons.

Each day at lunchtime, a different writer, storyteller, academic, or movement person was invited to take part in the COOLS. The week before, I was invited to speak about the top five achievements of ACT UP over the last twenty-five years. A few older veteran ACT UP folks showed up, two or three younger AIDS activists involved with transgender and international AIDS work, two members of the Occupy Farms working group, as well as two older gentlemen involved with Occupy from the very beginning. Working within the dialogical model of Paulo Freire's popular education, we ended up exchanging stories and information as I recalled ACT UP's zap on Wall Street a quarter century ago this March.

One of the men taking part in the COOLS, Bernie Venditto, had written a mimeographed book about "Happiness" arguing that happiness involved a holy combination of social connection, poetry, and socialism. I could not agree more. Quoting William Butler Yeats, he noted:

The good are always the merry.
And the merry love the fiddle.
And the merry love to dance.

In Occupy, many loved to dance as well as share stories. One of the great things about the COOLS sessions was the willingness of the participants to share what they knew with each other, so we could all learn something. Some weeks, the conversation linked the lessons of the feminist sex wars of the 1980s with the debates about safer spaces in the movement. Other sessions involved debates about the diversity of tactics stretching back to the days of broken windows in Seattle in 1999. Many discussed how we could support adding more voices and tactics to the movement, rather than attempting to stifle or censor those we found objectionable? Another session involved the history of May Day and general strikes. Sometimes we met at Zuccotti Park just to dance; on other occasions, to begin bike rides to community gardens and throw seed bombs into fenced-off vacant lots that could become community gardens. The conversations at the COOLS took countless forms and directions. On March 18th, the conversation was about the future of the movement in the face of repression.

Leaving the COOLS sessions, Erik and I rode over to 100 Center Street, where activists were being processed. A group of OWS folks was outside doing jail support. Many were still grumbling about the violence of the night before. Some had heard police saying, "They really fucked up that one." Word at the plaza was that no one would get out today or even the following day. With each day, the state seemed more intent on increasing the cost of participation in this clash between the 1% and the 99%.

The reality of police repression of the Occupy Wall Street movement has been a constant theme of the entire year. Police have arrested my friends for sitting on park benches, for chalking, for walking the wrong way on the sidewalk, and now for standing or trespassing in a park designated by zoning laws to be open twenty-four hours a day (and unlike the rest of New York that St. Patrick's night, without alcohol). Many joked about the absurd reasons they were arrested. One bragged he was arrested for looking at a policeman the wrong way. "They had a hard time figuring out a charge," he said. These days, I still spend one or two days a week in jail support for friends put through the system for speaking out as they were doing on Saturday. I spend countless hours going to and from court for those facing OWS arrests for offences such as trespassing in a park zoned for twenty-four-hour access and standing on the sidewalk. It would be funny if it weren't such an ongoing reality. Yet, we all smile and greet each other with hugs as we occupy the courts, where some of the most interesting people in town are hanging out.

On Saturday, March 17, 2012, the NYPD were out for blood. Around lunchtime, a policeman threw away loafs of bread from the old encampment's kitchen and started the crackdown on the group peaceably assembling in the park. Waves of my friends were arrested all day as they moved in and out of the park. A woman I know had the police grab her breast as she was arrested, before they violently pulled her wrists back to cuff her, breaking them. "They broke my finger, stabbed me in the eye…for standing in a park…for making a statement about this system," another man noted after he was arrested. Later, police claimed people were setting up tents to sleep in the park. With no tents in sight, people were just dancing in the park.

After doing jail support, Erik and I rode over to Judson Memorial for the beginning of Occupy the Empty Space. There, everyone looked rattled.

"I can't stop thinking about last night and the innocent people around me brutalized by police," confessed Monica Hunken, who started the show. "We cannot allow this to go on without accountability. It's time to kick out Bloomberg and Kelly. The NYPD is a sham. Let it be known, there was no clash. That implies equal action and reaction. There was only brute force used by the police upon peaceful protestors."

To be sure, the New York City Police Department can and will make every effort to shut down this movement, just as they did with Critical Mass! Over the years after the 2004 crackdown, cyclists litigated. And the city was found to be guilty of violating cyclists' basic rights. In fall 2010, the city agreed to pay the cyclists attacked on Critical Mass rides $965,000. Yet, instead of apologizing, the city targeted cyclists and later OWS protesters taking another stab at reclaiming public space.

Democracy is only as strong as the people who use it. The question is, will everyone else remain silent as freedoms gradually erode?

March 21, 2012 at 11:50 p.m.

Nearing midnight at Union Square after the "Million Hoodies" demo for Treyvon Martin, a young, unarmed African American man shot earlier in the year, clashes between police and activists could be heard and seen on the Global Revolution live stream:

"The park closes at twelve o' clock. You have to leave the park," warned the police.

"The NLG reporting over five hundred or more cops surrounding the park," noted the two activists filming the live stream, "There will be massive arrests. There is a massive police force." "You have to exit the park at midnight," police insisted.

"Whose park? Our park?" the crowd responded, echoing an anthem heard in standoffs dating back decades.

"It is important to note that every effort to quell the movement has failed," noted the videographers, "And now it's the American Spring. In eight minutes, there will be a mass arrest. I've never seen this many cops. This is similar to the raid the other night. You gotta know when to hold and when to fold 'em and when to walk away. This is the absolute meeting place for the park."

"Five, four, three, two, one," the crowd chanted as the clock turned midnight. People roared. "We have a right to peaceable assembly, freedom of assembly. You guys don't hurt us. We're not criminals. We're citizens of the United States," noted the videographers.

"Get up, get down, there is a revolution in this town," screamed the crowd.

"More high ranking officers than I've seen since the raid," noted the videographers, "While the NYPD can evict people from the park, the locals say this is open twenty-four hours a day. People are always here drinking, smoking. The NYPD can evict people from the park, but they cannot stop this movement. People are coming from around the country. This is bottom up."

"Take off that riot gear, we don't see no riot here," screamed the crowd.

"People were playing chess in the park last night, but their game was interrupted by a checkmate by the police," noted a cycling activist interviewed by those on the live stream, "Every time they try to sabotage us, they just make us stronger."

Conclusions

Social movements are fundamentally about public space. From Zuccotti Square to People's Park to community gardens, movements find inspiration in a place to meet, organize, share stories, break isolation, dance, plan, build mutual aid, and create a bit of care and civil society in an otherwise tough, alienating world.

In 1649, the Diggers, a group of landless commoners, claimed St. George's Hill, outside of London, as their own. "The symbolism of taking back as common land what had been enclosed (i.e., privatized) overshadowed the negligible material value of planting corn in barren soil," noted Steve Duncombe, "but what these outcasts of Cromwell's New Model Army did hold dear was the community created in their act of resistance; it was a scale model of the universal brotherhood they demanded in the future" (Duncombe 2002, 17). In New York City, these struggles are currently found in spaces where convivial social relations take shape, such as bike lanes, community gardens, public piers, parks, and pop-up occupations As the clock passed midnight on March 22, activists facing a line of police could be heard chanting: "One, we are the people, two, we are united, three, this occupation is not leaving. Where is my freedom?"

References

Duncombe, S. 2002. *Cultural Resistance: A Reader*. New York: Verso.

Nyceve. 2011. "FOIA request reveals Zuccotti Park owners Brookfield Properties heavily taxpayer subsidized," *Daily Kos*, November 1. http://www.dailykos.com/story/2011/11/01/1032061/-FOIA-request-reveals-Zuccotti-Park-owners-Brookfield-Properties-heavily-taxpayer-subsidized.

Ratner, S. 2012. "The rich get richer." *New York Times*, March 25.

Shepard, B., and G. Smithsimon. 2011. *The Beach Beneath the Streets: Contesting New York's City's Public Spaces*. New York: SUNY Press.

Sitrin, M. 2006. *Horizontalism: Voices of Popular Power in Argentina*. Oakland: AK Press.

Writers for the 99%. 2011. *Occupying Wall Street: The Inside Story of an Action that Changed America*. New York: OR Books.

"A Stiff Clarifying Test Is in Order"

OCCUPY AND NEGOTIATING RIGHTS IN PUBLIC SPACE

Gregory Smithsimon

ONCE OCCUPY WALL STREET marched into Zuccotti Park and made it clear that they would be staying a while, everyone was surprised to find out that there were more regulations specifying the color of the paving stones in a plaza than what you could do there.[1] The amount of seating in a plaza like Zuccotti was established by a precise mathematical ratio, but whether you could lie down on the benches, camp on them, or protest on top of them had never been established.

That lopsided set of rules isn't surprising once we think about what public space is. Public space is the parks, sidewalks, malls, buses, subways, and plazas where we meet and interact with people we don't know. But it is neither the places themselves nor the activities that go on within them. It's both: *Public space is the space where social conflicts are negotiated.* A location is a public space to the extent that it's where people go to meet friends for lunch, start conversations with people they don't know, play, sell newspapers, protest, drink coffee, watch, and be watched and where, in the course of doing so, they interact with others, come into conflict with them, and accommodate people in countless small and large interactions.

Sometimes those conflicts are about larger social issues like the role of banks in the economy and money in politics. Most often, the conflicts are over space itself—who had a seat first, whether one person's desire to listen to the radio is infringing on another's desire to take a nap, or whether ledges

---

1. Among other things, paving "shall be of non-skid durable materials that are decorative and compatible in color and pattern with other design features" (New York City Planning Commission 2007, Section 37-718).

are for sitting or for skateboarding (or, building owners would protest, for neither). The negotiation of these conflicts may be explicit and written, as in public meetings that lead to the creation of new rules that govern the contested behavior in a public space. Or the negotiation may be physical and impromptu, as people adjust their behavior to accommodate each other. Because public space is constituted through conflicts that happen in certain places, the rules that are written for a public space are the battle scars of the conflicts that have created that space.

In this chapter, I will discuss the rules regulating bonus plazas like Zuccotti Park to delineate distinct eras in the design of New York City's bonus plazas. I began studying New York office plazas a dozen years ago to understand why so many were barren and unusable (Shepard and Smithsimon 2011). Interviewing architects, planners, and building managers about those plazas, I found a fifty-year history of conflicts, rules, and regulations that defined several distinct periods in plaza development. Each set of rules resolved one round of conflicts, but inevitably set the stage for the new conflicts that would ensure the plazas remained public spaces. Recognizing how each era's rules set the conditions for the next set of conflicts makes the occupation of Zuccotti much less unexpected. Furthermore, the history of conflicts over public spaces gives indications of some of the rules and regulations that are likely to result from the most recent round of protests. Contrary to people's worst fears, if history is any guide, those new rules will not clamp down on political protest, but could actually more firmly establish our right to protest effectively in public space. To see why, we first need to observe the process of conflict and regulation in New York plazas.

Social Unrest and Privatized Spaces (1961–1975)

The conflict that created office plazas was originally between the new needs of business and a fifty-year-old zoning code. In the mid-twentieth century, developers were chafing against zoning regulations that required setback buildings or "wedding cakes" like the Empire State and Chrysler Buildings. Since floor plans shrank on each subsequent floor, the buildings were complicated to build and difficult to rent to companies seeking large, open floor plans. Likewise, architects were frustrated that they couldn't build more modernist towers like Mies van der Rohe's Seagram Building. The city responded with a "bonus plaza" program in the comprehensive 1961 zoning reform: In high-density areas, for each square foot of public space that developers created at ground level, the city gave permission to build up to ten square feet of additional usable office space (or floor area ratio) at the top of the building. The enticement was so sweet that every project that became eligible for the bonus took it. The new program constituted a contractual exchange: public space at ground level for more office space at the top of skyscrapers.

In the first decade of the program, the results were disappointing. Plazas were barren, windswept, empty places. Developers refused to allow seating or trees, architects hid some plazas in remote corners of the property or sunk them below ground level, management companies skimped on maintenance, and some tried to lock and gate plazas.[2] Richard Roth, whose firm at one point designed more than a quarter of all the plazas in New York City, explained to me, "The plazas got bleaker and bleaker and bleaker—less people-oriented. Because, again, the owners of the buildings didn't want a lot of people sitting in those spaces … The client kept saying, 'No, I want it as minimal as possible.'" A landmark survey of New York's bonus plazas found that among Midtown and Downtown plazas built in the 1960s, not a single one earned an "A" grade; 83 percent got a D or an F.[3]

The privatized spaces reflected developers' anxiety about the city in the 1960s. Politicians and others regularly described New York as a "jungle." Civil rights movements and protests against segregation and racial inequality had upset the old order of de facto racial disparity in public space. White flight was well under way, and the class of people who rented and worked in Midtown office buildings saw the city as threatening. Plazas reflected their anxiety and were built defensively, no-man's-lands designed to keep the public out. Those early plans make clear that developers and designers could conceive of no "legitimate" use for public space.

Thus the first conflict was between members of the public, who were owed adequate public spaces, and developers, who sought to keep people

---

2. Too often architects have been wrongly blamed for modernism's barren plazas—Tom Wolfe's *From Bauhaus to Our House* (1981) comes to mind. But my own research found that their clients and developers gave explicit instructions during the 1960s to develop designs that kept people away from the plazas, even firing landscape architects who failed to comply. See Smithsimon 2008a, 325-351.

3. On the survey, see Kayden et al. 2000. Analysis of the plaza grades is in Shepard and Smithsimon 2011.

Although the owners of 299 Park Avenue, at left, were richly rewarded with extra floor area in exchange for a public "bonus" plaza, management surreptitiously turned the plaza into a private driveway. At right, signs announce the public space is private, prohibit vehicles, warn potential users they will be under constant surveillance, and even go so far as to announce that the bike racks cannot be used by the public. *Photos by Gregory Smithsimon*

away. To their great credit, the New York City Department of City Planning proved to be a consistent advocate of the public's right to use bonus plazas. The department was influenced more by Jane Jacobs's vision of the city as a space of social order than by demagogues' shouts that the city was a place of chaos (Jacobs 1961).

New York City's commitment to public space is clear in the documents that first created Zuccotti Park (then called Liberty Park). The building at One Liberty Plaza was far larger than anything that would be permitted under the zoning for the area, so the builder, U.S. Steel, sought special permission by promising a public park across the street in exchange for unprecedented permission to build a tower that would cover an entire block. The city agreed, specifically because of the promise of public space: "The City will gain what amounts to a permanent open park in the heart of one of the most densely built-up areas in the world," they wrote in 1968. "It is principally because of this public benefit that the [Planning] Commission has viewed this application with favor" (New York City Planning Commission 1968). Like other public spaces, Liberty Park was, from its inception, a negotiation between competing interests: the desire of a corporation to build a massive headquarters and the interest of the public in having adequate open space they could use.

As the inadequacies of the first round of privatized plazas became clear, Jane Jacobs's one-time editor at *Fortune* magazine, William H. Whyte, patiently studied the failing public spaces and cajoled the NYC Department of City Planning into passing the first revision of the bonus plaza regulations in 1975. (The new rules were adopted when developers were too busy licking their wounds from a building slump to pay much attention to new regulations about plazas that no one was building.)[4] The new regulations mandated seating and other features to make plazas more usable. The first era of bonus plaza design, which had been characterized by privatized spaces, was over.

Gentrification and Filtered Spaces *(1975–2000)*

Paradoxically, the requirement that developers make plazas be more open and usable served building owners well in the next period. Citibank opened the first bonus space under the new set of rules at the base of the isosceles-topped Citicorp Building in 1975. The space was like a shopping mall, a design that conveniently seemed private enough to welcome well-heeled shoppers, but suggested to others that the space was private and they were not allowed. In this second era of bonus plazas, developers played a cat-and-mouse game with the NYC Department of City Planning, finding new ways to create spaces that might be attractive to the returning gentry, but seemed, from the street, to be private. Indoor spaces could be hidden behind mirrored glass, and plazas could be turned into a café's seating area. Saky Yakas, a partner at one of the leading plaza-designing firms, explained how architects met the needs of their clients:

> Although the intent of these is to be public, a lot of the design is geared towards making people think before they use them. A lot of people don't know that these are public spaces. I think a lot of developers like them to not know they're public spaces. And one of the ways is how you do your fencing or how you change the grade, how you situate them in relationship to the buildings, how you use your cameras. They want them to be used, but you want a feel of exclusivity.

---

4. For an engaging account of Jacobs's and Whyte's intersection, see Alexiou 2006, 57-64.

These new spaces reflected conflicts at the municipal and national level. They were components of the gentrification of New York City fostered by the fiscal crisis of 1975. During the fiscal crisis, the financial industry took firm control of the city from its industrial and union predecessors, deindustrialization weakened the old base of the city, and ascendant neo-liberalism took its first toll on New York's working class and people of color.[5] Gentrified plazas were among the beachheads from which elites reasserted control of urban public space.

The NYC Department of City Planning fought back once again, dog-gedly prohibiting the design features that made public bonus spaces look and feel private. The symbolic and physical barriers that developers had used to keep out less desirable users while offering amenities to the gentry were banned: mirrored glass could no longer conceal an indoor mall from the street and barriers that made it hard to enter were prohibited. The problem was so severe that planning eventually insisted that at least 50 percent of the street frontage of a plaza be unobstructed and open for entry; even where walls were permitted, they could be no more than two feet high.

These strict design regulations, incidentally, gave designers more crea-tive latitude, not less. As Whyte pointed out, under the original regime, de-velopers hadn't let planners do much of anything in the plazas. "Ambiguity as to what the developer must provide is an invitation to provide little," he wrote. Requiring usable features provided designers with a set of elements they could use and gave them license to actually design the spaces.

The End of History, Hubris, and Suburbanized Spaces (2000–Present)

As the next period opened, developers made little use of design as a means to exclude users. Plazas became striking for how much more open, accessible, and well appointed they were. New plazas were built with lush plantings (ar-ranged to allow easy surveillance of the space). Older plazas were retrofitted with seating, easier access, and flowers. Developers increasingly projected a placid image of the city that suggested that social conflict was over.

In the city at large, this was the period of zero-tolerance policing and the stop-and-frisk tactics in which police questioned and searched African

---

5. See Smith 1996. On neoliberalism, see Harvey 2005.

American or Latino men a half-million times per year in the city (Peart 2011). Filtering at the level of the individual plaza became redundant: aggressive policing, coupled with widespread gentrification, had convinced owners of plazas that business districts were once against the domain of white-collar professionals. In this period, plazas opened up, barriers disappeared, and developers saw plazas as a potential amenity for tenants. Falling crime rates and skyrocketing housing costs gave Manhattan the illusion of an urban playground at the "end of history" (the term Francis Fukuyama had used to predict the end of social conflict).

Those changes, coupled with the enthusiasm of the real estate boom, led to ever more ambitious public spaces. Confident that crime waves and personal insecurity were a thing of the past, spaces were built that ignored the hard-learned design lessons of Jacobs and Whyte, as the High Line soared above Whyte's caution that people won't climb steps to get to an open space and Jacobs's insistence that isolating any public space from the eyes on the street was its death warrant.

The bold plazas of this suburbanized era were premised on the misapprehension that conflict had been relegated to history. Recognizing that public space is defined by conflict, it wasn't hard to see that such spaces would be uniquely accessible to protest movements. In a 2008 review of these changes to public space, I noted that "people-powered social movements will no longer need to scale the citadel's walls to get noticed, but only march into the airy, accessible, well-appointed plazas, claim their space and be heard" (Smithsimon 2008b). The statement was by no means a prediction of Occupy Wall Street. It was simply a recognition that social conflict continued to exist, and that developers had built (and at Zuccotti, redesigned) bonus plazas without imagining that insurgent movements could ever make themselves heard again.

In this way, the fall 2011 occupation of Zuccotti Park was a fitting outcome of the previous set of rules that had opened up plazas, and the cultural shifts that had let developers—and corporations—ignore conflict and inequality.

Occupy Wall Street's actual message was neatly paralleled by their occupation of Liberty Park. The movement objected to corporate control over the public sphere (through campaign contributions that encouraged bailouts and financial industry deregulation), and their presence in Liberty Park confronted corporate control over public space. Many protesters objected

Even during the Occupy Wall Street protest, Zuccotti Park could still be used for multiple purposes. Above, construction workers from the World Trade Center site spend their lunch hour checking out the drumming circle. Below, tourists consult a map next to the park's well-known statue by J. Seward Johnson. *Photos by Gregory Smithsimon*

to government giving big bonuses to corporations, while they took over a park that had been built to secure a big bonus for a major corporation. Finally, people were frustrated by government's inconsistent enforcement of the rules—bailouts for indebted banks, but foreclosure for indebted homeowners—and were eventually evicted by government's inconsistent enforcement of plaza rules—police enforced ad-hoc rules against protesters (no sleeping, no lying down, no backpacks) but disregarded rules meant to protect the public (such as the requirement that plazas not be barricaded and that owners could not impose new rules by fiat).

Public Space and the Inevitability of Negotiation

Public space demonstrated its power to require negotiations throughout the protests. Negotiation is so inherently a part of being in public space that parties with no intention of negotiating do so. (This is perhaps what puts public space at the heart of democracy.) The mayor didn't want to negotiate with Occupy Wall Street. Occupy Wall Street hadn't come to negotiate with Mayor Bloomberg, much less with Brookfield Properties, the plaza's owner. Yet all sides were inevitably drawn into negotiations from the first moments of the occupation.

The protest began, after all, with a negotiation: The protesters marched to Liberty Park and announced, loudly enough for the police to hear, that if they were forced out of the plaza, they would march south and seek to occupy Wall Street itself. The police let them stay.

Soon, the mayor claimed the plaza had become dirty and that the protesters needed to be evicted so that it could be cleaned. Protesters responded by displaying a battery of brooms and mops and cleaned up the space. Then nearby residents objected to late night drumming, and Occupy Wall Street negotiated a curfew on loud noise. The fire department seized gas generators, claiming they were fire hazards, and so Occupy used pedal-powered generators instead. At each turn, the city made a complaint and Occupy successfully negotiated a resolution. Unfortunately for Occupy, the city was only willing to articulate superficial complaints—about dirt, noise, and fire hazards—that were intended to be pretexts to forcibly removing people. Had Mayor Bloomberg articulated his real wish—that the Occupy movement leave Liberty Park—it could have prompted a truly interesting, revealing, and potentially fruitful negotiation about what would be required in return:

The physical nature of public space imposes requirements on users. In September 2011 (well before the mayor's demand in October that the park be cleaned), Occupy participants autonomously cleaned and maintained the space, including sweeping up trash (left). Occupiers also developed a creative water recycling system for dishwashing (right). *Photos by Gregory Smithsimon*

The mayor might have offered to support a moratorium on foreclosures, a jobs program, a millionaires' tax or bank regulation, a permanent home for the movement, or even debt relief. We don't know what the content of such negotiations could have been. But had the city been committed to negotiation rather than eviction (which, like other forms of violence, represents the rejection of negotiation and of the opposing party's legitimacy and humanity), the more productive resolution of opposing interests would likely have been better for the city and the country.

Negotiating the Future of Protest in Public Space

What new rules will result from the recent conflicts in Zuccotti Park? Despite building owners' calls for draconian restrictions on public plazas, we should not be pessimistic about it because public space is not defined by state repression, but by the negotiation of conflicts. Even in the face of direct challenges to corporate and government legitimacy, that pattern has largely held.

William H. Whyte, the great champion of New York City's public plazas, had experienced firsthand the arbitrary restrictions owners placed on their private plazas. Bristling with populist indignation, he wrote that

The public's rights in urban plazas would seem clear. Not only are
plazas used as public spaces; in most cases the owner has been specifically, and richly, rewarded for providing them. He has not been given
license to allow only those public activities he happens to approve
of. He may assume that he has license, and some owners have been
operating on this basis with impunity. But that is because nobody has
challenged them. A stiff, clarifying test is in order. (Whyte 1988, 164)

It has been fifty years since the first bonus plaza legislation was put
into place, but that long-overdue test is now likely upon us. The zoning
regulations are unequivocal, if not especially detailed: "All public plazas
shall be accessible to the public at all times." But that rule was not enough
to prevent the police from closing the plaza, so people who were pushed
out may want stronger protections. Protesters who were arrested simply
for being in that space, people whose activities were summarily restricted
by police, and individuals and groups whose property was seized in Liberty
Park and destroyed are likely to call to strengthen requirements that plazas
be kept open.

The legacy of Occupy Wall Street will therefore be to press for a more
reliable guarantee of the public's access and the establishment of a range of
protected activities permitted in them. On the first point, there has already
been activism since Occupy Wall Street was evicted in mid-November 2011.
The New York Civil Liberties Union and protesters arrested when police
cleared the park have argued in court that the corporation that owns the
building does not have the authority to evict people from the public park
(Moynihan 2012). A group called Who Owns Space requested that people
complain to the NYC Department of Buildings that public access to Zuccotti Park was being abrogated. The city dutifully investigated and soon
after, the barricades around Zuccotti were removed.

From the other side of the barricades, the corporate demands are fore-
seeable and fall into three categories.

First are the preexisting demands: building owners will ask for the right
to close plazas at night—not because of recent events, but because they've
been asking for that for fifty years. But the NYC Department of City Planning has virtually always denied that request because the department has
rightly concluded that building owners can't be trusted: A plaza that can
close at night risks soon being closed in the afternoons, on weekends, and

any time management decides not to unlock the gates. In the extraordinary cases where owners are allowed to close plazas, pages of explicit requirements try to prevent closure creep. Such creep would be inevitable if broad permission to close at night were given.

Second are restrictions inspired by Occupy Wall Street, which are likely to have far broader consequences: prohibitions against serving food, sleeping, or lying down. There is reason to hope that groups unrelated to Occupy will also oppose these blanket prohibitions because they will inhibit so many other activities and are therefore overly broad.

The final categories of rules developers may pursue would seek to remove public plazas from the realm of public space altogether, by prohibiting them from being used for the only significant purpose they have found in a half century: as sites of political and anticorporate protest and First Amendment expression.

Maintaining and expanding access to bonus plazas for protest is important. For fifty years, the plazas have been created without a well-established public or a clear sense of their use. For the first time, the people of the city of New York have found a fitting use for these public spaces appended to corporate headquarters: protesting those corporations. Demands to tax the 1% made their way all the way up to the governor and even the president, demonstrating how the protesters shifted the public debate.[6] That level of influence is surprising for anarchists who weren't even making policy demands.

I use the term anarchists intentionally. Clearly, not all the protesters were anarchists, but we can now say that the movement has been strongly influenced by anarchism and in the best way. The culture was anarchist, the consensus decision-making style came from consciously nonhierarchical organizations, and the focus on direct action rather than on policy demands was consistent with direct-action anarchism.[7]

The political roots of the movement are significant in considering the regulatory outcome of Occupy. On principle, anarchists have little faith that government will protect their rights, anticipating instead that even a liberal democratic state will defend the claims of private property before the

---

6. See Stelter 2011; Kaplan 2011.
7. And anarchy was astonishingly effective. The consensus decision making did a better job of addressing the "Black Bloc" tendency to violence than other anticapitalist protests have done, and the decentralized structure somehow responded to hyper-rapid news cycle developments more quickly than most social movements can manage.

rights of regular people. But anarchist movements have a peculiar history of not believing that courts can be fair, using them only with great skepticism, and then, improbably, winning major gains in rights and liberties. The free speech fights of the early twentieth century in which the anarchist International Workers of the World were banned from speaking in public in Spokane, Washington, are instructive. First, they used direct action tactics, recruiting hundreds of members to speak, be arrested, and financially burden the city of Spokane through the costs of housing and prosecuting prisoners. Meanwhile, lawyers brought legal suits defending the right to free speech. While it was the direct action efforts that carried the day more than the legal challenge, the long-term result was that the anarchists' legal arguments about free speech were integrated into judicial understandings of First Amendment rights.[8]

A similar result could come from anarchist-organized protests in the age of Occupy. In the free speech fights, a favorable outcome for civil liberties occurred from legal challenges that took place simultaneously with disruptive direct action in the street. If renewed Occupy actions are ongoing while plaza rules are negotiated in court and in public hearings, we can expect advocates for protesters to argue several of the points already made to the city by the New York Civil Liberties Union (NYCLU). First, in a letter to the city in 2012, the NYCLU noted that "an owner's ability to restrict the public's use of a public plaza is constrained by zoning laws and by City policy." Second, they wrote that "An owner of a public plaza may not, of course, forbid conduct in public plazas that is otherwise protected by the constitution." Finally, the NYCLU quoted New York City's own zoning regulations, which state that an owner "shall not prohibit behaviors that are consistent with the normal public use of a public plaza."

These arguments are nothing more than the rearticulation of existing rules about bonus plazas. But the need to reestablish them more securely could lead to important expansions of the "right to the city."[9] If they can

---

8. Lawyers made innovative arguments about the streets as a "traditional public forum" and the need for any regulations to be neutral in their application to different messages. See Kohn 2004, 23-46.

9. The "right to the city" has been of growing interest in the US and internationally. David Harvey (2008, 23) defines the right to the city as "far more than the individual liberty to access urban resources: it is a right to change ourselves by changing the city. It is, moreover, a common rather than an individual right since this transformation inevitably depends upon the exercise of a collective power to reshape the processes of urbanization. The freedom to

prevail, the NYCLU's argument would prioritize the public's rights above the prerogatives of private plaza owners. It would, at long last, establish constitutional protections for people in bonus plazas. And it would definitively protect "normal public use." Decades after William Whyte, bonus plazas' greatest champion, called for a test to establish our rights in such public spaces, the rights we all have might finally be recognized.

Every day, public space demonstrates the power to transform mundane events into important ones. The negotiations of conflicts don't restrict a space, but define and distinguish it. Even when protests are repressed, they can ultimately produce greater liberty. Whatever the long-term contribution the Occupy movement makes to politics, it is likely to have a lasting impact on the right to the city in New York.

References

Alexiou, A. S. 2006. *Jane Jacobs: Urban Visionary*. Piscataway, NJ: Rutgers University Press.

Harvey, D. 2005. *A Brief History of Neoliberalism*. New York: Oxford.

———. 2008. "The Right To The City," *New Left Review* 53 (September-October). http://newleftreview.org/?view=2740. Jacobs, J. 1961. *The Death and Life of Great American Cities*. New York: Vintage Books.

Jacobs, J. 1961. *The Life and Death of Great American Cities*. New York: Random House.

Kaplan, T. 2011. "Albany Tax Deal to Raise Rate for Highest Earners." *New York Times*, December 6.

Kayden, J. S., New York City Department of City Planning, and Municipal Art Society of New York. 2000. *Privately Owned Public Space: The New York City Experience*. New York: John Wiley.

Kohn, M. 2004. *Brave New Neighborhoods: The Privatization of Public Space*. New York: Routledge.

Letter from the NYCLU to City of New York. 2012. January 9. https://www.documentcloud.org/documents/283014-nyclu-letter-about-zuccotti-park.html.

Moynihan, C. 2012. "Civil Liberties Group Joins Occupy Protester's Fight." *New York Times*, February 16. http://www.nytimes.com/2011/12/18/opinion/sunday/young-black-and-frisked-by-the-nypd.html.

New York City Planning Commission. 1968. *Between Promise and Performance: A Proposed 10-Year Program of Community Renewal for New York City*. New York.

---

make and remake our cities and ourselves is, I want to argue, one of the most precious yet most neglected of our human rights."

————. 2007. "Privately Owned Public Plazas Text Amendment." September 19. www.nyc.gov/html/dcp/pdf/priv/101707_final_approved_text.pdf.

————. 1968. No. 20222. March 20.

Peart, N. K. 2011. "Why Is the N.Y.P.D. After Me?" *New York Times*. December 17.

Shepard, B. H., and G. Smithsimon. 2011. *The Beach Beneath the Streets: Contesting New York City's Public Spaces*. New York: SUNY Press.

Smith, N. 1996. *The New Urban Frontier: Gentrification and the Revanchist City*. New York: Routledge.

Smithsimon, G. 2008a. "Empty by Design: Bonus Plazas and the Creation of Public Space." *Urban Affairs Review* 43, no. 3 (January): 325-351.

————. 2008b. "Sunset in the Imperial City: How New York's Public Spaces Presage the End of Empire." *Journal of Aesthetics and Protest*, no. 6: 230-24. http://newleftreview.org/?view=2740.

Stelter, B. 2011. "Camps Are Cleared, but '99 Percent' Still Occupies the Lexicon." *New York Times*, November 30.

Whyte, W. H. 1988. *City: Rediscovering the Center*. New York: Doubleday.

Wolfe, T. 1981. *From Bauhaus to Our House*. New York: Pocket Books.

Being There

Wendy E. Brawer and Brennan S. Cavanaugh

BEST KNOWN AS the founding director of the global Green Map System, Wendy E. Brawer is an eco-designer and social innovator focused on sustainable community development through local leadership, as seen at ecoCultural.info. An everyday cyclist based in New York, she met coauthor Brennan S. Cavanaugh through Time's Up!, the direct-action environmental group. Brennan is a photographer and member of the Occupy Wall Street Sustainability Working Group and the Occupy Wall Street Photo Team. With Time's Up!, he bikes to raise awareness of how we can live and cause less damage to our environment.

Wendy E. Brawer (WEB): Why and when did you go down to the occupation at Zuccotti/Liberty Park?

Brennan S. Cavanaugh (BSC): I went down initially on September 24, 2011 as a street photographer—I love to shoot chaos. The occupation had been there for a week, and it seemed unbelievable, so I had to see it for myself, and there was no press about it. On the first week anniversary, there was a large march planned, but it didn't return to the park after going to the New York Stock Exchange, it continued north, on Broadway, against traffic. This was very exciting. We're so used to planned, permitted marches, and this one went rogue. Everyone was on board.

Strangers made formations to thwart the New York Police Department (NYPD) at intersections. The slogans and signs were smart—this wasn't apa-

Marching against traffic up Broadway on September 24, 2011. *Photo by Brennan S. Cavanaugh*

Beginning the random arrests at Union Square on September 24, 2011. *Photo by Brennan S. Cavanaugh*

thy, this was action. People calling for real change—restore Glass-Steagall—that smart, engaged. The march went all the way to Union Square, where it splintered on its way back downtown because the cops wedged the march and then started kettling [corralling] people. As I was making pictures of people getting arrested, being put face down on the ground, and while white girls were being famously pepper sprayed on the next block, an unidentified plainclothes cop came out of nowhere and quickly handcuffed me. "I'm the press!" I demanded, but "no, you're a part of this" was his response.

So that's how I became part of it. In jail, we were all together, discussing ideas, plans. These were smart, action-oriented people from all over. Press. Direct action. Medics. First-time marchers. All were there. These are my friends now. I was released at 3 a.m. and went back to the occupation—at this point, sparse, with some scattered people sleeping in the warm open air. After that, I just made time to go back and photograph. The Media Center/Team formed quickly. Media never wanted photographs, only video, so a number of us still shooters formed Occupy Wall Street Photo, and we're still going, gearing up for spring.

WEB: Your compelling photos show how the Occupy movement evolved during those first exciting weeks. You were there—day, night, and over-night—shooting as the hard edges of the park changed, over and over. What made this a magnet for you despite being arrested right off the bat?

BSC: This was obviously not the typical march/protest. I always correct people and call it what it is, an occupation. That we were able to stay there, in Liberty Park, made this happen. We got to know each other and evolve

OWS Sanitation "WINNING" sign at Zuccotti Park in November 2011. *Photo by Brennan S. Cavanaugh*

ideas, work our experiences, show the world what a community of strangers can do. Of course, it had its difficulties that we didn't have time to work out by November 15th, when the NYPD raided the occupation and stole people's belongings. But ideas never stopped, about how exactly we could provide an alternative to the current system.

As for the camera, the night and early mornings were fascinating times to shoot—the revelry after a long day, then the peace as the sun rose and the city woke to meet us. Before the tents came, we all slept in the open air. One night, I left my bag with my laptop leaning against one of the marble benches, and later that day it was still there, with a tarp partially draped over it.

You'd wake up, in your sleeping bag, during the short time sunlight got into the park between two east-side buildings. People would bend down as you rubbed your eyes open and say, "I'm glad you are doing this, it's about time." I felt like every time I got to the park, I was walking into a dream campus of some fantastic grad program. I could learn intellectual economics or consensus rules and take photos of it changing daily. And every day, not just for an afternoon rally, but every time of day, we were a thorn in the side of Goldman Sachs, Chase, Bernenke, etc. and were justly expressing our frustrations of economic and other inequalities through our First Amendment rights. This was very exciting, very hopeful, and extremely photogenic.

WEB: Was all of this new to you?

BSC: I work with Time's Up! environmental, direct-action group, as a board member and as a volunteer, and we've been working on public space issues forever. The Occupy movement was exactly what we do. One of our group bike rides has us swimming in midtown corporate fountains in our bathing costumes to illuminate the POPS (privately owned public space) aspect of these open places. To take back, live in, and enjoy the commons.

Union support. *Photo by Brennan S. Cavanaugh*

March to Occupy Times Square in October 2011. *Photo by Brennan S. Cavanaugh*

Another thing we'd do, with Time's Up!, was the Decompress Occupy Wall Street Dance Parties. After being in that park all day, with the sound of the drummers, car traffic, and mic checks bouncing up the caverns, people would have to decompress. With Time's Up!'s sound system bike, we'd lead people to another unused and open POPS down the street, across from the Blarney Stone, and people would dance in this open air for hours.

And eventually the press and the people came. The messages from this curious event, this revolutionary encampment, were getting out. Weekends were crowded with tourists. Orange faced girls all wearing "we are the 99%" T-shirts. Radical, anarchist, and antigovernment folks, theory-headed kids, and post-genderists, all conversing with mainstream America right there. And the police didn't know what to do. For weeks, Bloomberg urged people not to go there as New York City tourism was losing money. But the community was something you couldn't buy. Even the screen printers making T-shirts gave their donations to Occupy Wall Street (OWS). It was a real "living."

WEB: The city refused to see how the Occupy movement drew tourists and positive attention. Denying the public health issue, they resisted providing toilets and water, thus burdening the whole community.

Occupiers clean the park before Bloomberg's threat is rescinded. *Photo by Brennan S. Cavanaugh*

BSC: Right. But it was *clean*. We had a crack sanitation team, and remember, all volunteer. The night of Bloomberg's first eviction threat, there was a beautiful and park-wide coordinated cleanup where sections of the park were cleaned at a time, and we proved we could take care of this land we'd legally "claimed."

And eventually a philanthropist donated Porta Potties, and a company loaned its loading dock so we didn't have to line up at McDonald's to use the bathroom. The occupation had a laundry team. Compost, garbage, recycling—all were taken care of by us. Dishes were all washed with eco-soaps. We were all working with the tools we've individually practiced with for years—actions and thoughts all working to make a better world, a cleaner world with equal representation.

WEB: We both took part in OWS Sustainability Working Group, which gravitated towards making the square itself greener and healthier rather than focusing on crafting a statement. This was a good move, especially as our group's energy-generating bikes, composting, and water recycling systems became iconic action statements impacting the collective image of Zuccotti/Liberty Park, and what the Occupy movement stands for. What was your role?

OWS Kitchen served in all weather. *Photo by Brennan S. Cavanaugh*

BSC: With a kitchen onsite, taking in donated foods and prepping mass meals on the spot, it became quickly apparent that we needed to be the change we wanted to see, so we started composting. We couldn't dig up the mums and set up composting there, so we formed a bike brigade with a shared Xtracycle (an extended bicycle with long panniers, which we locked next to our deli delivery bike that housed our bedding) and contacted local community gardens that were interested in taking the raw food scraps. By the time of the raid, we were taking up to two hundred pounds of waste out each day and had keys to several Lower East Side gardens.

We also brought in an energy-producing bicycle to the sustainability area (by the Liberty Street entrance, right next to the Sanitation crew station—I miss those folks). This was a stationary bike we outfitted, at the Time's Up! space, with a rollerblade wheel attached to a motor that spun, producing electricity that was transferred to a boat battery. It was a hit, coming in right after the New York City Fire Department had confiscated the nasty gas generators. When we were appealing to the General Assembly (GA) for funds to create more energy bikes to power the park, the kitchen was using the bike to light their station to prep food and feed people. The GA gave us the funds, and, soon, we had almost every station in the park outfitted with two energy bikes in the medic, kitchen, media, and even the

OWS Sustainability desk with gray water, recycling, and compost. *Photo by Brennan S. Cavanaugh*

The energy bikes, which soon powered the park. *Photo by Brennan S. Cavanaugh*

strong women's tent (no penises allowed) —only the library was left, and it was supposed to get bikes next, after their big tent was installed—then the raid happened.

The Sign Field in the first weeks of Occupy. *Photo by Brennan S. Cavanaugh*

WEB: That's when the NYPD destroyed everything, right? Were there any other projects in the works at that time?

BSC: We got most of our equipment back, but one bike was crushed like a John Chamberlain sculpture. The next project we were going to implement, but couldn't get to, was an OWS bike share program so the Medic or Kitchen could get supplies, bring goods to Jail Support, or just for getting people out of the park and onto a bike for healthy minds and bodies. We have to be healthy for the revolution!

WEB: Tell us about your before and after scenes that demonstrate how the multidimensional Occupy movement went beyond existing concepts of what we can manifest in privately owned public spaces.

BSC: Zuccotti/Liberty Park changed daily. The area that was covered with a forest of cardboard signs, facing One Liberty Plaza, gave way eventually to tents. By the end, everything gave way to the tents.

The GA relocated from the northeast corner (which was slowly taken over by the People's Library, as that expanded to five thousand books) to the amphitheater-esque steps by the Joie de Vivre (or Big Red Thing, as

Original site of the General Assembly at Zuccotti Park, November 2011. *Photo by Brennan S. Cavanaugh*

this sculpture was often called) to, eventually, off-site. The police had fun constantly pushing us back into the park. But it was a functioning town that changed organically, as devised by the needs for, and purposes of, that tiny city space.

The funny thing is that I never really realized how really ugly that little park is until after they emptied us out of there and closed it off (illegally)! The park even looks ugly on paper.

When the occupation was there, all the hard angles of marble and fluorescent lights set in the ground weren't readily seen—it was all bodies, and ages, colors, signs, all put together by people, not machines. And the trees didn't look so lonely and intentional. There was the sense of possibilities (like the sign "let's figure this shit out together") that bloomed amongst the sharp tables and chairs. And monocultured plant beds. The contrast between what Zuccotti/Liberty Park was then and what it is now is stark.

Zuccotti Park's west side, home to dancers, drummers, and well-placed signs for tourists and conversation. *Photo by Brennan S. Cavanaugh*

Role reversal on November 16, 2011, the day after the raid. *Photo by Brennan S. Cavanaugh*

WEB: Although I got to experience the ever-changing square early in the occupation, while it was in full bloom, and later when just small vestiges glowed in holiday lights festooning the plaza's valiant trees, your involvement was so much deeper. How would you like to see POPS throughout the city change?

November 16, 2011, the day after the raid. *Photo by Brennan S. Cavanaugh*

First Brooklyn Bridge march, with the roadway below seen from the footpath. *Photo by Brennan S. Cavanaugh*

BSC: I'd rather see the populace change their methods of interaction with the POPS. With our Time's Up! fountain rides, we exhibit friendly ways to enjoy our surroundings and reclaim our public spaces. I'd like to see more people enjoying our commons. My current favorite bumper sticker phrase is "the most radical thing we can do is introduce people to one another," and the commons will allow these meetings. When these POPS fill with people, they become beautiful with possibility.

WEB: I love that Fountain Ride video on Times-Up.org! Where can people see more of your photos about the ongoing Occupy movement?

BSC: Thank you. Spring is here, so there's going to be much to shoot. For now, on my flickr page at http://www.flickr.com/photos/brecav/ or at www.brennancavanaugh.com. Stay tuned!

Politics Out of Place

OCCUPY WALL STREET AND THE RHETORIC OF "FILTH"

Julian Brash

ON OCTOBER 15, 2011, NBC television's venerable comedy show, *Saturday Night Live* (SNL), aimed its sights on the growing conflict between Occupy Wall Street (OWS) and New York City's billionaire and ex-CEO, Mayor Michael Bloomberg. In the early days of the occupation, Bloomberg's reaction was muted and somewhat ambivalent. On the one hand, the mayor had dismissed many of the occupiers' complaints and warned against any disruption of business as usual in Lower Manhattan. On the other hand, he had acknowledged the right to protest and had refrained from using the kind of heavy-handed police tactics that might have been expected in such a situation (though, of course, they were used later on). But as September turned to October, Bloomberg made it increasingly clear that he was seeking to defuse the occupation, albeit in a relatively nonconfrontational way. His rhetoric focused more on issues of sanitation and cleanliness, and on Wednesday, October 12, the mayor made a personal visit to Zuccotti Park to inform the occupation that their encampment would have to be temporarily removed to allow for the cleaning of the park. This sudden interest in the cleanliness of public space was the centerpiece of SNL's send-up of Mayor Bloomberg: the climax of the piece and the biggest laughs came when, dismissing the contention that sanitation was being used as a pretext for ending the protest, comic actor Fred Armisen as Bloomberg made the transparently absurd claim that "New York City parks are routinely power-washed."

On initial inspection, this focus did seem suspect. While sanitation was clearly an issue for the occupation, it certainly hadn't reached crisis-level

61

proportions: though surrounding businesses had expressed annoyance at the occupiers using their restrooms. As of October 12, the NYC Department of Sanitation had not received any complaints concerning sanitation in the area, and the occupiers themselves had taken steps to deal with issues of cleanliness and health—among them the creation of a Sanitation Committee, the development of a gray-water system to deal with dishwashing contaminants, and the organization of a network that allowed occupiers to take showers and baths off-site, generally at the apartments of New York City supporters. Indeed, numerous observers (including myself) were impressed at the cleanliness of the park, noting that despite the mayor's concern Zuccotti Park appeared far cleaner than most other public parks in New York City.

So it is tempting to join the writers and cast of SNL in dismissing Mayor Bloomberg's focus on sanitation as little more than a pretext to disrupt or end the occupation with as little political fallout as possible. But there are three important reasons that we should resist this temptation—and that we might see this focus on sanitation as worthy of some attention. First, there is the simple question of why Bloomberg chose to deploy this issue and not others that might have had as much if not more substance—there *had* been complaints made to the city about noise and drumming, for instance. Secondly, Bloomberg's focus on sanitation was a (characteristically) more outwardly rational and technocratic instance of a broader discourse, most prevalent on the right, that depicted the occupiers as "dirty," "filthy," "nasty," "pigs," and so on. Indeed, two prominent right-wing memes concerning OWS that popped up repeatedly in blog postings, article titles, radio talk-show discussions, and social media were the phrase "the filth and the fury" and the case of one occupier (or at least someone who was spotted sleeping in Zuccotti Park) defecating on a police car. Finally, for cultural anthropologists such as myself, the sustained and repeated centrality of cleanliness, filth, pollution—in short, of *dirt*—to debates about OWS raised a red flag. Both empirical research and theoretical analysis have shown that this particular kind of talk is a sign that something very particular is going on, that the target of such talk has committed a very particular kind of transgression. What is the nature of that transgression, and what does this tell us about OWS, the response it generated, and the potential of the Occupy movement?

Mary Douglas' book *Purity and Danger: An Analysis of the Concept of Pollution and Taboo* (2002) remains the gold standard of anthropological analysis of beliefs concerning pollution, dirt, and uncleanliness. In it, Douglas makes three key points that allow us to understand why sanitary conditions played such a crucial role in the initial debate over OWS and the significance of that fact.

First, Douglas argues that pollution beliefs tend to address situations of moral ambiguity, in which categories of right and wrong cannot be easily or safely applied. And such situations, especially in our contentious and politically divided society, are all too common: "There can often be more than one view of what action is right," Douglas writes, "because of disagreement about what is relevant to moral judgment and about the estimated consequence of an act" (2002, 162). Attacking OWS on moral grounds, on the basis that its cause, its strategies, and its tactics were unambiguously in the wrong, would have been a difficult proposition. After all, the fact of increasing and increasingly entrenched inequality in the United States is absolutely undeniable. Moreover, the evidence is overwhelming that the majority of Americans—including the Republicans and the wealthy—consider the degree of inequality now found in the United States to be highly undesirable (Norton and Ariely 2011). Finally, there is the fact that OWS mobilization of the "99%" against the "1%" did not just evoke powerful critiques of aristocracy and plutocracy, but had the additional benefit of being an accurate diagnosis of the country's situation: as numerous analyses demonstrate, it is in fact that top 1% (and with that group the top .1% and .01% of the country's income distribution) that has reaped the vast majority of the economic gains of the past several decades (for a summary, see Hacker and Pierson 2010, 12–40). While some conservatives made an effort to dispute the occupiers' diagnosis of this situation and their demand that something (whatever that might be) be done about it, it was difficult for them to gain a foothold among a citizenry roiling with populist resentments. And if anyone would have a hard time defending the justness of the status quo, it was New York City's billionaire ex-CEO mayor, a paradigmatic one-percenter who had ridden a wave of cash and CEO hagiography into office (Brash 2011).

Second, Douglas argues that pollution beliefs can be invoked in morally ambiguous situations to sanction an individual or group when it might otherwise be difficult to do so. However, in order for this to work, the target of these beliefs must have committed a specific kind of offense: they must have transgressed not a moral system, but one of *social ordering*. All human societies require systems of classification and organization. While always changing and contested, as they tend to advantage some and disadvantage others, such systems create the basis for shared understandings and actions.

It is the transgression of these systems of ordering that is labeled as polluting or unclean. "There is no such thing as absolute dirt," Douglas writes (2002, 2); instead, she argues, drawing on an old definition, "dirt is matter out of place...No single item is dirty apart from a particular system of classification in which it does not fit" (2002, xvii, 44). This is the meaning of the red flag that pollution-talk throws up for cultural anthropologists: it says, "Here is a case in which someone is claiming that people or things are not necessarily wrong or bad, but are *not where they should be*." This "where" can be taken in metaphorical terms: sometimes offenses against order can entail phenomena that cannot be properly placed into abstract categories. But often it can be taken quite literally, as the organization and classification of *space* is crucially important to systems of social ordering.

In the case of OWS, charges of uncleanliness were a signal that the occupation had violated notions concerning the ordering of *urban* space, and in particular the proper place of urban political dissent. In the modern era, the city—and public space within the city—has functioned "as a key space for dissent and collective mobilization within civil society" (Graham 2010, xxi). However, in the past few decades shifts in urban governance and policing have drastically restructured the place of politics in urban space. The period since the early 1970s has seen the spread of what scholars have called urban neoliberalism: a policy regime centered around the attraction of investment, business, and desirable residents on the one hand, and the reimposition of order in cities after the turbulent 1960s and 1970s via increasingly punitive approaches to criminal justice, social welfare, and public space on the other (see Hackworth 2007; Wacquant 2009). Protest and dissent have come to be viewed by many urban elites not as signs of a healthy democracy or a vibrant civil society but as another symptom—along with rioters, muggers, the homeless, squeegee men, and other urban undesirables—of urban disorder, as well as a threat to the cities' ability to create and maintain an environment appealing to business, tourists, consumers, and the so-called "creative class."

As a result, urban elites have taken steps to tamp down dissent and protest, particularly when voiced in public space. While direct repression has been one means for this, in cities in liberal democracies like the United States a preferred strategy has entailed the use of various legal and administrative means to *domesticate*, rather than repress, urban dissent. So for instance, since the late 1980s, cities across the United States and the globe have set up so-called preplanned "free speech zones" during events likely to draw protestors: spaces demarcated, often via chain-link fencing and razor wire, as lawful sites for protests. At other times—including in Mayor Bloomberg's New York City during the 2004 Republican National Convention—ad hoc free speech zones have been set up whereby police surround and immobilize protests and marches that do not have official sanction. Cities have heightened the requirements for permits for protests and marches, increasingly denied organizers flexibility in determining the place and time of their actions, and in general reacted to proposed protests and marches in intransigent, uncooperative, and recalcitrant ways. All this has had the result of segregating protestors in space (and time) away from the targets of their protests or their fellow citizens.

By locating itself in a visible public space on a 24/7 basis, Occupy Wall Street violated the ordering principle of protest in the neoliberal city: that dissent should be permitted, but not seen or heard. Moreover, OWS occupied a park located directly in the heart of a district not only symbolizing but *named after* the industry—finance—that has been the economic driver of neoliberal urbanism. To return to Douglas's terms, OWS was *politics* out of place, a politicizing contagion that threatened the ostensibly inevitable centrality of finance, and of the profound inequality that has accompanied it, to the contemporary city. It was this transgression against the political ordering of the neoliberal city that generated the concern with filth, cleanliness, and sanitation that characterized the initial reaction to OWS on the part of the Bloomberg administration and so many others.

As October turned to November, OWS showed no sign of leaving Zuccotti Park, and Occupy encampments sprouted up in hundreds of cities and towns across the globe—regenerating not just the radical political energy that had ignited a global wave of antiglobalization protest in the 1990s but also the centrality of *urban space* to protest politics. Faced with a growing movement with a powerful message, Mayor Bloomberg overcame the initial uncertainty that SNL had mocked in that October 15 broadcast and ordered the dismantling of OWS's encampment and the effective closing of Zuccotti Park. He was accompanied by political leaders in Davis, Oakland, Portland, and many other places. As is often the case, defiance of the state itself became a trigger for state violence and punishment: emboldened by their peers, high-level officials unleashed the power of the state upon the occupiers, often without any compelling rationale, sanitation-related or otherwise. Raw political power vitiated the *cultural* forces that had made cleanliness and sanitation such a crucial issue in the initial response of officialdom to the Occupy movement.

Turning to the third of her relevant insights, Douglas argues that the invocation of pollution belief is not just indicative of moral ambiguity or a transgression of order, but is a sign that a particular transgression against order represents a *threat*: "Though we seek to create order, we do not simply condemn disorder," Douglas writes: "We recognise that it is destructive to existing patterns; also that it has potentiality...It symbolises both danger and power" (2002, 117). The organizers of OWS were keenly aware of the need to disrupt the (paradoxically) ordered nature of dissent in the contemporary neoliberal city in order to make an impact—and that is why they chose to *occupy* rather than *protest*. Moreover, they recognized, as Douglas does, that all "disorder" in fact contains the germ of an alternative order, and thus developed and foregrounded practices of mutual aid, self-organization, horizontal decision making, and so on. The reaction of Michael Bloomberg's mayoral administration, and of all those who condemned OWS as unsanitary, unclean, and polluting, demonstrated that defenders of the status quo knew this as well. Calling the occupiers "filth"—though meant as an insult—was in fact a profound compliment, an acknowledgment of the transformative potential inherent in OWS. Nevertheless, this initial response is worth remembering—and should give those of us broadly supportive of Occupy hope as the movement matures and reacts to changing circumstances.

References

Brash, J. 2011. *Bloomberg's New York: Class and Governance in the Luxury City*. Athens, GA: University of Georgia Press.

Douglas, M. 2002. *Purity and Danger: An Analysis of Concepts of Pollution and Taboo*. New York: Routledge.

Graham, S. 2010. *Cities under Siege: The New Military Urbanism*. New York: Verso.

Hacker, J. S., and P. Pierson. 2010. *Winner-Take-All Politics: How Washington Made the Rich Richer-and Turned Its Back on the Middle Class*. New York: Simon and Schuster.

Hackworth, J. 2007. *The Neoliberal City: Governance, Ideology, and Development in American Urbanism*. Ithaca, NY: Cornell University Press.

Norton, M. I., and D. Ariely. 2011. "Building a Better America—One Wealth Quintile at a Time." *Perspectives on Psychological Science* 6: 9–12.

Wacquant, L. 2009. *Punishing the Poor: The Neoliberal Government of Social Insecurity*. Durham, NC: Duke University Press.

To Occupy

Saskia Sassen

CURRENT UNSETTLEMENTS ARE breaking the cages into which territory and time have been pushed by the project of making nation-states. For centuries, national states worked at nationalizing territory, identity, security, power, rights—all the key elements of social and political existence. Those nationalizing dynamics assembled the pieces of what we now experience as the national and the natural. And what happened outside the borders of territorial states, whether the impoverished terrains of former empires or the earth's poles, was written out of history.

As time and territory begin to seep out of these century-old cages, notions of disorder and crisis dominate the debate. The current financial crisis is partly such a debordering of the old cages—the electronic space of finance and the escalating orders of magnitude and speed made possible by digitization break through the time and space of the national. Today's catastrophic conditions—the melting of the glaciers, the radicalness of poverty, the violence of economic inequality, the genocidal character of more and more wars—are often seen as part of a crisis. But it seems to me they are not. On the contrary, they are part of that putative no-man's-land that absorbed the costs of the making of national states and the more brutal side of capitalism. They are floating signifiers, speech acts that narrate the current condition in a far more encompassing manner than standard narratives about nation-states and "development." While these conditions have existed for a long time, they cross new thresholds and become more and more legible as the cages of the national begin to fall apart and reveal the landscapes of devastation on which they were built.

The flattening of territory into one singular meaning—national sovereign territory—is consequential. Territory is not ground or terrain, nor is it a given: it is made, collectively, through struggles and negotiations. Territory is a complex capability with embedded logics of power and of reclamation. In its beginnings, the work of making national territory was often the work of gaining autonomy from a dominant power—that was the goal of the early North American colonists, the independence movements in Africa in the 1960s, and other such struggles. Yet, more often than not, these original projects to gain the right to make a territory of one's own have gotten derailed into abusive power and fatigued claim-making.

The worldwide protests that took off in 2011 made visible the fact that there is life in the territorial, and that its meaning goes well beyond the one that has dominated our modernity. Tahrir Square, Los Indignados, Occupy Wall Street, each made novel territory by occupying what was merely ground within a national sovereign territory.

Street struggles and demonstrations are part of our global modernity. The uprisings in the Arab world, the daily neighborhood protests in China's major cities, Latin America's *piqueteros*, and poor people demonstrating with pots and pans—all are vehicles for making social and political claims. We can add to these the antigentrification struggles and demonstrations against police brutality in US cities during the 1980s and in cities worldwide in the 1990s and today. Most recently, over one hundred thousand people have marched in Tel Aviv, a first for this city—not to bring down the government, but to ask for access to housing and jobs. An important part of the demonstration was Tel Aviv's tent city, housing mostly impoverished middle-class citizens. The Indignados in Spain have been demonstrating peacefully in Madrid and Barcelona for jobs and social services since May of 2011; they have now become a national movement. These are also the claims of the six hundred thousand who went to the street in late August of 2011 in several cities in Chile. Taken together, these instances suggest a concept that goes beyond the empirics of each case. This has led me to the notion of the Global Street, one I develop elsewhere (e.g., Sassen 2011).

The Global Street takes making. It takes occupying. By *global street*, I mean a space not only for making claims but also for making the social and the political by those who lack access to formal instruments of power. The urban street as public space is to be differentiated from the piazza or the boulevard of the European tradition, a space for ritualized practices. I think of the space of "the street," which of course includes squares and any available open space, as a rawer and less ritualized space in which new forms of the social and the political can be *made*, rather than being routinely enacted. With some conceptual stretching, we might say that politically "the street and the square" are markedly different from "the boulevard and the piazza": the first, signal action, and the second, rituals.

Seen this way, there is an epochal quality to the current wave of street protests, no matter their enormous differences—from the extraordinary courage and determination of protesters in Syria to the flash mobs convoked via social media to invade a commercial street block, as we have seen in cities in the United States, the United Kingdom, and Chile.

Out of these shifts and unsettlements arise partial (often highly specialized and other times elementary) assemblages of bits of territory, authority, and rights that were once firmly ensconced in national institutional frames. These assemblages cut across the binary of "national vs. global," the usual way of attempting to understand what is new in our global modernity. These emergent assemblages inhabit both national and global institutional and territorial settings. They can be localized and denationalize bits of national territory. Or they can span the globe in the form of trans-local geographies connecting multiple, often thick, subnational spaces—institutional, territorial, subjective. These settings are the building blocks for new global geographies. They do not run through supranational institutions that take out that thickness and generalize across differences.

New York City's Occupy Wall Street made a new partial assemblage of territory, authority, and rights—pulling out elements from, in this case, the territory of global finance. Occupy Oakland occupied a bit of the territory of global trade when it occupied its port, the biggest in our very big trading country. These are just the two most visible and dramatically different among the many occupations that took place across the country. To occupy these places is to remake their territoriality and thereby their embedded logics of power by introducing logics of sharing and solidarity.

Reference

Sassen, S. 2011. "The Global Street: Making the Political." *Globalizations* 8 (5): 565–571.

The Office of the People

Gan Golan

DEMOCRACY REQUIRES PHYSICAL space. When people are allowed to assemble in physical space on a regular, ongoing basis, they forge more dense social networks, which in turn facilitate the creation of new institutions. In other words, having a physical space is a prerequisite to developing new forms of power—and sustaining them—the same way that all institutions require space in order to evolve, mature, and get the day-to-day work done.

Now, I hope the above statement elicits a "so what?" To me, it reads as an incredibly obvious statement and, to be honest, I mean it in the most boring, self-evident way. I think it's worth thinking about the boring aspects of space because in the analysis of the Occupy Wall Street movement (OWS), most of the focus is on how Occupy is some sort of radically different, aberrant kind of space—and yes, perhaps it is. But perhaps not enough is being said about the ways in which Occupy is actually a very typical, mundane kind of space.

All the dominant institutional sectors in society already have space, called offices. The public sector has its city halls, state houses, and the capitol building; the private sector has tens of thousands of offices in gleaming skyscrapers in cities across the nation; and the nonprofit sector has its nerve center located in pricey offices in Washington, DC. All these office spaces share one common shortcoming: they are fundamentally undemocratic, restricted spaces; particularly those that are meant to "represent the people." To have an office in government, you first need to raise millions of dollars to run for it. To have an office with any real power in the corporate sector, you need to be a manager or CEO. To have an office in the nonprofit sector, you'll first need to have a master's degree, and, of course, you'll need to have cozy connections to wealthy funders who'll pay for it.

This raises the question: If all these institutions have spaces, then where is the office space for everyday people? Where are the places where ordinary citizens can simply show up and automatically have a voice, without elitist filters and barriers to entry? Where can the ordinary citizens gather with others and speak their own truth, form their own social networks, make plans, and then get the work done? That space has long ceased to exist in our society. Occupy filled that need.

In short, Occupy is the "Office of the People." By recreating the town square in American civic life, Occupy has created a space where everyday people can come together without having to jump through institutional hoops or pay their dues to some existing form of power. It created a place where people, regardless of their access to power and privilege, could simply be heard. But it is also more than that. People don't just show up to speak. They stay. They meet. They return daily. They discuss, they strategize, they plan, and very quickly they begin forming their own institutions.

This reveals what is perhaps most important about occupying space, one that most movement theorists have overlooked. Occupying is far more than a "tactic," or "meme," or "campaign." Simply put, it is infrastructure. As such, it is a foundation for institution building, which in a very short time facilitated the birth of an entirely new institutional sector—a sector that very quickly began competing with existing political sectors. After all, one could argue that Occupy did more in three short months to shift the national dialogue on the economy than the entire progressive nonprofit sector did in the last three decades, after hundreds of millions of dollars spent.

One only needs to look at the number of OWS working groups that took shape, with their round the clock meetings at 60 Wall Street, the thousands of people participating, and their vast network of hundreds of new websites to keep them working 24/7. By producing an office space for the people, Occupy created a platform in hundreds of cities that allowed citizens to form institutions on their own terms, without the kinds of barriers and restrictions placed on such spaces. The absence of and the deep desire for such spaces is evidenced by the sudden, massive proliferation of occupations, reaching over eight hundred in number.

So, I think there is a very mundane way in which Occupy should also be acknowledged. It is not just some wildly different, insurgent space, but rather the birth of something natural and necessary. It is simply providing something for people that the elite and powerful already have. After being locked out of almost every office space there is, everyday people simply went out and created their own.

A Space for New Stories

Physical spaces tell stories. Every place inhabited by human beings is infused with narrative. The spaces we move through in our daily life are constantly telling us stories about "how to behave" or "who we are" within that space. They speak to us. Soothe us. Even yell at us. The stories that are told by the spaces that surround us shape us just as much as we shape them. It is in this dialogue—of creating space and it creating us—that we become who we are and who we hope to be.

Most spaces in our society are restrictive, regulatory spaces meant to maintain the status quo. More and more, these stories are neither created by us nor open to our revision. Their goal is to narrowly channel our behaviors into a fixed set of allowable activities. When outside, the privatization of public space has meant that we are mostly being told we are shoppers. In the privacy of our homes, we are told to eat and enjoy television. At work, we are told to work hard, keep our noses down, and play by the rules. The stories we are told by most of our daily spaces tell us we are consumers or workers, and not a whole lot else.

However, there are other kinds of spaces that societies have always needed that are transformational spaces (churches and universities, for example). We enter into those spaces to become someone different, and we leave that space with a new story of who we are. Occupy is one such space that has been sorely lacking from our political landscape: the public square. But while it falls into this tradition, it is also a very different kind of transformative space. Unlike churches and universities, the stories of transformation it tells are not delivered by hierarchies (priests and professors) but are rather self-created and open to interpretation and reinterpretation. In that sense, Occupy is also a space created so that people can begin to tell their own stories.

So Occupy has been part university (transforming the intellect), part church (transforming the heart), part town square (engaging the body, both individual and collective), and yes, even part laboratory (a place for experimentation with all of the above). People are not just "meeting" or "conversing" in Occupies, they are being deeply transformed at the most visceral level. They are emerging from Occupy as different people. They are leaving these spaces with a new, different story about their own agency, about their connections to other people, as well as a different story about what they expect from systems of power. And what's more, they are now taking these new stories into their homes, their workplaces, the streets, the shopping malls. This transformative capacity of Occupy is perhaps what makes it so threatening to existing institutions.

In understanding this capacity, it is important to recognize how Arts & Culture lies at the heart of this transformative process. Occupy was first and foremost a cultural movement. From day one, rather than seeking to argue its case with policy prescriptions, it ignited the popular imagination with a vision of the impossible made real, expressed through posters (the ballerina atop the bull) and short films (Anonymous's online videos) and then the massive art explosion that followed. The story that Occupy was telling—about the rejection of the system and the need for a radical, structural overhaul—is a completely different kind of storytelling than what most progressive organizations have been telling the public for three decades, which are all about working within the system and incremental change. It should not be a surprise that the visionary, unapologetic tone that defined Occupy is what actually inspired people to take action.

Arts and culture have also helped crucially define the spaces themselves. In Zuccotti Park, there was a functional library before there was a kitchen. People set up an art-making center before they had actual tents to live in. The Arts & Culture working group was the largest of the eighty or so working groups that formed, with over twelve guilds and five hundred members. What the art has done is help to immediately define these spaces as different, separate, and autonomous. The artistic spectacle that is Liberty Square puts anyone entering the space on alert, declaring loudly that "if you enter here, know that this space does not abide by the same rules as the rest of society." You are allowed to change it, make it yours, and allow yourself to become someone else. The story being told here is a different one. It is a story that you, along with everyone else here, get to create.

Some Unresolved Constitutional Questions

Arthur Eisenberg[1]

THE OCCUPY WALL STREET movement (OWS) brought attention to the growing disparity between rich and poor in this country and to the injustice of that disparity. Its message resonated widely throughout the nation and abroad. Beyond its compelling call for fairness, however, the occupation of Zuccotti Park in New York City by OWS also generated a significant set of difficult and unresolved constitutional questions that arose out of the effort by OWS to engage in protest activity in a privately owned park that had been created and maintained as a facility widely accessible to the public.

The ultimate constitutional question presented by the broad range of protest activities undertaken by OWS within the park was whether the various restrictions imposed upon the protest activity were consistent with First Amendment standards. But there was a threshold constitutional issue that needed to be addressed before reaching that ultimate question. That issue is was whether the First Amendment even applied in a privately owned facility such as Zuccotti Park.

1. The author would like to thank the staff of the New York Civil Liberties Union (NYCLU) for the work that it has undertaken in connection with Occupy Wall Street and for the research that has been of assistance in the preparation of this essay. Taylor Pendergrass, Rebecca Engel, Taurean Brown, and Katherine Bromberg of the NYCLU deserve particular recognition, in this regard. Despite their assistance, the views and opinions advanced in this essay are those of the author and do not necessarily represent the position of the NYCLU or of other NYCLU staff members. And any errors in judgment or analysis are, perforce, those of the author alone and not the NYCLU.

More than seventy years ago, the Supreme Court recognized that "[w]herever the title of streets and parks may rest, they have immemorially been held in trust for the use of the public and, time out of mind, have been used for purposes of assembly, communicating thoughts between citizens, and discussing public questions. Such use of the streets and public places has, from ancient times, been a part of the privileges, immunities, rights and liberties of citizens."[2] This observation appears to support the proposition that the First Amendment should limit any effort by either the City or the property owner to restrict expressive activity within the park because Zuccotti Park has long been recognized as a property "held in trust for the use of the public."

This conclusion, however, does not account for a potentially conflicting constitutional principle holding that, as a general matter, the federal Constitution limits only the conduct of government officials and agencies and that it does not impose limitations upon efforts by private entities to restrict constitutional rights.[3] This constitutional principle is often described by courts, lawyers, and legal scholars as the "state action" doctrine in that it requires that there must be governmental conduct, described as "state action," that limits individual rights before the federal Constitution will come into play.

The state action doctrine is one that has been much criticized for its inconsistencies and incoherence. Indeed, more than forty years ago, a Yale scholar, Professor Charles Black, decried the state action doctrine as "a conceptual disaster area" and described efforts to analyze and apply the doctrine as "a torchless search for a way out of a damp echoing cave."[4] A burden of this essay will be to cast a glimmer of light into that cave.

In addressing rights of free expression on privately owned property, Supreme Court precedent has swung widely from one side of the state action divide to the other. In 1968, the Court considered a controversy involving a privately owned shopping mall that attempted to prohibit a labor union from establishing a picket line directed at a merchant that leased space within the mall. The labor union claimed that the First Amendment protected the

---

2. *Hague v. C.I.O.*, 307 U.S. 496, 515 (1939).
3. *Burton v. Wilmington Parking Authority*, 365 U.S. 715, 721 (1961).
4. Charles L. Black, Jr., "Forward: 'State Action,' Equal Protection, and California's Proposition 14," 81 Harv. L. Rev. 69, 95 (1967), quoted in William R. Huhn, "The State Action Doctrine and the Principle of Democratic Choice," Hofstra L. Rev. 1380 (2006).

right to set up a picket line to protest the merchant's employment practices and that the exclusion of such activity from the mall was unconstitutional.

The Supreme Court agreed.[5] It held that, in contemporary society, the shopping mall serves as the "functional equivalent" to what, in earlier times, would have been an urban business district with streets and sidewalks; and that, therefore, the exclusion of protest activity within the shopping mall would violate the First Amendment, notwithstanding the fact that the mall was privately owned.[6] Eight years later, however, the Court overruled its 1968 decision.[7] In doing so, the Court reasoned that "the constitutional guarantee of free speech is a guarantee only against abridgement by government."[8] Since the restrictions on free expression were imposed in the shopping mall cases by private entities, the Court concluded that no First Amendment claim could be pursued.

The Court has warned, however, that a determination of whether "state action" exists will often turn upon a careful "sifting of the facts."[9] In applying the state action doctrine to Zuccotti Park, it is therefore important to consider how and why the park was created and how it was administered over the years.

The park was created in 1968, pursuant to a special permit granted by the New York City Planning Commission that allowed the owner of the property, U.S. Steel Corporation, to build and maintain a public plaza in exchange for a waiver of the rules that would limit the size of the building that the corporation was constructing just north of the plaza. The plaza was called Liberty Park and, in an agreement subsequently concluded between U.S. Steel and the City, the property owner agreed that it and its successors in interest would comply with the New York City laws governing the use of the park and that this promise would be "a covenant that ran with the land."[10] Accordingly, this commitment remains binding upon Brookfield Properties as the current owner of the park.

---

5. *Amalgamated Food Employees v. Logan Valley Plaza*, 391 U.S. 308 (1968).

6. *Amalgamated Food Employees*, 391 U.S. at 318.

7. *Hudgens v. N.L.R.B.*, 424 U.S. 507 (1976); see also, *Lloyd Corp. v. Tanner*, 407 U.S. 551 (1972).

8. *Hudgens*, 424 U.S. at 513.

9. *Burton*, 365 U.S. at 722.

10. *People of the State of New York v. Nunez* (Crim. Court of the City of New York, Docket Number 2011-NY-082981), "Memorandum of Law In Support of Motion to Dismiss" at 3-4. The City of New York Special Zoning Permit, CP-20222, No. 4 (March 20, 1968) is set forth as Exhibit C appended to the Memorandum of Law submitted by the New York Civil Liberties Union as *amicus curiae*.

The park was badly damaged on September 11, 2001. But in 2006, it was reopened by Brookfield Properties amid great fanfare and with new design features. It also was given a new name: Zuccotti Park. In 2007, New York City became significantly more involved in regulating the many privately owned public spaces that had, by that time, emerged throughout the City.[11] The City Council adopted an elaborate zoning law that imposed design standards and requirements in order to render such facilities more accessible and inviting to the public. With regard to physical access, the zoning enactment prohibited owners from erecting barriers that might impede open public space and required a certain percentage of frontage to remain unobstructed.

The 2007 enactment also provided for a continuing involvement of the City Planning Commission in the regulation of such facilities. Indeed, the law set forth both procedural and substantive limitations that essentially prohibited private owners from restricting public access without approval of the Commission: "All public plazas shall be accessible to the public at all times, except where the City Planning Commission has authorized a nighttime closing." It further authorized the City Planning Commission to permit closure "during certain nighttime hours" if it were to find that such closure "is necessary for public safety."[12] The procedural limitations required that a property owner seeking relief from the requirement that the facility remain open twenty-four hours a day must apply to the Planning Commission for such a waiver and must document significant operational or safety issues in support of its application.[13]

Brookfield never sought relief from the City Planning Commission regarding the twenty-four-hour access requirement, even after OWS began to occupy Zuccotti Park. Instead, on October 13, 2011, Brookfield issued and posted new rules limiting access to the park and the conduct that would not be permitted in the park. The rules stated that "Zuccotti Park is a privately owned space that is designed and intended for use and enjoyment by the general public for passive recreation," for the "safety and enjoyment of everyone," and that, therefore, the following types of behavior would not be permitted:

---

11. New York City Planning Commission, N-0704972RY (Sept. 19, 2007/Calendar 21) appended as Exhibit E to New York Civil Liberties Union Memorandum of Law as *amicus curiae* in the *Nunez* case.

12. Memorandum of Law in Support of Motion to Dismiss in *People v. Nunez, supra*, 4–5.

13. Ibid., 5-6

    (i) camping and/or the erection of tents or other structures;

   (ii) lying down on the ground, or lying down on benches sitting areas or walkways which unreasonably interfere with the use of benches, sitting areas or walkways by others;

  (iii) the placement of tarps or sleeping bags or any other covering on the property;

  (iv) the storage or placement of personal property on the ground, benches, sitting areas, or walkways which unreasonably interfere with the use of such areas by others.[14]

At the time that these new rules were issued, it appeared that Brookfield and the city officials were working closely in monitoring the protest activity within the park and in responding to the objections to such activity by others. On October 11, Richard Clark, the CEO of Brookfield Properties, wrote to New York City Police Commissioner Raymond Kelly claiming that Brookfield had "received hundreds of phone calls and emails from concerned citizens and office workers in the neighborhood." The letter further maintained that, because of the occupation, Brookfield was unable to undertake its cleaning and maintenance practices and that conditions in the park had "deteriorated to unsanitary and unsafe levels." The letter acknowledged that Brookfield and city officials were conversing "on a daily basis" about the situation in the park, and it requested "the assistance of the New York City Police Department to help clean the park."[15]

One day later, on October 12, New York City Mayor Michael Bloomberg told the OWS protestors that they would need to leave the park temporarily to allow it to be cleaned. And one month later, early in the morning of November 15, 2011, the Police Department cleared the protestors from the park. At the time, the mayor acknowledged that he had been consulting with Brookfield in the days before the eviction of OWS. He stated that "Brookfield asked the City to assist in enforcing the no sleeping and camping rules." Mayor Bloomberg insisted, however, that the "final decision" to remove the protestors from the park was, in his words, "mine and mine alone."[16]

---

14. *People v. Nunez*, "Decision and Order," Docket No. 2011-NY-082981.

15. See "Letter from Richard Clark to Commissioner Raymond Kelly." October 11, 2011, available at http://www.capitalnewyork.com/article/culture/2011/10/3722467/bloomberg-tells-occupy-wall-street-protestors-clear-zuccotti-park-fr.

16. See James Barron and Colin Moynihan. 2011. "City Reopens Park After Protestors Are Evicted," *New York Times*, November 15.

The question remains as to whether this history of joint participation between the owner of the park and the City of New York in the creation and administration of Zuccotti Park establishes sufficient "state action" so that efforts to regulate and limit expressive activity within the park should have been subjected to constitutional scrutiny under the First Amendment. In the 2001 Supreme Court decision in the *Brentwood Academy* case,[17] the Court suggested five sets of circumstances under which "state action" might be established so as to impose constitutional limitations on the regulatory efforts of a private entity: First, when the private entity acts pursuant to the "coercive power" of the State or is "controlled" by the State; second, when the State provides "significant encouragement, either overt or covert" to the private entity; third, when a private actor operates as a "willful participant in joint activity with the State or its agents"; fourth, when the private entity "has been delegated a public function by the State"; and fifth, when the entity is "entwined with governmental policies" or when the government is "entwined in [its] management or control."[18] The last three of these circumstances are potentially applicable to the relationship between the property owner of Zuccotti Park and the City of New York.

The first of these circumstances involves an inquiry into whether the private entity and government officials willfully participated in a joint activity. Such joint activity seems clearly to exist in the relationship between the owner of Zuccotti Park and the City of New York. The decision to create a public park at the current location of Zuccotti Park rested upon a joint agreement entered into between the City and the original owner of the property. Moreover, the City continues to maintain close administrative authority over the policies governing access to the park, by operation of a 2007 zoning law that requires the approval of the City Planning Commission regarding any request on the part of the property owner to deviate from the rules governing public access to the park. Finally, and most importantly, the apparent active involvement of the Bloomberg Administration in the policing and adminis-tration of access to the park during the fall of 2011—when OWS occupied the park—further reinforced the claim that the City and the property owner of the park were jointly engaged in creating, administering, and enforcing the rules governing public access. In this regard, the October 11 letter from

17. *Brentwood Academy v. Tennessee Secondary School Athletic Association*, 531 U.S. 288 (2001).
18. *Brentwood Academy*, 531 U.S. at 930.

the CEO of Brookfield Properties, coupled with Mayor Bloomberg's statement that the decision to remove OWS was his and his alone, confirmed the joint enterprise and established a basis for the application of the First Amendment to the restrictions that burdened free expression and political protest in the park.

The second circumstance identified in *Brentwood* that might have been found to bear upon the situation presented by Zuccotti Park involved the question of whether the City had delegated a "public function" to the owner of Zuccotti Park. In 1966, in a case entitled *Evans v. Newton*,[19] the Supreme Court considered a testamentary gift of a parcel of land to a Georgia municipality to be used as a park. The donor conditioned the gift upon the requirement that the park be maintained only for white residents. When it became apparent, in the 1960s, that the City's exclusion of African Americans from the park violated the equal protection clause of the Fourteenth Amendment, City officials ended the discriminatory policy. In response to the municipality's action, however, individual citizens then asked a state court to return the title of the park to private hands in order to fulfill the intent of the donor and restore the park as one that excluded African Americans. This request rested upon the belief that if the park were owned by private individuals, the Fourteenth Amendment's prohibition against racial discrimination would not apply because, as noted earlier, the Constitution does not limit private conduct. The Georgia courts ordered the return of the property to a group of private individuals who would serve as trustees of the park. The US Supreme Court then reviewed the decision of the Georgia courts and concluded that the discriminatory admission policies of the park remained subject to the limitations of the Fourteenth Amendment and were unconstitutional. The Court held that the creation and maintenance of a public park is a "public function" and that "the service rendered even by a private park of this character is municipal in nature."[20] The Court concluded, therefore, that "the public character of [the] park [at issue in the case] require[d] that it be treated as a public institution subject to the command of the…[Constitution] regardless of who [had] title under state law."[21] The *Evans* case has never been overruled. And under the *Evans* precedent, Zuccotti Park might simi-

---

19. *Evans v. Newton*, 382 U.S. 296 (1966).
20. *Evans v. Newton*, 382 U.S. at 301.
21. *Evans v. Newton*, 382 U.S. at 302.

larly have been regarded as performing a "public function" and, therefore, subject it to constitutional constraints.

Although never overruled, however, *Evans* has been narrowed considerably by subsequent Supreme Court decisions. One of those decisions involved a constitutional challenge to the employment decisions of a private school.[22] In reviewing the challenge, the Supreme Court rejected the claim that "education" was a "public function" and held that the employment decision of the private school would not be held to constitutional standards. In doing so, the Court concluded that only those activities that would be regarded as the exclusive responsibility of government would be considered "public functions." The Court reasoned that just as there are public schools there are also private schools and that, therefore, the administration of schools is not an exclusively "public function." So, too, with parks. Just as there are parks that are administered and owned by government agencies so too are their privately owned parks. Accordingly, the creation and administration of a park might not be considered an "exclusively public function."

The common understanding of this more recent case is that entities such as schools or parks or assembly halls which might be administered by private parties in some circumstances and by government agencies in other circumstances will not be regarded as performing *exclusively* public functions and will not, therefore, be held to constitutional standards when administered by private entities. So understood, the "public function" theory that was employed by the Court in the *Evans* case would, most likely, not have provided a basis for holding that the owner of Zuccotti Park was subject to constitutional limitations.

But the third circumstance identified in *Brentwood* could well support the claim that the restrictions directed at protest activity in Zuccotti Park should have been measured against the requirements of the First Amendment. This third circumstance arises when there is an "entwinement" between a private entity and governmental officials in the administration and management of a facility such as a park. Again, the facts, as discussed above and as commonly understood, support an entwinement theory in the case of Zuccotti Park. Over the past two decades, the Supreme Court has clearly moved away from an expansive interpretation and application of the state

---

22. *Rendell-Baker v. Kohn*, 457 U.S. 830 (1982).

action doctrine and has, instead, narrowed the circumstances under which constitutional claims can be advanced against private entities.[23] Nevertheless, in this case, the City and the owners of the park have been closely engaged in the creation and administration of the Zuccotti Park rules governing public access. Such close engagement supports the claim that the rules imposed governing access to the park for political expression should be measured against the requirements of the First Amendment. Even if the facts surrounding the joint enterprise between the City and Brookfield were found insufficient to establish "state action" and if, therefore, constitutional claims could not be directed at the administration of Zuccotti Park under the state action doctrine, there remains an alternative line of cases under which the protest activity in Zuccotti Park might have been found subject to First Amendment protection.

This line of cases draws upon a First Amendment concept called the "public forum" doctrine. Under the public forum doctrine, there are certain species of government property with attributes that make them inherently appropriate venues for expressive conduct. Such property, which includes streets, sidewalks, and parks, are regarded as "quintessential public fora."[24] And there is a discrete line of cases that extends the public forum doctrine even beyond government-owned streets, sidewalks, and parks to property that is owned by private entities in circumstances where such entities have agreed to create an easement for use by the public.

In a Michigan case,[25] for example, a private owner secured permission to build an office building in exchange for agreeing to create an easement for the public designed to facilitate vehicles that needed to turn around as they entered the property. The easement was found by a court to constitute a "public forum" for expressive activity even though it was private property. Similarly, a federal court in Massachusetts has held that pedestrian lanes inside a market owned by the City of Boston but leased to a private entity constituted a "public forum," in part, because the City retained an easement protecting "the public's access and passage."[26] Finally, in a case involving the

---

23. See, for example, *Rendell-Baker v. Kohn, supra; Blum v. Yaretsky*, 457 U.S. 991 (1982); *Flagg Bros. v. Brooks*, 436 U.S. 149 (1978). See also *Brentwood Academy*, 531 U.S. 288 (2001).

24. *Perry Education Ass'n v. Perry Local Educators Ass'n*, 460 U.S. 37, 45 (1983).

25. *Thomason v. Jernigan*, 770 F. Supp. 1195 (E.D. Mich. 1991).

26. *Citizens to End Animal Suffering and Exploration v. Faneuil Hall Marketplace*, 745 F. Supp. 65 (D. Mass. 1990).

Venetian Casino and Hotel in Las Vegas,[27] a court recognized that private property should be treated as a "public forum" where a property owner agreed to construct a sidewalk "dedicated to public use" in exchange for securing approval to build the Venetian Hotel, which necessitated widening the road and eliminating the original sidewalk. The situation presented by the Venetian Hotel is not much different from that at issue in Zuccotti Park. Here, as there, the property should have been treated as a "public forum" for First Amendment purposes.

This conclusion that Zuccotti Park should have been treated as a "public forum" and that restrictions upon free expression within the park are subject to First Amendment scrutiny does not, of course, end the constitutional inquiry. In order to decide whether the expressive activity undertaken by OWS in Zuccotti Park ultimately enjoyed protection under the First Amendment, closer consideration must be paid to the nature of the expressive activity and to the efforts by the administration of the park to limit such activity. In the aftermath of the November 15 eviction of OWS from the park, Brookfield, with support from the City, allowed OWS to return to the park subject to three regulatory measures that seriously curtailed OWS activity. First, the prohibition against the erection of tents and the use of sleeping bags in the park was reinstated. Second, to enforce the prohibition against sleeping bags and tents, Brookfield introduced a policy of searching those entering the park to make sure that sleeping bags and tents were not being brought into the park. Third, Brookfield and the City erected barriers around the park to funnel all those seeking to enter the park to the narrow entry points where the searches would take place.

Representatives from OWS claimed that the twenty-four-hour occupation of the park and the erection of tents within the park conveyed a symbolic message of solidarity with the homeless and with those who were losing their homes in these harsh economic times. Accordingly, OWS contended that the prohibition against sleeping overnight in the park abridged its First Amendment right to engage in symbolic speech. The Supreme Court has found that the First Amendment does, indeed, protect symbolic speech.[28] But

---

27. *Venetian Casino Resort v. Local Joint Exec. Bd.*, 257 F.3d 937 (9th Cir. 2001).

28. *O'Brien v. United States*, 391 U.S. 367 (1968). *Texas v. Johnson*, 491 U.S. 397 (1989) held that the act of burning an American flag during a protest rally was expressive conduct under the "symbolic speech" doctrine. The *Johnson* Court observed that for conduct to qualify as symbolic speech the speaker must intend to convey "a particularized message" and the "likelihood must

the Court has also upheld a prohibition against sleeping in tents in Lafayette Park and on the Washington, DC mall, even in the face of a claim that the prohibition prevented an organization from sleeping in the park to convey a symbolic message calling attention to the plight of the homeless.[29] In light of this Supreme Court precedent, it is unlikely that OWS could have prevailed had it litigated the constitutional question of whether the prohibition against erecting tents in the park violated its right of symbolic expression.

The second regulatory measure, involved the searching of those entering the park to prevent them from bringing sleeping bags and tents into the park. This measure clearly burdened the associational interests of OWS in that it undoubtedly deterred individuals from joining OWS protest activity in the park. The burdens imposed by this measure should, therefore, be evaluated against one of two alternative First Amendment standards.

If the regulatory measure were understood as having been directed against OWS because of the views expressed by the protestors or because of the content of the OWS message, the sleeping bag search policy would be subjected to what courts and lawyers describe as "strict judicial scrutiny."[30] Under that level of scrutiny, those defending the search policy would be required to demonstrate that the searches were necessary to the advancement of a compelling interest and that such an interest could not be pursued in a less burdensome manner.[31] The search policy could not have survived such scrutiny, for it is clear that a less burdensome solution existed. If Brookfield and the City were interested in preventing the use of sleeping bags they could have simply entered the park and confiscated bags if and when they were erected or being used. A blanket search policy was clearly unwarranted.

If, however, one were to conclude that the imposition of the search policy did not turn on the content of the OWS message, the restriction

---

be great" that those who view the conduct must understand the message that the speaker intends to convey (491 U.S. at 404). There have been a number of recent lower court cases in OWS-like situations in which activity has been found to constitute symbolic expression protected by the First Amendment. See *Occupy Fort Myers v. Fort Myers*, 2011 WL5554034 (M.D. Fla.); *Occupy Minneapolis v. County of Hennepin*, 2011 WL5878359 (D. Minn.); *Freeman v. Morris*, 2011 WL6139216 (D. Me); *Occupy Trenton v. Zawicki*, No. C-72-11 (N.J. Ch. 2011); *Occupy Columbia v. Haley*, 2011 WL6698990 (D.S.C.); *Occupy Boston v. City of Boston*, No. 11-4152-G (Sup. Ct. Mass., 2011).

29. *Clark v. Community for Creative Non-Violence*, 468 U.S. 288 (1984).

30. *FCC v. League of Women Voters*, 468 U.S. 364, 547-548 (1984).

31. *Perry Education Association v. Perry Local Educators Ass'n.*, 460 U.S. 37, 45 (1983).

might then be measured against a less rigorous constitutional test. Such a test would, nevertheless, inquire as to whether the search policy was "a reasonable time or manner" restriction. But the inquiry into the reasonableness of the search embraces a requirement that the restriction must be "narrowly tailored to serve a significant governmental interest."[32] And because the prohibition against the use of tents could have been more directly accomplished, the search policy should not have been found to be reasonable even under the less rigorous constitutional test, although this circumstance presented a closer constitutional question. Additionally, just as the search policy is likely to have been found unreasonable, the erection of an elaborate set of barriers around the park to effectuate the search policy should similarly have been found to pose an unreasonable burden on the rights of political association and expression.

Finally, public discourse regarding the occupation of Zuccotti Park raised the question as to whether OWS was entitled, under the First Amendment, to gather in such numbers and in such a manner as to preclude others from using the park. The "reasonable time, place and manner" standard imposed by the First Amendment provides, if not an answer to this question, a way to begin to think about an answer. A municipality can limit the numbers of those seeking access to the park consistent with the capaciousness of the facility. It can also reserve portions of the park for a variety of uses and users. And it can do these things so long as there are adequate alternative opportunities for a group such as OWS to convey its message. As always, the devil is in the details.

The constitutional questions raised here were never fully[33] and finally adjudicated and the answers set forth above rest largely upon a normative view

---

32. Ibid.

33. A New York City Criminal Court has rendered a decision in the case of *People v. Nunez*, Docket No. 2011NY082981 (2012) that, in dicta, has upheld the constitutionality of the prohibition of tents in Zuccotti Park. In doing so, the Court relied significantly upon the Supreme Court decision in *Clark v. Community for Creative Non-Violence*. The *Nunez* case, however, did not involve a direct challenge to the constitutionality of this restriction. That case involved the prosecution of Nunez for trespass for remaining in the park after the NYPD tried to remove occupiers who were violating Brookfield's prohibition against camping. Nunez moved to dismiss the trespass charge claiming that the trespass prosecution could only be sustained if Brookfield's prohibition against camping constituted a valid directive. Nunez further argued that Brookfield's directive was not valid because Brookfield never applied to the City Planning Commission for permission to alter its twenty-four-hour access obligations in order to impose the no-camping rule and that the City Planning Commission, therefore, never approved this

of the First Amendment. Many of the questions require a fact-intensive inquiry to be answered properly. Still, the constitutional lessons to be learned from that experience bear to varying degrees upon all privately owned public space. Accordingly, the OWS occupation of Zuccotti Park was not only about the protest message conveyed by that occupation: it was also about the constitutional protections that may extend more broadly to political expression in privately owned public space.

---

new limitation on what had been unfettered public access. The Criminal Court ultimately rejected Nunez's argument. In this regard, *Nunez* was primarily a case that turned on an interpretation of both the penal law prohibition against trespass and the obligations of private property owners of privately owned public space under the City Zoning Law. *Nunez* was not a direct constitutional challenge to the prohibition against camping, and the criminal court's conclusions on the constitutional questions occurred in passing and were not central to the decision.

2

*Emplacing Equity
and Social Justice*

Making Public, Beyond Public Space

Jeffrey Hou

IN CITIES AROUND the world, citizen actions to re-shape public spaces have long been an important ingredient of vibrant urban life.[1] On the streets outside the Yoyogi Park in Tokyo, for example, young musicians defy the official rule and transform the sidewalks to a linear outdoor performance space. In the ground-level entrance to the HSBC Headquarters in Hong Kong, Filipino guest workers congregate on Sundays and turn the anonymous corporate space into a carnivalesque gathering of friends. Every day, vendors in cities from Mumbai to Madrid change city streets into temporary markets—legal or illegal. In East Los Angeles, Latino residents retrofitted streets, buildings, and front yards of existing neighborhoods to support a more vibrant and culturally rich social life. In cities across North America, immigrant groups have created sanctuaries and refuges in suburbs, ethnic malls, and multicultural urban neighborhoods.

Besides these everyday acts, citizen actions in urban spaces can also blossom into significant and transformative political events. The year 2011, for example, brought us the Arab Spring, protests from Athens, Greece to Madison, Wisconsin, and the Occupy movement. In each of these events, individuals and groups have taken over an urban space and transformed it into a site of actions, meanings, and possibilities. The main components of these events included not only the space itself, but also the individuals who were responsible and instrumental for their transformation. These instances

---

1. The term citizen in this chapter is used in a broader sense that includes various forms of citizenship beyond the definition of nationality.

Young musicians outside the Yoyogi Park in Tokyo transform the sidewalk into a linear concert stage. *Photo by Jeffrey Hou*

Filipino guest workers turn the ground-level lobby of the HSBC Headquarters in Hong Kong into an active social space every Sunday. *Photo by Jeffrey Hou*

of citizen action suggest the possibility and capacity of human agency to modify the everyday structure of the city and the society. Through their individual and collective endeavors, the protestors mobilize not only themselves but also the very notion of "public" in the public space.

The distinction between public and space, or actions and vehicles for actions, is an important one as we examine the implications of the Occupy Wall Street protest at Zuccotti Park and beyond. In a recent series of forums organized in New York City to envision the future of public space in the wake of the Occupy movement, two familiar responses emerged: how to make public space truly publicly accessible and inclusive in the face of growing privatization and diminishing publicness; and how to create space for protests to take place, with all the necessary parameters, such as size, location, means of transportation, and so forth.[2] The focus on physical space is not surprising given the presence of architects and designers in the forums. However, if the failure of privately owned public space (POPS) in substituting for a true public realm in today's city is any indication, the focus on spaces and physical parameters alone is likely to lead to another misguided attempt to invigorate public space and public realm. In this chapter, I argue that the making and mobilization of the public as an actively engaged citizenry is what enables a public space to remain public and continue to serve as a vehicle and building block of our participatory democracy.

Two Public Spaces

In my edited book *Insurgent Public Space* (2010), I make the distinction between two kinds of public space—*institutional public space* and *insurgent public space*. Institutional public spaces include typical parks, plazas, squares, streets, and some civic buildings, as well as privately owned public spaces, that are defined and produced by governments and corporations. These spaces are by nature codified, regulated, and institutionally maintained. Furthermore, they often assume a generic public that may be served by these spaces, but for the most part is not actively engaged in their making. In contrast, insurgent public spaces are those created or initiated by citizens and communities, often outside or at the border of the regulatory and legal

---

2. The forum was titled Freedom of Assembly: Public Space Today. See http://cfa.aiany.org/index.php?section=calendar&evtid=3964. (Accessed April 3, 2012).

Occupy Wall Street protesters transformed Zuccotti Park into a space where strangers can engage in a political conversation. *Photo by Jeffrey Hou*

domain. Insurgent public spaces are frequently brought into being by those who appropriate, reclaim, or occupy a given space to gather, express their opinions, and engage in a wide variety of cultural practices. They include guerrilla gardens, flash mobs, "third places," street vending, street theater, and protests. The notion of insurgent public space suggests that public space is not limited to the archetypal and familiar categories of parks and plazas. It also suggests that the making of public space is not the exclusive domain of institutions. Instead, the making of public space can involve a much broader set of actors. In this way, the term "public" is no longer just an adjective but rather an active body of citizens in the broadest sense.

For obvious reasons, the Occupy Wall Street protests in Zuccotti Park, as well as in many other locations around the world, serves as a prime example of insurgent public space. Through camping out, making and putting up protest signs, setting up temporary libraries and stations for communication and outreach, collecting and preparing food, engaging in conversations with passersby, and participating in shared decision making, the protesters transformed an otherwise passive and mundane urban space into a site of active political expressions and collective actions. Rather than a violation of public space as characterized by the authorities, developers, and property owners, the occupation of Zuccotti Park is actually an act in the production and protection of public space—both physically and politically. More than the law enforcement, it was the protesters who safeguarded Zuccotti Park and other Occupy sites as public space, a space for political dialogue and expression.

Actions and Space

The capacity of individuals and communities to transform urban spaces has been a topic of considerable attention in recent literature. In *Loose Space*, Karen Franck and Quentin Stevens (2006) examine how people in cities around the world pursue a rich variety of activities in locations not originally intended for them. They argue that it's people's actions that make a space loose and give a city life and vitality, "with or without official sanctions, and with or without physical features that support those activities" (Franck and Stevens 2006, 2). Similarly, in her introduction to *Everyday Urbanism*, Margaret Crawford describes "everyday spaces" as distinct from "the carefully planned, officially designated, and often underused spaces of public use that can be found in most American cities…Lived experience should be more important than the physical form in defining the city" (1999, 9–10). In her contribution to *Companion to Urban Design*, Kristen Day (2011) suggests that women's use of public space can constitute resistance when they engage in self-determined, meaningful activities that define their own identities. Similarly, in an article that discusses feminists' recognition of the grassroots informal politics, Faranak Miraftab (2004) makes the distinction between "invited" and "invented" spaces of citizenship. Here, "invited" spaces are defined as "the ones occupied by those grassroots and their allied nongovernmental organizations that are legitimized by donors and government interventions," while "invented" spaces are those "directly confronting the authorities and the status quo" (Miraftab 2004, 1). The articulation of "invented" spaces makes clear the agency of individuals and groups in creating spaces of resistance and expanding existing notions of citizenship.

Emphasizing the human agency of placemaking, these discussions have in many ways challenged the familiar narrative of loss in the recent discussion of public space (see Sorkin 1992, Zukin 1995, Low and Smith 2006),

They reinforce Don Mitchell's claim that definitions of public space and the public are produced "through constant struggles in the past and in the present...for it is by struggling over and within space that the natures of 'the public' and of democracy are defined" (Mitchell 1995, 121, 128).

Making Public and Making Space

As we envision the future of public space in North America and beyond, it is clear that the focus of our efforts should be equally, if not more, on the making of the public than on the making of space. While space remains critical as a vehicle for actions and expressions, it is through the actions and the making of a socially and politically engaged public that the struggle for public space as a forum of political dialogues and expressions can be resuscitated and sustained. But how exactly can this be accomplished in the everyday life of today's cities? How can such processes occur with or without another occupation in places like the Zuccotti Park? Further, how can we look beyond the specificity of the Occupy movement and Zuccotti Park and examine the making of a socially and politically engaged public as a broad-based, everyday practice involving a wider set of actors and processes?

Recent experiences from Seattle offer some leads. In 1989, with Jim Diers as the founding director of the Department of Neighborhoods, the city launched a highly popular program called the Neighborhood Matching Fund. The program, which still exists today, provides different categories of funds (Small Sparks, Small and Simple Projects, and Large Projects) to support community-initiated endeavors, from community outreach and mobilization to design, planning, and implementation. Because communities can receive the funds through cash donations and/or volunteer hours, the program incentivizes community building and organizing. From 1989 to 2001, communities in Seattle have generated more than $30 million in matching resources for projects ranging from neighborhood public art installations and community gardens to the renovation and development of neighborhood parks (Diers 2004). The funds not only supported the improvement of the city's many neighborhoods, but also strengthened the social networks and the capacity of community groups to become more engaged in the city's planning process. Many of the citizen groups have continued to be involved in the programming and maintenance of the spaces after the projects have been completed. Some of the efforts have snowballed into greater initiatives, such as the Growing Vine Street project, which began in a community garden but has since expanded to include preservation of vernacular houses and greening of streets in Seattle's Belltown neighborhood.

Concerted efforts in Seattle to expand the city's parks and open spaces serve as another telling example. In an era of diminishing public resources for many municipalities, Seattle's support for parks and open space has also fallen behind the demands from residents and neighborhoods. Instead of seeking private support, however, park advocates and citizen groups worked with the city staff and campaigned to put new tax levies on the election ballot twice in the past decade. In 2000, voters in Seattle passed the Pro Parks Levy at a price tag of $198.2 million over eight years to fund parks acquisition, development, and environmental stewardship, maintenance, and programming.[3] In 2008, even in the midst of the economic recession, Seattle's voters approved decisively the Parks and Green Spaces Levy, a $146 million fund over six years to continue to support the expansion of public open spaces in the city, including funds for more community gardens. Aside from projects listed in the levy proposals, the two levies also included a "Opportunity Fund" that supported projects proposed by citizen and community groups. Through the successive parks advocacy campaigns, the network of citizen and community groups continue to lobby on behalf of progressive planning and transportation policies in the city. The campaigns have encouraged the formation of an actively engaged public with significant political influence on the city's policy and planning.

Seattle is not the only place where one can find experiences and inspirations. In cities throughout North America, as well as a growing number of places around the world, community-based and nonprofit civic organizations have filled the void between institutions and communities. In Oakland, California, the nonprofit Unity Council worked with community members and design professionals to undertake a transit-oriented development to spur economic development in a predominantly immigrant and minority community. The organization was also instrumental in developing a new waterfront park to increase open space amenities in a district with the highest percentage of children but least amount of open space per capita (Hou and Rios 2003). In North Philadelphia, the Village of Arts and Humanity started as a community art project to engage local youths and improve the neighbor-

---

3. See http://www.seattle.gov/parks/proparks/default.htm. (Accessed March 15, 2012).

hood's many vacant lots. Since 1986, the organization has transformed more than one hundred fifty parcels of vacant land into sixteen parks, gardens, and passageways.[4] Today, it offers a wide variety of community services, including job training and educational programs.

In Hong Kong, community activists and social workers in the Wan Chai District have not only secured the preservation of the Blue House, one of the last remaining old-style tenement buildings in the city, but are also using it as a base for outreach and mobilization through the creation of a local museum and guided tour. In addition, to serve the low-income residents in the rapidly gentrifying neighborhood, social workers have created a swap shop, a grocery store selling local products, and a community currency called Time Coupon that encourages residents to volunteer for community services in exchange for donated and second-hand goods. In the rural township of Meinung, Taiwan, activists from TransAsia Sisters Association have been working with immigrant women from Southeast Asia to create gathering places that host a variety of activities including language lessons, child care, and social events. By participating in the making of these places, immigrant women were able to become active members of a community beyond their traditional role as parents and housewives (Chen and Lin 2010).

In Guatemala City, the organization Camino Seguro (Safe Passage) has been working to serve and engage the children and families living in extreme poverty around the city's garbage dump, the largest in Central America.[5] Since 2006, it has brought in landscape architecture students and faculty from the University of Washington to work with local families to create outdoor gardens, playgrounds, and classrooms that are intended as places of learning, recreation, exploration, and healing. These places serve not only as a refuge for children and families from poverty, violence, and despair, but also as a vehicle for gaining confidence and skills.[6] Built by university students together with local residents, the transformation of the sites has brought a sense of hope and pride in the community (Winterbottom 2011).

Community-based organizations like the Unity Council and the Village of Arts and Humanities, as well as their counterparts in other locations, help engage individuals as active members of the community, moving them

---

4. See http://villagearts.org/place-making. (Accessed March 15, 2012).
5. See http://www.safepassage.org/about_us. (Accessed April 3, 2012).
6. See http://larch.be.washington.edu/features/design_build/guatemala/guatemala_2009.php. (Accessed April 3, 2012).

away from passivity and indifference. While focusing primarily on issues at the community level, these organizations have the potential of forming broad-based networks and coalitions with the capacity to change the political discourse and structure in our society.

Public Space and Beyond

The privatization of public space in North American cities today is only a small part of a much more entrenched political and institutional crisis—the privatization of our democracy through unequal taxation, institutional loopholes, and overpowering financial influence of multinational corporations. The root cause of diminishing public resources and the privatization of public space in our cities today is precisely the privatization of our political system, a deeper crisis that cannot be addressed by creating more public spaces alone or by making public space simply more inclusive and accessible. This crisis requires the attention and intervention of a much more active and engaged public, a public that is willing and capable of speaking up and mobilizing politically to change the system.

To create a more active body of citizens, public space in our cities and communities can still play a critical role. Specifically, public space can serve as a focal point of collective action and make such expressions and struggles visible to others. As in the case of Zuccotti Park and many other Occupy sites, public space can serve as a vehicle for galvanizing attention and mobilizing people. But as we also learn from Zuccotti Park and other Occupy actions, it is the actual "occupation" of public space that activates the agency of these places, enables mobilization and expressions, and catalyzes a movement. The occupation of these spaces and the continued occupation of the political sphere of our society require the ability of citizens to mobilize, network, and take actions in order to effect fundamental change beyond the public spaces of our contemporary cities.

References

Chen, H.-Y., and C.-H. Lin. 2010. "Making Places of Fusion and Resistance: Experiences of Immigrant Women in Taiwanese Townships." In *Insurgent Public Space: Guerrilla Urbanism and the Remaking of Contemporary Cities*, edited by J. Hou. New York: Routledge.

Crawford, M. 1999. "Introduction." In *Everyday Urbanism*, edited by J. L. Chase, M. Crawford, and J. Kaliski. New York: The Monacelli Press.

Day, K. 2011. "Feminist Approaches to Urban Design." In *Companion to Urban Design*, edited by T. Banerjee and A. Loukaitou-Sideris. New York: Routledge.

Diers, J. 2004. *Neighbor Power: Building Community the Seattle Way*. Seattle: University of Washington Press.

Franck, K., and Q. Stevens. 2006. "Tying Down Loose Space." In *Loose Space: Possibility and Diversity in Urban Life*, edited by K. Franck and Q. Stevens. New York: Routledge.

Hou, J., ed. 2010. *Insurgent Public Space: Guerrilla Urbanism and the Remaking of Contemporary Cities*. New York: Routledge.

Hou, J., and M. Rios. 2003. "Community-driven Placemaking: The Social Practice of Participatory Design in the Making of Union Point Park." *Journal of Architectural Education* 57 (1): 19–27.

Low, S., and N. Smith. 2006. "Introduction: The Imperative of Public Space." In *The Politics of Public Space*, edited by S. Low and N. Smith. New York: Routledge.

Miraftab, F. 2004. "Invited and Invented Spaces of Participation: Neoliberal Citizenship and Feminists' Expanded Notion of Politics." *Journal of Transnational Women's and Gender Studies* 1. http://appweb.cortland.edu/ojs/index.php/Wagadu/article/view/378/719. (Accessed March 12, 2012).

Mitchell, D. 1995. "The End of Public Space? People's Park, Definitions of the Public, and Democracy." *Annals of the Association of American Geographers* 85 (1): 108–133.

Sorkin, M., ed. 1992. *Variation on a Theme Park: The New American City and the End of Public Space*. New York: Hill and Wang.

Winterbottom, D. 2011. "Effecting Change through Humanitarian Design." In *Service-Learning in Design and Planning: Educating at the Boundaries*, edited by T. Angotti, C. Doble, and P. Horrigan. Oakland: New Village Press.

Zukin, S. 1995. *The Culture of Cities*. Cambridge, MA: Blackwell.

Freedom Corner

REFLECTIONS ON A PUBLIC SPACE
FOR DISSENT IN A FRACTURED CITY

Mindy Thompson Fullilove with Terri Baltimore

Occupy Pittsburgh March: Freedom corner (Hill District)
to Market Square

Occupy Pittsburgh Day of Action:

Saturday, October 15, 2011

Beginning Rally: 11:00 a.m. Freedom Corner

March from Freedom Corner to Market Square: 11:45 a.m.

Movement Kickoff Rally: 1:30–3:00 p.m. Market Square

Occupation of Pittsburgh begins 4:00 p.m. at Mellon Green,
Grant St. & Sixth Ave

(Progress Pittsburgh 2011)

ON OCTOBER 15, 2011, the Occupy Pitts-
burgh movement took to the streets, starting in a neighborhood called the
Hill District, in a place called Freedom Corner. Several hundred people
gathered there for a short rally, followed by a march to Market Square.
Accompanied by bongos, they chanted, "The banks got bailed out, we got
sold out!" and "This is what democracy looks like!" The crowd grew as
people arrived from all over the Pittsburgh region, drawn by many sources
of discontent and pleased to be part of the 99%. The rally at Market Square
ended at 4 p.m., and protestors continued on to Mellon Square, a private
square belonging to Mellon Bank, which had agreed to let the protestors

Figure 1: The Occupy Pittsburgh march and rally at the intersection of Centre Avenue and Crawford Street. *Photo by Renee Rosensteel*

stay. They pitched tents on damp ground and prepared to occupy Pittsburgh. This chapter will examine why Occupy Pittsburgh started its protest in this particular corner.

Pittsburgh, Pennsylvania, is an industrial city that was peopled by waves of migrants and immigrants as it grew. While there are many histories of this important American city, our focus here is on the story of the African American people fighting for full equality. As in other American cities, African Americans in Pittsburgh have faced many disadvantages and have organized relentlessly against them. One corner in the city assumed tremendous significance when it became the site of a famous billboard denouncing urban renewal. Over the years, the vacant corner lot evolved into "Freedom Corner," the place where marches started or ended and rallies were held. It has, since 2001, been the site of a Civil and Human Rights Memorial. In all these incarnations, this corner has served as a location for dissent.

The African American community was concentrated in the Hill District in Pittsburgh during the Great Migration, which began in 1916 and ended in 1930. The Hill was a segregated black neighborhood by then, and Freedom Corner, as it is now called, was located in the center of that space, at Crawford Street and Centre Avenue, in an area that was within the dense commercial area known as the Lower Hill. In Figure 2, we can see a photograph from the 1950s in which the plans for urban renewal were in-

Figure 2. Proposal for urban renewal in the Hill District. *Courtesy of the Pennsylvania Room, Carnegie Library, Pittsburgh, Pennsylvania*

dicated with pieces of transparent material, representing new roads and the Civic Arena that were proposed for the area, laid over an aerial photograph.

The urban renewal clearance started in the late 1950s. According to Sala Udin, a civil rights leader and former Hill District councilman, many of the civil rights leaders supported urban renewal in the 1950s, having been told that it was a program of renovation. As urban renewal progressed—and the African American community began to be displaced and no new housing was being built—the leaders realized they had been wrong. They realized that urban renewal was a program of neighborhood destruction.

By the early 1960s, the destruction had reached Crawford Street, and the community learned that the authorities, having destroyed the triangle of the Lower Hill, intended to extend the process for an additional sixteen blocks—up to Kirkpatrick Street—making it substantially larger than the devastating first section of clearance. Frankie Pace, owner of a store on Centre Avenue, just east of Crawford Street, that sold gospel sheet music, organized the erection of a billboard in protest.

Figure 3. Proposal for urban renewal in the Hill District.
Courtesy of the Pennsylvania Room, Carnegie Library, Pittsburgh, Pennsylvania

The Freedom Corner website states that after the city began to target the area from the new Civic Arena to Kirkpatrick Street, the remaining residents of the Hill rose up in protest:

> They erected a billboard reading "No development beyond this point!" at the corner of Centre and Crawford. Demonstrators gathered on the steps of St. Benedict the Moor Church, and, amid cries of "Not another inch!" and in the face of death threats, they marched to City Hall. The community succeeded in holding back the tide of further demolition and redevelopment in the Upper Hill. From that time on, the corner of Centre and Crawford was known as Freedom Corner and became the rallying point for local marches and civil rights demonstrations that reflected Dr. Martin Luther King's commitment to nonviolent protest.

As Sala Udin explained in a conversation with Mindy Fullilove, the 1960s fight against displacement merged with the national civil rights protests and became a fight for freedom. He related,

Ms. Thelma Lovette has in her possession a bus ticket for the 1963 March on Washington. The ticket says that the bus will be departing from Freedom Corner at 6 a.m. That is the earliest documentation that I have seen that the place had come to be known as Freedom Corner, and the name was popular enough that everyone would know where that was.

Throughout the 1960s, Freedom Corner served as the rallying point. When civil insurrection started after the 1968 assassination of Dr. Martin Luther King, Jr., leaders of the NAACP gathered people there and negotiated with riot police for a march to the Point, the city's park at the confluence of the Allegheny and the Monongahela Rivers that form the Ohio River. Thus established, named, and used, Freedom Corner became the official launching site for civil rights protests.

This brief history of the site reveals that it was massive change that brought this site into focus as a space for protest. Urban renewal was one of a series of policies that have contributed to sorting American cities by race, class, religion, sexual orientation, lifestyle, age, and gender (Hanchett 1998). The process of sorting the city undermines the ability of the city to function as whole; drives resources toward wealthy areas and away from poor areas, thus functioning as a fundamental cause of disease; and impairs the ability of the city to control greed and other kinds of misuse of people and land. Freedom Corner was erected at a critically important moment in the history of American sorting, but it also served as a site of protest for Occupy Pittsburgh, a movement originating in the US in 2011 to denounce the concentration of wealth. In the next sections, I want to reflect on geographic and social changes in the area and the erection of the civil rights monument at Freedom Corner.

Reflection 1: *What Is the Geography of the Site?*

In the heyday of the Hill, this intersection of Pittsburgh was part of the commercial hub of the Lower Hill and ran parallel to its main street, which at that time was Wylie Avenue. The destruction of the Lower Hill made two changes to the geography of the corner of Centre Avenue and Crawford Street. It was no longer in the center of the black ghetto but on the edge of it. In a striking series of maps, geographer Joe Darden depicted the shift in segregation in Pittsburgh (Darden 1973). Prior to urban renewal, the point of the Lower Hill is coded as a black segregated area. In the 1970 map, however, it was no longer so. Edges are extremely important to ecosystems, and urban ecosystems are no different from forests in this regard. The strategic placement of the billboard depended on the long view that the clearance had afforded.

The meaning of the site shifted in another very important way. Prior to urban renewal, the major street linking the Hill to downtown was Wylie Avenue. There is a documentary about that era called *Wylie Avenue Days*. Wylie Avenue was described as the "only street in America that starts at a church and ends at a jail." It was a commercial center for its entire length and the heart of the Hill. Urban renewal destroyed this main artery by chopping it off at the knees. At the same time, Centre Avenue, which had ended just beyond its intersection with Crawford Street, was extended to downtown and became the great connecting street.

At present—in 2012—Crawford Street has even greater potential for connection then Wylie had, as it continues east through many Pittsburgh neighborhoods, which is of critical importance for strengthening the whole urban tissue. Freedom Corner's visibility has grown as Centre Avenue has assumed increasing importance in the regional system of movement.

Reflection 2: *What Is the Sociology of Freedom Corner?*

Greetings All:

In a dramatic and historic move, organizers and supporters of the June 23rd Black Males Solidarity Day decided to take their message to heart and revise the route for the upcoming mobilization. In the long history of Freedom Corner, no demonstration has ever originated downtown and ended in Pittsburgh's historic Hill District Community. On Saturday, June 23rd, just that will happen. Organizers believe strongly that while public policy directions are of vital importance, the ultimate responsibility for addressing the challenges faced by the greater African American community must be shouldered by us. Our dramatic march from downtown up to the Hill symbolically reflects the serious nature of the charge we have taken on. Residents of the Hill District are currently in the midst of a struggle to address a broad range of issues that will dramatically affect the community for decades. That struggle is representative of the many struggles being waged in neighborhoods throughout the area. Black men and boys from across the county will assemble downtown, and in a dramatic expression of solidarity with the Hill's mostly African American residents, march to Freedom Corner at Center and Crawford St. (Brotha Ash Productions 2007)

Freedom Corner was born out of desperate efforts by the African American community to save itself. Prior to urban renewal, the Hill was tightly organized, made up of blacks of all professions, backgrounds, and social classes, and able to carry out the functions of community, such as caring for the vulnerable and recognizing problems. The clearance of the Lower Hill by urban renewal devastated the social system of the Hill. Thousands of people were forced to move, businesses, churches, and social organizations were destroyed, families were sundered, and the political strength of the Hill was greatly undermined. Thus, urban renewal had a massive effect on the social organization of the Hill.

Eva-Maria Simms (2008), writing about childhood in the Hill, found that growing up changed dramatically in 1960, which coincided with the destruction of the Lower Hill. Before urban renewal, in an era we shall call Simms I, the tightly interwoven community functioned so that a broad net of adults participated in the rearing of a broad net of children. Young people were surrounded with opportunities, their activities were carefully policed and organized in an age-appropriate manner, and they were expected to connect with all the other children in the neighborhood. People might have been poor, but they had a rich life.

After 1960 and after urban renewal, an era we shall call Simms II, the social networks shrank and the general engagement of the adults with the children began to shift. Pittsburgh entered into deindustrialization and the Hill, largely dependent on jobs in the mills and factories, began to suffer from the problems of long-term unemployment.

By 1980, which we shall call Simms III, the combination of urban renewal and unemployment had led to a dramatic shift in the social organization. One of Simms's interviewees said that what he experienced was "unexpectancy": when he went out of his house, he looked to the left, looked to the right, not knowing what would happen next. The neighborhood spaces that had offered vast support for youth development had shifted in their purpose. As one example, where youth had once learned to roller skate, a drug treatment program had been installed.

In the setting of Simms III, violence, addiction, family dysfunction, poor school achievement, and high infant and maternal mortality became the order of the day. The capacity to protest staggered as the social organization declined, but it did not disappear. Many people, especially but not exclusively elders who had lived in earlier times, became keepers of the flame of the history and hope of the Hill. They told the story of Freedom Corner and emphasized the role of protest as part of the armamentarium of problem solving. Teenie Harris's photo of the billboard was circulated and treasured. In 1998, Mindy Fullilove visited Sala Udin, then a councilman for the Hill. He proudly unwrapped a framed copy of the photo, which he had discovered in a small shop on Fifth Avenue. He remembered the erection of the billboard; it was a story he told with pride, and it was part of the inspiration for creating a civil rights memorial at the site.

Reflection 3: *Why Was a Memorial Created?*

The first district-elected councilman for the Hill was Jake Milliones. Sala Udin related to Mindy Fullilove,

> Jake had the idea to use new housing on Crawford Street as a bulwark against further redevelopment in the Hill. There had been no new housing created since the past century. He thought the place to start was Crawford Street. He set in motion a plan for new housing and part of the plan was to preserve a primary plot of land at Freedom Corner. He wanted to erect a sculpture that would be iconic and representative of the civil rights struggle in Pittsburgh.

Milliones died suddenly in office before he had been able to realize this vision, but the land had been secured. When Udin was elected to office, he undertook to carry out the mission of creating a memorial. Although developers for the Crawford Street area saw the corner as the most valuable piece of property, Udin remarked that "We said 'No.' We've never given up on that ninety square feet of land as Freedom Corner."

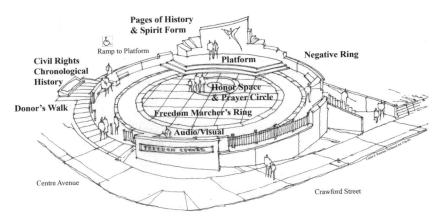

Figure 4. The design of the Freedom Corner Monument. *Illustration by Carlos F. Peterson*

As Udin and others prepared to create the memorial Milliones had envisioned, they expanded the idea to incorporate gathering space so that the marches, which were starting on the steps of St. Benedict the Moor, the church across the street, could gather at Freedom Corner.

Sala Udin and others proposed that the Freedom Corner site should be formalized. A memorial to civil rights activism in Pittsburgh was proposed. It was created by a community subscription that raised about $750,000. A design competition was held, won by the team of architect Howard Graves and artist Carlos Peterson. The soul of the design is the Spirit Form, a soaring figure that echoes the statue of St. Benedict, an icon of the Hill that stands atop the church just opposite Freedom Corner.

In the design, the names of twenty-five "fallen heroes" of the Pittsburgh civil rights movement were inscribed in an inner circle, while seventy-five "living legends" were inscribed on an outer circle.

In 2001, the memorial was dedicated, to the delight of many (Dyer 2001). As Phil Hallen, one of the "living legends" saluted in the memorial, shared with the authors, "Standing at the corner for the dedication was like a kaleidoscope of all those marches."

The memorial was envisioned with many bells and whistles and as part of Pittsburgh's History Trail. As time passed, people sometimes expressed disappointment that the most elaborate parts of the vision were not realized and the site was poorly maintained. Ownership of the site, which originally was in the hands of the Hill District Community Development Corporation, passed to the city, but this did not resolve all the problems of maintenance. The Freedom Corner website, visited on April 11, 2012, had evidently not been updated or expanded since it was first created. News of events at Freedom Corner was available on Google, but no links or postings were available at the Freedom Corner website. The memorial itself was, perhaps, not more neglected than other parts of the Hill, which was still largely declining from the inertial forces that had set the neighborhood on a downward trajectory, but it was not better tended either.

Time had taken a toll in other ways as well. "Of course, by now," said Udin, speaking to Mindy Fullilove in 2012, "about half of the living legends are gone. We want to add a black asterisk next to the names of those who have died."

But these concerns overlook a remarkable positive aspect of the space: it was established as a space of dissent in the 1960s and has remained available for that activity ever since. It is enough to say, "Meet me at Freedom Corner," for people to know where the demonstration will start.

Reflection 4: *What Does Ongoing Change Mean for the Area?*

Urban renewal cleared the Lower Hill and the space was used for the Civic Arena. In 2012, after many months of debate and protest, the Civic Arena was demolished. The burning question was: what would happen to the space that once was the Hill? If the Hill extends out, then Freedom Corner resumes a position tucked into the community. If downtown moves up to Crawford Street, then Freedom Corner becomes even more important as an edge of the African American neighborhood. In this regard, it is the position of a second space—a "truth and reconciliation" park—that emerges as a central issue. The proposal on the table in 2012, at the time of this writing, was to put the park at the point where the historic Hill met downtown. To do so would require an expensive project, one that would create a platform over a highway. Such a park is highly symbolic, memorializing the "lost limb" of a neighborhood amputated by urban renewal. It is not, however, likely that such a place would be highly functional in the movement system of the city, which might mean that, in spite of being full of meaning, it would be empty of people (see Proposed Park II in Figure 5).

Figure 5. Proposed locations for a truth and reconciliation park. *Courtesy of the Pennsylvania Room, Carnegie Library, Pittsburgh, Pennsylvania. Graphic design by Rich Brown*

Another idea was to put the truth and reconciliation park along Crawford Street, a proposal that included a link to Freedom Corner (see Community Reconciliation Park I in Figure 5). It is interesting to note that the rectangular box we used in Figure 5 to indicate this proposed park is a precise echo of the plastic form used to show the edge in Figure 2. By memorializing the long edge that Jake Milliones and others worked so hard to reinforce, this proposal honors the history of resistance. Furthermore, it highlights the edge that for fifty years has been the edge of the Hill District. Creating such a place to stand and watch the rebuilding process offers a psychologically healing bridge to the future.

Whatever location is chosen, it is essential that the park be a *meaningful* place—a place that draws on the location, history, and meaning of the site to maximize the ability to restore the urban environment. Consider, for example, the idea to develop "August Park" on the site in honor of August Wilson's cycle of ten plays about the Hill. It would be possible to create and install one sculpture a year for ten years. These sculptures would simultaneously acknowledge the truncation of the Hill, salute its resistance to destruction, and celebrate its great cultural treasure trove.

Given two choices, each powerful in its own right, how are the design and placement of the park to be decided? This is really the central question raised by the whole history of Freedom Corner, a history that played out while the progress of the civil rights movement was being undermined by urban policies of upheaval and deindustrialization. The decision to carry out urban renewal was made by powerful white leaders of the city. African American leaders were given misinformation so that they would endorse the process, but they were not real decision makers with voting power. Ultimately, the only power they had was in the street. The erection of a billboard was a potent pushback but not evidence of real discussion and shared decision making. Freedom Corner became an important site due to a desperate community's need to be heard. An open conversation about the placement of the reconciliation park would be the highest tribute we could pay to this historic spot.

Final Thoughts

In a long conversation with coauthor Mindy Fullilove, Pittsburgh activist Terri Baltimore described her experiences at Freedom Corner:

> Many activities start there, it's a place to get grounded. It's been a good place to look and see the Arena and understand what it did to the neighborhood. It's been a good place to look at the black fence along Crawford Street, which turns the neighborhood on its Western edge into a dead end. People get why the space is so pivotal. In my work, I do some projects with Duquesne University, which is situated in the neighborhood next to the Hill. When the students are at school, they are not looking at the Hill. When I take them on a tour and we stop at Freedom Corner, they can see that their school is right there.
>
> I've noticed that it's also just a pleasant space for people to sit and meditate. I'll go by and some soul is sitting quietly on stairs. While we were there for the ONE HILL demonstrations, I noticed that neighbors were caretakers of the site. One leaned out the window and joined a conversation about one of the heroes, Jim Henry, former director of Hill House. The neighbor said, "I love Mr. Henry. He saved my life."
>
> I was there on August 19, 2008, for the signing of a community benefits agreement between the ONE HILL Coalition and the city, county, and Pittsburgh Penguins. Tables were lined up in the plaza and ten copies of all the documents were laid out. A representative of

forty-five organizations was called up to sign multiple copies of the agreement. It was really cool, that moment, how the space was used to celebrate the community benefits agreement—seventy-five to one hundred people were there.

The decision to start the Occupy Pittsburgh protest at Freedom Corner was fortuitous, aligning this new movement against exclusion with older protests against the same problems. In sum, Freedom Corner held the line. It remains on the line. The question we face is this: lines define the sorted-out city; therefore, what shall we do about the line?

References

Brotha Ash Productions. 2007. "Announcement of Black Male Day of Solidarity." http://www.brothaashproductions.com/blacksolidarity07.htm.

Darden, J. T. 1973. *Afro-Americans in Pittsburgh: The Residential Segregation of a People*. Lexington: Lexington Books.

Dyer, E. 2001. "Freedom Corner dedicated in Hill District: Memorial marks battle for civil rights." *Pittsburgh Post-Gazette*, April 23.

Freedom Corner Memorial. n.d. "History." http://www.freedomcorner.org/history. html.

Hanchett, T. W. 1998. *Sorting Out the New South City: Race, Class and Urban Development in Charlotte, 1875-1975*. Chapel Hill: University of North Carolina Press.

Progress Pittsburgh. 2011. "Announcement of Occupy Pittsburgh." October 13. http://progresspittsburgh.tumblr.com/post/11394011744/occupy-pittsburgh-march-freedom-corner-hill-district.

Simms, E.-M. 2008. "Children's lived spaces in the inner city: Historical and political aspects of the psychology of place." *The Humanistic Psychologist* 36, no. 1: 72–89.

Occupying Dissent

A CONVERSATION WITH MAYA WILEY

Ron Shiffman

Ron Shiffman (RS): Can you describe the work you do at the Center for Social Inclusion (CSI)?

Maya Wiley (MW): The Center for Social Inclusion is a national policy strategy organization whose mission is to dismantle structural racial exclusion. We think about the ways multiple institutions, policies, and actions serve to exclude communities of color from opportunity and from full participation in society—politically, economically, socially—and what the policy strategies are that could change or transform that into inclusion and opportunity.

RS: Language can create space for inclusion in dialogue. The term "occupy" almost has a colonial connotation. What is your reaction to the phraseology and language of Occupy Wall Street (OWS)?

MW: On one level, it is a language and a naming that feels historically relevant because it is an effort to occupy space in order to take it back, psychologically and physically. But I also agree that it is also old language that harkens back to a history that does not have great meaning or relevance for some communities. For communities of color, this notion of "occupying" is neither positive nor negative, nor is it necessarily motivating. It's a language that becomes not sufficiently encompassing of all the Occupy movement's aspirations. For example, some leaders of color agreed with the Occupy movement in terms of its goals, but didn't feel that it was racially inclusive. That feeling spawned Occupy the Hood. But why do we need to occupy the hood when we are already there? It's the space we are in! Occupying Wall Street was really about claiming space people felt excluded from and dominated by. I don't think Occupy the Hood has the same meaning.

RS: OWS had a number of different strategies, and its use of spaces and places was one of them. Space is a place with an idea or a function. It is used to debate and communicate both frustrations and ideals. In what way does CSI address space as a place for expression or debate of race?

MW: We think of space in three interactive, interconnected ways. There is psychological space, political space, and physical space. They are all interactive, and none of them are race-neutral—they are highly racialized, even when we're not clear how they are racialized.

For example, the structure of physical space is driven by polities and attitudes. Once you say, "Occupy the Hood," everyone knows you're talking about people of color. The reason that is true is how we've racialized physical space through housing policies, land use planning, and many other public and private actions. Our politics are also driven by how our communities are defined. We have districts, and elected representatives represent a geographic area. To build political power, communities try to build racially identifiable districts. And that then racializes politics, although sometimes in positive ways. Space then drives psychological space around our identity and who "we" are. It's very difficult to disentangle the *idea* of space and how people see themselves in relationship to each other, and what sorts of problems we create and how we solve them. For CSI, none of those issues are race-neutral; they're not *only* about race, but they drive how we see space and who gets to be seen as part of the idea of that space. Those three realms of the physical, the psychological, and the political are all wrapped up in each other.

RS: How then does that translate into how we view spaces in our own city? How would you advise decision makers, urban planners, policy makers, or even urban designers in how they plan and design space, keeping these ideas in mind?

MW: In the interaction between physical space and social/political space, who we are and who we think we are is shaped by space: how we organize it, who we are in it, and how we include or exclude people from it. That is both in the process of creating it and what we do with it: what purposes does it serve, who should it be for, what solutions it should help create. At this point, people of color have to fight very hard to be included in real discussions and decisions about space: what it's for, how it should be used, and how it can be used to help us solve problems. If people of color are not formally included in a process of thinking about what spaces we need and what kinds of relationships they drive, then we will ultimately have not only racially identifiable and segregated space, we will have a fragmented social and political community. So much of how we identify who we are—who we should be in relationship with, and what their value is to the larger community, city, region, nation—is so often expressed in space. Who is the space for, and whose needs does it meet? All of those questions need to be part of the decision-making process.

RS: After 9/11, a number of New Yorkers went to Europe to look at public spaces and learn how they were used to memorialize major events. In Barcelona, we were introduced to the concept of "spaces of social inclusion." They sought to bring people together in the same space, to break down barriers. There is also the idea in Europe of social cohesion, which has both negative and positive connotations, of both inclusion and exclusion. How can spaces be used to build up solidarity in neighborhoods—even spaces in the "hood"—and be used to create social cohesion and political awareness?

MW: We actually took that term "social inclusion" from its use by Nobel Laureate Amartya Sen, so our idea of social inclusion comes from a global discourse. We named the Center for Social Inclusion around what we are for, because we have a vision consistent with that of the global south.

Having physical space is important. Fundamentally, most space is exclusive. People have to find and have ways of contesting that, and build on what we've got as assets in the community. There needs to be spaces for people to come together to contest that exclusion. I think about this as civic engagement…civic engagement is more than electoral politics. It's how we come together to solve problems we need to solve. In communities of color in particular, there are very few such spaces for that sort of civic engagement. The schools are actually one of the few institutions in communities of color, but it can be very difficult to access that space as a community space, outside of the school day or school use. Very few community centers exist, and there are very few parks and recreational spaces for people to gather—let alone whether they are comfortable gathering there, which is another issue. There are so few spaces that it is often difficult to create the opportunities for people to come together and do that level of civic engagement.

I'm reminded of one theorist who, in relation to the Black liberation struggle, said that space has to come together as critique of the dominant order, or else it is just idle talk. It's not just about physical space. Spaces that bring about the opportunity to think more collectively, to critique, and to challenge are the spaces we have the least of in communities of color. But we also need leadership and institutions that help that become a critical and constructive space, as well as celebratory space. We also need space for joy and appreciation of one another and the richness that is community, even if it's income is poor.

RS: There are also spaces like sidewalks, where an exchange can take place. Also policing, etc. has to do with that.

MW: You can design spaces in a way that creates much more opportunity.

RS: But a lot of that has to do with how it's programmed, how it's policed...

MW: This is part of the psychological aspect of space. You are deemed a criminal or dangerous too often, for people of color, just because of how you look or the street you live on, not whether or not you've actually done anything. The Center for Constitutional Rights documented that 90 percent of police stop and frisks in New York City don't result in any arrest. And of the arrests, many people are released later without charges. Almost all, 87 percent of New Yorkers stopped, are African American and Latino. I know one kid who wanted to be a lawyer, but dropped out of school because he was harassed regularly by the police when he had never even committed a crime, and police were in his school. To avoid the police, he dropped out. People of color have very small activity spaces. They don't go very far. Some of that is affordability—but some of that is psychological, because of the criminalization of space and an imposed order. This harkens to gang criminalization, and how just wearing certain colors can exclude you. Two people wearing certain colors cannot stand together on a sidewalk because they are deemed to be in a certain gang. That history of criminalization is so endemic to so many people of color's experience living in this country, without even addressing class. It does matter how the government mechanisms of control respond to the space.

RS: One of the problems young people have in New York City is that whenever there are more than three or four of them, the police break them up.

MW: Right, they think it's a riot! I watch huge groups of white teens walking around New York so carefree, and I mourn that black and brown kids can't do that without fear.

RS: OWS has tried to make the space for dialogue in physical space, but it emanated first in the virtual world. Both the virtual and physical have had barriers in communities of color. How should we go about addressing both of those issues?

MW: That's an important observation, and it's absolutely true. There are multiple levels of barriers at play. The Center for Social Inclusion has been doing work on high-speed Internet access for communities of color because it's become such a fundamental infrastructure for inclusion in society. If we're not testing our ability to have that access, it affects our ability to have, again, any form of civic engagement, which I consider OWS to be. Even more, it is how we are part of the deployment of that infrastructure. It is not just the ability to have broadband; it is having a community create broadband solutions, so that broadband itself creates more opportunity for coming together, engaging, and solving multiple community problems.

One level of solution is to say that the government should be not only investing in broadband deployment but also doing so in ways that enable nonprofit innovation and community-based infrastructure and deployment community wide. There is the technology, but also the space for engagement for doing multiple things, with all the opportunities that that infrastructure opens up. You colocate the actual infrastructure for an area with all the opportunities that the infrastructure gives you, such as workforce training, social uses of the Internet, educational programs, etc. The government could pilot ways of doing this so that you don't just have telecommunications companies building and profiting from infrastructure most communities can't afford. You can have alternatives that are much more locally based, and you can create opportunities for engagement along with the mechanisms that have become necessary in the twenty-first century, like broadband.

With OWS, the fact is that physical space became a place for storytelling about people's lives. There was a performative aspect certainly, but the goal was to get people who were walking by to stop and engage. It was an opportunity for a conversation. I took my daughters there so they could really understand what was going on, and we read people's signs, and they talked to people about their lives... that's pure gold! It doesn't matter what you think about OWS, but the opportunity to see how the recession is actually impacting people's lives was invaluable.

The issue for people of color is to have the time and space to physically go down to Zuccotti Park and be there all day—and not necessarily have a way to pick up your kids, take care of your family. All these transaction costs meant that the way the space was occupied—for long periods of time—was not necessarily accessible to many people including many people of color, who have all these other transactional limits on their time and space.

RS: That doesn't negate what they were doing...When I was younger, during the civil rights movement, people went on buses down to the South to...

MW: But there was a reason why it was usually college students, even then. Who has the transactional space for that? In Zuccotti Park, most of the people of color were young college students. It's not a critique of OWS, but an indication of what happens structurally...the guy who I stopped to talk to who was fifty years old was white and not black. He was out of work and didn't have children to care for. Most people I saw there were young, which meant they had the time and, I would guess, fewer obligations to others.

Another issue, at least in the first few weeks of OWS, was that because of where Zuccotti Park is located, many of the police were not white. They're Chinese, African American, and Latino, and, of course, there were many white cops. It was a very diverse group of police. Some protesters treated the police as bad enemies. This was very problematic for me, as a person of color. The police are the 99%. I thought the message and attitude should have been "we are here for you—the police, too—because you are performing a public service"... Instead, it was very antagonistic. Not exclusively with cops of color, but the mentality was very us-versus-them antagonistic, which was a missed opportunity in the use of the space. What would have happened in the civil rights movement is that you would have been trained in that interaction so that you could make a larger point. We don't have the same preparation and training vehicles in the strategy of OWS. What I loved about OWS is how organic it was, but there was downside as well.

RS: I actually experienced the opposite. I saw the folks in the hard hats, who in the civil rights movement would have been throwing bricks at the protestors, actually joining them instead and getting into discussions. The antagonism I saw in the antiwar movement in the 1970s and the civil rights movement in the 1960s was greater. The interaction I saw with the crowd and the construction workers coming off the construction site was completely different.

MW: Yes, it is quite complex, and those interactions were changing over time and were not static at all. The relationship with the police was changing the longer they were there. And of course, since then, OWS has been developing and conducting trainings of forty-five thousand people on corporate responsibility. I wish a stronger racial inclusion analysis had also been included in the trainings. As we know, the construction trades are very white. At many of the nonunionized construction sites in the area, there is a lot of racist stuff yelled about Latinos in nonunion jobs. It would have been interesting to see the physical makeup of the people in Zuccotti Park mirror the people in the city more, and what the dynamics would have been. There are not many spaces where people can come together and interact in that way across those noted differences—come together not just for simple cohesion, but to understand the structure of what is going on and why and how we can solve it. Why does the white construction worker have to care about the Latino immigrant, and vice versa? The problems are getting "solved" without everyone benefitting.

RS: Are there lessons you observed across the street in Zuccotti Park that should be applied across the city and in other spaces in the neighborhoods?

MW: First is the importance of having those big, public spaces and every community should have a large, central public space that can be utilized in multiple ways, including for dissent. The most tragic part of OWS is how it became shutdown to public use for dissent, under very specious circumstances—supposedly for safety, and not for inappropriate public use. We need to have those spaces, but we also need to be able to make use of them. It is almost as if we have to *dissent* about the constriction on our use of public space for dissenting purposes.

RS: You are an attorney, so you must be familiar with the public forum doctrine. Zuccotti Park was one of the only spaces the protestors could go, because, for example, City Hall Park is restricted, our public parks are fenced off, and so it is ironic that a privately owned space that was publicly accessible was the space chosen—and where there was a gap in the law. What do you think the initiative should be around expanding that doctrine, so you have the opportunity to raise these issues in public *and* private spaces?

MW: It isn't so much about what is legal, but about challenging the law to honor the Constitution's intent. Sometimes that means *doing* what is not legal in a peaceful and purposeful way. The fundamental strategy of the civil rights movement was demonstrating how the way we were treating African Americans, in particular, was antithetical to the Constitution. Think of *Walker v. Birmingham*, where Martin Luther King wanted to march the streets of Birmingham, but the lawyers told him he couldn't because it was not legal... and he said, that's not the point! That's why we have to march. Dr. King wrote his famous letter from the Birmingham jail, arguing for breaking the law peacefully to confront injustice.

These are such fundamental questions for all citizens. What does it mean when people can't quite physically find a space to congregate for expression and protest? The courts may not change this immediately or on their own, so we need to demonstrate those laws are against our values as a country by *breaking* them. It becomes its own form of dissent.

RS: What always hit me in many public meetings in New York is that they are comprised of folks predominantly from the white, middle-class community... that appears to be different around the country, from what I've seen, from Atlanta to Los Angeles, where there is less segregation in the movement.

MW: Around 9/11, there were only very young "mediating institutions," which become vehicles to cross and engage communities; they were fairly new and still trying to establish themselves at that time. Now, those groups are more mature, but that history is still relatively short. Oakland and Los Angeles, by contrast, have had a longer history of communities of color-led and -organized groups, and Occupy Oakland was much more diverse. That may have been a factor with OWS.

One more point we should make about race, particularly how it relates to physical space, is the changing demographics of the city. Even this notion of the "hood" is starting to change... where people are increasingly being priced out of not just their neighborhoods but also the city itself. People that fled the cities in the 1970s are now coming back into the cities, and the city itself is becoming wealthier and whiter, while inner-ring suburbs have become a place of low-income people of color. Dominicans from Washington Heights are moving to eastern Pennsylvania, and people from Williamsburg are being pushed up to Nassau County—they are physically leaving the city and not necessarily by choice.

RS: Many neighborhoods in New York City, such as the area surrounding the Gowanus Canal where I have been working recently, are back at the racial balance they were at the 1950s, before white people fled in the 1960s and 1970s and those neighborhoods became predominantly communities of color. The difference now is that those neighborhoods are much more economically stratified. The pressures on low-income people are felt in many ways beyond housing affordability... the businesses have changed and they can no longer find the services and goods that they need. So it's not only the civic spaces but also the space of one's own community, the streets and commercial businesses that need our attention.

MW: Right. When those small businesses that provide "cultural commodities" get priced out, this affects the identity of the community. On the one hand, we're happy to see the nice restaurant open up, but then you start to worry about the 99-cent store next door. We need to have different levels of affordability of commercial space, which is actually a pretty radical idea. We think about affordable housing that way—we have private housing, public housing, quasi-public housing, but we don't address commercial space in the same way. Those businesses serving and owned by low-income people need to be able to stay viable in the community.

AT CSI, we are trying to build this model of community economic development for social good. We are exploring how federal policy in broadband technologies can drive more opportunities for local employment in communities—everything from searching for and applying for employment using the Internet to the development of new job opportunities resulting from the technology itself. We believe that some of the money set aside for broadband activities should be going directly to communities to do this. We are also trying to help the elected officials, particularly ones representing communities of high need, to understand this, and we are also trying to help communities themselves understand the opportunities, so that community innovators can engage in this technological opportunity at the outset. We are working with lawmakers to find ways to support a federal-to-local-incubation strategy, a ground-up strategy that can get to scale and reach large numbers of people.

RS: In essence, you are trying to bridge the virtual divide, yet, at the same time, a new sort of physical divide is emerging—privately owned publicly accessible space is replacing public space. Those new privately sponsored, publically accessible spaces occur in high-rent income and commercial districts but do not exist in most neighborhoods. We see the emergence of all these park conservancies and business improvement districts, which enable the wealthy to entrench their privilege, instead of taxing them and spending those funds in an equitable manner.

MW: This is a longer-term strategy around tax and spending in the community. Race is often used as a wedge. For example, former presidential candidate Rick Santorum said that "our dollars are spent to keep black people on welfare." Who is "our," then? CSI has been starting a public conversation process focused on who adds value and who is an asset in this country. The person picking vegetables, who is not documented, is adding value by putting food on people's tables versus the investment banker who is not producing any value, but who is making money by shifting around other people's money. If we can stop using a racial wedge, we can ask how we use revenue to make an impact on people. I don't think we can have that policy conversation until we recognize who has value in this country, beyond pure economic units. We fundamentally have to start a conversation that humanizes and includes, as assets, people of color to talk about how we can invest in people. Part of the use of public space in OWS is to drive a conversation.

RS: That's a critically importantly point, on a macro-policy level. When you get down to the city of New York or Oakland, you begin to form alliances. It's much easier to build something like the High Line in Manhattan than build the Bronx River Greenway, which is taking decades to build. There is the sense that we don't have the access to improvements because we don't have the means to pay for their development and to sustain them. This also extends to schools. The disparity in schools to offset budget losses in a city is enormous from one school to the next. Why do we allow these things to occur? Is there a more equitable way to finance them?

MW: You are absolutely right that you have to have those alliances beyond the public discourse strategy. But it is not just a macro-policy conversation; it is local and national, applicable down to the community level. It has to start with how we challenge those structures, how we racialize them. We are the only industrialized country that locally funds our public schools. We've created a historical construct that is racialized for us. Our local resources are racialized from the beginning. Policy exclusions, failure to invest—these are very local issues, but we can't be thinking about them that way. It isn't just about geography, but also identity. Our kids need to be "all of our kids." We need to demand something fundamentally different than what we normally demand.

RS: Do you think OWS has created the space for that conversation to happen?

MW: Yes, the space is there. The challenge is that we need big ideas. We need our houses not to be foreclosed upon, we need jobs—these are important outcomes. Yet, the demands need to be bigger and more thought out. What are those big ideas? We need to assume that OWS can't come up with those ideas on its own. Progressives need to be more comfortable making those longer-term demands that might not fly in the next legislative session. Conservatives said forty years ago, "let's abolish welfare," and now they are saying, "hey, look it's happening." Populism, in its strongest days, was doing that. Like abolishing the electoral college—this is a demand that should have never gone away.

RS: So OWS…

MW: It probably makes more sense for OWS to be the discussion vehicle, but it has to speak to people beyond OWS over time.

RS: When I visited OWS the first time, I was reminded of the Pratt students strike in the 1970s, which addressed small, specific issues like chalk in classrooms, but quickly shifted to larger issues such as the role of the professions, their education/curriculum, what was happening to the communities around their institutions, etc. It seems to me that dialogue has been missing.

MW: You're right, we often feel like we have to have a formulated demand in advance. OWS demonstrated that well—you don't have to have a demand ready in advance. In law school, we were going to set up one of the first AIDS law clinics in the country… and then it was closed, and the school said it was about educating law students. We said, "no, it's about students engaging as citizens, and Columbia should enable that." We were not going to be told how we were going to learn.

RS: In many ways, that space becomes a space of learning, like a university. In many ways, that same function can happen in the local neighborhoods—in the Laundromat, in the barbershop, in the line at the supermarket, then you have to go to another space for a similar conversation.

MW: It's not just whether it's public space, it's space—sometimes private. We do need space for strategy. So that it feeds into those other spaces. The Highlander Center was one of these strategy spaces for the union movement and for the civil rights movement. Rosa Parks would not have been down there without the spaces for strategy. Septima Clark[1] and the organizing of the Citizenship Schools, where she taught black southerners who had been denied a proper education to read and write. Learning to read using a Sear's catalog, going to the black hairdressers—those were the spaces where you "got learned." We have to think about those spaces that sometimes are the

---

1. Septima Clark played a leadership role in the voting rights and civil rights struggle and became known as the "Queen Mother" of the civil rights struggle in the 1960s and 1970s.

local mom and pop businesses and sometimes are the institutions like the Highlander Folk School in Tennessee, a social justice-training center.

Recently, we met with Professor john powell, who is setting up a multi-disciplinary public center at the University of California at Berkeley—the Haas Center for Diversity and Inclusion—with faculty from across the university to participate in research projects together to generate big ideas about race, gender, sexual orientation, disability, and class. It's also about using the university as a space for this dialogue, its ability to contribute to something larger.

RS: Anything else?

MW: The only other point is that the demographics of many places change—becoming younger and with more people of color, where white people are predominantly sixty-five and older. If we don't think about these spaces, we really are going to create this new form of apartheid, where the vast majority of people will be excluded while they are carrying the remainder of the country. It is really quite scary, and quite real. We need to reevaluate the current trajectory.

RS: I know Alinsky and by extension community organizing has been demonized by the right as of late, but there has been lots of work about organizing. It seems that is something we need to address again, how do we build local leadership that leads to change.

MW: The wonky way to talk about it is to create mediating institutions, but it's about creating the spaces for organizing and relationship building that enables us to come together. However, it can't happen with the exclusion of people of color, or else, ultimately, the country will fail.

Whose Voice

THE LIMITED PARTICIPATION OF
PEOPLE OF COLOR IN THE OCCUPY MOVEMENT

Roland V. Anglin

THE OCCUPY MOVEMENT has largely lacked leadership and significant participation by people of color. This is not an indictment, but rather a recognition that the major social movements of the last century were led by and/or based on redressing the social and economic marginalization of Latinos, African Americans, Native Americans, gay Americans, and women. There is no question we have made major strides since the days when the world witnessed Alabama authorities unleashing dogs and high-pressure water hoses on blacks marching for their civil rights, or since the struggle for dignity and living wages by California Latino farmworkers in the 1960s and 1970s. Much, though, remains to be done.

Glaring issues such as political incorporation and civil rights, while not totally resolved, have made way for far more intractable challenges such as limited access to good schools, high unemployment, and limited wealth formation. These problems continue to exist and are exacerbated by the lack of fiscal discipline and accountability in the financial services community that lead to the subprime crisis. Many marginalized groups, principally Latino and black communities, lost a tenuous hold on the middle class when homes were lost and communities were economically devastated (see Mindy Fullilove's contribution in this volume).

While commanding voices were (and are still being) heard from these communities, the lack of a sustained voice, protest, and impact is significant. This paper argues that the lack of concerted oppositional force from communities of color in the fallout from the subprime debacle is partly a consequence of spatial and land-use trends that have been changing the

American political and metropolitan landscape since the mid-twentieth century. The result is both a challenge to coalition building across income, race, and ethnicity and an opportunity to transcend those challenges if properly understood.

The Occupy Movement as a Historical Moment

The Occupy movement offers a point of reflection, an opportunity to ask questions about the nature and transiency of social protest and what is and is not a social movement. Occupy burst onto the nation's consciousness not only because of the underlying protest against the near collapse of the financial system, but also because the evolving organization and dedication of the various mobilizations seem to presage the first real social movement of the twenty-first century. It is too early to say if this initial potential will bear out, but the movement (and the limited mass participation by people of color) prompts the following question: can the present challenges faced by communities of color be incorporated into the broader national feelings of disquiet brought to the public square by the Occupy movement?

Historical precedent and contemporary demographic trends cast doubt on the possibility that the Occupy movement will not only incorporate the challenges faced by communities of color but also be a vehicle that those communities can use or manipulate independently if they are so inclined. The Occupy movement can be classified as an oppositional movement targeting broad macro structures and general ideas but lacking a necessary focus on the relentless personal challenges that marginalized communities such as people of color, women, and gay, lesbian, and transgendered individuals face day-to-day.

The Occupy movement can best be compared to the student movement that swept not only the United States but also the world in the 1960s. Students for a Democratic Society and the student uprising of 1968 in Paris broadly argued that post-World War II industrial democracies possessed deep contradictions. For these and similar movements of the time, the democratic promise was never realized. However, fulfilling that goal within the context of a market economy was challenging, and with limited options for democratic socialism, the student movement did not achieve as much as it asked. Whatever history's view of the student movement of the 1960s, it was a significant part of the temper of the times, ushering in new personal freedoms and a healthy questioning of the powers of government.

The Struggle for Community and Opportunity in Post–World War II America

The broad democratic goals of the student movement of the 1960s were clearly successful as a coalescing force. Yet I would argue that in the post–World War II era the civil rights movement and similar movements based on group marginalization (for example, the women's movement, and the movements to acquire and solidify political and economic rights for Latinos) had a tactical advantage in terms of longevity. Racism and sexism, as we know, are often written into law or practiced through custom. They manifest themselves in the form of racial and ethnic segregation and their powerful sibling: unequal access to opportunity through public policy. It is easy to forget that the modern civil rights movement was first a local struggle against oppressive laws and customs.

The institutions that grew strong in opposition to racial and ethnic exclusion were community-based. Faith institutions, fraternities, and women's guilds were the scaffolding of resistance in the African American community. A powerful and enduring literature chronicling racial exclusion in the United States has shown that in the pre-civil rights era, enforced segregation encouraged communities of color to develop self-governing institutions.[1]

The great migration of African Americans, Mexicans, and Puerto Ricans seeking jobs in industrial centers after World War II was a flight from marginalized communities in one place to marginalized and segregated communities in another. The limited opportunities to create a mass-based movement in the rural context created the preconditions for an urban social movement.[2]

Segregation by law and custom cannot be defended, but the reality is that segregated communities of color in the postwar period were able to use the "agglomeration" effect promulgated in economics to fashion a collective voice that evolved into collective action. "Agglomeration" describes an economic process or ecosystem in which primary and secondary producers and consumers exist in close spatial proximity. Entrepreneurs reduce the transaction costs in the service/production life cycle by closely monitoring

---

1. Traveling the United States, one can find the historical remnants of strong African American communities such as the fabled Hayti community in Durham, North Carolina, or the Bronzeville community in Chicago. While testaments to human reliance, these communities were nonetheless marginalized by the broader American political economy.

2. It is important to note that the civil rights movement did find its roots and momentum in the urban South in places like Atlanta and Birmingham, which had been centers of finance and industry for decades when the civil rights movement emerged.

competitors, thereby calibrating prices, incorporating new ideas, and reducing connection time in the supply chain and in bringing their products to the market.

The agglomeration idea fits well with the emergence of the civil rights movement in the postwar period. Proximity reduces the cost of collective action. Organizing becomes easier if marginalized communities experience crosscutting challenges such as low wages, poor public services, and substandard housing. Moreover, segregation forces significant numbers of people to live and work together in a defined space, which increases the production of social capital. This social capital can be used in birthing and maintaining a social movement (again, see Fullilove, *infra*, on this point).

The civil rights movement succeeded in large measure because it was able to use a defined goal (social and economic inclusion) and spatial proximity to galvanize opposition to discrimination. The fact that the United States has created a significant African American and Latino middle-class community in the post-civil rights era is testament to the power of communities organizing for increased opportunity and participation in American society. Yet progress brings with it new challenges. Like whites in the postwar period, African Americans and Latinos have left cities in increasing numbers to seek the American dream encapsulated in low-density living. The consequences are many and nuanced.

The Contemporary Challenge

The challenges confronting metropolitan areas in recent years have been well documented. Issues related to inner-city poverty and increased crime rates are central to the debate over the overall health of large cities. The problems that challenge inner-city communities began to intensify during the 1980s as access to meaningful employment opportunities began to diminish. The decline of the manufacturing sector and the emergence of technological advancements eliminated many well-paying low-skilled jobs that inner-city residents depended upon. Separated from meaningful employment, many inner-city residents began to participate in an underground economy often involving drugs and violence. The real and perceived deterioration of city life encouraged middle-class residents, both nonminority and minority, to leave our nation's cities.

The high poverty rates in the inner cities of metropolitan areas is not a new occurrence, but the massive joblessness of the past thirty years and more that now accompany urban poverty is relatively new. According to William Julius Wilson, prior to the 1980s most adults in inner cities were not only employed, but enjoyed a relatively stable lifestyle:

> They invested economic and social resources in the neighborhoods, patronized the churches, stores, banks, and community organizations, sent their children to the local schools, reinforced societal norms and values, and made it possible for lower-class blacks in these segregated enclaves to envision some upward mobility. (1991, 462)

Today, however, inner-city residents are faced with a growing isolation from the economic structures of society, which deprives them of resources and conventional role models, as well as access to "social networks that facilitates social and economic advancement in a modern industrial society" (Wilson 1991, 642). The results all lead to concentrated levels of poverty and societal dislocations in the form of higher rates of teenage pregnancy, high school dropout, and crime.[3]

Spatial separation reduces the potential of political support for addressing the poverty both from a geographic and an individual perspective, presenting challenges for public policy and political organizing. The diffuse nature of the problems facing communities of color spatially limits the prospect of a coherent political movement that can address the manifold issues raised by urban poverty.

The problem of political organizing is twofold: the places where marginalized groups have moved to in the metropolis are often at the tail end of their economic life cycle. Often termed first-ring suburbs because many (but not all) were built during the first wave of postwar suburbanization, these places show varying degrees of economic strength and contain significant pockets of concentrated poverty. First-ring suburbs can be found

---

3. Disadvantaged neighborhoods diminish the life chances of their residents. Black and Latino neighborhoods are cut off from information about jobs. Teenagers growing up in the poorest neighborhoods often lack positive role models and are susceptible to negative influences in their surroundings. Schools in poor neighborhoods have higher needs and lower tax bases, which make it harder to hire and retain good teachers; and teachers in such schools often have lower expectations of their students.

in all regions of the United States, and they all share complex challenges such as trying to reduce the so-called achievement gap for their minority citizens while keeping neighborhood crime down to attract investment and middle-class residents. The political issue for minority residents is not so much local disenfranchisement, though some of that surely exists, but rather the problem of state and regional disenfranchisement brought by a weak tax base.

Suburbs and cities alike rely on property taxes, but suburbs depend more heavily on them. Property taxes may not have a plural economic base. If a suburban community houses a significant level of poor people, it has less to draw on in taxes to support needed services. Surrounding jurisdictions do not have self-interest in alleviating concentration, and the dilemma resembles the often-cited urban crisis of forty years ago. Now, however, the minority poor have less institutional and numerical strength to express a collective voice, and addressing lagging services has become more a question of tax-base sharing.

Focusing Occupy through Regional Opportunity and Equity

That the spatial dynamics underlying concentrated poverty and racial exclusion have changed should not limit the options for democracy-based reforms that encourage inclusion and opportunity. Experienced, longstanding community organizing groups such as the Gamaliel Foundation and emerging faith-based organizing groups are now offering coherent organizing principles for change that center on a "ground game."

The regional equity movement, as it is popularly known, relies on the dispersion of poverty in America's metropolitan areas as the basis to argue for educational, housing, and other opportunity policies centered on people and not tied to particular places, because the latter (and urban places especially) may not be where economic opportunity is located. Politically, first-ring suburbs have the potential to leverage change and reform. These suburbs are not totally poor. In fact, they still retain power if they can form a common agenda among themselves to secure fully funded, opportunity-focused polices through regional tax sharing.

Underlying the regional equity movement is a "deconcentration of poverty" agenda that grows out of the open housing movement of the 1970s. The movement for regional equity incorporates and mobilizes social justice advocates, civil rights organizations, labor unions, and community-based developers concerned with the often-unequal way metropolitan regions develop in the United States. This broadly defined movement responds to two challenges that poor and marginalized communities and neighborhoods face as they seek to improve their quality of life. The first is that larger patterns of metropolitan development (commonly called sprawl development) have undermined community-based efforts to address concentrated poverty and social, economic, and racial isolation. The second challenge is to find ways to link poverty alleviation to larger patterns of social economic and environmental development. Although advocates of regional equity find common cause with some in the environmental and "smart growth" movements, they have been critical of both for their lack of attention and responsiveness to issues of race, class, and poverty.

Similarly, there is no doubt that the core of what Occupy represents is relevant to communities where the financial services industry stripped hard-won equity through systemic fraud. But if you think through the interests of marginalized communities, just what is the incentive to commit time and attention if education is a challenge, unemployment is a challenge, and health is a challenge—along with the results of the market meltdown? Then again, where is the coordinating vehicle or movement that focuses voice when many marginalized communities are now spatially fragmented? One could imagine the evolution of a coalition, but the power of place-based organizing against poverty may not translate well for a strategy that relies on a direct challenge to corporate capital. Such a strategy has never been the spark in minority communities, and with notable exceptions it has been of limited value in rousing meaningful antipathy throughout American history. It takes a confluence of factors to challenge the "privileged position" of business.

The regional equity movement cannot claim overwhelming numbers nationwide, but it does have a strategic coherence and an organizing strategy lacking in the Occupy movement. The regional equity movement makes great use of faith-based organizations and churches to rally sustained numbers of people. Nationally, the movement has not captured the attention of the media the way the Occupy movement has, but its rootedness in existing movements for social justice, the environmental movement, and the growing rejection of unplanned growth argues for a longer tenure and impact.

Is the argument being made here for the Occupy movement to become part of the regional equity movement? Not necessarily. The Occupy movement, though, has to become more conscious that race, class, and ethnicity still ground the context for organizing for expanded economic opportunity in this country. What the Occupy movement has to do is place itself within an oppositional context that is firm, clear, and moves beyond capturing public spaces. Occupy must form coalitions with existing trends and movements that can give it a ground game. In some cases it has the potential to revitalize moribund movements, in other cases it can propel existing movements to new heights of accomplishment. The regional equity movement especially provides a vehicle not only to work with communities of color but also to advocate on issues that have broader appeal such as food security and climate change, not to mention equity issues.

In sum, the Occupy movement has rightly lifted up the possibility for sustained voice against the concentration of money that often distorts democracy. But spatially focusing opposition in proximity to government and corporate centers can only go so far. The problems that still challenge marginalized communities, especially marginalized communities of color, must be given increased attention. Politically, it makes sense to juxtapose the continuing plight of the poor and marginalized with the excesses of corporate power.

Occupy needs to establish a ground game the way that other social movements, including the Tea Party movement and the regional equity movement, have done. The latter movement is proceeding in a slow, methodical fashion, often engaging when necessary in the battleground that is local politics. Such local battles and organizing do not bring the excitement of marches and confrontations with the police, but if the ultimate goal is increasing opportunities through institutional and political reforms, Occupy needs to broaden its focus and appeal to include areas, such as older suburbs, which have much in common now with central cities.

References

Wilson, W. J. 1991. "Public Policy Research and the Truly Disadvantaged." In *The Urban Underclass*, edited by C. Jencks and P. E. Peterson. Washington, DC: The Brookings Institution.

Emplacing Democratic Design

Michael Rios

THE OCCUPY MOVEMENT has piqued interest within architecture and urban design circles about the role of public place as a setting for democratic action. Public space has become a battleground for issues related to terrorism, anti-immigration, and now urban austerity. The claiming of public space in the epicenter of Manhattan's financial district and the ensuing Occupy movement were a welcome sign to many, given the federal government's lack of response to ensure accountability in the face of growing disparities between the many and the few. The embrace of a nonhierarchical style of leadership, a consensus-based model of public assembly, and an innovative use of social media has drawn attention to novel forms of direct democracy. The Occupy movement has also revealed the changing nature of public space, which some scholars characterize as a state of exception—the indefinite suspension of laws and regulations by the government, and the extraordinary departure from existing policies that can be deployed to include as well as exclude (Agamben 2005; Ong 2006). Political philosopher Giorgio Agamben argues that the state of exception is not a provisional measure but an inherent part of government that perpetually transcends the juridical order in the name of public good. What is at stake, Agamben notes, is the relationship between law and violence as the state determines who gets to live and who gets to die. From this perspective, the truly political is only that action which is able to sever the relationship between violence and the law. In a similar vein, cultural anthropologist Aihwa Ong discusses the state of exception as a "technology of sovereignty" that differentially regulates populations through market forces and selectively produces entrepreneurial forms of citizenship in lieu of social rights. Those not subscribing to market-oriented policies are vulnerable to exclusionary practices and thus are not considered full members of a political community whose boundaries are delineated by market forces. Low-skilled migrants, undocumented individuals, and refugees with little or no formal education are among the populations whose status is disarticulated from rights, entitlements, and participation in political life.

This suspension of laws and rights manifests itself in US cities in the marketization, criminalization, and militarization of public space. Managing fiscal debt in times of economic restructuring, reduced taxes, and higher rates of unemployment has forced cities to borrow money from banks and use municipal bonds to service debt at higher interest rates, which further compound debt levels. This gives an exorbitant amount of power to city bond raters such as Moody's and Standard and Poor's, which determine a city's credit worthiness but ultimately instigate the introduction of market-based reform policies and cuts to government services. These policies and practices determine which parts of the urban landscape flourish and which parts cease to exist when it comes to the allocations of limited resources and the provision and maintenance of the public realm. In addition, the criminalization of urban space, the rise of the security industry after 9/11, and the increasing use of surveillance technologies to monitor spaces have further eroded the public realm in terms of freedom of movement, right of assembly, and the ability to voice dissent (Davis 1992; Giroux 2004; Mitchell 1995; Mitchell and Beckett 2008). This has caused many populations—especially immigrants, undocumented individuals, and the poor—to live in fear of falling into the surveillance net and being incarcerated or deported. However, this anxiety also extends to citizens whose rights are formally recognized, including the working class and people of color that struggled to gain political and economic standing over a generation ago.

The planning and design fields have proven ineffective in dealing with these matters, as they focused their attention on aesthetic and formal preoccupations with little thought given to the ethical and political issues arising from the changing public realm. A central focus in urban design is the ordering of a civic realm through a distinction between public and private functions that assumes universal access to the "public." However, the "public" in public space is both underspecified *and* overspecified: underspecified, because of a lack of attention to how public space is to be regulated and managed, which leaves such matters to the whims of politicians and policymakers; and overspecified through the articulation of highly formal and programmed spaces based on cultural and class norms of propriety and consumption.

The limits to current approaches are evident inasmuch as public space design often stays within the narrow confines of professional culture and fails to address claims by new social groups in the city. This complicity defines the current crisis of urbanism—an ambivalence about which public is being served, the reproduction of social structures that perpetuate exclusion and inequality, and the absence of ethico-political considerations.

In the following, I discuss how the field of urbanism—as practiced by architects, planners, and urban designers—maintains the illusion of public space while making invisible certain segments of the public. This includes the provision of public space as a market-driven amenity in capital-intensive projects that cater to the consumption of private goods in lieu of the creation of physical settings where citizens can deliberate about public matters that have material consequences. By contrast, I then turn to placemaking in marginalized communities and describe how the spaces found in these locations draw attention to issues of social inclusion and citizen rights. I conclude with some implications for urbanism and lessons for practice.

From Wall Street to Main Street:
Invisibility in the Image of the City

As a field that imagines the spaces of the city, urbanism identifies what is common to a public and the form of its visibility and its organization. Like art, urbanism can either repress modes of being or reveal new sensory possibilities that instigate novel forms of political subjectivity— which can be defined as the awareness of one's own (and others') political position and of how existing relationships might be changed in the future. However, power relations determine which parts of the city are made visible and what can be said about them. Representational regimes construct particular narratives of the city in the symbolic economy and influence how a place is to be valued, where capital is to be invested, what locations are to be marketed, and what policies are to be enacted. The power of these imaginaries is their ability to privilege particular places in the cognitive map of many urban dwellers.

Today, the field of urbanism is complicit in manufacturing an image of the city that equates democracy with neoliberalism and the public realm with spaces of consumption. A reading of the city as envisioned by architects, planners, and urban designers produces representations and future projections that, although not always intentionally, have the effect of concealing the sensibilities of multiple publics and the existence of unequal social relations. Henri Lefebvre (1991) called this "the illusion of transparency," which masks the reality that spaces of the city are socially produced to serve powerful interests. What are the political outcomes emanating from this exclusionary image of the city?

A central issue is how representations of urbanism facilitate and enable powerful interests to envision, plan, and regulate the city. One example is the use of architecture as a public relations strategy to convince the citizenry to underwrite and approve large development projects through high profile commissions. These urban spectacles are also used by place marketing campaigns to increase the competitiveness of a city's cultural economy, but often at the expense of investment in low-income neighborhoods and other parts of the city deemed as underperforming. Alternatively, urban design ensembles are pieced together to create a "sense of place" and market lifestyle experiences to targeted populations defined by race and class. The production of urban spectacles and aestheticized experiences, or the imposition of a civic spatial order in the case of New Urbanism, give the illusion of "publicness," but ultimately are the dictates of a cultural and political economy that serves the few while the burden of the costs is borne by the many. This contrasts with a different image of the city, one that is not produced by urbanists but practiced in the places of the excluded. These are the spaces of the marginalized that do not figure into the representations of the city projected by urbanists and whose presence disrupts normative visions of urban life. These places also present a different conception of public space that does not fit easily into regulatory frameworks, rule-bound management, or the law.

The Negotiative Spaces of Marginalized Places

Over the past several decades, demographic changes have contributed to the restructuring of regions and cities, resulting in greater social and cultural heterogeneity. Much of the recent growth has come from migrants and historical minority groups such as Latinos that are projected to reach close to 29 percent of the US population by the year 2050. For many immigrant and refugee communities, places provide a common sense of territorial identity despite these groups having roots elsewhere. A networked and expanded notion of home is inclusive of both material (that is, a house or piece of land) and immaterial qualities such as memory and imagination. In New York City, the Puerto Rican vernacular house, or *casita*, serves as a public place in a number of neighborhoods that lack such spaces. Similarly, in a number of California cities, community gardens have been established by Hmong refugees who find it difficult to assimilate into American culture and seek the familiarity of a life they left behind in parts of Laos, Cambodia, and Vietnam. Examples such as this underscore the need to recognize how groups perceive their belonging and how these understandings may differ from existing norms.

Placemaking ultimately reflects, and is the outcome of, various negotiations—belonging to a community, participating in local decisions, and navigating the political landscape at multiple scales. These negotiative spaces define the physical, cultural, and political spheres where marginalized groups struggle to create a *place* of their own. Different conceptions of belonging and rights of inhabitation raise questions about the way urbanists think about place and the fixity of boundaries between "here" and "there," "inside" and "outside," the "visible" and the "invisible," and what it means to dwell in place. Questioning the rigidity of physical and social boundaries also draws attention to more fluid and hybrid relations between public and private realms, challenging the binaries that historically define the public realm (e.g., domestic/political, feminine/masculine). Quotidian spaces such as streets and parking lots, but also vacant sites and other *terrain vague*—indeterminate zones in the landscape that are often perceived as indicators of decay and abandonment—are used for activities other than their intended function or designation in legal terms. These sites are often appropriated for spontaneous, improvisational, and creative uses, such as an abandoned gas station that serves as the backdrop of a semi-legal produce and meat market in Sacramento. They are the generative spaces that incubate emergent forms of social and economic activity seldom observed in regulated land uses and sites.

Other sites are transformed into public places for political purposes as marginalized groups struggle to gain legitimacy. These politicized spaces serve the purpose of anchoring solidarity and expressing explicit counter identities in the urban landscape, producing new symbols and meanings: an example of this is the reclaiming of San Francisco's Mission District through the development of El Plan Popular, or People's Plan, as a tool against gentrification and the displacement of this neighborhood's working-class population. Parts of this community-based plan included preserving a local industrial district and ensuring protections for blue-collar businesses, both of which were later adopted into policy by San Francisco's board of supervisors (Marti et al. 2012). Another outcome of these efforts was the creation of the San Francisco Community Land Trust, whose goal is to acquire and remove buildings from the speculative market through the conversion of rental buildings into limited equity cooperatives rather than condominiums.

The increasing diversity in cities has also prompted the rise of multiethnic and multiracial places that are produced by social groups as they negotiate their differences to create a more inclusive sense of belonging. These places can be viewed as microcosms of larger demographic and social changes and, as such, present a transcultural image of the city yet to come. One example is the relocation of a day labor site near downtown Seattle. Conflicts arising from its relocation into a largely Japanese American neighborhood instigated a Good Neighbors Agreement leading to the development of a new public facility to provide a location for day laborers. Also included is an event space and an outdoor plaza, as well as expanded programming to serve this racially and ethnically diverse community (Emerson and Hou 2012).

Emplacing Practice

Placemaking highlights the novel ways in which marginalized groups are developing their cultural and political identities through the claiming of rights. These types of engagement can be viewed as cultural forms of citizenship that represent "the ways people organize their values, their beliefs about their rights, and their practices based on their sense of cultural belonging rather than on their formal status as citizens of a nation" (Silvestrini 1998, 44). These negotiations are important inasmuch as they establish what groups can expect of one another, help to bridge differences between communities, and serve as the basis for coalition building. The ability of urbanists to produce a more inclusive and egalitarian image of the city rests on their ability to help groups envision new imaginings of place, represent these futures in ways to win over the hearts and minds of multiple publics, and facilitate the formation of political alliances. These goals will be determined, in large part, by the ability of architects, planners, and urban designers to serve as cultural brokers and provide leverage for these publics vis-à-vis government agencies, institutions, and private interests.

Places also provide a location for creative praxis that can help instigate the formation of new political subjectivities. Organizing campaigns and staging events that call attention to the unequal power relations in the present order of things exploiting contradictions and ambiguities in policy and regulation, and revealing the sublime in public places are some of the ways that link spatial interventions with political acts. In some ways, this describes the convergence of aesthetics and politics in Occupy Wall Street: creating an event and mobilizing a public through art and symbolism; occupying a "privately owned public plaza" as a legal right through a regulatory loophole; and producing an uncanny scene of pitched tents in the middle of a corporate landscape.

Seeing places in this light opens up a space for emplaced forms of engagement. Emplacement explores the relationship between material thinking, location, and human action (Carter 2004; Thrift 2008; Vaughan 2008). Situating action in places also alters how one thinks about practice. As geographer Doreen Massey suggests: "Place changes us, not through some visceral belonging but through the *practicing* of place, the negotiation of intersecting trajectories; place as an arena where negotiation is forced upon us" (2005, 154).

The "practicing of place" is a means toward democratic ends. By locating ourselves in communion with others, we can better work toward a more inclusive image of the city and give shape and meaning to the places people inhabit.

References

Agamben, G. 2005. *The State of Exception*. Chicago: University of Chicago Press.

Carter, P. 2004. *Material Thinking*. Melbourne: Melbourne University Press.

Davis, M. 1992. "Fortress Los Angeles: The Militarization of Public Space." In *Variations on a Theme Park: The New American City and the End of Public Space*, edited by M. Sorkin. New York: Hill and Wang.

Emerson, P., and J. Hou. 2012. "17th and Jackson: Relocating Casa Latina and Navigating Cultural Crossroads in Seattle." In *Diálogos: Placemamking in Latino Communities*, edited by M. Rios and L. Vazquez. New York: Routledge.

Giroux, H. A. 2004. "War on Terror: The Militarizing of Public Space and Culture in the United States." *Third Text* 18, no. 4: 211–221.

Lefebvre, H. 1991. *The Production of Space*. Cambridge: Blackwell.

Marti, F., C. Selig, L. Arreola, A. Diaz, A. Fishman, and N. Pagoulatos. 2012. "Planning Against Displacement: A Decade of Progressive Community-based Planning in San Francisco's Mission District." In *Diálogos: Placemaking in Latino Communities*, edited by M. Rios and L. Vazquez. New York: Routledge.

Massey, D. 2005. *For Space*. London: Sage.

Mitchell, D. 1995. "The End of Public Space? People's Park, Definitions of the Public, and Democracy." *Annals of the Association of American Geographers* 85, no. 1: 108–133.

Mitchell, K., and K. Beckett. 2008. "Securing the Global City: Consulting, Risk, and Ratings in the Production of Urban Space." *Indiana Journal of Global Legal Studies* 15, no. 1: 75–99.

Ong, A. 2006. *Neoliberalism as Exception: Mutations in Citizenship and Sovereignty*. Durham, NC: Duke University Press.

Silvestrini, B. G. 1998. "The World We Enter When Claiming Rights: Latinos and Their Quest for Culture." In *Latino Cultural Citizenship: Claiming Identity, Space, and Rights*, edited by W. V. Flores and R. Benmayor. Boston: Beacon Press.

Thrift, N. 2008. *Non-representational Theory: Space, Politics, Affect*. London: Routledge.

Vaughan, L. 2008. "Emplacing local intervention." *Studies in Material Thinking* 1, no. 2.

3

Reimagining Public Space

The Sidewalks of New York

Michael Sorkin

1. The Streets belong to the people!

2. So do the Sidewalks.

3. A minimum of 50 percent of the Street space of New York City shall be taken out of the realm of high-speed and mechanical locomotion and assigned the status of Sidewalk.

4. This minimum shall apply on a Block-by-Block basis.

5. The entirety of a given Street may be transferred to the status of Sidewalk with the consent of 75 percent of the membership of the Block Committee.

6. A Block Committee shall be comprised of all of those of voting age whose primary workplace or residence is accessed from a given Block.

7. All New York City Sidewalks, including these additions, shall revert to ownership by the City of New York, which shall assume primary responsibility for their maintenance. Notwithstanding this obligation, the right to control the disposition of uses on each Block shall be shared by the Block Committee and the City of New York, subject to the overriding general rights of Passage and Assembly.

8. A Block shall be understood to be the space from corner to corner defined by a single Street, not a square block, and shall encompass the Sidewalks on both sides of the Street. Each square block shall be understood as including portions of four different Blocks.

9. Block Corners, the junctions of Blocks, shall be assigned to one of the impinging Blocks such that each Block shall control two out of the four Corners it engages.

10. Such assignment shall be random.

11. The consolidation of Blocks for purposes of the administration by the Block Committees of elements of the blocks that exceed that space of a single Block shall be permitted as long as the consolidation is of Blocks that are contiguous.

12. In no case may this consolidation be permitted to exceed four contiguous Blocks.

13. All uses on the Sidewalk shall be public or accessible to the public.

14. Neither the Right of Passage along the Block nor the Right of Assembly within the Block shall be fundamentally infringed or impaired.

15. No Assigned Public Use (APU) shall impede walking or standing rest within the area of the designated minimum Territory Of Passage (TOP).

16. The use of Sidewalks, other than for Passage or Assembly, including loitering and standing rest, shall be determined by Block Committees, which may assign rights to their use other than for Public Passage or Assembly. Such subsidiary public rights shall be assigned on a rotating basis.

17. In no case may more than 5 percent of the area of any Block be occupied by a use that requires direct payment by the public to access its benefit.

18. Fees from the assignment of public rights shall profit the Block from which they are derived except in the case of High-Income Blocks.

19. A High-Income Block shall be understood to be a Block on which revenue from fees shall exceed by more than 50 percent the median fee collected from all Blocks, citywide.

20. 25 percent of the revenues from High-Income Blocks shall be tithed to the Block Bank.

21. The Block Bank, the directors of which shall be composed of representatives from the Block Committees, shall make Block Grants for improvements to Blocks that do not qualify as High-Income Blocks.

22. Permitted uses shall include sitting, the playing of games and miscellaneous other recreational activities, gardening and agricultural activities, the storage of bicycles, the capture of rainwater, the care of children, the management of waste, the planting of trees, public toilets, and the sale of books, journals, newspapers, and snacks.

23. The area of any Block necessary for access to the New York City Transit system, including both street-level and underground operations, shall be designated a *corpus separatum* and its maintenance shall be the responsibility of the Transit Authority.

24. Uses of sidewalks shall be classified as either Grandfather or Sunset uses.

25. Grandfather uses are to be permanent. Sunset uses are subject to annual review by Block Committees.

26. Grandfather uses shall include Minimum Passage and Street Trees.

27. Minimum Passage shall be a lateral dimension between ten feet and half the width of the expanded Sidewalk, whichever is greater, and shall be harmonized with the dimensions of contiguous Sidewalks. These dimensions shall be established by the Department of City Planning with the advice and consent of the Block Committees.

28. Street Trees shall be planted such that they shall, within five years of their planting, provide adequate shade over the full area of the Block during the months of summer.

29. The location and species of these trees shall be established by the Department of City Planning with the advice and consent of the Block Committees.

30. Sleeping on sidewalks shall only be permitted by permission of the Block Committees on application no less than one day in advance of bedtime.

Radical Imagination

Caron Atlas

IN THE EARLY morning hours when Zuccotti Park was raided[1], I was writing a blog about holding ground and thinking big. I was reflecting on a recent conference where people spoke about the importance of holding ground in times when our basic rights are under attack. Others said this is a time for big ideas and a radical imagination.

You can't evict an idea whose time has come.

This powerful message went viral even as the park was being cleared. You can evict the people, but you can't destroy their imagination. Later that day, the Arts & Democracy Project went ahead with our planned national conference call, connecting people involved in arts and culture in the Occupy movements. The energy was palpable.

Across the country, Occupy and the 99% movements have unleashed creative expression: Hip Hop Occupies' Rise & Decolonize events support community self-determination and solidarity. Occupy Broadway featured 24 hours of performances in a POPS (privately owned public space). Occupy Sound produced three volumes of soundtracks, including a custom mash-up featuring Noam Chomsky and Pharrell. Occupy Halloween brought over 500 participants to the country's largest Halloween parade. "Pay your taxes" was projected on the GE building on tax day. Occupy musicians and filmmakers were inspired by Occupy writers and filmmakers who pledged to support the movement. Occupy Dance's Ballet Barre on the Barricades brought

---

1. November 15, 2011

to life the iconic Adbusters poster of the dancer atop the Wall Street Bull. Live drawing documentation, stand-up comedy, flash-mob choreography, and street theater are happening across the country. Creative tool kits provide tips for small town occupations, and installations create common messaging for big cities. Occupy Art: The People's Movement in Visual's Facebook page is more than 6,000 strong and growing.

> *Seize this moment to create something new.*
> —activist Grace Lee Boggs

On another level, Occupy has generated new paradigms of democratized art and creative organizing, the language to express them and the resources to support them. The 99% meme has captured the public imagination. Some described the Zuccotti occupation as an art form in and of itself. You don't need to be an art collector or a season ticket holder to engage with this art, and you don't need an MFA to produce it. Art Is My Occupation shares information, resources, and "direct support for the culture workers of the 99%," while monthly InterOccupy Arts Calls build community and stimulate connections and opportunities across the country. A new Occupy art course at Stanford explores "the complex, contested, and shifting ideas associated with the word 'Occupation'" and how artists have "taken spaces— occupied them—in order to transform them."

Arts, culture, and grassroots media provide vital spaces to cultivate democracy and generate change in a time of inaccessible public squares and polarized political debates. It isn't surprising that creativity would play a leading role in this activism. After all, believing that another world is possible requires an imaginative leap, and cultural shifts often precede political ones. For longtime activist Grace Lee Boggs, the "next American revolution" of sustainable activism and humanity will be built on a shared "faith in our ability to create the world anew." This involves not only our minds, but also our hearts and emotional core.

Spaces of Intervention

> *The future of cities is less about buildings and more about the reconfiguring of social and economic relationships. Artists can really contribute to that.*
> —architect Teddy Cruz

Arts, culture, and grassroots media create spaces where people can tell their own stories in a manner that helps others to see what those in power don't want them to see. They shift narratives, reconfigure social relationships, and enact new forms of engagement that embody movement and change. Unlike organizing that replicates social inequities, cultural organizing embraces the wholeness of its participants, their unique contexts, and their agency in their struggles.

For artist and Occupy activist Gan Golan, this happens in transformational spaces:

> We enter into those spaces to become someone different, and leave that space with a new story of who we are. Occupy is one such space in that it is a traditional space, which has been sorely lacking from our political landscape for a long time: the public square. But while it

Foreclosure song sheet.
Poster by Liz Starin

falls into this tradition, it is also a very different kind of transformative space…a space created so that people can begin to tell their own stories.

Cairo's Tahrir Square was animated by art during the Arab Spring protests. Actor and filmmaker Khalid Abdalla describes how it was "an incredibly creative space through humor, painting, art, music, but also in the way that people shared the space." For example, at 3 a.m. one night, performance artists drew a circle and created and recreated the society they hoped to live in. For Abdalla, "transgression is the act in which you are projecting the possibility of something before you can create it actually in stone and institutions."

If you're not disrupting something—a system, an institution,
a business—you're not fully taking advantage of the moment.
    —journalist Jose Antonio Vargas

In New York City, Organizing for Occupation (O4O) has successfully stopped foreclosure auctions with their singing auction blockades. Performed in beautiful multipart harmony with lyrics by Luke Nephew, this song has made for a particularly effective intervention:

Mr. Auctioneer
All the people here
Are asking you to stop all the sales right now
We're going to survive, but we don't know how.

Says Organizing for Occupation: "We aimed to confuse the court with our loveliness. We use the power of song and bring a presence of calm and beauty into the auction…furthermore in doing something so beautiful in the midst of something so brutal and cruel we expose the system for what it is." The action is deliberately nonviolent in contrast to the violence of a foreclosure and serves to extend solidarity to the people who are losing their homes. "This action affirms our human right to dignity."[2]

Leveraging the tools of public relations and branding, and with a mission to "affect popular understandings of events, symbols, and history," the collaborative Not An Alternative appropriated the image of yellow-and-black police caution tape to create "occupy" and "foreclosed" visual

---

2. Video of singing auction blockade: http://www.youtube.com/watch?v=u3X89iViAlw

messages used across New York as part of bank and foreclosure actions. They have converted a storefront in East New York into an Occupied Real Estate office, with official-looking branding to correspond with a website and auction blockade brochures. The storefront will be staffed by volunteer members and neighbors from local community groups and used as an organizing hub and community space for trainings and meetings and for storing materials and props for actions.

Los Angeles Poverty Department (LAPD) is drawing attention to housing issues by reclaiming public space and human dignity on Skid Row in Los Angeles. "We want the narrative of the neighborhood to be in the hands of neighborhood people. We work to generate this narrative and to supplant narratives that perpetuate stereotypes used to keep the neighborhood people down or to justify displacing the community." *Walk the Talk* is a peripatetic

The Line flyer.
Flyer by Stefan Hagen

Demonstration for Jobs

**March 6, 2012 - 8am on Broadway
Bowling Green to Union Square**

http://theline2012.wordpress.com

Freedom of Expression National Monument. *Photo by Charles Samuels*

performance with a brass band, community dialogues, and public artworks that celebrate neighborhood residents whose visionary actions have reknit the social fabric of Skid Row. This includes the story of Justiceville, a 1985 Skid Row homeless encampment organized by more than seventy-three residents that survived for more than four months. Justiceville lived up to its name as a self-determined community offering shelter, services, and dignity to a diverse group of residents.

The Line, organized by theater artists and labor unions, focused on unemployment, creating the world's longest unemployment line in New York on Super Tuesday, March 6, 2012. For fourteen minutes, thousands of people lined up from the Wall Street Bull to Union Square silently holding up pink slips—one minute for each million of unemployed Americans. The Line was originally created as part of the Imagine Festival, which took place during the Republican convention in 2004, another time when freedom of assembly was in jeopardy.

Also featured in the run up to the 2004 election was the Freedom of Expression National Monument, an enormous red megaphone in Foley Square that enticed passersby to voice their thoughts, poetry, and grievances. Originally created on the Battery Park landfill by Los Angeles Poverty

Department's John Malpede, visual artist Erika Rothenberg, and architect Laurie Hawkinson, the Creative Time and Lower Manhattan Cultural Council invited a wide range of artists, writers, politicians, community activists, and individuals to engage with Freedom, a modern-day soapbox.

Spaces of Intersection

Through the transformative experience of the parade, they become owners of the street, at least for the duration of their performance
    —anthropologist Helen Regis

Spaces of intersection are often generative of change. The Arts & Democracy Project commissioned a series of conversations about these spaces and the change makers who cultivate them—strategic artists and creative organizers, activist anthropologists and poetic politicians. In these spaces, people come together outside of conventional social processes and norms and create new forms of solidarity. Longtime Bronx cultural activist Bill Aguado recalls the history of squatting in New York:

> Squatting was a type of strategy, a political community strategy, to empower, to take over, to assume…Squatting was a way for us to take over housing, to take over hospitals and improve the health care, to take over school boards, saying, "You don't listen to me, I'm taking it over." In communities like the South Bronx, Harlem, Bedford Stuyvesant, Lower East Side, and many others across the country, we had to take control of our space.

Squatting in East New York led to the transfer of four hundred units that were rehabilitated and legally occupied by low-income families.

The conversations also identified the power of transformative "third spaces" and the catalytic connections that happen within them. Cultural organizer amalia deloney describes the Mayan concept of "*Nepantla*, the space in the middle…a space to be and become at the same time." Carnivals and festivals are spaces where the world can be imagined anew. Says Ken Wilson of the Christensen Fund:

> Look at cultural traditions of carnival and festival in which public spaces are occupied for parody and independent representations of identity and freedom of expression. These types of activities are stron-

Second Line parade. *Photo by Eric Waters*

gest in contexts where subaltern groups and social movements have despaired of representation in public life and instead established the right to create living alternatives sustained and protected by art, beauty, humor and numbers. Legitimating themselves as an alternative in a small slice of time in the center of their home cities, such activities keep alive traditions and values and draw forward better times.

While some have dismissed Occupy Wall Street (OWS) because of its carnival atmosphere, others take its role reversal, subversive humor, and spirit of liberation more seriously. This includes the NYPD who, as described by Claire Tancons, reached back to a mid-nineteenth century ban against masking, "leaving little doubt about their fear of Carnival as a potent form of political protest." For Tancons, it isn't a coincidence that New York City Council Member Jumaane Williams was arrested both at a West Indian parade and at OWS, for it was "a tactical re-territorialization of public space and political discourse, of social formation and cultural production, carried out as a concerted effort to regain democratic rights and liberties" (Tancons 2011).

Mardi Gras Indians and second-line jazz funerals in low-income African American communities in New Orleans are also cultural forms that contest, transform, and challenge authorities. Writes anthropologist Helen Regis in "Blackness and the Politics of Memory" (2001):

> The majority of participants in the second-line tradition are not owners of homes, real estate, or large, public businesses. Yet through the trans-formative experience of the parade, they become owners of the streets, at least for the duration of their performance. This collective owner-ship of the streets that is experienced by participants of the second line, has important political implications. It works against the numerous forces that create atomization in urban neighborhoods. Among the most challenging of these forces are the entrenched patterns of police violence and corruption.

After Hurricane Katrina, New Orleans authorities tried to stifle the subversive power of these cultural forms by raising the cost of parade permits and through police harassment. Mardi Gras Indian Chief "Tootie" Montana tragically died while testifying at a city council hearing about police harassment.

Union Square after 9/11 became a transformational crossroads where people connected, held forth, and mourned personal and collective losses. It offered participatory forms of meaning and belonging, including a collective mural consisting of butcher paper and markers, altars, and the compelling stories and images of the missing. In Los Angeles, Cornerstone Theater's citywide Festival of Faith provided much needed spaces for public dialogue soon after and at a time when people felt like they "were unable to finish their sentences" (as I heard an Egyptian professor comment about the culture of silencing and self-censorship).

Spaces of Imagination

Every important social movement reconfigures the world in the imagination.
—writer Susan Griffin

Knowledge comes from taking apart and wisdom comes from rebuilding.
—activist Leroy Johnson

Democracy is an ongoing and dynamic process. "Beyond Zuccotti" means ensuring that the values of human dignity and economic justice that the occupation put on display are embedded in our daily lives and our social and political systems. This goes beyond a claiming of public space to an insistence on equity in the public sphere, and beyond Occupy art to inclusive cultural citizenship.

The Occupy movement's protests deconstructed a corrupt system that perpetuates inequity and consent. Its spectacles disrupted business as usual, reversed roles, and freed the imagination. Its processes offered an empowering experience of agency and participation. Now comes the challenge of rebuilding, of moving from compelling temporary interventions into sustained transformations toward a just democracy.

This rebuilding is taking many forms. It is the bridge-building between Occupy and long-standing organizing groups to build multiracial coalitions and the capacity for neighborhood-based and citywide organizing. It is the direct democracy of participatory budgeting where residents make decisions about how public money is spent and learn enough about the system to demand structural change. It is the reclaiming of the airwaves through the successful struggle for community radio licenses and the ongoing advocacy for an open Internet. In this rebuilding, radical imagination is rooted in our deepest values. The myth of austerity transforms into a demand for fairness. Our beleaguered public sector is regenerated into libraries, parks, and schools that are vital community hubs. Our numbing commercial culture is replaced by a culture of respect, humanity, and liberation.

References

Regis, H. 2001. "Blackness and the Politics of Memory in the New Orleans Second Line." *American Ethnologist* 28, no. 4 (November), 752-777.

Tancons, C. 2011. "Occupy Wall Street: Carnival Against Capital? Carnivalesque as Protest Sensibility." *E-Flux Journal* 30 (December).

Room to Grow Something

Paula Z. Segal

Marginality is today no longer limited to minority groups, but is rather massive and pervasive. Marginality is becoming universal.
—Michel de Certeau, *The Practice of Everyday Life*

THE FOUNDATION OF a civil society is space for civility. The development of culture hinges on spaces for people to simply be together, to talk, to eat, to work, to avoid work—all on their own individual terms that meld together into a shared culture. Change from the ground up, whether subtle or revolutionary, is only possible where people are able to get together, form relationships, negotiate difference, find similarities, and finally see themselves as situated in a community by the natural workings of our biological inclination to feel safe among familiar faces.

Liberty Plaza in lower Manhattan, also known as Zuccotti Park, for a short time provided such a space. There, the occupants (née occupiers) built culture from the empty concrete slab up. They ate, drank, slept, took out the garbage, recycled their used water, shared books, argued, made electricity, spent money, sought privacy, sought publicity, and, most importantly, got to know one another.

The freedom to build community and so to exercise governance over our individual and collective lives is our most fundamental freedom as human beings.[1] In its natural form, New York City is dangerously lacking in space for the formation of these crucial relationships. Many neighborhoods

---

1. See Sen 2008.

have no communal spaces at all: nowhere to be together with others that does not hinge on a commercial transaction. At community meetings, I hear again and again that regular New Yorkers don't talk to their neighbors; they're not sure they have anything in common, don't know what to say, are not sure that they are actually part of the same culture. The problem is more acute in neighborhoods where demographics are changing, where those moving in feel like guests and those who have been there a long time fear that they will be pushed out.

Cities are the ultimate tools of what Michele Foucault termed *biopower*—the power to make live and let die. On the map of the city, we can most acutely observe that governance is not a question of imposing law on people, but of regulating things so that individual conduct situates itself within a determined frame of possible actions. As Michel Foucault reminds us, "The finality of government resides in the things it manages and in the pursuit of the perfection and intensification of the processes it directs; and the instruments of government, instead of being laws, now come to be a range of multiform tactics."[2]

The city on a map shows us areas where resources are pooled and vast steppes where resources are scarce. The census tract with the highest median income in the country and the one with the lowest are both in New York City.[3] They are barely three miles apart. One could walk between them in the span of an afternoon. Neighborhoods themselves reproduce vulnerability despite a widespread rhetoric of diversity and inclusiveness. Capital and the things that make life pleasant flee from areas where they are already lacking. Deleterious conditions concentrated in certain New York City neighborhoods are not an accidental convergence, but rather a systemic deprivation enabled through the production of urban geographies. Power congeals in pools of inequality that carry with them their

---

2. See Foucault 1991, 87, 95. Foucault explains that modern populations are governed through "biopower" or "biopolitics," a regulatory control that acts over the population as a whole, i.e., the global mass of bodies that is affected by overall processes of birth, death, production, illness, and so on. Biopower is the power to make live and let die by controlling and harnessing "endemics": permanent factors that sap the populations' strength, waste their energy, and take away their time.

3. See Center for Urban Pedagogy 2009. The map shows median family income by neighborhood in 2006. The Upper East Side had a median income of $178,000 per year, while only three miles away and across the narrow band of the Bronx River, the Belmont neighborhood of the Bronx had a median family income of $22,500 per year.

own gravitational pull. Piling burdens on those who are already burdened is certainly an efficient means of sparing those with the best chances of survival from exposure to death.

The differences between neighborhoods are even more stark when one looks at where foreclosures are concentrated,[4] where vast numbers of people are who pay more than 50 percent of their income in rent,[5] where renters most often find themselves in housing court.[6] These places overlap to a shocking degree. These are also the areas from which jail and prison populations are drawn and to which they return,[7] bringing the trauma and violence of their experiences back home, as well as the neighborhoods to which you have to take a bus because the subway does not reach them,[8] the neighborhoods where few hospitals ever opened and those that did are closing,[9] the neighborhoods with few grocery stores[10] and fewer farmers' markets, the places without parks but with trash incinerators.[11] These are also, by the numbers, the places where one is most likely to be stopped and

---

4. See Bloch and Roberts 2009.

5. See Community Service Society & United Way of New York 2005a.

6. See Community Service Society & United Way of New York 2005b.

7. Overtly discriminatory policing and the connection between imprisonment and larger trends in late capitalist economic development intensify the creation of a geographically determined racial "caste system" (See Herbert 2010, A27; Davis 2003). The effects of mass imprisonment are felt disproportionately by a small number of New York City neighborhoods. Fourteen of New York City's fifty-nine community districts, home to only 17 percent of NYC's adult male residents, account for over 50 percent of all adult males sent to New York State prisons each year from NYC (http://www.justicemapping.org/). These neighborhoods are geographically concentrated in three areas: northern Manhattan, northeastern Brooklyn, and the South Bronx. As an example, the neighborhood of Brownsville, in Brooklyn's 16th Community District, is home to Brooklyn's highest proportion of residents living below the federal poverty line. The residents who live in District 16 are nearly all people of color. During 2003, one in twenty adult men in the district were admitted to jail or prison (not counting those living in the district who are on parole, probation, or other community supervision). Even more troubling, one in twelve young men between the ages of sixteen and twenty-four go to either prison or jail from this district every year. See also Clear 2007, 63–67.

8. See OnNYTurf, n.d. This is a subway map overlaid on a Google map showing the gaps in service that the MTA map's distortion hides. See also American Community Survey 2008.

9. See Opportunity Agenda 2005.

10. See Kavanaugh 2010.

11. See the Parks, Playgrounds & Open Space layers of the OASIS Interactive Map of New York City at http://www.oasisnyc.net/map.aspx (last visited May 6, 2010).

frisked.[12] The most burdened neighborhoods are also the neighborhoods where the majority of New York City's people of color live.[13]

Biopolitics pulls people with limited privileges toward blocks and neighborhoods that, despite their proximity to the rest of New York City's urban fabric, may as well be a world away. This is a sort of amputation, a more precise surgical version of Hitler's Telegram 71, an order to destroy the German people's own city (Berlin) in order to "save" it (Foucault 2003, 239, 241). Exposure to death is concentrated in certain areas, areas that simultaneously absorb the toxicity of the city and are deprived of its life-enhancing elements. The rest thrives.

A truly public and just city is one in which gravity evens out and there are no pools of plenty or barren steppes. Tactics for the formation of spaces in which a public can find shape is crucial to creating such a city. Those publics, once formed, can start the process of strategizing for a true rebirth of our shared culture and community.

> *[A tactic] takes advantage of "opportunities" and depends on them, being without any base where it could stockpile its winnings, build up its own position and plan raids. What it wins it cannot keep. This nowhere gives tactics mobility, to be sure, but a mobility that must accept the chance offerings of the moment, and seize on the wing the possibilities that offer themselves... It must vigilantly make use of the cracks that particular conjunctions open in the surveillance of the proprietary powers. It poaches them. It creates surprises in them. It can be where it is least expected. It is a guileful ruse.*
> —Michel de Certeau, *The Practice of Everyday Life*

The tools we have now are tactics that seize opportunities and slip through cracks, but our goal is to strategize and execute—to unify the margins and stockpile winnings of love and hope for the future. Participation in spatially based community projects is one of the tools we have as we move into a future of decentralized action with liberatory potential.

Putting governance tactics into the hands of the communities of people who are affected by the disposition of things is the goal of a truly demo-

---

12. See Robbins 2012.
13. See Opportunity Agenda 2005.

cratic society. Making self-governance possible allows people from any neighborhood to draw directly the resources they need. In this article, I describe three classes of tactics that my collaborators and I have tried and have found to work, despite an imperfect world, towards that end: (1) Go there and put a sign on it (govern your own city); (2) Use maps as megaphones; or spatially organized social networking; and (3) Draw pictures, with arrows.

These are ideas for how to pierce the city's concrete skins and form bonds as neighbors, to become the city we share and make room for a truly people-driven city strategy. Michele de Certeau described tactics as "currents" in a "sea theoretically governed by the institutional frameworks" that they "gradually erode and displace" (de Certeau 1984, 34). It's a hopeful thought.

1. *Go There and Put a Sign on It (Govern Your Own City)*

All space is occupied by the enemy. We are living under a permanent curfew. Not just the cops—the geometry. True urbanism will start by causing the occupying forces to disappear from a small number of places… The concept of the 'positive void' coined by modern physics might prove illuminating. Gaining our freedom is, in the first place, ripping off a few acres from the face of a domesticated planet.

—Attila Kotanyi and Raoul Vaneigem, "Theses on Unitary Urbanism"

In summer 2011, I started a project by getting my hands on a spreadsheet and a map that showed all the vacant public land in Brooklyn. "Vacant" land

Figure 1. 596 Acres physical interventions keep the digital placemaking relevant to real places. Here, we put up a sign demystifying the chain-link fence and weeds. *Courtesy of 596acres.org*

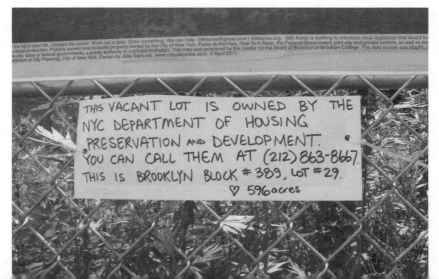

Figure 2. Before and after of a vacant lot where 596 Acres implemented a garden project. *Photo by Meg Wachter*

is land for which the NYC Department of City Planning has no use code on file, land that is literally, from the perspective of the department, not being used for anything. Public land is any land that is being held by a city, state, or federal agency. Adding up the rows in the spreadsheet, I came up with the number 596 acres of vacant public land in Brooklyn alone—an astounding total area of land slightly bigger than Prospect Park, the borough's celebrated giant park. I thought people needed to know; and so "596 Acres" was born.

In June 2011, 596 Acres began physically labeling vacant and available public land in Brooklyn, based on the entries in the spreadsheet. Since then, at least four new garden projects have been formed by passionate local citizens, who joined forces through local community meetings held by 596 Acres and received guidance on how to gain approval to implement projects in vacant lots scattered throughout New York City. Over two dozen projects started because someone walked by and saw one of the 596 Acres signs on the chain-link fence surrounding a lot that until that moment was indistinguishable from other vacant lots being warehoused by private owners in the same neighborhoods. People who saw these signs got together and decided how they wanted to fill the vacant property in their corner of the city. Making information visible to those whose immediate environment is controlled by that information creates power and the possibility of change.

To highlight the effects of a top-down revitalization plan for the city of Sao Paulo, Brazil, and start a conversation about gentrification with those who would be affected, the Spanish collective Left Hand Rotation organized a walking tour in which participants studied the plans put out by Sao Paulo's city hall, then went out to the streets hanging signs on buildings that described each one's specific projected trajectory: whether it would be demolished (many) or rehabilitated.[14] These walks and signs started conversations with the residents of Sao Paulo's downtown and the owners of businesses whose buildings were slated for demolition, most of whom had no access to the connection between the city hall's plans and their own spatial reality.

Sometimes signs are just the beginning. Guerilla gardens and renegade spaces are wonderful, but many folks we work with actually want their projects to be authorized and legitimized by the municipal bureaucracy. Permission is the key to resources and protection from law enforcement interventions. But getting permission can take a very long time. It's hard to hold the attention of the community and to communicate hope and possibility when the day-to-day reality is an unmoved locked fence. So—we plant pansies in plastic bottles we find in the local garbage cans. Right on the fence, attached with string or wire or zip ties. Pansies are hardy flowers that can live with just a little bit of soil. Here in New York they bloom in March, a welcome splash of color after winter's gray. And they are patient and long-suffering. Spending a Sunday afternoon with a bag of soil and a palette of flowers and a stack

---

14. See http://www.lefthandrotation.com/museodesplazados/ficha_luz.htm.

vacant lots (1027)
vacant lots being organized around (28)
vacant lots where groups have gained access (3)
lots that are part of community gardens (281)

Figure 3. This map shows vacant public land that is warehoused by New York City agencies for projects that have not been realized. Not surprisingly, this warehoused resource is concentrated in poor communities of color that cluster around North and Central Brooklyn, as well as near Coney Island. Sites that are preexisting community gardens are depicted as "vacant land" in the city's databases, making them vulnerable to offers by private developers. *Courtesy of the Center for the Study of Brooklyn at Brooklyn College*

Figure 4. A community is gathering resources digitally to create a real urban orchard on this sunny vacant lot. The picture shows that there is an organizer who has identified herself and four people who are watching any changes to this lot's page. Anytime anyone adds a note or other information to the page, all the organizers and watchers get a message. *Courtesy of 596acres.org*

of fliers is a wonderful way to break up the waiting and create a public space for the day. It serves as an entry point for neighbors to connect to the larger dreams of taking land (which already belongs to them) for the community.[15]

---

15. Fence pansies are the canaries of community-controlled space. We planted pansies on the fence that surrounds the space one community hoped would someday be Myrtle Village Green, a community space promised to be created atop a property that was acquired for building an access tunnel into New York City's newest aqueduct. Unfortunately for these pansies, they and the banners announcing the community intentions to make a green space were removed after five days, apparently swept up in NYC Sanitation Department's campaign to get rid of unpermitted election campaign advertising. Another set of pansies was planted on the fence surrounding a trash-strewn lot in Bedford Stuyvesant where a community is just beginning to organize. A young neighbor told us that his family had tried to plant a tree in the same lot the summer prior, only to face threats of trespassing charges from the NYPD. He now plans to join his neighbors in their efforts to gain control of the space officially, and start planting.

Figure 5. 596 Acres started as a poster that simply shared NYC Planning Department's data about vacant public land. We got the data, did the arithmatic, and added a summary. One thousand of these were distributed all over the borough, some as folded broadsheets and some, like here, as signs affixed directly to vacant public lots. *Courtesy of 596acres.org*

2. *Use Maps as Megaphones or Spatially Organized Social Networking*

Maps don't merely represent space, they shape arguments; they set discursive boundaries and identify objects to be considered.
——Institute for Applied Autonomy, "Tactical Cartographies"

596 Acres facilitates the creation of gardens and community green spaces by connecting people with the public land resources in their neighborhoods, supporting them in forming community organizations with the capacity to steward public land, advocating for these organizations' access to land with the government entities that hold title to it, and continuing to support the newly formed gardener coalitions by connecting them with resources and networks of experienced gardeners and farmers. Currently, there are over one-hundred people who actively use our site as a social networking hub to organize with their neighbors around specific sites of urban abandonment and municipal neglect.

Being able to organize geographically and to see the disparate distribution of vacant land in poor communities inverts the power imbalance.
While the NYC budgeting process inherently gives more life opportunities
to projects and people living in places where capital is pooled, the areas left
underfunded are no less likely to house people who want to live in a city and
neighborhood they are proud of. Letting those people find each other using
spatially organized social networking tools allows their voices to be heard.

> *A tactic is an art of the weak.*
> —Michel de Certeau, *The Practice of Everyday Life*

Like the human "mic" used in the Occupy general assemblies, whereby
everybody has the same right and power to speak and turn his/her message
into a powerful collective voice, the coming together of people living in
disadvantaged areas empowers them to express desires and concerns that are
usually silenced. 596 Acres's goal through collective action is to make the
weak and the marginal stronger, more capable of strategy, and of protecting their winnings. These are the acres where people can truly catch their
breaths, if only for a moment, or for the short duration of the notice that
allows them to access and steward the commons.

3. *Draw Pictures, with Arrows*

"Government" and "law" shape the fabric of daily life but are illegible from
that vantage point. There are databases to be decoded and a special legal
language to learn if you are to understand how law and bureaucracy apply
to you in your daily life. But not everyone has the interest, or the time, or
the education. Making law legible where it matters is key to creating an
opportunity for people to intervene in their own governance.

The collective #whOWNSpace re-revealed the prevalence of privately
owned public spaces (POPS) in Manhattan—as opposed to truly public
spaces like parks—and made visible their ownership by the same large corporations whose recklessness has affected so many people in recent decades
by publishing a two-sided map, designed by DSGN AGNC.[16] On one side,

---

16. From http://whownspace.blogspot.com/2011/10/whownspace-mapping-nyc.html:
"The 1% weOWNu map focuses on Privately-Owned Public Spaces (POPS) as well as institutions of private funding, specifying financial institutions that received bail-out funds in
2008. The goal of doing so is to direct attention to the constitutions that control the flow of

Figure 6. This image illustrates the barricades that surrounded Liberty Plaza from November 15, 2011 to January 10, 2012. It appeared on the #whOWNSpace website as part of call for direct action. *Courtesy of #whOWNSpace*

the POPS, and the other, the parks, with contrasting sets of rules and obligations for each. These maps were distributed at Liberty Plaza and are likely to resurface as planning tools for temporary spaces where people can come together.

The New York City Zoning Resolution governs the design of POPS. The resolution has been revised several times in the last fifty years; with each revision, design specifications have gotten more detailed. The original resolution included the requirement that at least 50 percent of frontage between a POPS and the sidewalk be unobstructed. Revisions have added the requirement that paths be provided through the space, and that those paths connect to adjacent sidewalks for circulation.

---

capital. These funding institutions are essential in the transfer of ownership from the city to private interests. The 99% weOWNu map focuses on publicly owned open spaces and the city agencies that control those holdings. Both maps provide a framework for a larger study to comparatively map POPS and publicly owned open spaces, identify their intentions, and understand the political, corporate, and economic entities that control them; and organize with community and activist groups so that designers can collaboratively strategize to advance the use of these spaces."

In the aftermath of the early morning demolition of the Occupy Wall Street encampment in New York City on November 15, the New York City Police Department and security personnel for the property owner turned the POPS into a police barricade cage. The barricades at Liberty Plaza clearly violated the law, but law is words in books and on computer screens. We decided that we needed to apply the law to the place it governed; the result was the literal illustration of the violation through a series of pictures (Figure 6).

The pictures made the error so clear that *anyone* who cared about the future of Liberty Plaza or the public right to "public" space (and not just zoning experts) could engage the municipal agencies in charge of enforcing zoning laws and make a complaint. The way citizens can enforce the public side of the POPS bargain is by complaining to the Department of Buildings (DOB) about the violation of the zoning regulations. The Department of Buildings will send out an inspector and if the inspector finds that there is a violation, a citation will be written and returned to the Environmental Control Board. The Environmental Control Board (ECB) then has the authority to impose a fine on the owners of the "public" space. This route is not particularly clear to see, nor are the institutions involved particularly concerned with the public's right to inhabit space in our city. Nonetheless, these are the institutions that exist.

#whOWNSpace gave people directions so that they could engage with the existing mechanism and "occupy the NYC Department of Buildings Commissioner's inbox." The directions simplified the process of engaging the city agency: go to this web address, put in your name, paste this text, you should get a response in fifteen days, and if you don't, contact us. Over one hundred people complained and were backed up with the weight and power of three major civil liberties organizations. The barricades came down and the park became again became a site of potential.

We are developing an arsenal of tactics that allow for the congealing of power in unexpected places. Relationships are built, resources stockpiled—and yes! Now we begin to plan the raids: occupy our government agencies, hold on to what is already ours, put a sign on a fence, meet the neighbors, write a letter, fight, win, lose, understand the system, meet our elected officials, invite strangers to our house. This is how we pull the margins to the center and erode the institutional frameworks that have resulted in neighborhoods that are pampered and others that are left behind.

References

American Community Survey. 2008. "Mean Travel Time to Work of Workers 16 Years and Over Who Did Not Work at Home." http://factfinder.census.gov/.

Bloch, M., and J. Roberts. 2009. "Mapping Foreclosures in the New York Region." *New York Times*, May 15. http://www.nytimes.com/interactive/2009/05/15/ny region/0515-foreclose.html.

Center for Urban Pedagogy. 2009. *The Envisioning Development Toolkit Online Map.* http://envisioningdevelopment.net/. Last visited May 6, 2010.

Community Service Society & United Way of New York. 2005a. "Renters In Most Low Income Neighborhoods Face Very High Rent Burdens." *Mapping Poverty in New York* 7. http://www.cssny.org/userimages/downloads/Mapping_booklet .pdf.

———. 2005b. "Housing Court Actions Are Concentrated In Poor Neighborhoods." *Mapping Poverty in New York* 9. http://www.cssny.org/userimages/downloads/ Mapping_booklet.pdf.

Clear, T. R. 2007. *Imprisoning Communities: How Mass Incarceration Makes Disadvantages Neighborhoods Worse.* New York: Oxford University Press.

Davis, A. Y. 2003. *Are Prisons Obsolete?* New York: Seven Stories Press.

de Certeau, M. 1984. *The Practice of Everyday Life.* Berkeley: University of California Press.

Foucault, M. 1991. "Governmentality." In *The Foucault Effect: Studies in Governmentality,* edited by G. Burchell, C. Gordon, and P. Miller. Chicago: University of Chicago Press.

———. 2003. *Society Must Be Defended: Lectures at the College de France 1975–76.* New York: Picador.

Herbert, B. 2010. "Jim Crow Policing." *New York Times,* February 2.

Kavanaugh, S. 2010. "New York's Neighborhood Grocery Shortage Map." *Gardeners Supply,* March 21. http://www.thecitygreens.com/2010/03/21/food-deserts-nyc -public-health-hazard/.

OnNYTurf. n.d. "NYC Subway Map." http://www.onnyturf.com/subway/.

Opportunity Agenda. 2005. "Citywide Hospital Status By Race/Ethnicity." http:// www.healthcarethatworks.org/maps/nyc/. Last visited May 6, 2010.

Robbins, C. 2012. "Top 10 Places To Get Stopped And Frisked By The NYPD." *Gothamist.com,* March 20. http://gothamist.com/2012/03/20/top_10_places_to _get_stopped_and_fr.php.

Sen, J. 2008. "Other Worlds, Other Maps: Mapping the Unintended City." In *An Atlas of Radical Cartography,* edited by L. Mozel and A. Bhagat. Los Angeles: Journal of Aesthetics and Protest Press.

Openhearted Cities

Lynne Elizabeth

The human heart is the first home of democracy.
　　—Terry Tempest Williams

A FAVORITE UNCLE passed away this spring, a man who modeled for me simple acts of grace. He lived next door when I was growing up and was one who took a little extra time with us kids. He read us the Sunday comics, led us on hikes, showed us how to tie rag tails on our kites, and turned a kind, allowing eye when we made our Giant Stew. Giant Stew was to us very young ones a magical brew, stirred together with shrieking delight in a rusty galvanized tub in the driveway on rare Saturdays when our uncle washed his car. Like apprentice sorcerers, my cousins, brother, and I mixed dirt and leaves and dead daddy longlegs into this hose water, adding next a pinch of grass from the driveway's edges, then scouring the woods for precious puffballs and mysterious bits of white and yellow tree fungus, taking laundry detergent from under our aunt's utility sink, and finally stealing a handful of cement powder from the garage for extra potency. The fearsome giant lurked in our minds, adding urgency to our scurrying about. I can only guess our uncle found our adventure charming. How else would he tolerate our noisiness, mischief, and prodigious mess?

Today, when boisterous outpourings of citizenry fill public squares, parks, and city streets, banging pots for social change, and stirring up a Giant Stew of transformation, I find myself wishing for kindly uncles and good-natured aunts to be the benevolent guardians of our cities' public realms.

Who will be the mayors, city managers, council members, parks commissioners, and police chiefs with the inner wisdom and sensitive caring for their towns and citizenries? Who will work with patience, who will understand that everyone demonstrating, whether playful or earnest, is still an innocent child at heart, thrilling in the joint endeavor, engaging a shared imagination, trying on a new kind of bravery, and living out a world-changing, heroic role? Likewise, I've been conjuring citizen activists able to let their consciousness shift, if only for a moment, to see the innocent, committed side of those in power, to recognize the parts and scripts that leaders have assumed, to understand the demanding archetypal roles they've taken, and to see the vulnerable humans behind the curtains and levers.

Building Respect, Building Community

I can gratefully point to a community in the United States where understanding has been mutually expressed by those in positions of authority and by resident activists, a place of uncommon cooperation in the Occupy era. Surely there are others. The example is in Salt Lake City. While there for a conference of planning educators in October 2011, I visited the Occupy encampment in Pioneer Park and learned that occupiers not only had obtained city permits to camp, but were showing unusual flexibility themselves by agreeing voluntarily to break down their tents in the park on Saturdays to accommodate the weekly farmers' market. This ostensibly simple act of cooperation was in fact no small feat, as the Occupy encampment had, like most Occupy encampments, unintentionally attracted a large number of local homeless, mentally unstable, and disaffected drifters, who were barely aware of Occupy Wall Street politics, let alone skilled in diplomacy.

Visiting Salt Lake City again in June 2012 for a community design conference, I learned that a loyal Occupy community still met regularly and camped on the grounds of the city's main library. Stopping by the cluster of a dozen or so tents on an early Saturday, I was told by a camper that they were about to pack up for a few weeks to make room for a seasonal arts festival. Occupy Salt Lake City wanted to support the arts, he explained, and not get in the way—they'd come back at the end of the month. They had permits.

Salt Lake City's bicycle-riding mayor, Ralph Becker, happened to be addressing our conference that same morning at the library. When I mentioned the friendly relations between the city and the Occupy activists, he gave all the credit to the open approach of the city's chief of police, Chris Burbank. A commitment to respectful, community policing had engendered a wholesome culture of neighborly communications and thoughtful cooperation, even within a volatile social movement.

Chief Burbank, I later learned, takes that kindly-uncle grace one step further—not only has he committed his entire police force to community peacekeeping, he has spoken to the US Congress in opposition to pressures to cross-deputize police officers as immigration enforcement agents. His June 17, 2010 address against racial profiling to the US House of Representatives Subcommittee on the Constitution, Civil Rights, and Civil Liberties noted:

> The essential duty of modern law enforcement is to protect the civil rights of individuals while providing for the safety of all members of the communities we serve, equally, without bias. . . The foundation of our republic is not based on the rule of the majority. Democracy and those elected to serve must guard against the tyranny of the majority or of mob rule and ensure the well-being of the downtrodden or underrepresented.

Burbank is an active member of the Consortium for Police Leadership in Equity that promotes police transparency and accountability. How inspiring to have a police chief who is also a brave statesman!

Speaking one's truth to those in power takes valor, even when it is expressed within the system of power. To those without access to forums, and to those living where enmity and repression run deep, speaking out *and* being heard by anyone in authority may seem impossible. Indeed, when conditions are rigidly restrictive or dangerous, when unjust, unsustainable systems ripe for reform are unresponsive to any kind of dialog, next steps may take the form of civil disobedience. Dramatic public actions, especially acts of disobedience, are of lasting benefit to a community and the greater society when they are undertaken with utmost compassion.

Thoughtful leaders of social movements in the past, like Gandhi, believed that respect was fundamental to effective action and communication. Gandhi was not selective in whom he respected—he believed respect must be unconditional and all-pervasive. He began every campaign with days of meditation, and, with clear intention, he would write a carefully crafted request for change to an individual with the authority to make that change.

After a reasonable time, if there was no response, Gandhi carried out an act of civil disobedience with a commitment to *ahimsa*, no harm to any.

Loving My City

I'd like to summon this level of civility, honesty, and authentic public thought-fulness. I'd like to attract action that derives from bighearted sincerity, a sincerity that originates in love. I can't help but invoke the spirit of the late Jane Jacobs, a citizen activist and truth-speaking writer who successfully stopped several city developers from eviscerating neighborhoods with freeways. In a *Parabola* interview on cities Jacobs (1993) exhorted, "You have to love your city and love the area you're trying to improve, genuinely love it, not regard it with suspicion, disdain, any of those emotions, or whatever you do, even with the best of intentions, will be destructive and disastrous" (20).

Pier Giorgio Di Cicco, as Toronto's Poet Laureate, expressed the same fierce wisdom in his 2005 monograph, *Civic Valentines*.

> People who are not in love are irresponsible. A town that is not in love with itself is irresponsible, and civically apt for mistakes. Responsibility is a cold duty; and it inspires no one. A citizenry is incited to action by the eros of mutual care, by having a common object of love—their city. A town that is not in love will cut corners, lose sight of the common good. It loses sight of the common good because it has lost sight of what is commonly beautiful, and the beautiful is not landscape, or cityscape or architectonic; the beautiful is what people have built in the spaces between each other—a reciprocity, an exchange of ideals, a shared vision.

The call to be a civic lover is also a call to straddle tensions, to creatively hold opposing views with an open mind, to admit contradictions without judging them. It holds an open space for the voices of prison abolitionists touting books, not bars, and also for the prison guard unionists needing jobs; for the anarchists seeking overthrow in black teargas rags and for the bank CEOs intent on preserving established order; for the Japanese mothers marching to shut nuclear power plants and for the government officials trying to prevent panic; for the homeless veterans begging space to sleep and for the city parks' managers grooming lawns for children's play. The civic lover sees that each of these people is motivated to protect something or someone, each is caring even though one is pitted against the other, each interest group has simply, or rather complicatedly, a different and competing idea of how to serve the community.

Sitting Face-to-face with the Other

In the 1980s, as a peace activist, I was invited by an organization called Beyond War (later, Search for Common Ground) to attend a small training conference near Taos. Each participant was asked to bring someone of an opposing viewpoint. I joked with a friend that I'd like to invite the commanding officer of the nearby US Marine base and was dared to do it. To my amazement, the colonel commander accepted my invitation. It was an epiphany. In contrast to my preconceived idea that everyone in the military was bloodthirsty and ignorant, this incredibly amiable, sophisticated, and open-minded man was truly committed to peace on earth. I also discovered that we both believed in a motto of that era: "peace through strength." The colonel, however, defined strength as military prowess, and I defined it as domestic health. We talked at length about these issues and became eventual friends.

Like everyone else, I can imagine a better world based on the ideas I have collected throughout a lifetime. In many cases, my cherished visions are surprisingly compatible with those I think oppose me. Who doesn't want healthy convivial neighborhoods or clean water, land, and air? Where we differ is the means of achieving those goals. It is in meeting and sharing visions that we open up to the possibility of finding common ground. And discovering our shared visions opens us up to the possibility of reaching agreement on the means of realizing them.

What a huge stretch out of my comfort zone it takes, however, to sit down face-to-face with the Other, someone whose methodology I am convinced I dislike. Too often, we look at the obstacles to discussion and instead decide on confrontation and fighting, whether it is neighbors suing neighbors without first meeting to talk or nations launching military attacks without calling for mediation or a summit.

Buddhist teacher Thich Nhat Hanh exhorts us to write a love letter to our enemies. Even if the letter is not sent, the practice of looking deeply within and lovingly expressing ourselves can in itself transform the situation. And actually sending the letter may also bring about change.

In this time of the largest public demonstrations that the world has ever seen, in this era of colossal upwelling of systemic self-correction, I'm calling for a cadre of benevolent ones to bring about change with the kind of courage that originates in love for our communities. From the public heart centers of cities, may free participation and free creative expression be celebrated no matter how untidy. I'm blessing city plazas filled and bustling with rich discussion about shared visions for an equitable and just society, a healthy environment, and a stable economy. I give thanks for the vibrant and generous spirit of the Occupy movement, with its nightly general assemblies, working groups, people's libraries, first aid stations, services to the homeless, free kitchens, interfaith ministries, information tables, and people's universities. I give thanks for the irrepressible Occupy messages amplified in cardboard placards, projected "bat signals," and "people's mics" that has broken a toxic trance of business as usual and revealed to activists, who had been laboring in relative isolation, the potential for a transformative global movement. I implore city parents and all those in a position of responsibility to show calmness and empathy during this unfolding process. With open hearts, we can bring about necessary evolutionary changes in our society without causing harm to any. I envision letting go of blame. I see the 99% writing love letters to the 1% and the 1% writing love letters to the 99%. I see everyone remembering that we are 100% earthlings, 100% air-breathing, 100% in this together.

I see recognition that we are brother and sister, aunt and uncle to each other. I see public spaces as welcoming places for each person to tell what is on his and her heart, regardless of their heritage, gender, affiliations, or worldview. I see people lending each other their better ear, receptive and listening, refraining from finishing each other's sentences. I see us giving ourselves ample time to breathe between thoughts, to slow down long enough to offer the yes of our being.

Space to Heal

I believe this is also a time for cities to offer safe spaciousness for acknowledging the deep suffering we each experience—a time to sit with grief, to be with pain together. I invite cities to lend a tender shoulder in the shape of pleasant park benches, verdant lawns, plazas open to the sun, or stone-stepped amphitheaters for those who have endured much to tell their story. Let cities offer public space to grieve after tragedies, removing not too quickly the hundred little altars to beloved ones lost, the mementos, candles, flowers—let us respect the instinct to heal. Let people's messy expressions spill onto sidewalks and bus stops and city hall verandas.

Like a thoughtful friend, let cities offer solace in the form of open forums for those afraid to speak, for those needing encouragement to get something painful off their chest—we're not all brassy actors. And I see cities building public stages for the actors, too, to let their dramas recount the misery and the joy, frustration, and humor of this life. If we're not allowed to playact, anger explodes and becomes destructive. Better to work out old and new ideas in the form of theater, where natural feedback and revision feed the process of evolution.

We are all essentially tenderhearted. It is our natural state to empathize with others, unless we have suffered great pain and been ignored, unless we've been rejected, unless we've been cruelly punished. Those who are neglected, shunned, and maltreated can turn numb, hardhearted, armored as protection from further hurt. It is the way of human souls to respond so. Much gentleness and love are required to give the hardened heart space and time to soften and restore trust. Some place that feels safe, some place that feels like home is called for.

Profound social repair may not happen in a lifetime, given how deeply injured many have been, given the ubiquitous violence and relentless machines of punishment and repression we live among. One in one hundred adult US citizens were behind bars in 2008, an onerous imbalance contributing to untold suffering. And within the greatest system of organized tyranny the world has ever known, the US military, the suicide rate of personnel in 2012 is averaging one person per day.

While prisons and the military are the most obvious examples of hardening of the heart, it's also not a secret that municipal police have become increasingly militarized, especially in the wake of 9/11. Homeland Security, despite its cozy-sounding name, has foisted upon cities tens of billions of dollars worth of armored vehicles, riot gear, arsenals of weapons, and military-style training. The mayor of New York City brags he has the seventh largest army in the world, his police department, which is used against its own residents. Oppression and meanness hide in the private places of our culture, too. Countless among us have been seriously harmed, turned unfeeling by a lack of compassion, an absence of gentleness, in their living environment.

And so, in order for our city centers, our town squares, our common spaces to become places of healing, a *very* large grace is called for. The grace of our truest human nature. Such grace comes from a brave kind of vulnerability, a poise and dignity arising from someplace calm inside. Someplace quiet and strong. No special intelligence or schooling is needed to acquire it. Our unschooled inner selves can be so wise. What it does take is a large dose of peace in the acceptance of what is. A recognition of life in its preciousness and the mystery of who each of us might be.

When my imagination soars, I see a mayor as kind as Saint Francis, a chief of city peace officers as compassionate as the Dalai Lama, and public spaces as inviting as warm hearths. It need only be evoked. So let us call forth the Chris Burbank, the Gandhi, the Martin Luther King Jr., the Nelson Mandela in each of us—citizen and civil servant alike. Let us make a welcoming home of our public spaces. Let us host public assemblies and celebrations of every creative kind with warm support. Let us nurture goodwill. Let us attend to the well-being of each and of the whole in our central squares. Let us open the hearts of our selves and our cities.

References

Jacobs, J. 1993. "Where Trade Began." *Parabola* 18 (4).

Di Cicco, P. G. 2005. *Civic Valentines*. www.toronto.ca/culture/pdf/poet/civic_valentines.pdf.

Life and Death in Public Places

Nikki Stern

I FIRST SAW the smoldering remains of the World Trade Center (WTC) on September 20, 2001. Nine days after the terrorist attacks that killed my husband Jim, I arrived by ferry, along with a flotilla of armed soldiers, therapy dogs, and fellow mourners to witness firsthand the devastation at Ground Zero. While others cried and deposited teddy bears and flowers, I stared, mesmerized by the terrible beauty of the sculptured ruins. Waiting by the crumbled steps leading to what had been the World Financial Center, I began to kick at the loose stones. "You died here, but you didn't live here," I muttered, over and over, throwing in a profanity or two for good measure. I continued to kick and mutter, kick and mutter, until my toe ached and a concerned volunteer led me back into the line of anxious passengers staring at the crazy lady with the badly scuffed shoe.

My husband spent the better part of five days a week at the World Trade Center complex, toiling away on the 94th floor of Tower 1 as an information analyst and project manager for insurance giant Marsh McLennan. Between 8:30 a.m. and 5:30 p.m., and sometimes longer, he lived life as a back-office cubicle dweller. There were elements of working at the center he enjoyed—the mix of people, the convenience of retail shopping. We both loved Windows on the World; who didn't like to be high above the world imbibing overpriced drinks with the movers and shakers (and tourists)? Jim found the contrast between the still-shiny WTC zone and the crooked, narrow downtown streets endlessly fascinating. He was taken with the history embedded on the sides of buildings and in the sidewalks, and especially with the *potential* of the place. An amateur photographer with an abiding interest in architecture, he had an eye for detail and a creative sensibility. During our occasional lunches together, we'd stop at Liberty Plaza Park, a remarkable (and rare) open space with tables and seats. Over sandwiches or pizza, he'd talk about design integration, open space, and the *potential* of the area to deliver on its unfulfilled promise to become truly people-friendly.

I worked part-time in neighboring Soho, as the public relations director for a corporate architecture firm, and preferred that neighborhood. I couldn't relate to the cold impersonality of the World Trade Center, whose towers seemed nothing more than concrete monuments to the power of commerce. The place was notable for what wasn't there: grass, light, culture, access to the water, elements that were important to both of us. Nothing in that world suggested color or light or appeared to promote the creation or exchange of ideas except as they pertained to making money.

The towers in life and in death held no appeal for me. They didn't represent my husband. Neither was I taken with the idea of sacred ground; the sixteen acres appeared to me as a version of hell. Instead, I was fiercely attracted to the idea that a reimagined area might actually honor the memory of my husband not by focusing on death but by celebrating life.

Early on, I found myself at odds with those 9/11 family members determined to see Ground Zero left untouched, so that it would be a sort of sixteen-acre cemetery upon which no living people might engage in any activity that was not about remembering the dead. While I wanted to respect their beliefs, I fervently believed that in order for all of us—family members, New Yorkers, and all Americans—to heal, we had to create a kind of "living monument," a place where people engaged in the business of life: working, discussing, learning, watching, interacting, playing, relaxing, contemplating, celebrating, and yes, remembering. My voice was unique among family members lobbying for a far different sort of place, and most of the time it was overwhelmed by the outrage of the more forceful among them.

Instead, I discovered common ground with a number of other people, a few relatives and a great many New Yorkers who participated in several public forums I attended. Their goal was the restoration of their beloved skyline and the creation of an accessible public space that combined remembrance with affirmation. The details varied, the emphasis on life did not.

Returning to downtown, I plunged into the heart of the efforts to rebuild. I attended assemblies, conferences, and regular meetings held by the committees I'd been invited to join. I spent more time close to the site than

I would have thought possible, often at the headquarters of the newly created Lower Manhattan Development Corporation (LMDC) at One Liberty Plaza, adjacent to the decimated remnants of Liberty Plaza Park.

I was something of an outlier—an out-of-state resident with a passionate commitment to a geographic area I'd previously ignored, a so-called family leader at odds with other family members, a non-architect associating with talented planners and designers, and a grief-laden, childless, disconnected newly hatched widow who spent as much time away from the crushing silence of her house as possible. But I was engaged in what I felt was a project for the future—a future inspired by the tragedy of loss.

In December of that first year, I huddled with members of the Regional Plan Association and New York New Visions in raw space at the South Street Seaport during a three-day intensive design session. We were challenged to come up with plans that would complement and enhance those put forward by Mayor Bloomberg and the deputy mayor, Dan Doctoroff. The sessions produced some truly innovative ideas, plans that created opportunities for improved transportation, educational facilities, small businesses, creative arts, new media enterprises, and street-level retail establishments. Some of the ideas included a museum of tolerance, a business school for global entrepreneurs, satellite extensions of New York schools and universities, relocated cultural institutions. The concepts emphasized public spaces that promoted interaction and movement and gave back to the neighborhood. Someone even proposed a sort of Hyde Park corner. We tried to accommodate what we imagined were real estate considerations—replacing lost income, generating new revenue sources. We took security and safety concerns seriously. We envisioned world-class architecture harmonizing with park-like landscaping. The memorializing outside the memorial itself would be accomplished by discrete signage visible to those who worked in the surrounding offices or traversed the space—and by the mere fact that the realization of an idealized, multipurpose space might be our collective Phoenix-moment. Our answer to terrorism would be resilience. Our response to death would be rebirth. Our counter to devastation would be the creation of a place of unsurpassed beauty.

Naïve? Maybe so. I don't know if any of us anticipated the extent to which the site would be plagued by untenable delays and cost overruns, and demands and counterdemands from various parties. Certain elements, like the Performing Arts Center, have been delayed; others have been excluded. There is, for instance, no university presence, although the Memorial Museum, under its ambitious director, is seeking to institute 9/11-related educational programming. There has been controversy: over the treatment of the remains and over the proposed Freedom Museum, whose opponents feared would appear to "tolerate" terrorism by delving into root causes of discontent. In 2009, the site again made international headlines when plans for a Muslim-run community center several blocks away resulted in protests at the site. The objectors insisted the project would insult the memories of the dead. I wrote an op-ed piece at the time about how disappointed I was that Ground Zero for some would commemorate not only death over life, but also prejudice over tolerance, grief over hope, and a backwards, stuck-in-place mentality that trampled the visions of a better future some of us once had. But I didn't visit.

Another two years passed before I returned, not during the tenth anniversary of the attacks but just after. The memorial was open to the public and I went because, I suppose, I was curious to see how I would feel. I'd left time to stop by another, much smaller site I remembered well: a 3300-square-foot slip of green my husband and I visited so that he might escape the long shadows of the World Trade Center. Reopened in 2006 as Zuccotti Park for the philanthropist and chairman of the realty company that provided for its restoration, it had hosted the annual 9/11 anniversary commemorations. At that point, it was hosting Occupy Wall Street.

It was another one of those stunning autumn mornings, with another cerulean sky visible through half-built towers that aspired to reach higher. Hundreds of people were going about their business, their numbers augmented by thousands more whose presence suggested this was, if not yet a world trade center, then the world's visiting center. Not that most of the people actually went to the visitor's center, which might have provided some much-needed context. At that point, the memorial could be viewed without knowing much about what had happened or why a memorial was built.

As a family member, I was directed around the astonishingly long lines (history perhaps, but apparently a must-see destination). Without warning, which is to say without much in the way of signage, I was in the space, which consists of two massive waterfalls conforming to the footprints of the original towers and ringed with low granite walls bearing the names of the nearly three thousand people who died.

Using the guide I'd been handed, I made my way to the far side of the north pool and located my husband's name. I touched the engraved stone and whispered, "Well, here you are." And waited. But the rush of emotions

I anticipated—grief, perhaps; but also reverence, awe, inspiration, a telescoping of past, present and future, even a thrill of having been part of the planning—never came. It was all very lovely but somehow...static.

I ran into an acquaintance, a still active family leader who asked what I thought and, without waiting for a response, let me know how disturbed he was by the atmosphere. "Some of these people are just wandering around," he complained. "They don't even seem to know why they're here."

I left the memorial to walk over to Zuccotti Park, where the mass of tourists appeared to vastly outnumber the protestors. Another destination, I thought. The park looked overrun, no doubt about it, but not really disheveled. The bedding was neatly stacked, except when someone was still sleeping. An older gent played a pretty good rendition of "God Bless America" on the bagpipes. I made my way tentatively into the center, past the showboaters and picture-takers, and found occupiers talking quietly or texting or reading. I saw several meetings taking place, conducted in relatively quiet tones, since neither megaphones nor sound equipment was allowed.

I couldn't hear what was being said, although I picked up on the passion and the earnestness. By now, we've all read that the occupiers have been trying to draw attention to the economic inequities in the United States. We've also been told by various sources they're slackers or whiners, as if being young and out of work was a failing. Actually it is, not of this generation, but of a system that rewards banks and businesses that don't create jobs and CEOs who don't produce dividends.

What struck me about that little slip of green on that day is how utterly suited to its temporary purpose it seemed. A privately funded public space had been appropriated in order to make a point. Some may argue the protesters disrespected the park by misusing it. Since the park doesn't appear to have been injured, the purported abuse or misuse of public space is in the minds of the beholders. To me, Zuccotti Park was in full use, alive and teeming with good intentions and honest efforts.

I've given some thought to that little slip of green and the contrast with the acreage on which the 9/11 memorial sits. What did I expect of the latter? It is, after all, a place designed to encourage reflection and contemplation, remember the past and honor the dead. The gently cascading water at the memorial walls and the trees, many of them still to be planted, serve to juxtapose living nature against the starkness of death, I guess. True, if one looks up, one sees the outlines of blandly functional commercial buildings taking shape, but that is the nature of real estate in New York.

These are nothing more than plots of land, one converted to a platform from which to demonstrate democracy in action before being returned to its former state, the other reconceived as a place of remembrance. Still, they're iconic and that counts for a lot, even when it comes to dusty history. Looking back, I wouldn't have guessed it would be the former Liberty Plaza Park that would end up as a visual and visible symbol of life-affirming resilience.

4

Public Space Over Time

The Grass Is Always Greener

A BRIEF HISTORY OF PUBLIC SPACE AND PROTEST IN NEW YORK CITY AND LONDON

Lisa Keller

AMERICANS ARE FOND of talking about their cousins "across the pond"—the "special relationship" between the United States and Great Britain is warmly referenced in modern geopolitical conversations. We derive many of our foundational concepts from the English. Men such as John Locke, William Blackstone, and John Stuart Mill carved out critical concepts that helped form American society: the rights of the individual, the notion of freedom as intrinsic to society, the contract between the individual and the state for governance, and the cementing of clear and fair law as the basis for justice.

But, as the song goes, "You say tom-AY-to and I say to-MAH-to." In two different mouths, the same words can sound very different. And despite our common heritage, America and Great Britain express their ideas about freedom and liberty differently; while sharing essential beliefs, each country has acted on them in ways that highlight their historical differences. There is perhaps no better example of this than the place of protest and demonstration in each society. Great Britain, governed by common law, generally has shown greater tolerance for using its abundant public spaces for free speech. The United States, governed by codified law, has shown less toleration and has fewer public spaces dedicated for it.[1]

Public demonstrations have long served as the cornerstone of modern democratic societies. They have been critical mechanisms for nourishing democracy, an innovative political system established in fifth century Athens.

---

1. For a more detailed discussion of the material in this essay, see Keller 2008.

In order to work, democracy demanded popular participation in all levels of state governance: citizens had to participate not only to show interest in how the state was run but also to input ideas and show disagreement so that public opinion could inform the political process. In Greek and Roman societies, large outdoor assemblies where people voiced opinions were common; they were sometimes orderly and sometimes rowdy, but always considered necessary. It is easy to forget that democracy, as a working political system, existed only for a few centuries in the classical era before becoming dormant for more than a thousand years. During that hiatus, large public assemblies aimed at voicing political opinion faded away, yielding to a less politicized popular expression.

The difficulties that the Occupy Wall Street (OWS) demonstrators face in staging their demonstrations bring to mind this larger transatlantic historical framework regarding public protest during the past hundred and fifty years. The OWS issues are typical of those that any group in the twenty-first century will face in mounting a demonstration: availability of public spaces, public acceptance of large crowds on streets and in squares, societal acceptance of dissenting voices, unknown legal parameters surrounding free speech, the limits and roles of politics and government, and the toleration of disorder. When comparing the United States' and Great Britain's leading cities, however, there is a vast difference in the way free speech has developed. In Great Britain, there is a predisposition to favor public speech and protest, even when it is messy or becomes a nuisance. In the United States, despite our proclaimed belief in the concept, citizen rights tend to be more like a NIMBY ("not in my backyard") issue. In principle, we all think freedom of speech is a great idea, one that we firmly believe in; but the reality of enacting it is inconvenient, like the group home down the street from where we live. London and New York differ in the way they act out their freedom and in the way political will emerges in the interaction of police, government, and demonstration dynamics.

Interestingly, most of what happens today is not new, but a continuation of policies set almost a century ago. By 1900, both New York and London had established policies regarding demonstrations and public speech that remain consistent to the present time. These policies were formed through a complex process of societal conversations on the issues, though not all parties were fairly represented. During the critical period from 1850 to 1900, public officials determined what was in the best interest of citizens; lawyers interpreted legal codes; the public debated in speech and print what were valid objectives and methods; and the police followed the mandate set by the government to keep cities orderly places. The net result was that in New York and London, lines were drawn about where people could and couldn't go to express their free speech rights. The pressure to set those boundaries was a reaction to the raucous and flourishing political atmosphere of the nineteenth century. Public assemblies in the age of new democracies echoed the characteristics of similar gatherings in ancient Greek and Roman societies: loud, large, and challenging to authority, but also necessary to ensure that democratic political expression be heard.

Unfettered free speech, however, came with consequences. Democratic voices at times ran into conflict with the perceived need to protect the city from disorder. So authorities in London and New York enacted rules aimed not at preventing free speech and assembly but at limiting or controlling it. Both cities tried to strike a balance between freedom and order, but London protected what it considered its "birthright" freedoms more zealously in practice and preserved them better than New York. In London, the Metropolitan Police enforced government policy that vacillated between tolerance and repression of public demonstrations, but in the end tolerance prevailed. New York was more pragmatic and put daily life concerns foremost: here, there was a tighter hold on such demonstrations, more concern with order, and a greater toleration of the abrogation of rights.

The density of these great world cities is an important factor in this argument. In the mid-nineteenth century, London was the world's greatest metropolis with 2.6 million people; by 1900, greater London surged to 6.5 million. New York had a spectacular growth rate, from less than 80,000 in 1800 to almost 700,000 in 1850 and nearly 3.5 million in 1900. To make these cities sustainable—decent to live in and desirable to go to— and cope with the increasing complexity of urban life, authorities had to enact massive numbers of regulations. To a large degree, physical challenges were at the heart of the metropolis, and sewage, water, housing, and public thoroughfares were reengineered in both cities. These developments were not contentious at the time but considered signs of progress, optimism, and prosperity.

A different challenge to urban success was disorder, as both cities were rife with crime. The acknowledgment by city leaders that public order was a priority resulted in the formation of police systems in both places. London's was first, a model force in 1829, followed by New York's in 1845. London's Peelers were given an important mandate: "the principal object is 'the Prevention of Crime'… the security of person and property, the preservation of the public tranquility." The emphasis here is on prevention—that was more important than "detection and punishment after…the crime." That the police were to be a civil body was critical; no military were to be involved. Both in London and New York, the neophyte police had to find their way into their new roles and faced an extraordinary array of responsibilities: besides catching "crooks," they were also required to catch dogs, find lost children, arrest drunks, ticket cabs, oversee licensing, chase vagrants, monitor food adulteration and pollution, keep track of diseases, get rid of dead animals, lodge the homeless, and prevent riots and control public disturbances.

How to control demonstrations was an unchartered course in London and New York in 1850. The public used whatever space it could in each city to sound its voice, and the authorities reacted to the use of those spaces in varying ways. In London, Trafalgar Square became an enduring center for demonstrations, which is ironic given its history. When the grand square was developed in the 1830s and 1840s, it was meant to eliminate a dense, poor neighborhood and replace it with grand government buildings and academies. The layout of the space was designed to discourage public meetings: Nelson's column and the fountains were placed to prevent assemblies. Even the land's legal status defied the intent: while technically Crown land, its care and management fell under the public domain. Such a change in the use of Trafalgar Square proved critical for all of London, as many of its parks and squares followed a similar path in midcentury and increasingly provided public access.

London's multitudinous public squares, commons, and parks, along with the city's streets, became the destination for protestors in the nineteenth century. This created an interesting institutional dynamic. As London was for most of the century administered by a central government, the policies that emerged about public spaces were indicative of broad principles; they shifted depending upon which political party was in power, and there were numerous occasions when such changes were abrupt. Yet, government lawyers maintained a mostly consistent policy of backing broad common law rights of assemblage. The Metropolitan Police followed Home Office orders concerning free speech and specific demonstrations; but at times even the police became frustrated by the lack of clear policy.

In the 1880s, the playwright George Bernard Shaw decided to use London's streets as a testing ground for free speech, sparking off what would become a popular tactic for others. Shaw took to speaking at street corners to enunciate his brand of socialism, Fabianism. He nicknamed his tactics the "Dod Street trick":

> Find a dozen or more persons who are willing to get arrested at the rate of one per week by speaking in defiance of the police. In a month or two, the repeated arrests, the crowds which they attract, the scenes which they provoke, the sentences passed by the magistrates and at the sessions, and the consequent newspaper descriptions, rouse sufficient public feeling to force the Home Secretary to give way whenever the police are clearly in the wrong. (Shaw 1892, tract no. 41, 9)

He noted that oftentimes the police were his only audience, and always listened politely (though they didn't arrest him). As the "trick" became more popular, audiences increased to the point where there were at times tens of thousands in attendance, which did create street obstruction problems. Shaw was joined by other "celebrities" who wanted to call attention to issues. Artist William Morris became a fervent advocate of free speech and demonstrations at Trafalgar Square. After his arrest, Morris was embarrassed when the police court magistrate asked him who he was. "I am an artist," Morris answered, and "pretty well known…" (Thompson 1955). It was in these decades that the Speaker's Corner emerged as a meeting place for those who wanted to vent their opinions in public.

In the 1880s, during a time of increased unemployment and labor agitation, demonstrations in Trafalgar Square as well as in other areas of London increased significantly. While the government attempted to clarify the legal status of such meetings, it occurred to no one to ban them. The police themselves had been skeptical about preventing public meetings and made their opinions known to the government for quite some time. Only following one particularly violent gathering in the late 1880s was such a ban attempted.

"Bloody Sunday," a demonstration for working-class rights, was certainly not very violent by American standards. Three people were killed, seventy-five injured, and fifty arrested. The British public reacted strongly. Initially, reaction was split: many expressed relief at the containment of political "radicalism" and return to order, while many expressed frustration at the curtailment of basic rights. "Bloody Sunday" called attention to issues about liberties and unwarranted authority in a way that had not been seen before. Newspapers, officials, and citizens debated an issue long taken for granted but now perceived to be under attack. Free speech and assembly was no longer a tacit right but one that required bolstering. However, when the scales were tipped and the call for authority and order became too weighty, the need for balance became clear. The net result was the reassertion of the right of assembly in public, one that became modified in the twentieth century but was never curtailed.

Shaw's "Dod Street trick" would not have met a happy reception in New York. In the 1870s, Tompkins Square had become the center of the new dense immigrant population that aggregated below 14th Street, replacing The Park (City Hall Park) as a gathering spot. But as New York's population swelled, and its politics became more vocal and challenging, public assemblies became the focus of concern.

This worry about potential turbulence in the streets resulted in one of the most defining pieces of legislation regarding public assemblies ever passed. In 1872, the New York state legislature passed its first regulation of street processions and assemblies in cities across the state. From this point on, until the present day, assemblies of more than twenty would require a permit. There had been numerous disturbances during the 1840s to 1860s that had public officials worried, but two events in particular precipitated the creation of this law.

One was the severe trauma that New York experienced during the 1863 Draft Riots. What started out as a protest by working-class men who were frustrated that they could not afford to buy out of Civil War conscription turned into five days of chaos that turned the city upside down and resulted in massive destruction of property and more than a hundred dead. It was the Orange Day marches of 1871, however, that turned out to be the breaking point. Ostensibly a civic celebration by Protestant Irish, the event was a provocation to Catholic Irish and resulted in terrible clashes. A combination of police and militia couldn't prevent sixty-three deaths during the parade. Midst public fury, politicians scurried to prevent a reoccurrence. While politicians, the press, and the public maintained for the most part a theoretical right to demonstrate, the large number of deaths and wanton property damage also ensured that new limits would be placed on public gatherings. The law requiring a permit for assemblies was quickly passed in the state legistature. At the same time, between 1850 and 1900, public parks and squares were reengineered and new regulations enacted to limit where citizens could demonstrate. A few places, such as Union Square, did remain active for many decades, but, with a few exceptions, most parks and squares were slowly eased out of availability for political gatherings.

Indeed, Gotham had a dearth of public spaces. The 1811 Commissioner's Plan known as The Grid favored private and commercial development and failed to provide for parks or squares—with the exception of a reservoir, a marketplace, and a parade ground. This lack of public space in New York would prove to be defining in terms of limiting free speech and assembly. By the time Central Park opened in 1859, there were eleven public squares and parks below 42nd street, serving the bulk of Manhattan's population: the already mentioned Tompkins Square, which served a working-class neighborhood and was an important meeting place for decades, and Union Square, which became the sole sanctioned place for events; Washington Square, which had been a potter's field with more than twenty thousand people buried there, and was then made into a parade ground in 1826; Madison Square; Abingdon Square; The Battery; Bowling Green; Gramercy Park; Hamilton Square (no longer existent); The Park (City Hall Park), the main meeting place during the first half of the century; and St. John's Park (no longer existent). Central Park, the city's preeminent green space created in mid-nineteenth century, was from its outset defined as a leisure space not to be used for demonstrations, as was the case with these other open spaces.

By the early twentieth century, when the labor movement and radical politics gained momentum, only Union Square remained as a significant staging area for demonstrations. Named after the conjunction of streets that met at 14th Street, the Square (originally called Union Place) started as a potter's field. After prominent real estate developer Samuel Ruggles, who lived there and developed parcels around it, pushed for improvement of the area, the square opened as a three-and-a-half-acre park in 1839. In mid-nineteenth century, the square was the geographical heart of New York and a logical place for festivities such as the 1882 Labor Day, the first of its kind. The celebration of the workingman was not contentious, and it marked the beginning of an interesting bifurcation in public street activity: celebrations are acceptable, political speech is questionable.

The open-air rhetoric of the Industrial Workers of the World, better known as the Wobblies, helped fuel the labor movement in New York, and

Union Square became a symbol of free speech in the first few decades of the twentieth century, despite the fact that few events there were without contention. After the 1908 bomb blast in the square, the city ensured that large numbers of police were present at all demonstrations, and some felt their actions were carried out with heavy-handed tactics. One irate protestor commented, "Let us remove Madam Liberty from Bedlow's island and put there instead Inspector Schmittberger with his club" (*New York Times* 1908).

These meetings, such as the one in 1910 in Union Square attended by more than one hundred thousand people, were, for the most part, legal, with police issuing permits. But Wobbly demonstrations were contentious, and police monitored content carefully. By the eve of World War I, these demonstrations had become routinely raucous and prone to dispersion, as crowds were always large and police incapable of handling them. Even New York Police Commissioner Woods (1914) noted that people "have a constitutional right of free assemblage and of free speech... It is the duty of the police, not merely to permit this, but to protect people in the enjoyment of free speech and assemblage" (30–31). Such a right, he said, was dependent upon the peaceful nature of the meeting, which couldn't annoy others, obstruct streets, or produce violence. Much room was left for interpretation as to whether public speech was provocative and should be stopped. New York Chief Magistrate and former Police Commissioner McAdoo defined such speech "as inciting to riot if it was 'provocative of immediate violence.'"

Many people (such as this author's parents) recall vividly going to Union Square to demonstrate for political causes. But by the 1930s, there was increasing pressure to control such gatherings. Permits could limit the number of hours of a demonstration, for example, and police could keep people moving. The World War II era marked a halt to protest in public, replacing it with patriotic rallies. By the 1950s, the Cold War and McCarthyism turned Union Square into a "graveyard of memories," as a former demonstrator saw it, which prompted him to look longingly across the sea at Hyde Park, where "anyone with something to say and a will to say it may speak in perfect safety from everything but hecklers" (Wisotsky 1958). The changing place of public expression was obvious when only 2,500 turned out for the 1955 May Day parade.

Insufficient space for demonstrations in New York was only one of the many factors complicating the issue. Confusion regarding legal guidelines was another. Few people realize that First Amendment protection of free speech in our cities really began in 1925 with the Gitlow decision, which applied these rights to the states. Under pressure to keep cities orderly, the local application of federal protection of speech and assembly was honed in courts in order to create what might be called "tolerable" conditions for demonstrations. In cities like New York and London, the demands of the city are great and have resulted in modifications of rights, which are sometimes expanded and sometimes contracted, but always limited. Those modifications in London are just that—spaces remain open and available, though not at all time. The need for a permit in London was also added in the twentieth century. New York's fate reflected the larger national one: free speech became subject to time, place, and manner rules, which were then interpreted by local courts, and often resulted in severe limitations.

By the late twentieth century, New York was cemented into a rigid structure regarding public speech. There had been some loosening of restrictions in the late 1960s and early 1970s, during the liberal mayoralty of John V. Lindsay; but this was an exception to a more general tendency to restrict public events of a political nature. The need for a permit was added in the twentieth century in London, too; but public spaces remained open and available most of the time.

Nothing is a better example of the difference between policies in New York and London than the most recent manifestations of political speech. In 2003, anti-Iraq war protests drew at least three-quarters of a million people to London's Hyde Park, a royal park smack in the middle of the metropolis. In 2004, demonstrators who wanted to voice their opinions at the Republican Convention at New York's Javits Center found themselves on a forced march around Manhattan after the courts upheld the city's decision to bar them from the vicinity of the convention center. Since the destruction of the World Trade Center on September 11, 2001, fears of terrorism have also contributed to increased tightening of permission for political demonstrations, an irony given the fact that it is those very "American" freedoms that terrorists seem to hate so much.

Union Square, reengineered in the 1980s to be a larger park, has little space for demonstrations in the twenty-first century, but it does have plenty of room for green markets, where farmers come into town to sell their produce, and Christmas fairs, both of which take up most of the non-green space in the square. The shift in the use of public spaces is almost total: celebratory, civic, charitable, or commercial events are usually given permits. On almost any given weekend in New York, there can be up to a dozen events of this nature, which involve closing not just a few streets but often large areas of the city. This brings to mind several questions: Are such large gatherings less threatening to public order? And, notwithstanding the use of city resources during these events, are they more justifiable because of the income generated? It seems most curious that a royal park in London can accommodate three quarters of a million people, but in New York, the long-standing answer to the request that meetings be held in Central Park is that the park is for leisure and the grass would be damaged. New York City Parks Commissioner Adrian Benape reiterated a time-honored sentiment when he commented: "You can have unlimited, large-scale events, or you can have nice grass, but you can't have both" (Williams 2005). One wishes that lawn maintenance would take a backseat to free speech.

References

Keller, L. 2008. *Triumph of Order: Democracy & Public Space in New York and London.* New York: Columbia University Press.

New York Times. 1908. April 5.

Shaw, G. B. 1892. *The Fabian Society: Its Early History.* London: The Fabian Society.

Thompson, E. P. 1955. *William Morris: Romantic to Revolutionary.* London: Merlin Press.

Williams, T. 2005. "Parks Department to Limit Size of Events on the Great Lawn." *New York Times*, April 27.

Wisotsky, I. 1958. "Echoes of the Union Square That Was." *New York Times*, October 12.

Woods, A. 1914. "Reasonable Restrictions Upon Freedom of Assemblage." In *Papers and Proceedings*. Ninth Annual Meeting, American Sociological Society. Chicago: Chicago University Press.

The Romance of Public Space

Marshall Berman

THIS ESSAY BOTH explores and enacts what I want to call the romance of public space. This is one of the primary ideas of what historians came to call the Age of Revolutions, and finds its origins in ancient Greece, particularly Athens. Before I delve into that, however, I want to distinguish public space from the many large spaces in which, as long as human societies have existed, people have been assembled. In these spaces, rulers have assembled their subordinates and given them orders about how they should act. We get a glimpse of one of these assemblies in Book Two of *The Iliad*, in a passage called "The Great Gathering of Armies." Thersites, "a common soldier," challenges Agamemnon: "What are you panting after now?" Haven't these warlords accumulated enough treasure, bounties, and young women to bring back with them? Odysseus responds: "Who are *you* to wrangle with kings…You and your ranting slander—*you're* the outrage." The climax of his tirade is to "crack the scepter across his back and shoulders." Thersites "doubled over, tears streaking his face," his blood flowing. The soldiers' "morale is low, but the men laughed now, good hearty laughter breaking over Thersites's head…." Other generals now speak: "Not until you…razed the rugged walls of Troy" will there be even the thought of going home; any soldier who repeats Thersites's complaint" will be instantly killed. The threats, violence, and the soldiers' "hearty laughter" combine to end the assembly—and to silence the Greek common people for the next five hundred years or so. But then, from the sixth century BC till the fourth, the Athenian common people gained more and more power, established a

197

political form that called democracy—"power to the people"—and asserted themselves, above all in a giant outdoor space called the *agora*. Thersites is a textbook case of the people intended as *objects*, defined by what is done to them. "Public space" is something else: a stage for the people as *subjects*.

The "Old Oligarch" (in Kagan 1966) is a pamphlet written sometime in the fifth century BC. No one knows who the author was, but he was the first writer to describe the Athenian agora, a space completely different from the ones in his own city. (Which city? Some say Thebes, but we really don't know.) The Old Oligarch is fascinated by the Athenian agora's sloppiness. Here people dress down, social distance is minimized, one cannot even tell masters from slaves; Athens is the only city with a law forbidding masters to beat their slaves. The Old Oligarch is amazed that any city can hold together without a strictly visible social hierarchy. He concludes that informally defined spaces like Athens's agora, and peaceable practices like shopping and related cultural activities, can make people feel comfortable with each other and nourish peaceable bonds between them, so that everybody learns both how to rule and how to obey. To have the ability *both to rule and to obey*: Sophocles, Pericles, the Old Oligarch, and various orators and philosophers, all came to see this as the formula for democratic citizenship. Athens's agora appears as an ideal place to learn this contradictory behavior. It makes sense for us to call this gigantic mess the world's first democratic space.

Not everybody liked it. Sophocles's tragedy *Antigone*, first put on in 441 BC, features Creon, a politician and "man of the moment" who transforms the agora into an antidemocratic political theatre. Sophocles sets his story in Thebes; many of its characters are descendants of Oedipus, and could be said to share his complex. One of Antigone's brothers tries to overthrow the city government; her other brother fights him, and the twin brothers end up killing each other. Creon saves the city, only to destroy it inwardly. He decrees that only the "good" brother can be buried; the "bad" brother's corpse must lie outdoors, till his corpse is picked apart and eaten up by wild animals. Creon creates an agora for terror, using public space against not only a guilty man, but also his whole family. Creon's agora is one of the earliest examples of a totally political space, a stage where families are collectively punished for individuals' bad acts. He imagines political power as the capacity to define protest as treason, and to publicly destroy the traitors. Before Antigone dies, she and the chorus (and the prophet Teiresias) proclaim that stage directions like Creon's are toxic to urban democracy.

One more crucial thing we need to remember about Antigone is that she is a *woman*. It was a nineteenth-century cliché that women were excluded from the agora. Any reader of Greek comedy, or of Plato, should be able to see that women were banned from many things in Greece, but never from shopping. (In the twentieth century, archeology made it clear that Athens's agora was a giant shopping mall.) Antigone stakes out a claim to it. She says, in effect, that a totalitarian agora is a travesty of public space. She gets the point of a democratic agora better than the man who has her killed.

Creon's agora is not like the one in Athens, messy but overflowing. It resembles more the design created by Hippodamas of Miletus, the first known city planner. Hippodamas's model (described at length in Aristotle's *Politics*) was grid-like and functionally zoned; it seems to have existed in various forms from city to city, but they all shared the presence of rigid boundaries for people in different ethnic, economic, sexual, and political groups. There was a strong (and apparently often successful) attempt to put clamps on the ultra-agoric activity of hanging out. Hippodamas lived long, and shopped his model around the Greek world for years. The planner didn't say this, but anybody who (like Aristotle) saw his model in operation over the years saw the catch: it couldn't work unless democracy was overthrown and the army took total control of everyday life. The Athenians seem to have said, no thanks. For a couple of hundred years, they preferred their chaotic model to a rigidly clean one. Athenians fought a great deal with each other, but they were at home in democratic space. They didn't want to become a militarized Miletus. They preferred a mess.

One of the first Athens's self-celebrations can be found in what we call "Pericles's Funeral Oration," delivered in 431 BC at the start of the long war with Sparta, and contained in Thucydides's *The Peloponnesian Wars*. This speech is, among other things, a hymn to Athens's public space. Pericles talks about the city's openness: its lack of walls, he says, enables anybody to see and enjoy all there is, it brings in tourists who are thrilled by the city's openness, and helps attract original people who were kicked out of the cities they grew up in. People can explore and expand their identities, and fulfill themselves as a whole.

The paradox of public space in Athens was that the city couldn't seem to live with the radiance that its public space generated and bestowed on mankind. The Old Oligarch, delighted with the phenomenology of democracy, can't understand why so many Athenian citizens get so mad at each other. After they killed Socrates, many Athenians and many other Greeks kept asking, how could this smart, sophisticated city—Pericles had called it "the school of Greece"—kill its most devoted citizen? Of course, Athens was used to killing its own. It killed Pericles's son and his fellow admirals, after they won a spectacular battle against Sparta but failed to destroy the navy and kill all the enemies. In the postwar decade, it would very likely have killed Euripides, along with Socrates, if the playwright hadn't got out of town fast.

Socrates refused to go, and so provoked his enemies. He warned the city (*Apology*, 39c-d) that if they killed him, they would be afflicted with a generation of critics who, unlike him, felt no love for them. If we read Plato long enough to pick up the emotional tones, we can see what he meant. In many early dialogues, we find a sensibility that is radically critical of Athens, but clearly loves it. We find similar contradictions in Socrates's arguments with Thrasymachus in the *Republic*'s first two books. But as the *Republic* unfolds, it offers us a very different mix. By the middle of the book, we find the most vicious criticism ever written against public space, and we find a critical tone devoid of love:

> Whenever the populace crowds together, at any public gathering... and sits there clamoring its approval or disapproval, both excessive, of whatever is being said or done; booing and clapping till the rocks ring, and the whole place redoubles the noise of their applause and outcries...In such a scene, what will become of a young man's mind? What...will give him the strength to hold out against the force of such a torrent, or save him from being swept downstream, until he accepts all their notions of right and wrong, does as they do, and becomes just such a man as they are?

Most of what we know about the lower-class Socrates comes from dialogues written by the upper-class Plato. We can't say for sure where one ends and the other begins. But if we focus on these two views of the agora—a place that is defined as lethal poison, and a place that Socrates refuses to leave, despite its risks—we see the difference between being at home in public space and being radically alienated from it. Fifth-century Athens is often seen as a city that defined public space as a place where people could feel (like Socrates) "at home." This is true, but if we see it in depth, we will also see a place that could kill the man who was most at home in it; a place that could force the rest of us to feel (like Plato) radically alien. Athens's creativity is ambiguous, paradoxical; it lays out vocabularies for both.

Socrates's execution seems to have put Athens on the defensive about itself. In the 390s BC, Athens passed a series of laws that recognized its own capacity to create talk. From now on, the city would not kill anybody who was not guilty of a violent crime; it grew willing to listen to people who talked and who made others talk. The idea of "atonement" was not usually a part of the Hellenic vocabulary; but some of the post-Socratic laws do sound like an attempt to atone for what Athens had done to its public space and to itself, and to give that space a new life, to nourish it again by creating what modern citizens and thinkers, especially in England, America, Holland, and France, would come to call the beginnings of a Bill of Rights.

Beyond Athens

After Athens and all other Greek cities were conquered by Alexander the Great in the 330s and the 320s BC, the very idea of democratic space faded away and didn't come back into Western (or any other) culture till modern times: the eighteenth century, the Enlightenment, the Age of Revolution (see Robinson 1994). Many of the thrills and human difficulties first seen in Athens's agora have reappeared in modern times; but in the more than 2,000 years in between, Western culture has gone through plenty and become a lot more. The rest of this essay will be brief, too brief to explore this complex history. But it will open up diverse possibilities.

I'm Talking about Jerusalem

If there is one word to convey the romance of public space in both Jewish and Christian culture, that word is *Jerusalem*. Our earliest vision of Jerusalem as a special place comes in the first Book of Kings' narrative of the reign of King Solomon. In a dream, God asks Solomon what he wants, and is impressed when he asks for "an understanding mind to govern the people" rather than for riches or revenge. God gives him "a wise and discerning mind" and a "largeness of vision." In the course of his reign, the Bible says, "Judah and Israel were as many as the sand by the sea, they ate and drank and were happy." The Book of Kings gives an endlessly detailed account of Solomon's building projects, a temple and a king's palace standing directly opposite each other. It also describes projects that are likely to seem much more important to us: a tremendous population shift, to be obtained by sending thousands of Jews to Lebanon ("Tyre") every year and filling Jerusalem with an equal numbers of Lebanese, especially people with construction skills. Solomon's many marriages, too, must have brought not only "foreign women" (the "pharaoh's daughter" may have been the biggest scandal), but also great crews of servants, tailors, craftspeople, priests, and—this may have been his central idea—non-Jews. Solomon seems to have worried about Israel's smallness and lack of resources, and aimed to strengthen it by opening up channels of cooperation with other, better-situated peoples. (Later, when God is preparing to destroy Israel for its unrighteousness, the prophet Amos convinces God to be merciful by saying, "But my Lord, Israel is so small.") Like Pericles, Solomon grasped the strength of a mixed population, and sought to make Jerusalem as diverse and multicultural as he could. But Solomon's children and successors lacked his "largeness of mind"; Israel gradually split and then was "taken," first by Babylon. In post-Solomon incarnations it will be pulled to pieces. Later on, and stretching up to today, Jerusalem became a city specially consecrated as "redeemed"; but we can't understand the spiritual meanings of "redemption" without simultaneously grasping the meanings of "damnation." Jerusalem shows us that cities can be embodiments of both.

Talking about Jerusalem puts us on a distinctive wavelength, part of a spiritual drama: we imagine a city in radically contradictory ways, simultaneously as a sinkhole of depravity and a light unto the nations. But most of our accumulated talk about Jerusalem, from the fifth century BC till 1948, has been about a glorious city that has, for whatever reasons, been *lost*. Psalm 137, one of the first documents of *exile*, proclaims the duty of thinking about the city we have lost. The vow "If I forget thee, O Jerusalem" announces one of the primary forms of urban romance: the romance of *nostalgia*. Classical Christianity gives a dramatic twist to urban self-criticism. After two thousand years of Christian culture, anybody who thinks about cities inherits the twist, whether we are Christians or not (I am not). In the Gospel of Matthew (6.1-6), just after the Sermon on the Mount, Jesus disparages people who pray "in the synagogue." Unlike Saint Paul, he does not criticize them on behalf of some other public space (the early Christian church), but rather on behalf of *no* public space. He says:

> Beware of practicing your piety before men, in order to be seen by them. For then you will have no reward from your Father, who is in heaven. Thus, when you give alms, sound no trumpet before you, as

the hypocrites do in the synagogues and in the streets, that they may be praised by men...Do not let your let your left hand know what your right hand is doing, so that your alms may be in secret...

What is he saying? That we should be punished for self-knowledge—for our left hand knowing what our right hand is doing—but we get spiritual credit for ignorance of ourselves?

And when you pray...you must not be like the hypocrites; for they love to stand in the synagogues and in the street corners, that they may be seen by men...But when you pray, go into your room and shut the door, and pray to your Father who sees in secret and will reward you.

This is a remarkable passage, which has evoked little commentary. It says that any desire to be seen or praised by other men, "in the synagogue or in the streets," is poisonous; God will show respect, Jesus says, only to people who lock the door. It appears that the gesture of *locking the door* is the paradigmatic spiritual act. The desire to be with people, to be loved by them, is vicious, corrupt, inauthentic. The Jewish God required a *minyan*, a congregation of ten, to make prayer valid. This version of the Christian God demands a congregation of one, and that's all. He shrinks away from public space. He is open only to those souls who reject community with other men or women.

Now, it is impossible to live this way! Saint Paul prided himself on his celibacy, but accepted the overall legitimacy of people's need for each other. But Matthew's Jesus rejects it, at least for a while. What are we supposed to make of this? Is it an early form of nihilism? I don't think many readers have ever been willing to take Jesus's implacability as a model of how to live; yet, the idea that only aloneness is authentic has carried a long shadow even in the hearts of people who believe it's absurd. When we are in public space today, even in the sun, we are still partly in that shadow; the cloud rarely leaves us.[1]

---

1. Ironically, though, this cloud has been incorporated into secular, middle-class culture. Dr. Benjamin Spock, writing after World War II, may have been the first child care expert to say that all children deserved "rooms of their own" where they could elaborate their own fantasy lives, create their own worlds. Spock, a founder of peace and antinuclear movements, and an official criminal in the Vietnam War years, always argued that people who grew up with more private space as children would become better citizens as adults.

The Enlightenment and Modernity

If the Platonic and Christian utopias of radical alienation gave us a twist, a great deal of modern thought and culture, starting with the Enlightenment, has been a project to untwist us. Modern romantic poets on the street like Walt Whitman, and fighters for civil rights who sat down in the midst of traffic like Martin Luther King Jr., believed it was urgent to love, to overcome, and to do it together, openly, in public, and they believed that it could help us lift our own inner shadows.

A little while ago I talked about how Athens experienced its killing of Socrates as a trauma and passed a series of laws to ensure that nobody else would get killed for talking. This was a great expansion of public space, in the city that already had the most developed public space in the world, and it was an important moment in the history of human rights. But in its earliest incarnation, its scope was limited. For the most part, Athenians didn't see these as rights for all human beings, but only for Athenians. They didn't oppose them for other cities, they just couldn't imagine that other cities would care about them.

The concept of universal human rights couldn't emerge until centuries of Stoicism and Christianity had passed, and until the beginnings of modern science. The great leap forward that we call the Enlightenment featured the idea of a world public, and a demand for human rights for everybody everywhere. I don't mean that this idea has been fulfilled anywhere. But today, in the twenty-first century, we may have reached the point where it is *imagined* everywhere.

Montesquieu's novel *The Persian Letters* (1721), maybe the first great book of the Enlightenment, shows the connection between the idea of human rights and the forms of public space that have emerged in the modern city. Montesquieu sees immigration as a central feature of Paris, which thanks to immigrant diversity becomes a microcosm of the whole world. A world city takes some getting used to. Compared with the spaces the Persians have grown up in, it is a grotesque mess. But they come to feel the immense human vitality that is overflowing and creating this mess. They walk and talk through the streets, amazed at the variety of *the crowd*; after a while they see that they themselves are part of the crowd, and they are glad. Women come over to talk to them. At first they think these women must be whores selling themselves, but the women tell them they just want to talk, and there is this new thing, invented by women but bringing both sexes together, called *conversation*.[2] Later on they learn about salons, and have some terrific conversations there. By and by they are received at Versailles, and they discover that not everybody loves Paris. They learn that the French monarchy, since Louis XIV, has felt degraded and threatened by this city that is so enchanting to them. The kings are happier in their royal theme park, Versailles, and at home in their gardens full of statues, rather than in a city full of live people. Political conflict in France, both before and after the Revolution, was often imagined as "Paris versus Versailles." One of the distinctive ironies of modern times in France is that so many grand buildings and outdoor spaces, especially in Paris, were built by the monarchy to sanctify the grandeur of the state. But the monarchy was terrified by its own creations, and ordinary people found ways to make themselves more at home in those grand spaces than their kings had ever been. In what turned out to be the French Revolution, the image of the people taking over the Bastille Prison established itself immediately as a canonical vision.

The Enlightenment, however, thought big: it wasn't only about France, or about any particular place, but about the whole world. It showed a world public and a dream of world citizenship coming into being. In the years between the early Enlightenment and now, it has become clear that Paris is winning. (This is why, even if we have never been to Paris—as I had never been at age fourteen, when I saw the movie *Casablanca*—we know instinctively what Humphrey Bogart means when he tells Ingrid Bergman, "We'll always have Paris.") But it will always be a struggle, even in Paris—maybe especially in Paris. Modern city life has rarely been serene. Indeed, since the middle of the eighteenth century, modern cities have been explosive and revolutionary. But the people who meet on modern streets, or who just look at each other on the streets and in the parks and on the metro, and feel they recognize total strangers, are increasingly citizens of the world, with the capacity to imagine the world, to wear blue, and to imagine themselves with an identity as big as the sky.

A century of electronic mass media has expanded and deepened this world identity. When I was a kid, there was a vast literature explaining why

---

2. This is a central theme in my first book, *The Politics of Authenticity* (originally published in 1970), also elaborated by Dena Goodman (1994).

electronics had killed people's desire to travel. I thought, it sure hasn't killed my desire, and it's easy to see now how silly this was. Electronics hasn't killed anybody's desire to move. Tourism is the world's greatest industry, its bottom lines eclipsing even armaments. Photographs, movies, televisions, computers, and Skype give people at least a chance to see what other people's public spaces look like, and it makes them want to go. Even if we can't go, we can read and see and feel in some crucial way these distant cities as ours.

Here, then, is the romance of public space. Pericles, in ancient Athens, argued that Athens had got there first. Most of the world can imagine it now—if only we can survive to enact it! But we have moved beyond Athens in crucial ways. We have an idea of universal humanity; we can see now that the desire to live in public space is a central part of being human. We can also thank the Enlightenment for helping us imagine we can organize to make the sun rise. When we read about, and see pictures of, the women of Cairo, fighting to be and to stay in the streets, and shouting, "I exist! We exist!" we know they are talking to us, as well as to the priests and police holding them back and trying to push them back into their houses. We know their need: to have a place in the street, to be recognized as the people they are. We share a conversation, struggling for a public space we all can inhabit.

References

Goodman, D. 1994. *The Republic of Letters: A Cultural History of the French Enlightenment*. New York: Cornell University Press.

Kagan, D. 1966. *Sources in Greek Democratic Thought*. New York: Free Press.

Montesquieu, C. L. 1721. *The Persion Letters*. Cologne: Pierre Marteau.

Places that Matter

ZUCCOTTI PARK BEFORE / AFTER / NOW

Alexander Cooper

BEFORE ZUCCOTTI PARK there was Liberty Plaza Park. Liberty Plaza took its name from its bordering street, Liberty Street, in Lower Manhattan. Brookfield Properties owns the site, and through an extended public process transferred the development rights to the adjacent block on the north side of Liberty Street. The site became the subject of a City Planning Commission Special Permit, with the city granting approval for the transfer and the design even though the park property remains privately owned. The original design for the park, realized in 1973 by Skidmore, Owings, and Merrill, dealt with the sixteen-foot change in grade from Broadway going west to Church Street by having a stairway drop eight feet from Broadway to the park, which then extended as a flat surface to another stairway dropping another eight feet to Church Street. There was a bosque of trees and seating throughout. An unfortunate effect was seen from Broadway, the park appeared to be a hole, or a depression; while from Church Street, it looked like an imposing mound, or a hill.

The tragic events of September 11, 2001 destroyed Liberty Plaza Park. In the aftermath, the site became a staging area for rescue workers: a first aid center, a rest stop for first responders, and the gathering place for daily assignments to police and firefighter units. Following the cleanup, one year later, Brookfield suggested that work proceed with all possible haste to restore the land to public use. The design was accelerated, zoning approvals secured, the budget set, the contractors selected, and the art program initiated, all within a three-month period. Careful attention was paid to previous uses in the park: 25 chess tables, over 1,000 linear feet of granite

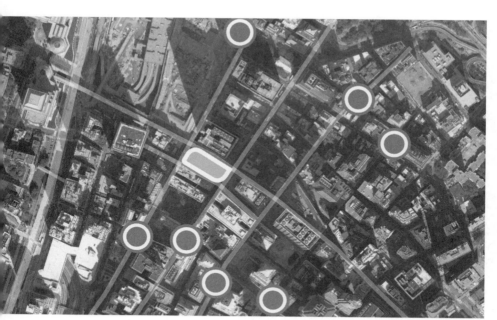

New York City. *Map by Cooper, Robertson & Partners* Protest Locations Rail Transit Stops

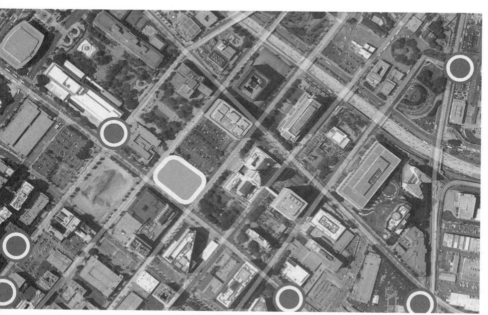

Los Angeles. *Map by Cooper, Robertson & Partners* Protest Locations ◉ Rail Transit Stops

Washington, DC. *Map by Cooper, Robertson & Partners*   Protest Locations   ◉ Rail Transit Stops

benches, a canopy of 57 honey locust trees, and over 500 in-ground lights were arranged to facilitate both casual and formal day and nighttime use. The grading within the park now slopes uniformly at 2.5 percent, so that the maximum grade change from Broadway and to Church Street is only three feet. A curving geometry allows a walk through the park, from Broadway to Church Street, without a single step to navigate. The accelerated time table, the flexible use of space, and the spirited response of all participants were critical to the renovation of the park, which was renamed Zuccotti Park in 2006 in honor of John Zuccotti, formerly chairman of the New York City Planning Commission, first deputy mayor of New York City, and currently chairman of US Commercial Operations, Brookfield Properties. The project, realized by the architectural firm of which I am part, Cooper, Robertson & Partners, also won the 2008 American Institute of Architecture (AIA) National Honor Award for Regional and Urban Design.

On September 17, 2011, the Occupy Wall Street movement (OWS) took possession of Zuccotti Park. The question naturally arises as to why Zuccotti Park was chosen. Part of the answer is that because it was privately owned, the city could not legally force visitors to leave. The architectural

New York City. *Map by Cooper, Robertson & Partners*

 Protest Locations Financial Centers City Hall

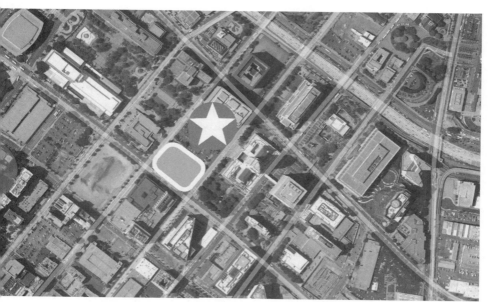

Los Angeles. *Map by Cooper, Robertson & Partners*

 Protest Locations Financial Centers City Hall

Washington, DC. *Map by*
Cooper, Robertson & Partners

 Protest Locations   Financial Centers   ⭐ City Hall

answer lies beyond the obvious proximity to Wall Street itself, as there were numerous other candidate parks close by. There are several compelling reasons to suggest that the choice was not accidental. A survey of nine protest sites across the country (Boston, New York City, Philadelphia, Baltimore, Washington DC, Chicago, Denver, Oakland, and Los Angeles) reveals an eerie commonality among them, including adjacent uses, size, and physical context. Not surprisingly, all nine protest sites are within a two-block walk from the cities' financial districts, and seven of the nine sites are visible from City Hall. Equally predictable is the immediate proximity to rail transit stops in all nine cities. They range from eleven stops in Chicago to a single one in Denver, but most with multiple stops. Clearly, mass transit access was a critical factor.

It appears that small size was another key determinant in choosing a site. Zuccotti Park is the smallest of the nine sites, at three-quarters of an acre, while the largest is City Hall Park in Los Angeles at 3.6 acres. This constitutes a strikingly different strategy from the large-scale protest sites in the Middle East and in China, but is in line with the political dictum of "always hold your meeting in a room that is too small."

Zuccotti Park before Occupy Wall Street, 2011. *Photo by Cooper, Robertson & Partners*

Zuccotti Park during Occupy Wall Street, 2011. *Photo by Francesco Fiondella*

Another common characteristic is that the sites tend to be surrounded by large, tall buildings. These protective walls provide enclosure; similarly, tree canopies provide further protection from prying eyes and supply a much-needed cooling effect in too-warm weather. The combination of tall surrounding buildings and layers of trees contributes to the idea of each site as a refuge. Moreover, if these sheltering devices are common, so too is the urge for exposure to the media. So views into the space, rather than from it, serve the purpose of presenting even a small gathering of protestors as a vast crowd for maximum media effect.

So therein lies a curious conflict. Zuccotti Park was designed to maximize the personal, intimate, small-scale activities afforded by an urban oasis. Yet, it has been called upon to broadcast a very large-scale, public message to the world. It has served both equally well.

Public Space and Its Disconnects

Rick Bell

THE TRADITION OF free speech in public space is of long standing. Examples in New York City from Union Square and Washington Square Park have continued in other places of public assembly, such as the Center for Architecture and the Occupy Wall Street sites. Regulations about the use of public space are vague but linked to questions of design intent. Long-standing concepts about the design of public space include durability, functionality, and amenity. To this, a fourth precept, community, needs to be added. Transportation infrastructure is important to public space in that it allows for connection and congregation. Subway lines and linear parks can link neighborhoods, while walls and highways can divide them. How people come together to create their city, and change it, determines its character. Government support through infrastructure stimulus, zoning bonuses for privately owned public space, and provisions of space for public activity, including plazas and bike lanes, needs more attention.

Architects, landscape architects, urban designers, planners, sociologists, and activists have learned from the Occupy communities. The spaces chosen by the Occupy movement have attributes in common, including the importance of location and scale. Each Occupy site created the core of a new city, with spaces devoted to habitation, information, and care. There was also a focal point, around which people could gather or rally. The spaces used by people coming together to demonstrate the right to freedom of assembly and free speech were not limited to the Occupy sites, but included and will include other locations appropriate to the occasion. Below are twenty points

People coming together at Occupy Wall Street. *Photo by Tom Bell*

of comparison between the mini-cities created by the Occupy movement and the attributes of the larger cities around them.

1. *Free Speech in Public Space*

The tradition of free speech in public space, whether at Hyde Park in London, the People's Park in Berkeley, or Zuccotti Park in New York City, is of long standing. People standing up to express their opinions, and rally consent, concurrence, and action, requires courage, space, and, usually, some means of amplification. Garry Trudeau's cartoons, starting in the late 1960s, had a character armed with a megaphone. London street corners had a tradition, carried forward to New York's Union Square and Washington Square Park, of speakers standing atop a soapbox—to be better seen and heard. At the Center for Architecture of the American Institute of Architects in Greenwich Village, a block from Washington Square, we have a literal wooden soapbox—to overcome the design of our lectern—which works well only for about 1 percent of our many speakers. But the Center for Architecture itself is a kind of soapbox, a place to broadcast ideas and, in turn, have them influenced and expanded on by debate and discussion. Since opening its doors in October of 2003, the Center for Architecture, as a public space, has hosted over a thousand events each year that are open to anyone who wishes to participate. With our recent physical expansion to the south, extending our storefront presence in LaGuardia Place, the place of public assembly has broadened. The "breakthrough" addition makes possible more meetings by larger numbers of people, brought together by the common goal of wanting to discuss how to make our city, our nation, and the world, better now, and for the future.

2. *Definition of Occupy*

Architects, urban designers, landscape architects, civic activists, and public officials gathering at the Center for Architecture discuss many different things, not only about the aesthetics of building facades or the environmental issues arising from innovations in energy conservation and building system design. Programs at the Center for Architecture have, on December 17, 2011 and February 4, 2012, addressed the very nature of public space and freedom of assembly. We have focused on how the Occupy Wall Street movement, unfolding a mile from the Center for Architecture, brings into sharp relief the sense of seizing the moment. The word "occupy" itself comes, by means of Old French, from the Latin word *occupare*, or "to seize."

Occupying a space for common cause, whether the Center's Tafel Hall, a public park, such as Duarte Park, or a privately owned public space, such as

Confrontation on Broadway over the right to occupy Zuccotti Park. *Photo by Tom Bell*

Zuccotti Park, is controlled by rules that are not often clearly known, posted, or rationalized. Tafel Hall, for example, has hosted a New York City Council hearing about the redesign of the dog runs at Washington Square Park. Dogs were allowed into the hearing to stand shoulder to shin with their leash holders, clamoring for a less species-specific use pattern at the park.

3. *Rules about Public Space*

Whether in the Latin of ancient Rome or the lingo of Lower Manhattan, the de facto regulations attempting to limit the right to free speech is not clearly de jure. At Zuccotti Park, microphones, megaphones, and amplifiers were forbidden. A human chorus designed to echo the oratory arose, reminiscent of Greek choruses in theater or responsive reading in the sanctuary. Reporters got their scoop du jour on the rebound.

The attempt to make clear rules about the design of public space and public buildings is not new. Vitruvius wrote the *Ten Books of Architecture* over two thousand years ago, attempting to codify, concoct, and market the wisdom of precedent. His text, still skimmed by virtually every architecture student in the world, ranges from site orientation, wind direction, and geology to materials and appropriate means of construction. Sections on walls

Communications and sound control were issues at Occupy Wall Street. *Photo by Rick Bell*

and fortifications, not to mention hydrologic and mechanical devices, give a sense of the spirit of the day. Today, the book is most often remembered for the triad of firmness, commodity, and delight, translated from the more resolute *firmitatis*, *utilitatis*, and *venustatis*.

4. *Vitruvian Rules and Community*

Do the terms of Vitruvius, and the attempt to codify the nature of design, make any sense in discussing the use and creation of public space in New York and other urban centers today? If we look closely at the encampment at Zuccotti Park and the one-day occupation of Duarte Square on December 17, 2011, it can be said that the three terms are a starting point for an understanding of the role of design, but they are not sufficient. To the *troika*, a fourth term, *communitas*, should be added, as suggested by the French semiologist Gwenaëlle de Kerret. Creating a rhetorical *carré*, or analytic square, of four precepts broadens the discussion by adding people to the mix.

Debate at Occupy Wall Street 2.0 alongside the park rules sign. *Photo by Rick Bell*

Occupy Wall Street 2.0 demonstrated durability and persistence. *Photo by Rick Bell*

5. *The Base*

Firmitatis talks to the base, the foundation, the underpinning. The solidity, stability, and durability of the substrate guarantees safety. The pavement of Zuccotti Park was perhaps hard, but it was easy to clean and took on the many people who did not want to trample the grass of the Sheep Meadow. The base, though, was not of concrete or macadam but of people, congregating for collective action. Their space recalled and re-created settlements and towns that started small and survived. Seventeenth-century New Amsterdam had a maximum population of nine thousand people by 1664, all camping out within a stone's throw of Zuccotti Park.

6. *Functionality*

Utilitatis talks to the function, the purpose, and the character of the design that makes it usable for some or many different activities. At Zuccotti Park, there were tents for information, for a library, and for medical care, not to mention those used for sleeping at night out of the wind and rain. The question to architects, urban designers, and landscape architects is how to create the functionality of community with or without governmental support. The *favelas* of São Paulo and a hundred other cities have not, historically, been aided by municipally funded infrastructure. Was Zuccotti Park a kind of

The removal of Occupy functions created a social vacuum. *Photo by Tom Bell*

favela, lacking only in permanence the imposition of settlement on the edge of a prosperous and polarized *polis*?

7. *Design Matters*

Venustatis addresses the aesthetic pleasure or attributed beauty that is appreciated as a function of proportion, material selection, and form. Zuccotti Park, with state-of-the-art design features by Cooper, Robertson & Partners and Ken Smith Landscape Architect, is also graced by the bright red focal point of *Joie de Vivre*, the extraordinary marker at the park's southwest entry point by populist sculptor Mark di Suvero. This sculpture became a flash point of argument and discussion as well as the backdrop for town hall participatory democracy. Does all designed public space require a symbol—such as the evanescent barn raising or blue tarp at Washington, DC's Occupy site? Larger towns and big cities such as New York have it—the red steps at Times Square or, perhaps, formerly the clock at Grand Central. How can the skill of the artist, architect, or urban designer create the context for people coming together?

Symbols of gathering can be large focal points or small signs. *Photo by Rick Bell*

8. *People and the Agora*

Hence, from the term *communitatis*, or the creation of community, Zuccotti Park was given the new name of Liberty Square. Some at Occupy Wall Street recalled the coming together of five thousand people during the *Listening to the City* events at New York's Jacob Javits Convention Center. There, with the whole world watching, a diverse group of people discussed the future of Lower Manhattan, New York City, and the region. Perhaps a convention center in Queens will serve equally well as a point of congregation. But the creation of community is location specific, as the ancient Greeks learned in positioning the agora at the intersection of commerce and culture. Hence, ease of gathering influenced the decisions about where Occupy sites should exist, near the Federal Reserve Bank and South Station in Boston and in the precincts of the city halls in Philadelphia and Los Angeles.

In New York, the beauty of the Occupy site was manifest. Located between the financial district and civic center, the rules of this privately owned public space danced to a different drummer. It may not have been crucial that it was also adjacent to the site of the World Trade Center Memorial or

Community building starts with picking locations. *Photo by Tom Bell*

the burial place of Alexander Hamilton, but, for many, it was critical that Zuccotti Park was well served by public transportation. The Fulton Street subway stop, a block away, has thirteen lines, linking this "new town in town" to all five boroughs.

9. *Importance of Infrastructure*

New York City's success as a city, from the Erie Canal to the development of the subway, is a function of designed infrastructure. Descending into the massive excavation that is the future Second Avenue Subway, one is struck by the enormity of the future public space and the sophistication of the drilling equipment. The tunnels needed to relieve the overcrowding on the Lexington Avenue line and, according to Metropolitan Transportation Authority of New York City's Final Environmental Impact Statement, the improvements in "mobility for all New Yorkers" will stretch some 8.5 miles from 125th Street to Water Street at Hanover Square. But it is not the volume or the length that captures our imagination. It is the future station, its walls carved from Manhattan schist that takes on the poetry of survival, resilience, and permanence.

Daniel Libeskind, whose architectural firm Studio Daniel Libeskind was selected in 2003 to rebuild the World Trade Center site, described the power of infrastructure to inspire and animate: "The most dramatic part of the Trade Center to survive the attack was the great slurry wall, an engineering wonder constructed on bedrock to hold back the Hudson River. Somehow

Fulton Street Transit Hub under construction near Zuccotti Park. *Photo by Rick Bell*

it had withstood the unimaginable trauma of the twin towers' destruction, asserting, as eloquently as the Constitution, the durability of democracy and the value of human life." The public space created by Michael Arad and Peter Walker at the World Trade Center site starts with the on-grade plaza that contains the two voids of the lost towers. How it will be used when the barricades disappear and those coming to pay respect mingle with those who live and work in the neighborhood has been the subject of much discussion. Ten years ago, workshops led by the American Institute of Architects (AIA) New York Chapter and the New York City Council brought together family members of those who had perished on 9/11 with Battery Park City residents to discuss the qualities of public space that were common to all. The current barricades, bollards, and bifurcation between memory and tumult were prefigured in the workshop with distinctions between sacred ground and living memorial. The goal of the interaction, however, was to break down the semantic and literal walls between such terms and to imagine a future where "the events of the day"—the day being September 11, 2001— would be able to coexist with the present day's events for those who live, work, or visit the place.

10. *Up Against the Wall*

The word "wall" comes from Old English *weall*—and thence from the Latin *vallus*, meaning "stake" or "palisade." The earthen wall on de Waal Straat was the northern limit of New Amsterdam. The Dutch West India Company

Scaling the wall at Occupy Wall Street 2.0 in Duarte Park. *Photo by Tom Bell*

needed not so much to mark a political limit as to create a barricade against the Native Americans who gave Manhattan its name and who had very different notions about property rights, trade, and profit. It also served to keep the cows in and, we're told, the expected regiments of British foot soldiers out. The four-meter tall stockade on Wall Street was maintained by the Dutch by means of a sin tax on imported beer. Since then, Wall Street has become less of the symbol of infrastructure and more of the metaphor for the conjunction of capital and consternation, hence the logic of the Occupy settlement at Zuccotti Park. Between this park and the street, at 111 Broadway, the AIA was founded on February 23, 1857 at Richard Upjohn's office. That was the year of the Panic of 1857, which, according to Marx and Engels, was the world's first worldwide economic crisis. Virtually all construction stopped for lack of capital and investor confidence. In that year, "commercial credit had dried up," writes historian Michael A. Ross, and unemployment was rife. Yet, major infrastructure projects in New York City, most notably Central Park, stretching some 843 acres, were opened.

11. *The Future Is Now*

If our infrastructure determines our future, and its interstices become our public space, New York City—with the occupation of the former rail spur known as the High Line and the start-up of significant new public transportation systems including East Side Access, the Second Avenue Subway, and

Occupy Wall Street 2.0 at Duarte Square in February 2012. *Photo by Rick Bell*

the #7 Line Extension—has shown that the future is now. And yet, we duck the issue of the infrastructure needed to prepare for significant sea level rise, as Columbia Professor Klaus Jacob decried at a program of the AIA New York Risk and Reconstruction Committee at the Center for Architecture. Do we build sea walls and sea gates to limit the risk of storm surge damage? Or do we count on the softer reinsertion of mitigating wetlands, as shown in the Museum of Modern Art's *Rising Currents* exhibition, to shortstop Gotham's tsunamis? In the 1950 novel, *Un barrage contre le Pacifique*, Marguerite Duras writes the more-or-less autobiographical tale of her mother trying to use a mangrove dyke to hold back the sea in French Indochina. It didn't work, and her failed wall became a refrain for trying to do the impossible. The major public parks and esplanades that, in New York, replace lost maritime, transportation, and industrial uses, are significantly and visibly vulnerable to flooding. Our new public space may be occupied by striped bass and scuttlefish long before the turn of the next century.

12. *Connection Point*

The ultimate piece of infrastructure—and divider of public space—is the wall. This can be the Berlin Wall, the Great Wall of China, the restored city walls of Jerusalem, or the barriers created by our elevated railways from Chicago to Queens, from Stillwell Avenue to the High Line. Walls can divide: Mongolia from China, East Berlin from West Berlin. But they

Many people gather on the High Line. *Photo by Rick Bell*

also connect. Without a traffic light or on-grade crossing, one can walk three miles on the Promenade Plantée in Paris. Similarly, with the High Line in New York, it is possible to walk from the bridge and tunnel bars of Gansevoort to the edge of the Hudson Yards train holding area. Matthew Johnson of Diller Scofidio & Renfro, a lead designer of the firm's High Line Project, described the possibility of the railroad reversion of the city's most popular park, funded in part by Rails-to-Trails money. It won't happen, but it could. It is almost miraculous that the massive infrastructure of the High Line survived the antipathy of Mayor Giuliani's city hall and the insurance-driven fears of CSX Transportation, which ultimately donated this important part of our infrastructure to New York City in 2005, creating a public space previously occupied only by intrepid birdwatchers and streetscape escapees.

13. *Stimulus and Occupy*

On any given day, hordes of tourists, New Yorkers, activists, and acolytes swarm the High Line and, in a significantly different manner, have occupied Zuccotti Park. What are both groups demanding? Do we all still agree that the Depression-era New Deal Works Progress Administration mentality of job creation can carry forward into present-day stimulus plans? Can we use the American Recovery Act money to guarantee social equity and bring design quality to our infrastructure? Some of the answers to these and other

Philadelphia's city hall was the site of Occupy Philadelphia. *Photo by Rick Bell*

questions came from Teddy Cruz, speaking at a conference of the Association of Architectural Organizations and the Association for Community Design. Cruz spoke from the lectern of the Friends Center on 15th and Cherry Streets, near the Occupy Philadelphia encampment at the city hall building designed by Scottish-born architect John McArthur, Jr. Before suggesting that those present join the demonstrators on the public plaza, he led a human megaphone chant of fourteen demands, including three that particularly resonated with the present situation in New York and other cities across the globe:

1. We demand that the municipalities rethink their own fragmented bureaucratic silos and resources.

2. We demand intelligent public spending on education, culture, and transportation.

3. We demand the right to culture and education not as expendable commodities but as civic responsibilities.

14. *Who Designs New York?*

Is this a platform or a foundation for validating the role of architects in society? When Mark Strauss, FAIA of FXFOWLE Architects, was president of the AIA New York Chapter, there was a debate, held at a bar in the East Village, between architects and civil engineers. The topic was "Who should

Bicycles are occupying the streets and sidewalks near Moynihan Station. *Photo by Rick Bell*

design our infrastructure?" After many jokes and jibes, by popular vote of those attending, we architects were sent packing. Now, with the American Recovery Act funds acting as stimulus for public space and transportation infrastructure projects from the Fulton Street Transit Hub to Moynihan

The People's Library table at Occupy Wall Street 2.0. *Photo by Rick Bell*

Station, the terms of engagement are different. The elected officials were assembled at Eighth Avenue and West 32nd Street, not with shovels to try to dig into the post office pavement, but rather with sledgehammers to symbolize the connection of breaking through barriers to connection. The goal was to allow for public occupation of spaces in the Farley Building previously used to store or repair broken mailboxes. Occupy Farley wasn't the Twitter message that day. But the post boxes that had survived rain, sleet, and snow fell before the onslaught of Skype, smart phones, and social networking. In June of 1987, an American president visiting Berlin exhorted his Soviet counterpart to "come here to this gate" and to tear down a certain wall. The common theme I hear in New York, from City Hall Park to Zuccotti Park, is, perhaps, more aligned with the Athenian Oath quoted by Mayor Bloomberg in his last inaugural: "We will transmit this City, not only not less, but greater and more beautiful than it was transmitted to us." That starts with people and the public space we use.

15. *People and Public Space*

Jane Jacobs (1961) wrote, "Cities have the capability of providing something for everybody, only because, and only when, they are created by everybody." *The Death and Life of Great American Cities* was published fifty years ago and has, perhaps more than anything written since, led to a discussion of the civic aspect of what goes as public space. When the AIA was founded in 1857, just two blocks from Zuccotti Park, public space was scarce. In the chapter called "Enhancing the Public Realm" in his book *Urban Parks and Open Space*, Alexander Garvin wrote that in the 1850s, "The public realm in the United States consisted of unpaved streets, barely landscaped squares, rudimentary marketplaces, and vast territories of wilderness. Everything else was in the hands of property owners whose actions were virtually unregulated" (Garvin and Berens 1997).

16. *Logic and Proportion*

What are the lessons that architects, landscape architects, urban designers, and civic activists can learn from the sense of community that was visible at Occupy Wall Street? How did the design of public space contribute to people coming together in Liberty Square/Zuccotti Park? In *The Occupied Wall*

Street Journal, Cornel West (2011) wrote that "justice is what love looks like in public." And, in the same broadside, David Graeber (2011) suggested that "the direct democratic process adopted by Occupy Wall Street has deep roots in American radical history." He added that "in parks and squares across America, people have begun to witness it as they have started to participate."

At Liberty Square, the overall design of the space made a difference in its usefulness as a place for people to visibly make the case for a more humane political environment. Vitruvius could have been writing about Zuccotti Park: "The size of a forum should be proportionate to the number of inhabitants, so that it may not be too small a space to be useful, nor look like a desert waste for lack of population. To determine its breadth, divide its length into three parts and assign two of them to the breadth. Its shape will then be oblong, and its ground plan conveniently suited to the conditions of shows" (Morgan 1960).

Sense of community at Occupy Wall Street. *Photo by Rick Bell*

Returning to Zuccotti Park on November 14, 2011. *Photo by Tom Bell*

17. *Details*

Similarly, design matters in the details. Discussing his work, sculptor Mark di Suvero has said, "Scale is one of the essential working parts. It is not just larger or smaller. There are different kinds of intensity. I try to change, compress or enlarge space—individual space itself" (Lloyd 2005). Back in the 1960s, di Suvero was one of the activist artists who started the Park Place Gallery, originally on Park Place, not far from Liberty Square, but relocated in 1963 to 540 LaGuardia Place, just two doors north of the Center for Architecture. Di Suvero has talked about how public space "has the capacity to charge the [surrounding] architecture and turn it into an aching reality, which makes us come to different levels of existence" (Lloyd 2005, 1). With the removal of the tents in the early morning hours of November 15, 2011, the public nature of Zuccotti Park changed again. People were displaced, shocked, enraged, expelled, and defiant. The dispersed community moved north and then returned, or tried to, down Broadway.

The Library tent at Occupy Wall Street. *Photo by Rick Bell*

18. *Some of the Parts*

In *The Empire City: A Novel of New York City* (2002), Paul Goodman describes the urban crowd that gathered the morning after the SS *Normandie* sank in 1942 at its pier on 45th Street. Goodman (2002, 165) wrote:

> There was a difference between the crowd and the sum of its persons. This was something beyond his previous experience, and he didn't like it: for he was used to hearing each person speak out his mind, in conversation or in large committees run according to the rules of parliamentary procedure. But here the people had gathered at random and had been stunned, and what he noticed was the following: that each person was reacting in his own way to the spectacle of the giantess brought low, according to his own character or powers of interpretation or peculiar circumstances; but the people collectively were reacting in a different way altogether, with a unanimity in which no one seemed to take a part and with a passion of which no one was aware.

Similarly, at Occupy Wall Street, the collective rage against a culture of indifference found a place of individual reflection and expression.

A solar panel at a tent in Occupy Washington, DC. *Photo by Rick Bell*

19. *Other Cities*

The First Amendment to the United States Constitution was ratified on December 15, 1791. It was drafted near the site of Occupy Philadelphia. In that same week, the first one-way street in the country was created in New York City. Today, in both Philadelphia and New York City, we are seeing a taking back of the streets to be used for public plazas, bicycle lanes, and, with or without permits, political expression. Even without the focus point of Zuccotti Park, subsequent actions, including the December 17, 2011 temporary occupation of Duarte Park just north of Canal Street, indicated that political expression is place based.

For visibility, media attention, and collective reinforcement, design matters. And transportation access is key. Occupy then becomes a metaphor for all urban settlement. The Occupy Boston site at Dewey Square is near the newly created BSA Space—the architecture center of the Boston Society of Architects. Such encampments and design centers are described and used as public gathering places to deliver a message about the future of our cities, our country, and our world. In Los Angeles, the tents of Occupy LA were removed from the park adjoining the landmark city hall tower

Occupy Los Angeles site at the Los Angeles City Hall. *Photo by Rick Bell*

on December 1, 2011. At city hall, one thousand riot police came down the steps, and those present in the public space were, essentially, pushed back into the street. Some graphics remained, including a poster that read "lucky to have been born a corporation." The mayor of Los Angeles, Antonio Villaraigosa, had been very supportive, but his backing disappeared after receiving accounts of health concerns about families with kids living in some of the tents.

20. *Common Sense*

In the pamphlet titled *The American Crisis*, Thomas Paine (1776) wrote: "I call not upon a few, but upon all: not on this state or that state, but on every state: up and help us; lay your shoulders to the wheel; better have too much force than too little, when so great an object is at stake. Let it be told to the future world that, in the depth of winter, when nothing but hope and virtue could survive, that the city and the country, alarmed at one common danger, came forth to meet and to repulse it. Say not that thousands are gone, turn out your tens of thousands." Paine died in 1809 at 59 Grove Street, next to Sheridan Square, in Greenwich Village, a half mile from the Center for Architecture. The park that bears his name, amidst the govern-

Common concerns and *joie de vivre* at Occupy Wall Street. *Photo by Rick Bell*

ment buildings in the civic center, was the scene of a demonstration on the anniversary of the ratification of the Bill of Rights. The Occupy movement demonstrates that Paine's eloquence has contemporary relevance—that people coming together for a common cause makes sense and is not much easier now than during the American Revolution. The spaces created by Occupy across the country show that we shape free speech by design.

References

Garvin, A., and G. Berens. 1997. *Urban Parks and Open Space*. Washington, DC: The Urban Land Institute.

Goodman, P. 2002. *The Empire City: A Novel of New York City*. Boston: David R. Godine Publisher.

Graeber, D. 2011. "Enacting the Impossible." *The Occupied Wall Street Journal*, October 23.

Jacobs, J. 1961. *The Death and Life of Great American Cities*. New York: Random House.

Libeskind, D. 2003. "Memory Foundations." *Studio Daniel Libeskind: Ground Zero Master Plan*.

Lloyd, A. W. 2005. "Aesop's Fables, ll." *Public Works*. Cambridge, MA: MIT.

Morgan, M. H. 1960. *Vitruvius: The Ten Books on Architecture*. Mineola, NY: Dover Publications.

Paine, T. 1776. "The American Crisis." *Pennsylvania Journal*, December 19.

West, C. 2011. "A Love Supreme." *The Occupied Wall Street Journal*, November 18.

Public Space Then and in the Future

Lance Jay Brown

*In designing sustainable communities, high priority should
be given to generating places that enable communication
and interaction among people.* (Copur 1997)

WHAT IS THE ORIGIN of public space? How has it developed historically, and how might that evolution inform how we understand, appraise, and consider the role, the use, and the design of public space as we move deeper into the twenty-first century? Furthermore, how can unearthing this history help us to evaluate New York City's urban design from a new perspective and provide a lens for understanding the forms of protest—including but not limited to Occupy Wall Street—that happen within the city's public spaces?

This article traces the history of shared urban space from the primitive widened market street to the more familiar formalization of space typified by the Tuscan city of Pienza and, finally, to the contemporary public spaces of the twenty-first century American city. This progression has produced a rich typology of spatial phenomena that both promotes and responds to issues of ownership, function, use, topography, climate, ritual, tradition, and dynamism. In this era of the greatest expansion of the urban realm since the beginning of human civilization—when more people will be living in more types of urban agglomeration than ever before and in increasing and accelerating human heterogeneity—what are the most profound functions to be considered when planning for human congregation?

Public discourse is beginning to address these issues, in part forced by the events instigated by Occupy Wall Street. As excerpted from the text for the Urban Intervention: The Howard S. Wright Design Ideas Competition for Public Space (2011), a 2011-2012 competition for a new public space in Seattle:

> How must public space perform in the coming century? Ecologically? Socially? Economically? How can public space evolve to better meet the needs of our changing social and natural systems? What kinds of public spaces will be needed in the future and how can activation and use be encouraged and accommodated in new and inventive ways? Can we generate ideas today that will inform a new generation of cultural centers and public places?

These fundamental questions are addressed in the second half of this article by nine distinguished urban design professionals who help to illuminate the physical reality of our cities and the social manifestations they produce.

Origins

The origins of urban civilization surely begin with the spaces in which people assemble—what we call public spaces. This is hardly debatable. The evolution of urban form and function, the use and meaning of the spaces created, and even the language and laws that developed to identify and describe this rich tapestry has been extensively discussed, documented, and written about by professionals, scholars, and civil societies. As R. E. Wycherly writes in his chapter on the agora in *How the Greeks Built Cities* (1976), in no case has the occurrence of shared space been divorced from the purpose or will of those who participated in its designation or provision, formally or informally. Philosophy, commerce, industry, politics, beliefs, mythology, religion, science, ritual: the entire universe of human interaction occurs in the consciously or casually created public spaces of human civilization. This range of uses and design functions can be demonstrated by exploring four concrete examples, both historical and modern.

Once upon a time in Anatolia, a site was developed that many refer to as one of the earliest examples of a city, or in architectural historian Sibyl

Figure 1. Drawings of Pienza, Italy. *Drawings in Ray Gindroz 2003*

Moholy-Nagy's terms, an "incipient" city. The most urban aspect of this early city, Catal Huyuk, is *"the clear distinction between public streets and plazas, and interior spaces* of a great variety of shapes and purposes" (Moholy-Nagy 1968, emphasis added). While Moholy-Nagy (1968) says that "no history was made in villages," there is surely evidence that villages did create public space, if only the widening of the thruway for passage and commerce. Moholy-Nagy's statement illustrates how history is made in cities and in the space of the city, for both good and bad. For many regions around the world, we have early records that are inconsistent, intersecting, and constantly evolving via ever-more sophisticated archeological data. These records continue to reveal early examples of how humanity first settled and then developed its urban mosaics. So much of our urban history is focused on the architectural monuments we inherit, from pyramids, temples, palaces, fortresses, and cathedrals, that the spaces between seem less significant. Nothing could be further from the truth.

The Tuscan town of Sienna, our next example, is the perfect medieval city, with its winding streets and medieval buildings. It is just one of the many perfect towns that dot the landscape of Italy. The walls of the map room at the Vatican are a painted landscape of the Italian peninsula with a multitude of small hill towns, each ruler of its own domain. These towns, ancient and medieval, have their own winding roads, defenses, and portals. Some have sprawled, but often they are protected from doing so.

To imagine the evolution of our next small town, let's travel back in time: In 1465, a stranger arrives at the outskirts of the Tuscan town Pienza. This stranger is familiar with Sienna, but something stops the stranger, transfixed by a sense that this is something new. The way to the center of Pienza is clear and unobstructed. The streets and spaces are organized and balanced. The buildings relate to the space in a formal manner and, at the center, there is the first consciously created Renaissance public gathering place (Figure 1). This is a beginning. This is conscious, explicit urban open space. It is urban design.

In excavating the history of city and town planning the role of public space and spaces of assembly is revealed. From Roman military towns to the Laws of the Indies and Oglethorpe's Savannah, town-planning instructions gave the size and position for a variety of spaces no longer informal and certainly not arbitrary. The small river settlement that preceded New York City began with a path that developed into New York's Broadway and its few attendant triangles. These corridors were, from the outset, the great organizing principle behind the city—at first, unintentionally, and then very intentionally so. For someone familiar with or knowledgeable about mid-twentieth century New York, before the streets were truly given over to the automobile, it was the great gridded city in which the streets were the open space. The basic network of New York City did not include the plazas and parks where people could gather. It was only after concerned citizens drew attention to this lack of public space that urban parks such as Bryant Park were built. Look at a photograph of the Grand Concourse in the Bronx in 1940, the empty Champs-Élysées of America. In the 1950s, as New York City expanded outward and the boroughs were platted, the unbuilt lots, sidewalks, curbs, parking lots, driveways, and schoolyards became used as the public space of the city. None were designed for the use they were put to and none were in any way particularly attractive. Certainly not like the Place de Vosges in Paris. Venturing into the heart of New York City, no grand open space could be found there, certainly nothing neutral, paved, and defined in the terms that the Viennese humanist Camillo Sitte used. Writing in 1889, Sitte decried the loss of "artistic" space to traffic, to newspapers replacing word of mouth, to the dominance of commerce and real estate pressuring the role of the town square for meeting purposes, and to the demise of fountains because plumbing was bringing water directly into the home. "Life in former times was, after all, decidedly more favorable to an artistic development of city building than is our mathematically precise modern life" (Sitte 1965, 106). The reference to traffic was profoundly prescient.

New York City Today

The New York of today still awaits the complement, the full range of public spaces that were omitted from its grand plan. Perhaps it was from its origins, an emulation or even copy of the pattern of Amsterdam, a city where water was the open space, where more varieties of open space between private property and public open space were omitted. In 1966, Edward Seckler, the renowned urban design professor at Harvard Graduate School of Design, said, in a session of his Urban Design course, that there was only one notable example of a "great space" in New York—Rockefeller Center (though he did recognize the special nature of the Brooklyn Heights Promenade)—and from a classical point of view, he made sense.

What he failed to understand is that until the mid-1960s, when he made the comment, it was the streets of New York City that were its great spaces. Unlike the narrow passageways of the classical European city where relief was found in the opening up at squares and plazas, New Yorkers had their streets and avenues on which to gather for playing stickball and football, for holiday marches and parades, for homecomings, and for social and political protests and demonstrations. With 30 percent of New York's land area used for streets, it was a luxury for a while. Today, those same streets are covered with cars parked and moving. In 1810, the year before the great grid of Manhattan was overlaid on the island, the population was roundly 97,000; by the beginning of World War II, it was just under 7.5 million, and today, it is pushing 8.5 million.

In 1901, 954 vehicles were registered in New York State, in 1910, the Yellow Cab Company was founded, and in 2012, 12.5 million cars were registered in the state.[1] In the past hundred years, the automobile has become ubiquitous and has claimed much of that 30 percent of public open space

---

1. See http://www.dmv.ny.gov/Careers/history.htm.

that existed between the between city's building walls. Today, the recapturing of some of this open space by the NYC Department of Transportation Commissioner Janette Sadik-Kahn is truly to be celebrated. Outside the dense urban core, the automobile and its terrain are critical for socialization; there are parking areas by sports fields, campgrounds, NASCAR tracks, and other areas. What you drive, in part, defines who you are. But in denser areas such as New York City, we socialize differently—and need public spaces that support and promote such use.

Typology and Definitions

The contemporary study, definition, and typing of urban space, open space, public space, and place has been greatly illuminated in the past fifty-plus years, since the early works of Paul Zucker (*Town and Square: From the Agora to the Village Green* 1959), Gordon Cullen (*Townscape* 1961), Jane Jacobs (*The Death and Life of Great American Cities* 1961), Kevin Lynch (*The Image of the City* 1960), and Camillo Sitte (*City Planning According to Artistic Principles, US Edition* 1965) were published. These and other books, articles, and talks served to awaken a new awareness of the role played by open space in the American city.

More recently, a new generation of publications has taken the mid-century rediscovery of the importance of open space and public space as both art and science and further explored its function in society. There are serious, ongoing debates about uses, dimensions, and definitions, and valuable and fascinating research on the subject. Too many to mention, the worthwhile books include *Public Space* (Carr, Francis, Rivlin, and Stone 1992), *On the Plaza: The Politics of Public Space and Culture* (Setha M. Low 2000), *Privately Owned Public Space: The New York Experience* (Jerold S. Kayden 2000), *New City Spaces* (Jan Gehl and Lars Gemzøe 2003), and *Life Between Buildings: Using Public Space* (Jan Gehl 2011).

The typology of open spaces crosses time, geography, and cultural barriers. Words migrate with people and end up enriching the urban fabric. A recent conversation among friends, slightly augmented by online dictionaries, yielded the following terms for urban open spaces: Agora, Plaza, Field, Terrace, Place, Placa, Platz, Square, Public Square, Qaui/Quay, Float, Jetty, Landing, Levee, Pier, Dock, Wharf, Roof, Atrium, Central Square, Piazza, Chowk, Maidan, Parade Ground, Green, Commons, Muse, Alley, Court, Yard, Schoolyard, Courtyard, Hard Space, Soft Space Promenade, Ramblas, Corniche, Sidewalk, Walk, Walkway, Street, Road, Avenue, Boulevard, Carrefour, Crossing, Bridge, Pont, Ponte, Piazzate, Garden, Park, Vest Pocket Park, Mall, Pedestrian Mall, Arcade, Boardwalk, Greenway, Forest, Bois, Arbor, Parterre, Steps, Stairs, Cours, Esplanade, Skatepark, Parking Lot, Street Corners, Market Square, Entryway, and Lawn.

The list can be augmented still. In many cases, the phrases that denote the sites carry architectonic spatial connotations. "In the street" (dans la rue) or "on the boulevard" (sur le boulevard) suggest that the cross section of the location can indicate a greater or lesser sense of enclosure, expansiveness, and potential. On the corner, on the sidewalk, in the park, etc., are further examples. A careful, clear, and structured "Typology of Urban Open Spaces" can be found in the book *Public Space* (1992) by Stephen Carr, Mark Francis, Leanne G. Rivlin, and Andrew M. Stone. Categories included Public Parks, Squares and Plazas, Memorials, Markets, Streets, Playgrounds, Community Open Spaces, Greenways and Linear Parks, Urban Wilderness, Atrium/Indoor/Marketplaces, Found Neighborhood Spaces, and Waterfronts. Which of these are available for open and free assembly is an interesting question. Not only which, but when, and in what manner. The space of power and the power of space are intricately entwined and constantly redefined. In the authors' summary of the chapter, they note, "The term public open space implies the freedom to use a place, but there are numerous constraints that prohibit or discourage members of the public from exercising their rights. We have identified a number of qualities essential to the promotion of these rights. Freedom of access...freedom of action...The right includes both freedom from disturbance and interference and freedom to use a place in a desired manner." The chapter concludes with a discussion of claims between groups, shared uses, and individuals who have the freedom to change settings, to modify settings, and to express "ownership and disposition as the ultimate exercise of rights."

In his essay "Occupy and the Provision of Public Space: The City's Responsibilities," Peter Marcuse (2011) goes into this issue in depth and notes, "It is axiomatic, we believe, that the concern of city planning is not only promotion of the efficient use of the city's built environment and the health and safety of its users, but also the extent to which that environment, and generally planning for and allocation of land uses in the city, furthers the interests of democracy and participation in the affairs of the community." The reference to spaces and places for public use only gets richer as we delve more deeply: formal or informal, real or ideal, fixed or flexible, local or civic. Even the simplest references are not simple. And it is not simply a matter of semantics.

The American Experience

John Brinkerhoff "JB" Jackson was a lifetime observer of the American landscape, its history, its use, and its meaning. In 1966, he defined the public landscape, writ large and distinct from the physical infrastructure that serves us. "A more correct term would be the political landscape; but since we associate that term not with citizenship as we should, but with politicians and politics, the term public is more effective" (Jackson 1970, 153). Jackson goes on to discuss the public meeting function of his public landscape as distinct from public buildings, parking lots, parks, and children's playgrounds. He says that is was in the nineteenth century that many public assembly spaces were transformed to such other uses.

The well-worded Seattle public space competition statement quoted in the beginning of this article, occurring simultaneously with the Occupy Wall Street movement and the forums, writings, and myriad of programs that have sprung up concerning our rights and our freedom to assemble, raises so many political, moral, and ethical questions that it is clear we have "hit a nerve" in the evolution of American society and its continued urbanization.

The Ongoing Evolution

What is fundamental to the design, the governance, the maintenance, and the overall creation of the spaces and places in which we gather? To delve further into these issues I asked nine accomplished American urban design professionals the following questions about urban open space: *With regard to the changing notions of public space relative to protests and demonstrations that often test the boundaries of public property and First Amendment rights, what are the limits to the use of public space? Who gets to decide? How can design play a role in creating parks and spaces that serve a variety of functions? What other issues impact the design of public space today?*

I had hoped their responses might help guide our movement to an ever more equitable civic landscape; however, many of their comments serve rather to underscore and illuminate critical questions raised throughout this volume.

Donlyn Lyndon, FAIA, architect, urban designer, educator, and founding editor of *Places Magazine*:

> The public and the private are intensely intertwined in the US; their intersections are the stuff of politics. The essential issue for designers concerned with the public realm is to recognize that entanglement… to think beyond boundaries. For each design process to begin with the confinements of property…for buildings and spaces to be conceived first, as they usually are, without regard or accountability to a larger setting, is a most destructive thing for our cities. As educators we need to think differently.

Ray Gindroz, cofounder and principal emeritus of Urban Design Associates, who pioneered participatory planning processes for neighborhoods and downtowns:

> My initial thoughts are based on the very old-fashioned term "common ground." In the common ground, anything goes. But how is it defined? During the Occupy London movement, the settlers camped in the spaces in front of and next to St. Paul's Cathedral. No one seemed to mind too much because the paths to the cathedral entrances were kept clear. Those spaces are adjacent to the main thoroughfare, so they are very public. Paternoster Square, a privately owned series of public spaces, was closed off and the Occupy group was not allowed in. Ironically, closing it off turned out to be bad for business. In the design of public space, it is critical to define the paths through the space. These are open to everyone. There are usually "areas of influence" within the space that are identified with individual uses. Appropriate definition is needed for these. And then the common ground that is shared by these uses and by the general public is the main focus of the space. History has useful lessons, such as Piazza Ducale in Vigevano. Designed by Leonardo da Vinci and Bramante as the forecourt to the huge Castello Sforzesco, its approaches led directly to the huge tower and entry ramps. Two hundred years later, the focus shifted to the cathedral. The cathedral façade became the dominant element and the castle tower was partially covered over. The area of influence changed but the patterns of circulation remained the same, and the common ground was further reinforced.

Diana Balmori, FASLA, landscape scholar, author, and design principal of the landscape and urban design firm Balmori Associates:

> It's a peculiar time for public space. On the one hand, everybody seems to have bought into the idea that its maintenance is expensive and difficult and that public agencies can no longer do it. They need the private sector to help. But in itself that privatizes the space in some way. The argument puzzles me because these spaces cost much less than maintaining any public building. My conclusion is that public space is not important enough to our culture.
>
> Yet, it is crucial to our culture, an equivalent to the freedom of the press—think Tahrir in Cairo, Zocalo in Mexico, Tiananmen in China, Occupy Wall Street in Zuccotti Park, and then worldwide. And there are so many reasons for closing them, from security to homeless people to curfews.
>
> But, of course, public space is also for the enjoyment of life, and that you can see in any park on a Sunday, including yesterday in Washington, DC with all the magnolia trees in bloom. Yet, even there, in attempting to cross Lafayette Square Park, I was told very politely that the park was closed. This was at 5:30 p.m. because there was a big state dinner for David Cameron, and it was closing for security reasons.
>
> It is true that some private/public partnerships work well—conservancies and trusts spring up because the partners care for public space. Even they need to work by clear rules, but they are the best of the alternatives of bringing private money in precisely because they are its advocates.
>
> Do we care enough as a culture for public space?

David Dixon, FAIA, principal of Goody Clancy Planning and Urban Design, and recipient of the 2007 AIA Thomas Jefferson Award:

> We can't restrict use of public spaces as forums for free speech. We can protect people and property from threats associated with protest, but not access to places that are meant to be truly public. We can design and designate portions or all of certain public spaces as places for gathering and speaking, but we have to take full responsibility for making sure that the spaces are located in appropriately civic settings, and not out of sight and mind.

Robert Campbell, journalist, architect, and Pulitzer Prize-winning architecture and urban design critic for the *Boston Globe*:

> I was staying in Times Square once on a night when the hated Yankees won a world series. The cops closed off all the side streets and there was an endless informal parade of honking cars with guys standing up waving their shirts, beer bottles, whatever, coming down Broadway—I'm sure directly from the game. It dawned on me that the best open space, at least for any kind of demonstration, is one that normally has another use but has been appropriated by the demonstrators. The act of annexation becomes a metaphor for the energy of the cause. I'm sure there was an official ticker-tape parade downtown in a day or two, but it can't have had the same spontaneity or vitality. The opposite extreme is the open space that is deliberately planned for a public purpose, e.g., City Hall Plaza in Boston, which seems to be endlessly, sadly waiting for something to happen. There would be no fun, no triumph in taking it over.

Richard Dattner, FAIA, architect and urban park designer, and recipient of the 1994 AIA Thomas Jefferson Award:

> In a time of increasing disparities in income, opportunity, housing, and neighborhood conditions, public open space becomes even more important for a civil society.
>
> Much of what we consider public space is actually privately controlled—in malls, arcades, building plazas, occupied sidewalks, etc. The Mike Davis book, *City of Quartz: Excavating the Future in Los Angeles* (1992), describes this trend—in his words: "Even as the walls have come down in Eastern Europe, they are being erected all over Los Angeles."
>
> Designers can help by creating varied scales of public spaces for assembly, from neighborhood "green streets" open space to venues for large assemblies.
>
> Mixing landscaped areas with hardscape allows for assembly on hard surfaces, while landscaped areas can remain off limits for intensive uses. Providing varieties of surfaces—level, sloped, stepped, shaded, enclosed—also helps guide public events to appropriate areas. New York City's recent pedestrianization efforts are a good prototype

for increasing public space.

The obvious problem is balancing the need for unfettered public access with issues of inappropriate uses, gathering by homeless persons, and antisocial behavior. Increasing the amount, variety, and scale of public space can help public agencies guide public events to appropriate venues while protecting landscape and neighborhoods from destructive activities.

M. Paul Friedberg, FASLA, landscape architect, author, and educator who founded the Urban Landscape Architecture Program at City College of New York:

The look and use of public open space is informed by context, chronology, and culture—three dynamic factors that are in motion and indicate the impossibility to identify a universal form or program for space. In my mind, there are no physical mandates or imperatives, only accommodations. The designer creates the situation, one that facilitates opportunities and not insistent on specific use. The designer is a facilitator accomplished in adjusting the physical to create opportunities.

The richer the opportunities that space provides, the more successful the design. When the visitor can interpret the environment they occupy and employ their creative energy, they take possession of their environment enriching their experience. This would imply that the less specific, more universal the design, the greater the opportunity for engagement by the user client. This notion is in direct contradiction to the objectives of most designers who are taught to seek or impose their signature on their work.

As painful as it is, let me suggest less ego and more humility.

Denise Hoffman Brandt, landscape architect and director of the Urban Landscape program at the Bernard and Anne Spitzer School of Architecture, City College of New York:

The Bill of Rights formalizes the right to free assembly. Nineteenth-century American public spaces, such as plazas, squares, and streets, were often designed with a monumental civic scale that enabled them to accommodate large crowds. In New York City, Central Park, Union Square, and Broadway are such examples. Broad cultural shifts in the twentieth century altered the public realm to essentially curtail the capacity of civic space for civic expression. Two aspects of the change in our material culture are human-scale cities and private/public spaces:

1. Human-scale cities: When you cease to design big, you cease to design for civitas. Efforts to humanize the city, through downscaling spaces and filling them with program, undermine the development of new civic arenas. Areas that were once a latent opportunity for collective expression have been filled with ball fields, tot-lots, dog parks, and gardens or divided up to create pleasant small-scale enclaves. Recreation is the opium of the people. The end result is an urban fabric that is nearly uniformly tight, lacking the big gaps that could be filled by large public gatherings.

It is no accident that the Occupy occupation was always portrayed as "spilling over" and intruding on the life of the city. Cities are bigger and the spaces for public civic events have not grown commensurately because there is little value attached to them in contemporary culture. There are very few locations now that can accommodate expression by a population sector of a city.

2. Private/public spaces: The Occupy movement has been situated in public/private territory in some cases. Zuccotti Park is a privately owned public space, and this is subtly ironic given the movement's positioning against co-option of the public good by private enterprise. It is an oversimplification to attribute the increase in public space financing through public/private partnerships to a lack of city capital.

Many of the valued civic spaces that we revere today were funded by industrial magnates as a gesture of civic noblesse oblige. That gesture, aside from grandiose naming and direct political clout, was not attached to direct benefits, such as variances for taller structures, and, in turn, the municipality retained management costs and benefits of the space. Authority for use and "occupancy" was clear, and the city could be held accountable for limiting access to citizens acting on First Amendment rights.

The events around occupying Zuccotti Park reveal the loss of civic capacity in these "public" realms, as the city and the corporate entity responsible for the park played off each other and positioned the occupation as a violation of the American ideal of sacrosanct private land rights. It is not the partnership that is problematic; it is the terms that are set by the municipality that have blurred the line between acts on public and private land.

Laurie Olin, FASLA, landscape architect, and recipient of the ASLA Award for Lifetime Achievement:

No urban park since their invention in the nineteenth century has been intended to have people camp in them. It is not their purpose, nor are they equipped for it. To use them thus is to deny their use to the citizens for which they were constructed. This is true for political protests as well as for the homeless and indigent, no matter how unfortunate their situation. Parks are not hotels or toilets. To use them thus is to degrade them and engender the need for their repair at public expense. I am an advocate of civil disobedience as outlined by Thoreau and practiced by Gandhi and Martin Luther King, Jr. I am in sympathy with recent demonstrations against Wall Street, and I have witnessed encampments at Saint Paul's in London, the Embarcadero in San Francisco, city hall in Philadelphia, and Zuccotti Park in New York City. I feel the style and form of these protests were not as effective as they could or should have been, and that, like several protests at recent economic summits, they were in part co-opted or infected and negated by various anarchist and nihilist groups. Legitimate protest—and there is an awful lot that is legitimate—makes many people, even me and most of those in government, uncomfortable.

Confrontation is unpleasant and painful. Effective protest causes inconvenience, makes business difficult, and can or must at times bring everything to a halt. It must not, however, cause property damage or injury. It also should not make matters worse for those already burdened or struggling. Any situation where one group seeks concessions or retribution from another always leads to a complex moral discussion and debate. It is easy with private land. IBM can have trespassers removed from a site it owns—plaza, headquarters, or factory. In the case of the federal government, it shouldn't be difficult either, as the land belongs to the people and, as such, should be open to them. Whatever the requirements to make federal and other properties secure from terrorism, they should in no way preclude or deter peaceful protest. By this, I mean assembling, marching, and presenting or addressing

Figure 1. Independence Park in Philadelphia. *Photo by Laurie Olin*

grievances. I do not, however, see a justification for overnight camping. Coming back, day after day, to the same place with an undeterred message, yes. Just because protesters feel frustrated, an "in your face, I'm not leaving" mood doesn't make it right anymore than it was for the Black Panthers and Students for a Democratic Society to turn to violence in 1968–69.

I have learned that attempts to design facilities to accommodate or manage protest are somewhat futile. At Independence Park, I designed the park to accommodate crowds of thousands for the Fourth of July, President's Day, and awarding a Freedom Medal. Part of the program from the National Park Service included a paved area that could hold several hundred people especially for the exercise of protest and demonstration (Figure 1). It includes a monument inscribed with the First Amendment to make the point. This area is situated so that TV cameras set up to focus upon a group at this spot will also have

Independence Hall and the Liberty Bell Pavilion as a backdrop. Over the past five or six years, I have watched it from our office nearby. Groups almost never use the space intended to accommodate protest. They inevitably move to the center of the lawn and as close to Independence Hall as they can get. For big events, groups take over the entire sloped lawn of the second block, but not the designated space (Figure 2). I conclude that it is in the nature of protest to be contrary, and that attempts to say "protest here, but not over there" are met with scorn and withering sarcasm. People vote with their feet.

We have designed a number of antiterrorist barriers for various federal and institutional facilities that are effective and have enhanced the public realm. One must be careful about design for protest. Those who design a park or plaza so the homeless are uncomfortable and unable to use it inevitably design something so negative and brutal or vacuous and unusable that ordinary middle-class citizens, regardless of age or gender, shun it as well. Attempts to control or discourage the

Figure 2. Group gathered at Independence Park. *Photo by Laurie Olin*

public from protest in a public place are equally fraught. Nearly any sort of barrier or physical crowd manipulation smacks of not wanting citizens to approach or have access to their government.

The above responses cover a broad range of concerns: overprogramming of available space; appropriately using the public landscape; acknowledging open space and democratic process; accepting public-private partnerships; appropriating; and understanding rules, among others. It was gratifying that the question posed allowed for wide ranging answers and encouraging to note that some suggestions were made focusing on ways in which current conflicts might be addressed.

As for New York City "beyond Zuccotti Park," there is much to be hopeful about. Under the current administration, more space has been reclaimed for public occupancy and use than anyone can recall. It remains somewhat curious that the NYC Department of Transportation has taken the lead in this initiative, but this is not a problem and it does control much of that 30 percent that is the city's open space. However, it may be that in time the true priorities of urbanity, civility, and open space will surface and a new department will emerge. Such a department would work to serve the people of the whole city and their right to its use. It would create and maintain parks, plazas, sidewalks, pocket parks, and markets in the full range and scale of spaces and places needed by a civil society. It would reclaim the space usurped inappropriately by the automobile. It would create grand spaces for large gatherings and small ones for local, intimate use. It would be called, of course, the Department of Public Space.

References

Carr, S., M. Francis, L. G. Rivlin, and A. M. Stone. 1992. *Public Space*. Environment and Behavior Series. New York: Cambridge University Press.

Copur, U. 1997. "Sustainable Environments; Holistic and Incremental Processes." In *Ecopolis: An Opinion for the Future*, edited by K. Lapintie and M.-L. Mäsä. Tampere, Finland: University of Tampere.

Cullen, G. 1961. *Townscape*. New York: Reinhold Publishing Corporation.

Davis, M. 1992. *City of Quartz: Excavating the Future in Los Angeles*. New York: Vintage.

Gehl, J. 2011. *Life Between Buildings: Using Public Space*. Copenhagen: Danish Architectural Press.

Gehl, J., and L. Gemzøe. 2003. *New City Spaces*. Copenhagen: Danish Architectural Press.

Gindroz, R. 2003. *Pienza: Dream City*. From *Pages from a Sketchbook* by the Marilyn and Ray Gindroz Foundation. Norfolk, VA: Marilyn and Ray Gindroz Foundation.

Kayden, J. S. 2000. *Privately Owned Public Space: The New York New City Experience*. New York: Department of City Planning and Municipal Art Society of New York.

Jackson, J. B. 1970. *Landscapes*. Cambridge, MA: University of Massachusetts Press.

Jacobs, J. 1961. *The Death and Life of Great American Cities*. New York: Random House.

Low, S. M. 2000. *On the Plaza: The Politics of Public Space and Culture*. Austin: University of Texas Press.

Lynch, K. 1960. *The Image of the City*. Cambridge, MA: MIT Press.

Marcuse, P. 2011. "Occupy and the Provision of Public Space: The City's Responsibilities." *Peter Marcuse's Blog*, December 1. http://pmarcuse.wordpress.com/2011/12/01/occupy-and-the-provision-of-public-space-the-citys-responsibility/.

Moholy-Nagy, S. 1968. *Matrix of Man: An Illustrated History of Urban Environment*. New York: Preager.

Sitte, C. 1965. *City Planning According to Artistic Principles*. New York: Random House.

Urban Intervention: The Howard S. Wright Design Ideas Competition for Public Space. 2011. "Call for Entries." www.aiaseattle.org/urbanintervention.

Wycherly, R. E. 1976. *How the Greeks Built Cities*. New York: W. W. Norton.

Zucker, P. 1959. *Town and Square: From the Agora to the Village Green*. New York: Columbia University Press.

Pushing Back Boundaries

HOW SOCIAL MOVEMENTS ARE
REDEFINING THE PUBLIC SPACE

Sadra Shahab and Shirin Barghi [1]

IN THE THREE YEARS that I have lived in New York City, I have crossed the Brooklyn Bridge only twice. The first time was back in 2009, when the bridge served as a platform for Iranians to protest the reelection of incumbent president Mahmoud Ahmadinejad. The second time came around last year, when the Occupy Wall Street movement was in full swing.

A few months after the post-election violence in our country in 2009, we organized the Green Scroll march in which Iranians carried a mile-long green banner across the Brooklyn Bridge in solidarity with the Iranian people. This was the first time the Brooklyn Bridge was serving an Iranian cause, and perhaps the first time I had occupied public space in the US.

Then there was November 2011, when thousands of Wall Street occupiers marched from Liberty Plaza and Foley Square across the bridge to Brooklyn. Despite attempts by the police to disperse the crowd, we managed to venture into the pedestrian walkway of the bridge and take it as our own for the next few hours. This was the first time I fully grasped the unique power of public space in securing a sense of unity, solidarity, and belonging even in a country other than my own.

But my main fascination with the bridge rises beyond nostalgic recollection of its role in social and civil rights movements, such as the Green movement and Occupy Wall Street (OWS). What intrigues me most about the

---

1. While this essay is the result of a joint effort between the two authors Sadra Shahab and Shirin Barghi, it is Sadra Shahab who is speaking in the first person.

Brooklyn Bridge is how it has served as more than a simple transportation corridor or a mere urban landmark resting on the boundaries of Manhattan and Brooklyn. All the more, it makes me think about the relationships between social movements and public space and how they are defined in the face of state-inscribed boundaries and frontiers.

As an Iranian, I know only too well about the importance of frontiers and boundaries. I was born in the midst of a devastating eight-year war between Iraq and Iran (1980–1988). Sparked ostensibly because of a border dispute, the war left irreparable scars within the Iranian society that have lingered on until today. I have vague memories of the war itself, but I grew up with the sociopolitical and financial consequences that continue even after more than twenty years. No one wants to have the sovereignty of his or her country to be compromised, but at the same time, we always wondered why our government let the war drag on for eight years. We were told that it was a matter of national interest, but looking back I see that it was mostly about the interests of the newly established government, which in its first years relied heavily on its territorial integrity and was willing to safeguard it at all costs.

The war left me with an entirely different notion of the term "occupation." For me, it evoked a top-down hegemonic force of action, bringing to mind examples such as the Israeli occupation of Palestine or the Chinese invasion of Tibet. But in New York, I found that "occupation" does not always have a negative connotation. Sometimes it could be a form of resistance. Occupation as a form of resistance is not a new phenomenon. In 1969, the Alcatraz occupation raised awareness of Native American rights and broken treaties. Although the US government forcibly ended the island's takeover, which lasted more than year, it was a giant leap in the history of American Indian protest actions. Perhaps OWS is the best modern-day example of occupation as a means of bottom-up resistance, which has not only swept through the entire United States, but also inspired many others worldwide.

I believe such occupations, which take the form of resistance, have two main components: the location of the occupation, which is normally the public space, and the territorial behavior of humans, which unlike that of animals is highly influenced by culture. In this sense, the attempt to seize control of a specific territory is aimed at securing the survival and prominence not of individuals, but of an idea.

Much has been written and discussed about the inherent "territoriality" in human nature—whether against the backdrop of war, in which humans defend their land against a foreign invader, or that of a soccer match, in which they defend their side of the field against the opposing team. But what has particularly engaged me is the strong and key presence of territorial behavior in social movements and how public spaces become the setting of a power struggle between citizens and the state.

From the beginning of OWS in September 2011, my friends and I would discuss the extent to which the survival of the movement depended on the small piece of land they had occupied on Liberty Plaza. Some believed that the movement would die upon the New York City Police Department's evacuation of the premises. Others disagreed, arguing that the movement is an idea and therefore not spatially bound. I remember taking a picture of a poster that read, "You cannot evict an idea whose time has come." The message is powerful and I totally agree with it. However, I also believe that the ground in which we raised our flags, chanted slogans, and stood up for a common cause has a value that cannot be overlooked. I believe the intangible potency of the idea and the corporeal realms of the public space go hand in hand.

The value of that space was the opportunity to collectively envision an alternative to the current system. Occupiers provided free public services, including health care, education, a library, food, and an open space for the people to create a general assembly and practice direct democracy.

It stands to reason that the public space was and continues to be an indispensable part of the Occupy Wall Street movement, but what about the other sociopolitical movements taking place across the globe in recent years? This is a question many Iranians have been grappling with since the electoral coup that reinstated Ahmadinejad back in office in 2009. The violent crackdown against demonstrators in public venues in Tehran, such as the Azadi Square, has been seen as a major blow to opposition groups such as the Green movement. Many wonder if the Green movement would have survived, had it managed to stay on the streets. Indeed, many believe that the main reason the Egyptian revolution of 2011 was a success was that the Egyptian people were able to seize and retain control of the public space for eighteen days, forcing Mubarak into resignation.

Some believe that the Green movement is an idea deeply rooted in the collective consciousness of the Iranian people that will continue to live on. Whether it is the Green movement, Occupy Wall Street, or even the Egyptian revolution, it would be shortsighted to suggest that they are all limited to bringing some sort of change through the act of occupation. In the case of the Egyptian revolution, for instance, it has managed to topple the Mubarak regime, but it still has a long way ahead to realize its main goals. It is true, however, that having a stronghold in the public realm is an effective way to keep the movement going.

But it is not only the citizens who try to reap the socio-spatial benefits of public spaces. There has been a persistent effort by the ruling elites to co-opt these civic arenas largely because of the historic significance of place-bound resistance politics in revolutions. Since the 1979 Iranian Revolution, the theocratic government has kept a short leash on public spaces in defiance of the Iranian constitution, which grants people the right to protest peacefully and by the same token entitles them to occupy public spaces. Not only has the government deprived the people of this right, but it has also treated Iranian individuals as public property—in other words, a component of the landscape. Meaning that the Iranian people's appearances, just like urban spaces, should not flout the principles of the Islamic Republic.

For the past thirty years, the Iranian state has gone to great lengths to control both public spaces and the presence of citizens within those realms. Public spaces were segregated, and revolutionary ideology was injected into the city landscape by means of murals, flags, posters, and banners scattered around main squares, landmarks, and other venues. Government intervention was not limited to the cityscape and people's presence in it, but extended to the monitoring of people's appearances, which can also impact the general atmosphere of the public arena. A strict dress code was imposed, which required Iranians to adhere to a set of Islamic rules and principles in public. It went even beyond that and led to the creation of a "moral police" tasked with ensuring the "appropriateness" of the public conduct of women and men. In Iran, it was first about checking lipsticks, hairstyles, and eyeliners, but now even water fights, which are not at odds with Islamic values, are deemed illegal in Tehran. I am referring here to reports of a Facebook-organized social gathering at one of the city's parks last summer in which young Iranians would use water pistols and plastic bottles in a water fight with one another. The initiative drew criticism of conservative factions within the

Iranian government, who labeled it as a "shameful disgrace to the Islamic Revolution," and it wasn't long before the police raided the park and brought the fun to an abrupt end. The crackdown was ordered by the government out of fear of losing its grip on public spaces.

But contrary to general belief, this does not take place only in totalitarian societies, but also in liberal societies such as Europe and the United States—albeit in a different form. The recent NYPD spying scandal on Muslim communities and organizations, some of which took place in public spaces, is a blatant example of privacy invasion. I have been a victim myself when the NYPD made an uncalled visit to my home. This experience leaves you with a rather unsettling feeling of being followed. I was constantly looking over my shoulder for a while. Another example, also a violation of constitutional rights, is the recent ban of face-covering veils and mosques in some European countries. Amnesty International reported in April 2012 that the bans on face-veil chadors are denying women jobs and education, particularly in France and Belgium.

I believe the Occupy Wall Street movement was compromised in much the same manner. One of the pretexts the police used to justify its excessive force against the nonviolent Occupy movement demonstrators at the UC Davis campus last year was that they were blocking the walkway and thus disrupting the public order. You can't help but wonder why Black Friday enthusiasts camping out on sidewalks don't get the same treatment? There are many instances in which the police violated the rights of people to demonstrate peacefully in American public spaces, which came to the fore during the Occupy Wall Street movement. From the very outset, the police tried to intimidate occupiers by bringing cameras and taking photos. This is ironically similar to the techniques used by the Iranian government during the 2009 uprising in Iran: here too, police would take photos of opposition demonstrators to instigate fear of being documented for retribution later. In both cases, the public is expected to toe the line and act within the statist promulgation of their roles in the public space. Any attempt to push the boundaries will ostensibly be seen as a threat to the public security, while in reality it is a threat to the clout of the state.

At times of social unrest, authorities tend to quell voices of dissent in the name of the law. It has been engraved in our subconscious that, as citizens, we must abide by the law for the sake of social welfare and peaceful coexistence. This is where there is a difference between the law that exists to secure public interest and the law that is used by the state as a leverage to confront nonconformists. The law is very malleable in itself. Those in the position of power have the leverage to shape and manipulate the law to gain the upper hand. Dissidents are painted as hooligans or hippies throwing the society into chaos and disrupting the public space. In light of that, the public has no choice but to turn to civil disobedience as a means to get their voice heard. Public space provides a platform whereupon they can lock horns with oppressive supremacy. In the words of the Iranian scholar Khashayar Deyhimi, "A citizen who is weak, gutless, and afraid is not a citizen, but a serf." Social agency can be defined by standing in the face of the supremacy. Sometimes an oppressive force can take the shape of a totalitarian government and other times it can rear its head as a corporation discriminating against its employees—or it can even be a developer abusing its ties and financial weight to construct an unwanted building against the will of the residents.

The power struggle over territory is not limited to the physical public space, but with the technological leaps and bounds in recent years, it has shifted to new dimensions. The Internet and the many wonders of cyber technology have redefined the boundaries of "public space" in the traditional meaning of the word. We now see how even an Internet domain, for instance, can emerge as a digital territory and become a scene of struggle between the government and the citizens. The significance of digital space is proven by its entanglement in power plays between the state and the citizens. Governments such as Iran and China have resorted to stringent Internet filtering mechanisms to patrol the actions of their citizens in the so-called digital space. In the same vein, Internet guerrilla groups have launched counter cyber attacks against the websites of government, propaganda news outlets, financial institutions, and corporations. One group, dubbed Anonymous, over the past year has launched systematic hacker attacks against a variety of websites, including Visa and MasterCard. Law enforcement authorities have been actively hunting down members of the group and last summer, according to reports, they managed to round up some twenty-five people allegedly connected to the group. That's how important cyberspace has become.

Those in power, whether at the helm of a corporation or of a government, have exploited mass intimidation in a bid to control and monitor any development transpiring in public spaces. In the US, there has been a deep-seated fear of so-called terror attacks since 9/11, which has led to the re-fashioning of not only the architecture of the cityscape, by means of barriers and police patrols, but also the state security apparatus that sometimes even goes as far as violating the right to public space under the Constitution.

Given the symbiotic relationship between public spaces and social move-ments, we reach the conclusion that the significance of civic sites in terms of civic service, as repeatedly highlighted by urban planners, sociologists, and architects, is much broader than what was previously envisioned. A public space designed initially for recreational purposes may end up having a key role in mobilizing the masses, amplifying their voices, and bringing socio-political change. In many instances, public spaces—whether Tahrir Square in Cairo, Christopher Street in New York, or Tiananmen Square in Bei-jing—have appeared at the forefront of social movements and uprisings. Thus, they have been able to solidify a social movement in its nascent stages through their mere existence. Public spaces have not only emerged as sites of tension between citizens and the oligarchic power, but also prepared the ground for sociopolitical actors to begin a dialogue and raise awareness about a certain cause.

That said, we must take into careful consideration the various rules and regulations imposed on how civilians can access and use the public space while also joining forces to improve both the quality of these spaces and the prevailing laws and constraints. Even if authorities do not apply these reforms, they will be claimed by the public at a grassroots level and within the context of each society. For instance, the young generation of Middle Easterners are resisting authority and ensuring their rights in the face of state patriarchy.

Whether in the Middle East or in the United States, the redefining of public spaces and the restructuring of rights by citizens who act out-side state-legislated control is a remarkable form of resistance. As seen in OWS, people are collectively, not to mention actively, testing state-inscribed boundaries and renegotiating the framework of rules and rights in a bid to create a new and unique definition of "public space."

5

Responsive Change

5.1

Public Sector Agents of Change

Occupy and the Provision of Public Space

THE CITY'S RESPONSIBILITIES

Peter Marcuse

THE OCCUPATION OF key public spaces by Occupy Wall Street as a means of calling attention to more basic problems raises questions about the role of public spaces that need to be urgently dealt with. The basic questions about the organization of society, democracy, inequality, social justice, and public priorities have deep roots and require long-term answers. They should not be preempted by the immediate needs for space, nor should any space be fetishized.[1] But spatial issues need to be dealt with immediately.

• • •

The Zuccotti Park affair and similar forcible evictions of protesters from public spaces in cities across the country reveal a deficit in the provision and management of public space. The courts may ultimately rule that the constitutional provisions guaranteeing the right peaceably to assemble and petition for the redress of grievances imply a constitutional duty on states and their cities to make such assembly possible through the provision of public space for its exercise. Until there is a change in the composition of the US Supreme Court, however, it is left for other branches of government to accept that responsibility as a matter of good democratic policy. The issues raised by the Zuccotti Park affair concerning the need for, and

---

1. For comments on the specific significance of space for the Occupy movement, see pmarcuse. wordpress.com, blog #5, "The Purpose of the Occupation Movement and the Danger of Fetishizing Space." As to options for New York City, see blog #4, "What Space To Occupy in New York: A Two-Site Solution?"

the function of, public space should therefore be confronted directly as a question of democratic governance. The following discussion suggests the possibilities in New York City, focusing in particular on the appropriate concerns of the NYC Planning Commission and its staff.

The occupiers of Zuccotti Park clearly had a message they wished to convey to the wider public, one that concerned issues of governance, social justice, public policy, the conduct of the affairs of the city. It was perhaps a controversial message, one affecting a wide range of subjects. There is widespread interest in what the occupiers have to say, both pro and con. They found Zuccotti Park a feasible location in which not only to express their opinions but also discuss them, look at alternate formulations, educate themselves, and in the process develop a model of discussion and transparent decision making that is itself of great potential value to the development of urban democracy. They claim the right to occupy a particular space not simply on First Amendment grounds—they do not wish simply to yell and scream for its own sake, but to participate in the democratic governance of the society in which they live. They are in a notable modern tradition of the use of central spaces for democratic action, a tradition that goes from Plaza de Mayo to Tahrir Square, including US spaces such as the mall in Washington, DC. An even older tradition goes back to the Athenian agora and the medieval cathedral square (as St. James is used in London today). Their availability for political use is generally taken for granted, if sometimes limited by undemocratic regimes or used for repressive purposes, as with Nazi plazas and Soviet squares.

In a city as dense as New York, and with the kind of market-dictated property values it reflects, there is a real need to face the lack of such spaces directly and to plan for their use as part of the essential city planning process and governmental regulation of land uses. We believe that the city government should, in confronting uses such as those of Occupy Wall Street, welcome their initiative for public involvement and consider carefully how the city's planning process might promote the occupiers' ability to participate, actively and peaceably, in the city's public life.

How might this be done?

An open and democratically motivated city leadership might provide communication facilities like radio and TV access; sponsor public fora; have transparent discussions on the issues raised in governing circles; and call for an open and supportive conduct by city officials in all matters related to the occupiers' abilities to make their voices heard, encouraging a public debate around their views. But even short of such actions, making space available for such activities is a primary need that should be addressed by the city, a need that requires it to examine the possibilities for the use of space within the city to encourage democratic activities. The demands of the First Amendment set a minimum threshold for the exercise of the right to free speech, but what is needed is not the ability to speak freely out in the desert, inaccessible to most and heard by few. Rather, what is needed are publicly available spaces that can fulfill the functions of the traditional agora, places where free men and women can meet, debate, speak to and listen to each other, learn from each other, confront issues of public concern and facilitate their resolution.

Zuccotti Park was not ideal for the purposes of speech and assembly, but by an almost heroic effort it was made into one in which such uses thrived. New York City could have supported the occupation: it could have done things as simple as providing sanitary facilities, as it has in other parks; it could have provided sound systems that would both have facilitated wide participation and minimized disturbance to neighbors; it could have consulted on health and safety measures, provided fire extinguishers and safe connections to power lines, even efficient sources of heat and protection from the elements. Facilities for the provision of food and water could have been supplied too, as they are in many parks. It could have arranged with the occupiers that they could speak and meet in safety and security. The availability of spaces such as the atrium at 60 Wall Street could have been a model. But the city did nothing along these lines at Zuccotti Park; it did not even explore their possibility.

But it is not too late to recognize the problem and plan for its immediate amelioration and long-term solution. The city has developed other plans that include the provision of public spaces, and has had them since the city was founded. Those plans need to clarify further what those publicly available spaces are for, what purposes they should serve, where they should be located, how they should be designed and equipped. We have plans for spaces and facilities needed for other purposes. We have waterfront plans of which we are proud, transportation plans, environmental plans, social service plans, recreational plans; we need public spaces as part of a democracy or public participation plan, one which would look at the spaces and the facilities needed to make a healthy democracy thrive. We are able to plan and make space available for ticker tape parades, community gardens, street fairs, farmers' markets, political rallies; we provide for commercial and recreational use of parks; we even arrange for seating for large numbers in the middle of Times Square in the heart of the city's busiest intersection at the peak of rush hour. We build and/or subsidize convention centers and sports arenas for large crowds. We plan special restrictions and special opportunities for various holidays. We provide office space and meeting space in numerous locations for the transaction of city business, from community board meetings to public hearings to electoral events, and we rent space in municipal properties and on public sidewalks to all kinds of activities, public and private, and at all hours of the day and night.

Further, New York City, through zoning regulations, building codes, tax and subsidy policies, antidiscrimination laws, environmental controls, infrastructure provision, transportation policies, and the exercise of other normal governmental functions, has substantial control not only over publicly owned spaces, but also over privately owned ones. Many of these deal explicitly both with restricted and with favored uses, whether negatively as with nuisances or positively as with theaters or community facilities or spatial bonuses for open spaces and public facilities. Spaces for public uses may be publicly owned, or privately owned and subject to public influence and regulation; it is the use, not the bare ownership, which is the issue. A Public Spaces Plan concerned with a specific component dealing with the spatial requirements for the exercise of democratic functions should deal with the use of space both in public and in private ownership. Should we not do the same kind of planning as we do for other spaces in the city to provide space for the functioning of the democracy to which we are constitutionally committed? Should not the imagination, the technical skills, the design experience, the collective experience of the diverse body of our citizenry and our guests, the knowledge of our educational institutions, the competence of our business community, and the creativity of our artists be now harnessed in that effort? The issues involved in dealing with Zuccotti Park are all within the city's power to manage and do so relatively easily. In Newark, for instance, "the city's police chief...said she would waive the permit ordinarily required to assembling in Military Park, telling protesters that her officers' task was 'to make sure you're safe'...members of the city's Municipal Council said they supported lifting the 9 p.m. curfew that typically governs the plaza" (Flegenheimer 2011).

The use of many of the city's spaces is already governed through appropriate time, place, and manner regulations, and such regulations, if reasonable, may be applied to spaces for democratic assembly and speech, keeping in mind the constitutional importance of the particular uses involved and making sure their adoption is consistent with a democratic decision-making process. In implementing such a Public Spaces Plan, consideration must be given to explicit criteria for the management of such spaces. Two different groups or individuals cannot conduct two different activities in the same space at the same time, certainly not without careful prior understanding as to their rules of behavior. Developing or applying such rules is a common everyday task for those in charge of many spaces, both public and private; the examples above suggest the many situations in which such rules are already established and enforced as to public spaces, streets, parks, with relatively wide public agreement.

The Zuccotti Park experience suggests two further points that require special notice. One is that in determining priorities among possibly conflicting claims on the use of a specific space, a particular consideration should be given to uses that increase the ability of the populace to participate actively and in an informed way in the democratic governance of the city. Detailed research would be useful to see how criteria are now framed in various cities for the regulation of various types of spaces. Transparency and ample opportunities to be heard should be a sine qua non for the adoption of such rules.

The Zuccotti Park case also shows the potential for an open discussion among users and affected non-users of public space concerning the creation of shared rules of conduct. The agreements between the occupiers and Community Board 1 for the regulation of noise at the park show that even in difficult circumstances, discussion can achieve satisfactory results. The experience at Zuccotti Park also shows that the absence of discussion can have very undesirable results, as demonstrated by the clearance of the park by the city in the dead of night, without notice or oversight, and with substantial property damage and infliction of unnecessary personal hardship. Occupiers waive no rights by entering into negotiations over time, place, and manner regulations on their use of a particular space at a particular time in a particular manner. The city, on its side, should be sympathetic to the prospective users' needs, and not meet them with expressed hostility. Agreement with their goals is not a requirement, but civility and common sense are.

There should be an end to the handling of the democratic outpouring we have seen at Zuccotti Park by forcible evictions and quasi-military police actions. These should be replaced by a forward-looking and responsible planning and implementation process that will allow the flowering of a vital and constructive democracy in the city.

Why should the Planning Commission take a leading role here as far as New York is concerned? Apart from its purpose to plan broadly and comprehensively for the long-term welfare of the city's people, there is a realistic political argument for it to take a leading role in the matter. All political leaders have a vested interested in staying in power; it goes with the territory. They have no incentive to tolerate protest, or certainly to encourage it, unless it may lead to a loss of voter confidence such as to threaten their continuation in office. The NYC Planning Commission, by contrast, is specifically created as a nonpartisan commission, and has very limited powers; its members are not dependent on their position for their livelihood or status. Those concerned about the uses of adequate space in the city for purposes that include political protest can attempt to persuade a sitting mayor that a negative attitude will incur a political cost to him or her. Directing the attention of the city's leaders to the somewhat less partisan Planning Commission may facilitate the beginning of a constructive discussion.

References

Flegenheimer, M. 2011. "In Newark, a More Welcoming Response to Occupiers." *New York Times*, November 27.

Is "Public Space" Possible?

David Burney

IN A SMALL VILLAGE in northern England where I often spend time, I walk up to feed the ducks at a large triangular meadow about the size of a football field, with a small duck pond surrounded on two sides by cottages and one side by a road. No one "owns" this field; it is the "village green," where you can sit on a bench under an oak tree and watch the world go by. In Britain, a "green" is any land on which a significant number of inhabitants have indulged in lawful sports and pastimes for twenty years as of right. There are no signs telling you what you can or cannot do, nor signs indicating ownership or jurisdiction. As far as the village is concerned, the green has always been this way. I don't quite know what would happen if someone tried to enclose it or take it over for some private use. No one has ever tried. If you continue up the hill from the commons, you come onto a vast area of grass and bracken, unfenced and unmarked, with sheep and the occasional cow grazing. These too are "common land" on which local farmers are free to graze their sheep, although they do not own the land. Farmers mark each of their sheep with a dye to distinguish them from those of other farms.

Some days I walk from my village to the next—about a forty-five-minute walk, through both common land and private fields. The path is well marked, with stiles to get over fences and drystone walls. This path is one of the nationally recognized trails in England and Wales, designated and managed by the Countryside Agency or the Countryside Council for Wales. They include some of the best-known routes in Britain, passing through some of its most beautiful countryside and areas of great historic interest. They are

271

all clearly indicated by a standard acorn symbol and described in a series of official guidebooks published by Aurum Press and easily obtainable from bookshops. The surface of the path is for most purposes considered to belong to the local highway authority: what this means is that the authority owns the surface of the way and as much of the soil below and the air above as is necessary for the control, protection, and maintenance of the highway. The rest normally belongs to the owner of the surrounding land. Before legislation was introduced to protect these trails, common law required that they be used at least once a year to keep them in the public domain. Many of the walking and hiking clubs in Britain (the Ramblers Association in particular) used to organize hikes to complete this requirement each year and keep the trails open.

There are also unmarked routes along existing public paths that have been described in print but are not specially indicated on the ground. They can be created by anyone who is prepared to research and publicize a route, and many fade into obscurity, but others find a gap in the market and can become as popular and well known as the National Trails. Many of the presently marked routes began as unofficial paths created by individuals and walkers' groups.

There are some rules associated with the trails as they pass through private land. Walkers are allowed to pass without hindrance, but they must not damage crops or fences other than what is necessary for passage through. By the same token, private owners may not obstruct the reasonable and free passage of walkers. For example, a farmer may keep "a bull of up to ten months old" in the field, but bulls over ten months are banned unless accompanied by cows or heifers. If any bulls act in a way that endangers the public, this is considered an offense under health and safety legislation.

There are 1.3 million acres of common land in England and Wales, divided in over nine thousand separate units covering all types of landscape and habitat. Common land is unique. It is historical land that has remained largely undisturbed through the centuries, a remnant of medieval times when people relied on a commons for their survival. The main reason for Britain's legacy of common land and public rights-of-way through private property is that before the agricultural revolution most land was common land, freely used by famers to graze animals and grow crops. Each village would be surrounded by several large open fields, usually not physically divided from each other, with each field containing a different crop as part of a three-field crop rotation. The fields would be split into sections a furlong (220 yards, about 200 meters) wide, each of which would be subdivided crosswise into strips covering an area of half an acre (about 0.2 hectares) or less. Under their commoner's rights, each villager was allocated a set number of strips in each field (traditionally about thirty), which they would use as a subsistence farm. The strips were generally allocated by lot in a public meeting at the start of the year. The individual holdings were widely scattered so that no single farmer would end up with all the good or bad land. In addition to the three fields, there would be large common meadows (allocated in strips in a similar way), common pasture land or "waste" where the villagers would graze their livestock throughout the year, woodland for the pigs and for timber, and a communal village green for social events.

As populations increased, the land available for each family diminished. From the late Middle Ages onwards, a gradual movement towards consolidation took place as small plots were amalgamated into fewer but larger holdings, with a corresponding increase in the power of the landowners. The enclosure movement in Britain ended traditional rights such as mowing meadows for hay or grazing livestock on common land. Once enclosed, these uses of the land became restricted to the owner; by the nineteenth century, unenclosed commons had become largely limited to rough pastures in mountainous areas and to relatively small parts of the lowlands.

The history of land ownership in the United States is, of course, quite different. In America's "ownership society," there seems to be a fear of the "un-owned." Someone, it seems, has to own everything; no land can be an orphan. This approach was painfully implemented by the early European settlers who appropriated and fenced land for exclusive private use, seizing it from the American Indians for whom the concept of land ownership had no meaning.

By the time of the Industrial Revolution in Britain, with its increased urban density, common land was largely unknown and the "village green" had been replaced by the town square associated with a church or a market. This is the most common urban form of public open space that we still see today. It seems that most of the large urban public assembly places began for commercial purposes and later became convenient venues for social or political gatherings. The fact that these public places were not in individual control or ownership no doubt contributed to their suitability for public gatherings. With the rise of capitalism and urbanization, organized labor started to use public spaces as a venue for mass demonstrations to advance their agenda.

There has always been resistance to the free use of public space for demonstrations, from Baron Haussmann's deliberate widening of the Parisian boulevards in order to prevent demonstrators from barricading them to the notorious suppression of freedom in Tiananmen Square. The Occupy movement has recently brought this issue to the fore once again: what is public space, who owns it, and who has the right to control its use? The 99% may be deprived of an increasing share of societal wealth, but do they still retain the right to occupy public space in the manner of medieval times? And what is public space? It would seem that the First Amendment should require some accommodation for groups who want to assemble in pursuit of their right to free speech, and the urban public plaza would appear to be the obvious choice. So why are so few of our plazas conducive to that right, and why was that choice ultimately denied at Zuccotti Park and other urban public spaces?

As Peter Marcuse (2011) put forth in his recent blog:

> The demands of the First Amendment set a minimum threshold for the exercise of the right to free speech, but what is needed is not the ability to speak freely out in the desert, inaccessible to most and heard by few. Rather, what is needed are publicly available spaces that can fulfill the functions of the traditional agora, places where free men and women can meet, debate, speak to and listen to each other, learn from each other, confront issues of public concern and facilitate their resolution.

Marcuse goes on to list a series of minimum services that public spaces should provide to support First Amendment rights, such as sanitary facilities, sound systems, fire extinguishers, safe connections to power lines, and even efficient sources of heat and protection from the elements. In other words, we could easily make arrangements for groups such as "Occupy" to speak and meet in safety and security. But we don't. Are we so afraid of dissent?

A major reason often cited for the restriction of free access to public space is security. This became a clarion cry used not just after the 9/11 attacks, but also after the 1995 bombing of the Oklahoma City federal office building. The prevention of terrorist attacks on civilians is a serious business and one that often involves necessary restrictions on certain freedoms. We are caught in a dilemma: the resistance to terrorism ends up forcing us to infringe the very liberties that we are defending from terrorism. Nowhere is this irony more apparent than in the public realm—our streets, airports, public buildings, and public spaces. But there is a sense that we are always caught "fighting the last war" and that we erect pedestrian and vehicular barriers into our public spaces because it is the only thing we know how to do, even when we know that it will not defend us from the next determined attacker with a "backpack" or "dirty" bomb. More recent and sophisticated counterterrorism relies on surveillance and prevention more than physical barriers, and we may have to give up some of our traditional privacy if we are to return our public spaces to a more normal civilian use. The fear of terrorism is real and it has sadly transformed our public spaces into potential targets. But we have to preserve our right to use our public spaces for legitimate social purposes.

It is not just political demonstrations that need support. Public space is a vital component of urban life, an indicator of the health and life of a city. A healthy and vibrant city needs a variety of public spaces that support a wide range of social activities. Such public spaces should be designed to meet certain physical criteria such as size and proportion, with well-designed buildings to enclose and define them. At the same time, however, public spaces should also retain an element of ambiguity, an ambiguity that is not easily usurped by authority. As Marshall Berman has commented, democracy thrives on a certain degree of "sloppiness"—and this is also true of successful public spaces. (See also Marshall Berman's essay in this volume.) It might even make sense, even though it goes against the grain of designers and planners, to leave some parts of public space unfinished, so as to allow for the spontaneous and the unexpected.

We have to stop thinking about public space as something that has to be captured and tidied up, and think of it as an enabler—what Jeffrey Hou (2010) calls "insurgent public space." (See also Jeffrey Hou's essay in this volume.) We should design public spaces *for* political protest, not to prevent it. One thought might be to provide more of the open-air "band shells" where we currently allow music performances. Why not allow them to be used for public debate, and provide more of them? We should also review the ever-increasing list of "rules" that we allow our government to impose on our right to assemble in public places: from restrictions of use to certain times of the day to the prohibition of many of the amenities that emerged in Zuccotti Park. Ideally, as a society we should be able to support the modern equivalent of the village green and the commons—areas where we not only allow but also support and encourage the unexpected and the insurgent. A healthy city needs such spaces. A healthy democracy should demand them.

References

Hou, J. 2010. *Insurgent Public Space: Guerilla Urbanism and the Remaking of Contemporary Cities*. New York: Routledge.

Marcuse, P. 2011. "Occupy and the Provision of Public Space: The City's Responsibilities." *Peter Marcuse's Blog*, December 1. http://pmarcuse.wordpress.com/2011/12/01/occupy-and-the-provision-of-public-space-the-citys-responsibility/.

Making—and Governing—
Places for Democracy

Brad Lander and Michael Freedman-Schnapp

WHEN OCCUPY WALL STREET (OWS)
landed in Zuccotti Park on September 17, 2011, the movement cast a bright
light on many contradictions in American democracy. The "occupiers" successfully refocused the nation's popular anger about growing income inequality, the outsize role of money in politics, and the fact that banks were
not held accountable for their damage to the global economy.

The venue and methods of the occupiers' protests also raised compelling questions about the space we make for participatory democracy in
our society—about where, when, and how we allow and encourage protest,
democratic debate, and expressive action. While important elements of this
movement took place online and via social media, much of it took place in
physical space. One key to the success of OWS—and also to the strong negative feelings it evoked in critics—was embedded in the form of the protest,
the occupation of quasi-public space. Many of those drawn to OWS were
electrified by the conversion of a park space into a robust, public, democratic
dialogue. Many who were repelled by OWS were traumatized by the same
conversion of Zuccotti Park.

As practitioners of community planning and local democracy, we have
frequently been struck by a broad hunger—extending far beyond Zuccotti
and those who participated in the occupation—for a more dynamic public
realm that offers and encourages more active democratic civic engagement.
We hope that in addition to continuing campaigns against inequality, against
money in politics, and for genuine financial reform, a legacy of OWS will

be a renewed sense of the possibility for enlivening our democracy with vibrant physical spaces for democratic action.

For urban planners who delight in zoning arcana, one particularly poignant professional irony surrounding OWS was the prominent cameo role played by the privately owned public space (POPS) of Zuccotti Park. The occupiers brilliantly exploited a loophole that made the whole endeavor possible since they would likely never have been allowed to camp out in any official New York City park, where both remaining past 1 a.m. and camping at any time without permits are illegal. The contradictions that played out at Zuccotti among constitutional protections for free speech and assembly, private property rights, police enforcement, and the city's zoning law offer a great starting place for thinking about a broader range of issues.

In this essay, we therefore begin with an examination of the policy contradictions surrounding POPS and suggest more democratic processes for setting rules there. But the call for a more engaged public realm extends far beyond POPS. We go on to explore policy opportunities for re-enlivening public places for democratic expression—in our parks and (newly emerging) plazas, in our public libraries, and in new models like "participatory budgeting" (which we are helping to pilot in New York City) that offer democratic engagement in planning not only *in* but also *for* the public realm.

Zuccotti Park: Your Pop's POPS

In the United States, privately owned public spaces (POPS) have been a tool for real-estate-led urban development ever since the creation of Rockefeller Plaza in the 1930s. In Manhattan, especially in the financial district, POPS offered in exchange for density bonuses on adjacent developments often helped to open up a number of narrow streets to add more space for pedestrian circulation as well as much-needed light, air, and open space (Garvin 2011). In some cases, these spaces helped anchor the revitalization of whole urban districts. Despite these benefits, POPS in New York City have often been operated in such a way as to exclude some or all members of the public. The examples are myriad, but even after several years of consistent work by the NYC Department of City Planning to fight violations, many still remain off limits to the public.[1] Many urban practitioners and planners questioned

---

1. A particularly egregious example from March 2012 that outlines the difficulty in enforcing

if the sizable benefits offered to developers were worth the meager spaces that had been created in exchange (Stern, Fishman, and Mellins 1997, 103).

As POPS are, by definition, owned by adjacent property owners, there are inherent tensions between the maintenance of POPS for maximum public access versus owners' desires for orderly management of the space. The public is noisy. The public generates trash. Members of the public can often be disruptive. The public often looks different from the tenants of the owner's building. Hence, owners of POPS often desire to closely manage or minimize public usage of the space in ways that are inconsistent with robust public usage.

Because a complex set of interactions between idiosyncratic deed restrictions, zoning laws, and constitutionally protected property rights underlie the legal framework in which POPS sit, the state has limited authority to control or enable activities on these spaces. The extent to which the police powers can be legally used to either uphold property owners' rights or to enable active public usage of POPS is a murky area that was brought to full display in Zuccotti Park.

The regulations that govern older POPS in New York City need a closer look. For those created before 2007, the process for posting park rules was left especially murky.[2] Witness the vagaries of what rules can be posted at Zuccotti and how they are enforced. At one point, users of the space were camping in violation of posted rules without fomenting police action. At another, users were harassed for bringing in pizza boxes, lest they become caches of food (although who wants to eat old pizza in downtown Manhattan when dozens of sources for fresh thin-crust pizza are within a short walk?).

We should not leave this complicated balance up to the courts to decide on a case-by-case basis. In an ongoing court case regarding an arrest for trespass at Zuccotti Park on the morning of November 15, 2011, the court's

---

POPS integrity involved an Upper East Side luxury residential tower that closed a vest pocket park that previously held a playground. The NYC Department of Buildings, upon receiving a complaint, initially found "no public space" and did not write a violation for the building until a reporter, following up on a tip from a community member, called the NYC Department of Buildings for comment. Cf. Zimmer 2012.

2. The NYC Department of City Planning implemented a 2007 comprehensive revision of the POPS plaza rules in the NYC Zoning Resolution, along with a 2009 follow-up corrective action, that disallowed all rule of conduct signs except for a single, one-square-foot sign in plazas built after the effective date of the revision. See the NYC Zoning Resolution, Section 37-752.

decision focused more on Brookfield's potential liability as a property owner than on the value of any expressive conduct.[3] (See also Arthur Eisenberg's essay in this volume.) This is the kind of public policy decision that either needs to be made by an elected body or a public rulemaking process that balances the exercise of police powers versus the need to maintain a robust environment for speech and assembly along with the public's ability to give input to that decision. We also should not delegate private owners as proxy for the government in deciding whether they are complying with constitutional requirements.

However, it is not a simple task to achieve this balance between public access, constitutional freedoms, and property rights while still respecting the underlying agreement that enabled the plaza in the first place. Those who have taken a basic property law course are familiar with the notion that there is a "bundle of rights" associated with property ownership and that these rights can be separated from each other (e.g., mineral rights, air rights, or easements for utilities). But at its fundamental level, land ownership typically means that the owner has "exclusive" control over the space—that is, he or she controls access to the space and can exclude any or all people from it. The creation of a privately owned public space means, at a minimum, the partial, if not total, waiving of the owner's right—you can't have a park or plaza and still exclude people.

This waiver of exclusive access is memorialized in a restrictive covenant, declaration, or easement that accompanies the property. This agreement is typically made for perpetuity and is binding for both the landowner and the municipality. Any changes to the legal agreements underlying POPS after their signing must be further negotiated between the landowners and the municipality.[4] Because the creation of POPS are almost always initiated by

---

3. *New York v. Ronnie Nunez,*. Crim Ct, New York County, April 6, 2012, Sciarrino, M., Docket No. 2011 NY 082981.

4. There are further questions of who speaks for the municipality and its interests that are tangential to this issue but still quite interesting. For purposes of simplification in this essay, we discuss a unitary municipal interest that is interested in balancing order and freedoms. In reality, there is a multiplicity of municipal interests that seek to achieve these balances at different levels—the many members of the New York City Council might seek to protect constitutional rights to assemble at a higher level than the mayor and his agencies, which might prize order slightly more. And within the administration, there is also a multiplicity of interests. The NYC Department of City Planning, which strongly directs the actions of the City Planning

the landowner seeking a benefit (say, building a bigger building than allowed as of right), any modification to the agreement that pushes in the direction of additional public access (say, increasing the hours of access, revoking rules of conduct that are burdensome on particular desirable activities, or seeking the removal of gates that are in conformance with the agreement) can only be achieved if the owner of the space wishes to gain more benefit. The public interest for such changes to older plazas is not a consideration under current law however much policy makers may wish it to be. The land remains owned by a private entity that continues to enjoy the private rights that remain pursuant to the original agreement.

This is the legal context in which Zuccotti Park/Liberty Plaza lies. It is a direct product of the plaza section of the 1961 NYC Zoning Resolution. The original law gave a great deal of flexibility to the design and operation of the space to the property owner. As urbanists, beginning with the pioneering work of Holly Whyte, learned more about how public spaces work best and as the NYC Department of City Planning gained more expertise in administering the program, the zoning code was revised in 2007 and 2009 to implement new design and rule guidelines for operators of POPS.

However, the NYC Zoning Resolution has a quite conservative grandfathering of nonconforming situations (one that brings perhaps as many benefits as burdens for a city as complicated as New York), which has been carried forward in new revisions of the law. Therefore, the new plaza rules do not apply to the older plazas, and the same laws that governed the earliest plazas (those created in the era of the international style, Robert Moses, superblocks, and *Mad Men*) still remain in effect. By comparison, other cities have more aggressive zoning codes than New York City's that may require the adoption of newer design guidelines and regulations for plazas at the time their related building undergoes a major renovation or expansion.

Ironically, the POPS formerly known as Liberty Plaza—originally opened in 1972—was damaged in the 9/11 attacks, briefly reopened for a couple of years, and then reopened in 2006 as the newly-christened Zuccotti Park.[5] The newer plaza rules did not apply because the underlying build-

---

Commission, might seek to uphold the integrity of the POPS zoning text, whereas the Police Department might emphasize the restoration of order regardless of the zoning rules.

5. See the affidavit of Edith-Hsu Chen in support of *Amicus Curiae* City of New York, *People v. Nunez*, March 5, 2012.

ing was not rebuilt; rather, the special permit from the NYC City Planning Commission that underlies the legal existence of the plaza was modified in 2005 to allow the redesign. Even though we knew so much more about design of good urban spaces than was known in 1972, the NYC City Planning Commission's hands were handcuffed in moving the plaza toward those ends.

This issue concerns not only design but also the rules governing conduct in those plazas and, as very visibly demonstrated by Occupy Wall Street, what can be done for cases in which a private landowner is calling for police action in response to violations of posted rules.

Some of the trouble with the 1961 plaza standards[6] derives from the NYC Zoning Resolution's silence on the rules that can be posted and enforced. In response to this issue, the 2007 modifications adopted rules that allow only one "prohibition" or "rules of conduct" sign. These signs cannot prohibit "behaviors that are consistent with the normal public use of the public plaza such as lingering, eating, drinking of nonalcoholic beverages or gathering in small groups. No behaviors, actions, or items may be listed on such sign that are otherwise illegal or prohibited by municipal, State, or Federal laws."[7]

Regardless of what signs can be posted, and looking beyond the issue of enforcement at Zuccotti, a series of questions remain that must be asked about when the police can be called to enforce plaza rules in general. For example, if it is a posted rule that plaza users cannot wear red hats, is it within the power of a police officer to enter the plaza and enforce that rule on his or her own recognizance? If a security guard employed by the plaza owner asks a police officer to enforce the rule, is that officer on more solid ground? Or are the police limited to enforcing the law of trespass? If so, when is it trespassing on a plaza whose owner signed away his or her right of exclusive access to the city? Is it only when a user is in a plaza outside the legally mandated hours? Or, by breaking a posted rule, does a user become an uninvited guest who can be legally evicted by the owner? What if the posted rule that users are breaking is the use of their rights to peaceably assemble and free speech?

While the exact legal answer to these questions can only be (and may

---

6. See NYC Zoning Resolution, Appendix E, Section 27-50.

7. See NYC Zoning Resolution, Section 37-752. This piece of the NYC Zoning Resolution does not apply to Zuccotti Park because it is a "plaza"—the legal term for the category of pre-2007 POPS that applies to it.

be) tested by a series of court cases, we take the view that it would be good to proactively answer them. We need a clear, public process for promulgating rules for POPS similar to the way that plaza owners must seek public review by the NYC City Planning Commission to establish nighttime closing hours. A public hearing, a review for rule consistency across spaces, and a review of the impact on free speech and assembly rights should be required. That way, when the public relinquishes rights of access to the owner of a POPS for the sake of safety, it is through a form of public review that is supervised by an agency charged with maintaining public access to the POPS, such as the NYC Department of City Planning under review from the NYC City Planning Commission and with input from the community boards and borough president. And most importantly, such a process would be able to roll back any rules that prove to be troublesome to administer and turn out to be constitutionally suspect in practice.

The interest in clarifying these rules is not limited to a narrow band of civil libertarians, urban policy wonks, legal theorists, and occupiers. The managers of business improvement districts certainly want vital urban spaces, but they also want to have clarity about the rules of the spaces that are throughout the areas they cover in New York City. Police departments can make up their own internal guidelines about when to intervene in POPS, but further clarity for line officers about when they should be doing the bidding of landowners would be helpful.

Furthermore, the public deserves clarity about the expectations of conduct when in a space that appears to be a public space. The lines between a sidewalk, a park, and a POPS are not always clear to a layperson, especially during times of protest when free speech and assembly rights are tested. To the casual observer, Zuccotti (especially post-renovation) appears to be a piece of the urban environment that is indistinguishable from the sidewalk or a park only in its design. After all, the ground rules would have been extremely clear (although quite strict) had Occupy Wall Street started off in a city park—in a citywide park, any camping or remaining in most parks after 1 a.m. would have been swiftly addressed by the authorities.

What About Our Public/Public Spaces?

While Occupy Wall Street's occupation of Zuccotti Park most directly highlights the governance issues in quasi-public spaces, if we want free expression—expressly political gatherings, but also cultural and civic events that bring people together to debate, learn, and create in diverse ways—to flourish in New York City, we need to take a hard look at our fully public spaces as well. If we want to have "civic squares" in our diverse city, we can't simply assume that democratic free expression will take place there. If "active recreation" means only volleyball (or even cricket), if filling up new plazas with activity means only delightful folding tables for drinking coffee (or even eating samosas), and if renewing our libraries focuses exclusively on providing much-needed computers for job seekers, we will miss an essential opportunity to enliven democratic, cultural, and political expression.

This is partially a question of regulation, but not only that. New York City lacks a place like Speakers' Corner in London's Hyde Park, though it is certainly not prohibited. The challenge is not simply one of government regulation that prohibits or allows; we also need a deeper democratic culture that supports speech and activism that matter. One thing that has been striking in the first six months of Occupy protests is a profound ambivalence about the kind of out-loud, public, "human mic," messy, political speech and protest. On the one hand, mainstream media and political discourse has patronized OWS as something self-indulgent, radical, and weird (and many Americans who share some of OWS participants' political critiques feel the same). On the other hand, the form of expression has clearly been fascinating and compelling to hundreds of thousands of people who came to rallies, follow OWS in social media, or were captivated by the message. What might it look like (regardless of what happens with Occupy in the coming months) if we looked to create Speakers' Corners in places throughout the city, providing more direct access to political debate and protest?

Parks

We often take our New York City parks for granted as open and available public spaces. They are indeed magnificent spaces for an extraordinarily diverse range of activities that incorporate people from every race, religion, community, and background—including a wide array of cultural events, from sports to concerts to drum circles to cultural festivals. But in recent years, opportunities for free expression have been restricted. Large-scale protests have been made elusive by park officials. Concerns about grass,

Figure 1. The Expressive Matter Vendor logo. *Courtesy of the New York City Department of Parks & Recreation*

trash, and maintenance are of course real. But if they can be answered for concerts, we should be able to answer them for protests as well. If the city cannot provide a space where truly large-scale protests can take place (or insists on penning protests into spaces that are too small and ill suited), we should not be surprised when protestors break the rules and occupy other spaces.

Park rules matter for freedom of expression in areas beyond protests. In 2010, the NYC Department of Parks & Recreation (DPR) promulgated new rules to restrict the spaces where art vendors could operate in Central Park, Union Square, Battery Park, and the High Line, arguing that areas of these parks had become too congested. According to the department's website, in these parks, "expressive matter vendors may only vend expressive matter at the specifically designated spots identified by the commissioner." These designated zones are marked with bright white lines and a logo (Figure 1).

Artists fought back, arguing not only that the policy unnecessarily restricts free expression but also that the "first-come-first-served" system (no permit is required) has resulted in a "survival of the fittest system," which has a discriminatory effect on women, the disabled, and the elderly, as some vendors sleep out overnight nearby in an effort to get the spots. There is a public interest in making sure that a wide variety of spaces in our parks is available for a wide variety of uses. And of course, art vending is a commercial activity, not solely one of free expression. But the Bloomberg administration's impulse to restrict reveals a less-than-fully-embracing understanding of New York City parks as spaces that have a core mission of welcoming, nurturing, and encouraging free expression, popular education, cultural production, and community organizing.

These tensions have emerged as well in public parks created outside of the DPR's jurisdiction, as the Bloomberg administration has done with Governors Island and Brooklyn Bridge Park. In the fall of 2010, officials from Brooklyn Bridge Park sought to evict an art vendor, initially arguing that the rules established by their Board of Trustees trumped city and state laws.[8] The park's leadership later agreed that they would follow the DPR's expressive matter policy (though it is not at all clear that they are legally obligated to do so).

Plazas

Beyond the parks (whether public or private), one important new resource for a more community-based approach to cultural and political activity are the plazas that have begun to flourish under NYC Department of Transportation Commissioner Janette Sadik-Khan. As part of her effort to make New York City's streets safer and more livable, the NYC Department of Transportation (DOT) has converted spaces that were previously part of streets into spaces for public gathering, beginning with Times Square, which is now full of tourists and workers enjoying coffee and engaged in conversation in places where cars once reigned. (See also Janette Sadik-Khan's essay in this volume.)

In 2008, the DOT expanded their plaza effort to focus on creating neighborhood plazas in low-income communities with too little open space through a request-for-proposals that offered city design and construction funding to "transform underused streets into vibrant, social public spaces." New plazas now exist in Jackson Heights, Corona, and Fort Greene and are planned in dozens of neighborhoods around the city. They offer space not only for drinking coffee but also for neighborhood programming—cultural performances, concerts, games, movie nights, speakers, etc.

Of course, many of the same challenges exist for these plazas as for other public spaces as well as some new ones, such as the frequent complaints by drivers about lost parking spaces. The new plazas have been most often used for commercial activity (albeit diverse commerce, like food vending), only sometimes used for cultural programming, and more rarely used for political or civic activity (although our office held a vigil against Islamophobic graffiti in a new plaza space we helped to create in Kensington).

While business improvement districts maintain Manhattan plazas, the DOT's concept is that not-for-profit partners will maintain and program

8. Brooklyn Bridge Park is not part of the NYC Department of Parks & Recreation, but instead governed by a not-for-profit corporation where the mayor, outside of normal city council oversight, appoints a majority on the board of trustees.

the outer-borough neighborhood plazas. But this has proved a significant challenge. There is not much money to be made in licensing out the use of these neighborhood plazas, and community-based not-for-profit organizations in low-income neighborhoods are already stretched. As it is, they can barely come up with the resources to provide for basic sanitation and maintenance, much less dynamic programming. Hopefully in the years to come, new resources—financial, volunteer, cultural—will be developed so that these spaces can truly become the "vibrant, social public spaces" envisioned by the DOT.

Libraries

One other hidden—and not yet fully realized or appreciated—treasure of New York City civic spaces are our public libraries, which are at a crossroads moment. As sad as it is for many of us, over the next few decades, libraries will cease to have as their primary purpose serving as a repository for beautiful tomes of paper and binding. Rather than be nostalgic, we need to look at this as an enormous opportunity. Public libraries have already rapidly become the gateway to the Internet for millions of New Yorkers who lack good connections at home, for research, reading, job searches, and entertainment.

But the transformation of neighborhood branch libraries should go beyond this. At their best, libraries are places where knowledge and culture are both *consumed* and *produced*. This has always been true to some extent, as many writers and poets have written in public libraries, and readings (for kids and adults) often taken place in library community rooms. Digital technologies create new opportunities to extend this tradition. Some libraries are starting to not only lend out e-books but also video cameras and editing equipment, allowing people to create their own work—and some are offering classes to help people learn to use these technologies, which will be ever more critical tools in the future.

With modest additional resources, libraries can be civic and cultural gathering spaces as well. Many of New York City's neighborhood libraries have community rooms with a stage and enough space for neighborhood performances, readings, and civic meetings. At the same time, artists are constantly looking for affordable space to rehearse, to create, and to perform, and community groups constantly struggle to find good spaces for meetings. The resources needed to equip these rooms with a decent wireless network and Internet access, a sound system, and a system for easy reservations are modest. In many cases, "Friends of the Library" groups are eager to help out. But we need a deeper civic and governing commitment. For too long, public libraries have been first on the chopping block at budget time. As a result, few neighborhood branches offer adequate evening or weekend hours, the times that are essential for bringing many neighborhood residents into the branches.

Yes, let's get five hundred thousand people in Sheep's Meadow to rally and protest, but let's also get thirty-five young people in the branch library talking about the problems with stop-and-frisk activity in their neighborhood, or a diverse group of artists curating a neighborhood exhibition, or a group of freelancers using rooms for collaboration, or a class where people are learning to create and edit video and radio programs of local interest. Community organizing meetings can take place anywhere, but we submit that something magical happens when they take place in the public library.

Democratic Expression about (and not only in) the Public Realm

Finally, democratic expression doesn't only have to be *in* the public realm—it can also be *about* the public realm. We have seen a great hunger amongst our constituents to plan for, dream about, and concretely improve the streets, parks, subways, sidewalks, and libraries in their neighborhood.

Inspired by this interest, we worked with three other New York City Council Members' offices in 2011 and 2012 to bring "participatory budgeting" to New York. Participatory budgeting is a democratic process in which community members directly decide how to spend part of a public budget. Participatory budgeting was initiated over two decades ago in Brazil (Porto Alegre) and has been used in over three thousand cities around the world. However, it has been used very little in the United States, where the first pilot program was undertaken by Chicago Alderman Joe Moore, and the recent program by council members Lander, Mark-Viverito, Ulrich, and Williams was the largest to date. The process gives citizens real decision-making power over real money—in our case, one million dollars from the council members' capital budget discretionary fund, money that can only be used for "physical public improvements."

Voters examine their potential choices on how to spend $1 million in the 2011-2012 Participatory Budgeting Process. *Photo by Michael Freedman-Schnapp*

Across the process, we were strongly impressed by the desire for and engagement with a more robust public realm across the diverse communities of our district and New York City. The process began with a series of neighborhood assemblies where hundreds of members of the community came out to suggest ideas for improving the neighborhood. Volunteer "budget delegate" committees then met over several months to develop the ideas into concrete projects, figure out which were the most needed, meet with city agencies to establish feasibility and cost, and prepare the projects for the ballot. In the last week of March 2012, residents of the four districts came out to vote. More than 2,200 residents of our district, and more than 6,000 citywide, came out to have their say.

Participatory budgeting is not only about the projects—it is about involving people more deeply in democracy. We extended voting rights so that any adult living in the neighborhood could vote regardless of immigration or criminal justice status, held voting across several days, translated ballots into the languages spoken in our communities (including Spanish and Bengali), and partnered with community groups like Community Voices Heard to conduct extensive outreach and "get-out-the-vote" operations. The results were encouraging. As documented by the Urban Justice Center, participation was deeper and more diverse than typical elections. In our

Community members discuss potential Participatory Budgeting projects. *Photo by Alex Moore*

district, the Bangladeshi community in Kensington came out in a far higher percentage than in any previous election, especially Bangladeshi women:

> "Men felt like they have a power that they can make a choice, but for the first time the women felt like, 'Oh, I can do that too,'" said a resident, Annie Ferdous, who translated the voter information into Bengali. "They saw the ballot in Bengali and thought, 'O.K., maybe I can understand and get involved.'" (Sangha 2012b)

Across the four districts, the proportion of voters with household incomes below $25,000 was nearly ten times higher than in the last municipal election. More Latinos came out in East Harlem as well as more people from public housing in East Flatbush and the Rockaways. The scene at the Windsor Terrace Library, where Bangladeshis, Latinos, long-time residents, and young families came out in large numbers, patiently waited in a long line, met their neighbors, and had a chance to talk about the twenty projects on the ballot across lines of race and class was one of the most inspiring examples of participatory democracy that many voters had ever witnessed.

While bread-and-butter projects like road paving or increased street lighting were very popular, so too were a variety of projects that sought to enhance the public realm—rebuilding a subway station entrance, adding more benches in commercial strips, having digital displays to tell you when the next bus arrives, and converting a little-used street segment into a public plaza or enhancing the local park. In East Harlem, the biggest winning project will bring playground improvements in public housing complexes. In Queens, voters chose new equipment for their volunteer fire departments and projects to preserve the community's beaches from erosion and flooding. In East Flatbush, where crime makes some neighborhood parks so unsafe that many residents fear using them, they chose security cameras and lighting. In our district, voters chose to improve decrepit bathrooms in a public school, add technology in two others, create a new community composting site, plan new street trees, and make repairs to the path system in Brooklyn's Prospect Park.

There were more than a few challenging projects that were popular but failed to fit neatly into a specific mechanism that the city has at its disposal— creating and installing local public art, creating a monument to the mother languages of a diverse immigrant neighborhood, or installing a community Wi-Fi network. The rapidly growing local Bangladeshi community, for example, came out in large numbers to vote for an "International Mother Language Monument" to commemorate the movement that led to Bangladeshi independence and to celebrate the broader struggle (recognized with a UN holiday on the same day, February 21st) of people around the world preserving their mother tongues. While this project did not win, it has sparked community organizing that will likely help bring about the full renovation of a neighborhood park, including the monument.

It is clear to us that people desire both a better public realm and more inclusion in the governance that shapes the public spaces they use every day. More importantly, the process of participatory budgeting for concrete improvements in the public realm can help transform individuals and deepen our democracy. As sixteen-year-old Marcus Monfiston, a student at Tilden High School who worked together with classmates to create and campaign for a proposal to add lights to their ball fields, told a *New York Times* reporter: "I was like, I can really make a change…We're not just here to go to school. We can be more, do more" (Sangha 2012a).

Conclusion

In his recent book on the New Left of the 1960s, *Participatory Democracy: The Dream of Port Huron*, Tom Hayden (one of the authors of the Port Huron Statement and a founder of Students for a Democratic Society, and later a state legislator in California) identifies the deepening of participatory democracy as a key element of the students and civil rights movements of the 1960s and an important link to Occupy Wall Street. As the New Left showed then, and as Occupy shows now, it is not only the substance of a social movement that matters but also the process of deepening participation, of enfranchising more people to believe that their voices can matter.

These opportunities for democratic engagement, for participatory democracy, can also extend well beyond the spaces of protest and into the lives of millions. As our libraries, parks, community theaters, and plazas show—as we saw again in participatory budgeting—there is a great hunger to be part of achieving things together. We believe that this will largely answer those who seek to drown government in a bathtub, to make us doubt what we can do together, to trick us into thinking that our shared vision will be swallowed by bureaucracy. In the creative, energetic, sustained, diverse, and sometimes messy partnerships between government and civil society, people take voice and action with neighbors (and, through social media, with people halfway around the world) to create the communities that support, sustain, and inspire us.

An essential element of these efforts is the places where participatory democracy can occur. As C. Wright Mills taught, we cannot have "democracy without publics." These need not be uniform—they are at least as varied as Zuccotti Park, the neighborhood branch library, a participatory budgeting delegate meeting, and the Internet—but they must be protected and nurtured. Beyond Zuccotti, we must learn not only to occupy but also to be—together—creators and stewards of our public realm.

References

Garvin, A. 2011. "The 1961 Zoning Resolution: Evolution in Response to Changing Conditions." Lecture, November 15.

Sangha, S. 2012a. "Putting in Their Two Cents." *New York Times*, April 1.

———. 2012b. "The Voters Speak: Yes to Bathrooms." *New York Times*, April 8.

Stern, R., D. Fishman, and T. Mellins. 1997. *New York 1960*. New York: Random House.

Zimmer, A. 2012. "Luxe High-Rise Owner Cited for Locking Community Out of Public Plaza." *DNAInfo.com*, March 15. http://www.dnainfo.com/20120315/upper-east-side/luxury-highrise-owner-ticketed-after-locking-community-out-of-public-plaza.

Making Cities Work

Janette Sadik-Khan

ONE OF THE GREAT CHALLENGES
we face in making our cities work in the twenty-first century is leveraging their potential not only as the central incubators of cultural, social, and economic development but also as the places where most people on the planet now live. In the broad global scale, making cities work is critical to improving sustainability and confronting the challenges of climate change because cities are so much more efficient than any spread-out form of development. Making cities work for more people also means making them great places to live and great places to do business.

New York City's efforts in this regard stem from PlaNYC, the long-range sustainability and infrastructure plan launched in 2007 by Mayor Bloomberg. The plan's main premise was to use the city's growth as a lever to modernize many of its basic systems like housing, energy, and transportation; to address environmental challenges by upgrading and updating these systems; and to forge a better city overall. It challenged a lot of long-held practices in city government.

The strategies that we developed in the NYC Department of Transportation's policies and action agenda have three major dimensions—making mobility efficient, treating city streets as important public places, and making our streets safe for everyone using them. To realize these goals, we have instituted significant changes to New York City's streetscape in the last five years.

Prior to 2007, our streets primarily reflected the mid-twentieth-century ethos of making cities adapt to ever-increasing volumes of car traffic. Other urban planning considerations like the public nature of streets, urban open space, and neighborhood quality were crowded out by the singular engineering focus on moving vehicles. In rethinking our streets, we are grappling with the fact that a singular reliance on traffic engineering has left them ill designed for the many different demands put upon them today. It's long past time for an update. Our general point of view today is that city streets are incredibly valuable resources that are far from being used to their full potential or efficiency. To keep a growing city moving and thriving, and to make it an even better place to live, we need to change that.

These aren't just principles vaguely held by a few people—they are articulated as city policies in PlaNYC, which now must by law be updated every four years and set out as a detailed action plan in the NYC Department of Transportation's strategic plan. The plan has over 250 specific targets, and we've met or made major progress toward 95 percent of them. In practice, we found that many of these goals—safer streets, streets that welcome all types of users, and streets that reflect the social, entrepreneurial, and cultural vitality of New York—are mutually reinforcing.

For example, when in 2009 we tackled a problem that had been hidden in plain sight for decades by creating major new pedestrian spaces along Broadway, we not only created new signature public spaces in Times Square and Herald Square and a green corridor running through the heart of the city, but we also unlocked great economic value. Creating more pedestrian space plays to New York's strengths, and more people on foot, unharassed by crowding and traffic, have been great for business. Six months after the project was implemented, we counted an 11 percent increase in Times Square's pedestrian volume. Surveys showed that 84 percent more people engaged in activities there like reading, eating, or taking photos. Not coincidentally, in the fall of 2011, Times Square made Cushman & Wakefield's list of top ten retail locations in the world for the first time. Also for the first time, realtors are listing properties below 42nd Street as "Times Square South."

The area is also a nicer place in other ways. Before this transformation, Times Square had some of the highest concentrations in the city of nitrogen oxide and nitrogen dioxide, two pollutants closely associated with traffic. But after the conversion to a pedestrian plaza, our air quality monitors found that these levels plummeted, with nitrogen oxide down by 63 percent and nitrogen dioxide down 41 percent. Times Square is visited by over a quarter of a million people each day, so this is no small improvement regarding exposure to these pollutants.

As in other areas of our work, our goals and action plan for the city's public realm are spelled out in a clear policy document, World Class Streets, released in 2008. It reviewed our early projects along Broadway and in Madison Square and pointed ahead to the full transformation of Times and Herald Squares. New public spaces and plazas are in fact in demand by business communities and citizens all across the city. Our partnership model has business improvement districts and other local entities taking care of the spaces and the street furniture. Clearly, there has been a hunger for more places to enjoy the city—the plazas are extremely well used, as are the linkages along Broadway that create a pedestrian-oriented necklace through Midtown and south to Madison and Union Squares.

But interest and the embrace of new public places are not confined to one corridor, or to the Manhattan central business district. In the summer of 2011, we worked with local businesses and officials to reclaim New Lots Triangle in East New York—the site of a local business corridor and busy subway hub. There was great support—the opening was a big celebration—and there was an instinctive reaction about why you would do something like this to help improve the neighborhood.

These transformations can now be found all over. In Chelsea, extra lanes of traffic on 9th Avenue are now a popular public space. And in Brooklyn's DUMBO, in one of our earliest examples, it's very clear that with paint and large planters or pieces of stone, we can implement changes to these public areas quite quickly. By using temporary materials, we can change a project back to its original state if something doesn't work out, but that hasn't happened. This approach has since been taken up in other cities, especially San Francisco. In every case, these new plazas will be rebuilt with attractive, high quality materials. That will also begin to happen in Times Square later this year.

The NYC Department of Transportation (DOT) has two distinct plaza programs that lead to the creation of high quality public spaces around the city—the "quick" plazas, with paint, epoxied gravel, and large planters or pieces of stone, which can be installed rapidly and then transformed over time with high quality materials, and another set of plazas that start out as community-based applications to DOT's capital program. So far, the programs have approved fifty-four new sites, and there is widespread demand across the city. Construction is currently underway at two sites in Brooklyn and is about to start in the Bronx.

New public space is so popular in part because New York has long represented the contradiction of being a walking city with no place where you can just sit down and talk with a friend or people watch. Space can be at such a premium that basics like that go wanting, and this is why people materialize within minutes in places that we've opened for them.

Our early surveys of the city's streetscape concluded that New York is essentially a "city without seats." Frankly, that's not great for retailers, it's not great for neighborhoods with growing numbers of seniors, and it can be tough on parents with younger kids. We're trying to remedy this problem not only in places where we find opportunities to develop public plazas but also throughout our streetscape. Through our CityBench program, we will install one thousand newly designed benches across the city in the next two years.

We've also allowed curbside businesses to change curb lanes into strips of public seating in Midtown, Lower Manhattan, and Brooklyn. These pop-up cafés and capital program plazas are strictly application-based programs. This focuses new initiatives into places where people want them, dramatically reducing project negotiation and development times and bringing implementation into reasonable time scales.

An additional dimension to creating an interesting and welcoming set of public places is to use city streets for different purposes at different times. The past few summers, over two dozen city neighborhoods have created their own weekend pedestrian streets with a variety of noncommercial community-organized activities and performances through the Department of Transportation's Weekend Walks program. Our centerpiece here is Summer Streets—the traffic closure of Park Avenue and connecting streets on Saturdays in August, creating a seven-mile corridor for walking, running, dancing, skating, cycling, or just people watching. It's proven enormously popular, drawing an estimated eight hundred thousand people since the project's launch in 2008.

Ultimately, everything comes down to space—every square inch of the space on our streets is contested. Fortunately, these spaces can be versatile, and we're striving to make our streets work better and be safer, for pedestrians, cyclists, and drivers alike. Cities around the world are beginning to recognize their streets for what they can be—dynamic, livable spaces that balance the needs of everyone who uses them.

Our experience in New York City shows that with vision and commitment, you can change a city at minimal expense and bring vibrant, healthy green spaces to communities across a city in close to real time.

5.2

*Designers and Developers
as Agents of Change*

*Blurring the Boundaries
to Keep Public Space Public*

Paul Broches

THE OCCUPY WALL STREET movement
raises so many issues! The following essay includes selective observations
about the architecture of public space. There are many wonderful books
on the history and design of public spaces and parks. They include analyses of form, landscape, aesthetics, context, and programmatic content. Of
great interest to me are those that extend the analysis to the sociology of
cities and architecture as a social art. The intention of these remarks is to
explore access, invitation, and "ownership" of public spaces; and to examine

Figure 1. Occupying public spaces for assembly is about creating
opportunity and capturing the moment. *Photo by Paul Broches*

Figure 2. The doorstep is the ultimate threshold between the private and public domain.
Photo by Paul Broches

the differences between public spaces where we feel like guests and public spaces where we feel a strong sense of well-being, belonging, and, finally, possession.

We know that we have taken possession when public space allows us to feel comfortable strolling through it, sitting on a bench, throwing a Frisbee, or gathering for a family picnic. We raise the bar on ownership when we take part in large gatherings, collective social action, and protest. When the gathering threatens social order—a very subjective moment—this is often called an "occupation." When freedom of assembly and protest challenge authority to the point of retribution, we must recognize that good design loses any benefits it might otherwise have.

Not surprisingly, as a practicing architect, I do believe that good planning, architecture, and landscape design can do much to create successful public spaces; however, before design can serve to make or remake public spaces function at the highest level, we must, as a society, buy into a social contract of civility. By this, I mean that a willing and collective process of socialization is necessary to enable us to coexist in the dense fabric of urban life.

It strikes me that we, the "citizens," are more effective on an informal level than those who are vested with the authority to manage good behavior, such as the police. The tools of intimidation, crowd control, and obscure rules of behavior that are invoked when we least expect them generally have the opposite intended effect. Until these matters are reined in and citizens take responsibility for their own social behaviors, even the best intended design will be ignored and rendered moot.

Many factors enter into the creation of successful public spaces. For the purposes of this discussion, I will focus on public spaces in relatively dense urban settlements. And, for this discussion, public space begins just outside the doorstep to our homes.

When we cross the threshold between home and the public domain, we relinquish the personal, private, intimate place in which we feel protected and in control to enter a world of shared experiences. We navigate through our daily routines around our families, neighbors, and complex social hierarchies. It is in this context that we strive for collective understanding and community. Our physical surroundings play an important part in helping to define comfort zones on the sidewalk, in the street, and in open gathering spaces.

Due to recent experiences with Occupy Wall Street and Zuccotti Park, questions have come into focus about what designers can do to accommodate large social gatherings, facilitate politically motivated assembly, and diminish the likelihood of a police bust. What went wrong at Zuccotti Park had nothing to do with its architecture or landscape design. It is a perfectly fine place that provides a respite for office workers in the shade of a diagonally placed bosque of honey locusts. The trees help to mitigate the otherwise canyon-like setting as the park is surrounded by skyscrapers. The landscape is a sensible choice to support the vast number of people who pass through the park daily. The awkward natural slope of the site has been expertly handled with a platform along Broadway that steps down to a nearly flat parterre with extensive wide stone benches and planters (see Figure 3). On a recent sunny lunch hour, several musicians stood on the high ground and looked out over the rest of the park, creating a natural stage.

Figure 3. Zuccotti Park. *Photo by Paul Broches*

It occurs to me that the Occupy Wall Street label may become Zuccotti Park's legacy. Like other public spaces in New York City, it has earned an historical hook that will make it more than just a POPS, or privately owned public space. As the tension surrounding the Occupy movement settles down, Zuccotti Park will become an enduring attraction and will hold up well for many different kinds of use. Memorable public spaces usually do have a commonly known history that derives from historic events that have occurred there.

Other important determinants of successful public spaces are their location in the city fabric, the sociology of the community around them, and their capacity to bring us fresh air and big skies and provide each of us, alone, a sense of sharing a special experience. Other factors that will be raised in the following paragraphs include the buildings that give form to the public space and its topography, traffic patterns, access to public transportation, and serendipity. To study such public spaces, as an anthropologist or sociologist might do, provides useful empirical evidence to inform our designs.

Memorable public spaces in urban settings are also the result of the right plan dimensions and the clarity of the architecture that surrounds them. They convey order and calm, often with a satisfying landscape and implied intention of use: generally conducive to passive recreation, children's playgrounds, and small gatherings. Sometimes the goal is to bring a woodland setting into the city (e.g., Gramercy Park in New York City); sometimes it is to create a palace garden (e.g., Place des Vosges in Paris); sometimes it is a neutral landscape simply to provide a respite from the dense urban fabric. Parks of this scale may attract picnics but are not likely to attract large social or political gatherings.

On the opposite end of the spectrum are those open spaces that bring the country into the city, providing both active and passive recreation: Hyde Park in London, Central Park in New York City, Bois de Boulogne in Paris, Rock Creek Park in Washington, DC, Golden Gate Park in San Francisco, etc. A special opportunity provided by these parks is to create spaces that accommodate sports events, concerts, and political demonstrations of up to one hundred thousand people and sometimes more.

Less common are formidable public spaces that were (and sometimes still are) the settings to demonstrate military might. They are frequently surrounded by monumental public buildings, important symbols of power. These spaces are usually not a promising setting for community. The Mall in

Washington, DC, Tiananmen Square in Beijing, and the Zócola in Mexico City are impressive, if somewhat troubling examples. While they are more overwhelming than appealing, these spaces are a great boon to social and political activists.

The towns and cities that warm our hearts do so not because of their monumental spaces and enormous parks; rather, they have a fine balance between the public and private realms where streets, squares, and parks weave between and around places of work, home, and celebration. In these cities, the texture is complex and the parks and less defined public spaces are filled with surprises. The boundaries between buildings and open space are blurred and the edges between passage and place are often ambiguous.

On a visit to Havana, Cuba, last year, I was impressed by an event that took place in the Parque Central in the old city. A rock concert celebrating the birthday of the nineteenth-century revolutionary José Martí was located on the edge of the park, but the crowd gathered on a side street perpendicular to it. The street was lined on both sides by buildings that had arcades along the full length of the block. To be on this street was to be in an intimate space where the energy of the crowd was palpable and the music resonated with great intensity. When a speaker held forth, there was a close connection between the speaker and the assembled crowd.

The rectangular Parque Central is heavily planted; nevertheless, a large paved swath aligns with the wide street. Park and street form an intersection. The two are merged. The street becomes the park and the park becomes the street! On the side street, the boundary between building and street is

Figure 4. Parque Central in Havana, Cuba. *Photo by Paul Broches*

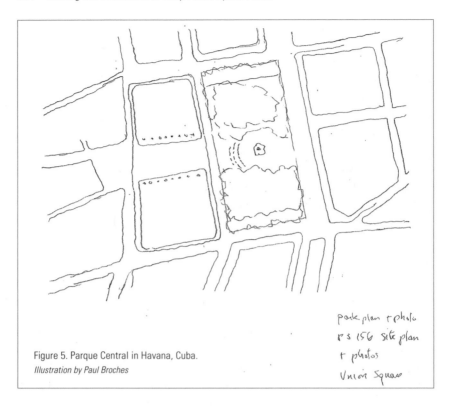

Figure 5. Parque Central in Havana, Cuba.
Illustration by Paul Broches

park plan + photo
P S 156 site plan
+ photos
Union Square

softened and blurred by the arcades. The arcade provides an ambiguous boundary between building and street. Their ambiguous situation allowed for a dynamic occupation. Precedents like the Parque Central are very informative in resolving contemporary design challenges.

Architects are obliged by their clients to create boundaries between their building or property and the public domain. The corollary, I believe, is that we are also obliged by an unspoken social contract to contribute to a hospitable urban fabric. The buildings we design are almost always bounded by a sidewalk, a street, or a defined public space. That boundary or edge will color the experience of the public space and the behavior of the people who interact with it. The more ambiguous the edges, the more easily a public will adapt to small and large gatherings.

Blurring the boundaries and overlapping public and private spaces proved to be useful concepts for the site planning and design of a primary school in the very tough Ocean Hill-Brownsville neighborhood of Brooklyn. Whereas playgrounds often end up in the back of a school building in favor

Figure 6. Primary School, Ocean Hill-Brownsville, Brooklyn. *Photo by Kevin Chu*

of the requisite pedimented portico on the street, in this case, the playground was consciously placed on Sutter Avenue, the main commercial corridor through the neighborhood. The school is the anchor of the neighborhood, a positive symbol for the multigenerational and diverse community, at least in part explained by its controversial history as the hotbed of school decentralization and community participation struggles that occurred in the 1960s.

The school functions as a 24/7 community center, merging playground and street life. Always populated with school children during the day and pickup basketball games after dark, the playground and public street behave as one and, in spite of the tall fence that separates them, create a safe haven for multigenerational gatherings day and night. The positive energy is celebrated and reinforced by a large illuminated mural that was created under the auspices of the New York City Department of Education program, Public Art for Public Schools. Engaging the school administration and PTA in the selection of artist was instrumental in its success. Blurring the boundaries, engaging community in the process, and celebrating their history epitomize architecture as a social art.

An important lesson learned from this public school project was how critical freedom of access is, both psychological and real. Access gives rise to ownership. Ownership of a public space empowers its occupants.

Conversely, one becomes skeptical about spaces where we can be fenced out or fenced in. As Figure 7 illustrates, the steps of Federal Hall across the

Figure 7. Wall Street occupiers at Federal Hall. *Photo by Paul Broches*

street from the New York Stock Exchange, a great stage for protestors, has been severely truncated by police barriers. The more complex the public space is in its boundaries, the more suitable it becomes for a wide variety of activities.

As I reflect on New York City parks, I am drawn to those that have resulted from the wonderful "defects" in the universal grid that resulted from the country lane, Bloomingdale Road, which survived the imposition of the grid in the 1811 New York City Master Plan. Through various accidents of history and city planning, Bloomingdale, now Broadway, celebrates the cuts that occur at major thoroughfares—most notably, at Times Square through Union Square, and at Strauss, Verdi, and Herald Squares.

The great, persistent New York City grid is reviled by some as having been created by profit seekers—and it is celebrated by others as creating a brilliant democratic framework within which to create an infinite variety of community design propositions. In my opinion, the grid is a wonderful foil for special moments and urban drama that are created by interrupting its repetitive rhythm. The paradigm, of course, is Times Square—described by Marshall Berman as a place "with a superabundance of meanings" (Berman 2009, *xx*).

Union Square's success is proven by its long and prominent history in supporting a great variety of public gatherings and social causes. In the midst of a neighborhood known in the early 1900s for its sweatshops and labor unrest, the square hosted numerous labor protests. Designed by Olmsted and Vaux, the designers created an ambiguous open space at the north end that is perhaps the least attractive part of the park, but the most successful for the public, accommodating public gatherings for protest or celebration, green markets, carnivals, and so forth.

The tension of the interrupted Broadway diagonal is always palpable. The streets that do not pass through the square are slightly annoying to automobile traffic but enrich the goings-on in the park.

The designers of Union Square employed many tools to give variety to the park and thereby invite many different uses. While the park seems relatively flat, topography was an important device. Used by entrepreneurial merchants and soapbox orators to garner attention, level changes were an important design tool for Olmsted and Vaux in their design to mediate between the desire for dynamic social space and pastoral garden. On the west side where there is no grade change, the intersection of park and road create opportunity for collective events, whether they be organized markets, ad hoc musical presentations, political demonstrations, etc. The center of the park is raised to create a quiet, protected, passive, interior, formally landscaped park between the collective gathering places at the north and south ends of the park. Benches and plantings provide a respite from the otherwise densely populated and dynamic mixed-use area. It is remarkable how significant a two-to three-foot change in elevation can be to change the character of experience and expectations of visitors to the square.

The recently renovated south end of Union Square incorporates an inspiring place to see and be seen, an amphitheater for the ad hoc occasion and appropriate for more "intimate" gatherings than might be considered at the

Figure 8. Aerial view of Union Square in 2012. *Illustration by Paul Broches*

north end of the park. On a recent TV newscast, a small but energized group of students from a nearby high school made an impressive show, protesting the tragic planned closing of their school. What emboldened the students was their position atop the stepped "theater." They stood on high ground and gained authority by their physical position. From Speaker's Corner at London's Hyde Park, we know that an elevated position gives one advantage.

Witnessing this brief event demonstrates the importance of topography as a design tool. We design in both plan and section and, together, they are important design controls. Once plan and section give form to space and define edges, it is important to introduce some ambiguity to provide alternative interpretations by the public when there are opportunities to use, control, and occupy the space.

However, given the variety of uses of public spaces, one can never fully anticipate in the final analysis where the right place for a raised platform should be or even the right configuration of any of the design elements, for that matter. And if one could anticipate all possibilities, the potential for surprise and empowerment—fundamental attributes for drama in public assembly—would be lost. While history and iconic symbols of prior events may give substance to a public space, it is probably the unpredictable, ad hoc setup that best suit those moments.

What we can do as architects and planners in the making or remaking of any public space is to study its boundaries, its defining edges, its topography, and its place in the larger urban context. With that background, we can use our palette of ambiguity between inside and outside, blurring the edges between public and private and creating spaces that have complexity and contradiction to confound and mask the instruments of control and to make vital, dynamic, accessible public spaces—public spaces that are not easily eviscerated by authority.

It should go without saying that in addition to the above considerations, we have not done our job as designers if we have not also created public spaces that provide compatibility with the surroundings, durability, human comforts, the art and craft of built form, and civic delight.

Reference

Berman, M. 2009. *On the Town*. Brooklyn, NY: Verso.

When Domestic Space Meets Civic Space

A CASE FOR DESIGN POPULISM

Michael Pyatok

I FIND IT MOST uncomfortable to be writing about my own work, especially after a career that has been critical of architectural egos and the damage they have done to our cities in the service of both private and public powers. But when Occupy Wall Street (OWS) arose across the country, I could not help but make connections to the 1960s, when, as a young professional freshly graduated from Pratt and Harvard, I spent almost every weekend in some demonstration against the Vietnam War in New York City's Central Park or at the Whitehall Street draft center, or in Washington, DC, at the Pentagon or the Washington Mall for the Poor People's March in the spring of 1968. The 1960s indelibly shaped my career goals so that by the time I opened my own office in 1984 after years of teaching and working for others, it was inevitable that my firm would be mission-driven, focused on the needs of lower-income communities, with a client base of nonprofit development corporations.

By now, my office has designed over thirty-five thousand multifamily dwellings, but the two projects I recalled the most during the recent OWS efforts were two that seemed to have nothing to do with housing. Instead, they focused on the design of civic spaces, both having been competitions sponsored by cities wanting to develop their city halls and the surrounding open space. Working with a former Harvard classmate, Yui Hay Lee, also known primarily as an architect of multifamily housing, we won first place for the Oakland City Hall Plaza in 1985. The second one I entered was in West Hollywood for a civic center and park, where I placed second. The former was built, while the winning solution for the second competition was not.

While each seemed to have nothing to do with housing and neighborhood design issues, our special concerns for everyday domestic needs required for multifamily residential design, particularly in lower-income communities, inspired our approach to Oakland's plaza and my approach to West Hollywood's civic center. The Oakland plaza/park has allowed comfortable public gatherings, both cultural and political, since its completion in 1998. As a resident of Oakland since 1978, I have seen the space in front of city hall both in its earlier configuration and in its present one as they were used for daily rituals and special occasions. I have watched it gradually become the natural setting for its citizens to respond to local and national events, including OWS. The civic center and large park I proposed for West Hollywood assertively pursued a similar "populist" approach, but a more formal government complex outranked it. However, that was stopped from moving forward by a lawsuit instigated by the Sierra Club for failing to provide an adequate replacement of a public park and its everyday activities formerly on the site.

Architects of housing focus on the domestic needs and aspirations of people in the more casual moments of their lives. Architects of high-profile buildings and public spaces are often asked to reflect the expectations of sponsoring agencies, public or private, and use open space as a means to celebrate the buildings that define it, which, in turn, glorify the institutions within. As a result, public spaces are not always ideal for entertaining the everyday needs of people, or for those moments when citizens need to express their opinions en masse.

This article explores how an approach to domestic space can inform civic space and result in public places that are more useful not only for meeting the needs of everyday life but also for supporting those major, catalytic events that attempt to shape our political future.

The Schooling of Design Professionals

Given the many schools of architecture and landscape architecture in the US, it is difficult to generalize about their methods of education. But the differences between architecture and landscape architecture as professions seem to have their genesis in their respective educations. The differences are not only that one creates buildings and the other creates outdoor places within and around buildings. It is really the differences in their attitudes and priorities that evolve from primarily focusing on one or the other project type. Not to simplify, but, nearing a half-century as a practicing architect and as an educator in schools that catered to both, I have observed some recurring differences.

Architects envision their buildings as special objects in the landscape (urban, rural, or anywhere in between), which must be celebrated while displaying a poetic vision that is unique to the author, sometimes regardless of a place and its people's social history and intentions. Even in this age of "sustainable" design, the pursuit of noble efforts to integrate with natural systems can often be used as an excuse to create exotic, technologically self-conscious monuments. Open space is used in a subservient way to help display the presence of an ingenious building, with some efforts to process rainwater from rooftops, or gray water for irrigation.

Landscape architects see themselves ideally as guardians of things natural, and they wish to celebrate not only a region's flora and fauna but also the past and present cultural history of its people. In general, there is a somewhat less personal "branding" of places as there may be in architecture. Places are designed not as technological responses to living systems but as real living systems, where both nature and people are expected and encouraged to gradually change the places over time and leave their own special mark on them. In contrast, architects hope their creations will be frozen in their original state for generations to come.

There is one realm of architectural practice that seems to bridge these differences in attitude and method between landscape and architecture: the design of domestic settings. Regardless of density, whether single-family or multifamily communities, open spaces are designed as an integral part of the domestic setting. In fact, a case can be made that the higher the density, the more cherished and rare the open spaces are. These spaces receive more attention by designers to ensure their full use by residents across all ages and at all times of the day and evening.

An added requirement to the design tendencies of architects of residential settings includes the participatory engagement of residents and neighbors, which is essential to working in and with lower-income communities. Years of participatory engagement workshops leave an indelible mark on the values and instincts of architects: the everyday needs of people come first, before the expression of any abstract, symbolic purpose or the urge to create personal stylistic brands.

Designing Civic Places

Nowhere can these differences be seen as clearly as in the design of civic buildings and the open spaces that surround or embed themselves within buildings. Collaboration between the architecture and landscape architecture professions is quite close and coordinated, and it would be a gross simplification to say that the design of open spaces is always submissive to the intentions of building design. But when the combination of buildings and open spaces is designed to serve the interests of government centers, even in democracies like the US, these professions often conspire to idolize the governmental institution itself and not the source of a government's legitimacy and power—its own citizens.

For example, Boston City Hall (Figure 1), completed in the mid-1960s, was a culmination of architectural tendencies of the era: a powerful display of brutalist form and fortress-like edges meeting the public realm. The city hall faces more than eight acres of brick-covered plaza, perhaps a reference to Siena's plaza in Tuscany, Italy, but without Tuscany's gentler climate.

Figure 1. Boston City Hall. *Photo courtesy of Pyatok Architects*

Figure 1a. Boston City Hall Plaza. *Photo courtesy of Pyatok Architects*

In 2005, the Project for Public Spaces ranked the plaza at the top of the organization's list of Squares Most Dramatically in Need of Improvement in the United States. It is often criticized as a space not for people due to the cold, wet, and wind of winter and the wind, dust, heat, and humidity of summer. In fairness, for large crowds attending short-term performances, the hardscape plaza works well. But for quiet, relaxing, everyday lounging or for long-term sleep-over demonstrations, it is extremely inhospitable.

A more recent city hall plaza, in a more forgiving climate, is in Austin, Texas, and designed by Antoine Predock. While there are no large open spaces, the assemblage of smaller open spaces—soft ones for processing rainwater from roofs and paved ones for various types of smaller gatherings—lends itself to a variety of everyday uses. One in particular, a stepped bank of terraces shaded from Texas's hot sun by solar voltaic panels, seems to have served well the needs of sleep-over demonstrators participating in OWS (Figure 2).

Figure 2. Occupy Wall Street at the Austin City Hall. *Photo courtesy of Pyatok Architects*

It is this attention to the detailed needs of people's everyday lives, even in important civic settings, that I would like to address. In the 1990s, Yui Hay Lee and I were commissioned to execute the design of the Oakland City Hall Plaza once the city raised sufficient funding to restore the city hall and other buildings and historic structures in the plaza district following the 1989 Loma Prieta earthquake. Bob LaRocca of San Francisco was the collaborating landscape architect during the competition; Pattillo Garrett Associates of Oakland was later selected by the team as the landscape architects to help refine and execute the original ideas. This was the first civic space that either of us as architects had designed after establishing our own offices. We both had primarily been designing higher density multifamily housing developments and their associated open spaces.

Oakland City Hall and Frank Ogawa Plaza

Built in 1914 and standing at the height of 320 feet, Oakland City Hall was designed by the New York architecture firm of Palmer and Hornbostel in 1910 after winning a nationwide design competition (Figure 3). It was

Figure 3. Oakland City Hall in 1917. *Photo commissioned by Oakland Chamber of Commerce, Publicity Bureau. Photographer from Cheney Photo Advertising Co. Original photo part of Oakland Public Library, Oakland History Room*

the first high-rise government building in the United States. At the time it was built, in the Beaux-Arts style, it was also the tallest building west of the Mississippi River. A triangular-shaped lawn area, at sidewalk level, spread before it, separated from the building's main ceremonial entrance by Washington Street. The triangular shape was the result of the intersection of San Pablo Avenue, a major diagonal north-south street that runs through several East Bay cities, as it terminated in Oakland's downtown at the corner of Broadway and 14th Street. In 1917, a coast live oak tree was planted in the lawn by the widow of Jack London in his honor, one year after his death. Jack London had spent much of his childhood on the Oakland waterfront, and it was in Oakland where he started his literary career and developed his socialist leanings.

In 1985, the Oakland City Council sponsored a design competition to redesign the area in front of city hall. It had become a collection of disjointed spaces and invasive auto-dominated streets, including parking lots and a reduced version of the original lawn that was not well used or maintained. The Jack London oak tree still stood firmly in its place, by then with a sixty-foot diameter spread. After reviewing approximately twenty design teams, the city invited five to compete, and the winner of that competition was the team of Lee-Pyatok-LaRocca. Without finances to build the new design, it remained simply an idea. Then, in 1989, the Loma Prieta earthquake seriously damaged city hall and destroyed its neighboring annex of offices. Several historic buildings around the plaza were also damaged and vacated. During the early 1990s, the city devised a financial strategy to seismically upgrade and renovate city hall and the adjacent historic structures and build a new annex along with the plaza as originally conceived in the competition.

The city council thought it appropriate to name the new plaza space after Frank H. Ogawa, who had passed away in 1994. As a Japanese American, he and his family had been detained in a relocation camp in Utah during World War II. When he returned to Oakland after the war, Frank Ogawa worked as a gardener and eventually saved enough to open his own nursery.

Figure 4. Oakland City Hall in 1999 with the Jack London oak tree prominently displayed.
Photo by Michael Pyatok

He had served on the Oakland City Council for twenty-eight years and was known for his soft-spoken approach to representing citizens while steering the city.

The design team conceived the new plaza to be primarily used as a park and secondarily as a plaza. As a housing design team, we recognized that there were several single-room occupancy apartment buildings in the area of city hall that had no open spaces of their own and no park space for the relaxation of their low-income residents. In addition, both government office buildings and private offices surround the space, and together they employ thousands of workers needing a noontime place to relax with their brown-bag lunches. A nearby hardscape plaza surrounded by offices partially serves this function, but this was an opportunity for a more park-like setting. We saw the existing lawn as a potential asset for these everyday activities, but because it was at sidewalk level, it had become a shortcut that could be passed through in a semidetached manner and not a destination in which to relax. We decided to raise the lawn two to three feet above the surrounding streets, just enough to discourage shortcuts and enough to make it a destination place in its own right (Figure 4). We edged the raised lawn with stepped seating to allow for casual gathering and people watching (Figure 5).

We also removed the parking lots that had accumulated over the years at the terminus of San Pablo Avenue, which allowed for an expansion of the lawn area by as much as 50 percent beyond its historic size. Two other streets that originally crisscrossed the area (15th and Washington Streets) were also closed to traffic and absorbed into the enlarged pedestrian-friendly district. For the first time, city hall's entrance was directly connected to its open space, no longer separated by traffic

Figure 5. Stepped edges for seating. *Photo by Michael Pyatok*

We recognized that not all the users of the park would be able to physically sit or recline on the lawn (which we soon nicknamed "the people's mattress"), so we surrounded the lawn with a series of living-room-sized seat-

Figure 6. Benches for seniors.
Photo by Michael Pyatok

ing alcoves (approximately 12' x 12'), equipped with benches with backs to be comfortable for older people (Figures 6 and 7). To improve security during evenings, each seating niche is marked on its four corners by light posts that are modern interpretations of the original pole lights gracing the side entrances to city hall. Ramps lead up to the lawn level, and a paved path around its entire edge allows people in wheelchairs to have access to the park and its activities.

In addition to the everyday, informal activities associated with the lives of the surrounding residents and workers, the space was also clearly the "front

Figure 7. Living-room-sized seating niches, equipped with benches, are decorated during the Christmas holidays. *Photo by Michael Pyatok*

yard" of city hall. As such, it was expected to host a variety of public events: cultural performances, festivals, campaign speeches, important public announcements, ceremonies, and celebrations. This, of course, included expected protests and demonstrations, not just about local issues, but also those affecting the state and nation as a whole, so crowds at times could be large. To accommodate these activities, we located a semicircular stepped forum directly in front of and on an axis with city hall's main entrance (Figures 8 and 9). To understand the intimate scale of these spaces, the paved forum, including seating and stage, is only about 0.15 acres, and the raised lawn is only about 0.75 acres. With a loosely assembled crowd (about ten square feet per person), the forum and lawn could accommodate about four thousand people, while a dense crowd (about five square feet per person) could almost double that.

We protected the Jack London oak tree with a circular seat wall running along its outer drip line. This provided another opportunity for people to sit and relax in the shade of the tree, either facing inward toward the quiet of its sweeping canopy or outward toward the park and streets. Two other coast live oak trees had grown over the years to the north of the main lawn area, and both historic preservationists and open space advocates encouraged us

Figure 8. The Forum. *Photo by Michael Pyatok*

Figure 9. Seating in the Forum. *Photo by Michael Pyatok*

to save them. We did so, but within a paved area that could host less formal events than those in the main forum. Ground-floor restaurants surround this northern zone of the triangle and spill into it during good weather. Its north corner is defined by a fountain with a vertical sculpture that serves as the terminus of the San Pablo Avenue corridor.

Oakland is a city of about four hundred thousand residents, but it is more or less the administrative center for the East Bay with its collection of physically merged smaller cities like Berkeley, San Leandro, Emeryville, Piedmont, Albany, and El Cerrito. Oakland's downtown contains the Bay Area's governmental headquarters with major state and federal office buildings, along with an administrative center for the Bay Area Transit Authority (BART), East Bay Municipal Utility District (EBMUD), and the statewide headquarters for the University of California Regents. It is home to the Alameda County Courthouse and the county's administrative offices. It should also be noted that Oakland has one of the most important public open spaces in the US, built in the 1960s and reflecting that era's populist tendencies. The Oakland Museum, at the east edge of downtown, designed by Roche-Dinkeloo, is partially embedded in the ground for approximately two city blocks to allow people walking on adjacent streets to freely enter a composition of people-friendly garden terraces built on top of the museum.

So it is inevitable that of all the cities in the East Bay, Oakland would attract the largest political demonstrations. But in none of these other locations is there a combination park and plaza to attract either casual, informal relaxing or intentional larger gatherings. Some may have plazas, but none host a park-like setting as well. This shortage of people-friendly public open places is also true of the major banks and corporations located in Oakland. The city hall park/plaza would become the location for the East Bay's version of Occupy Wall Street (OWS). With few other options of supportive public spaces in the downtown to choose from, its convenient combination of park and plaza became a simultaneously "domestic" and civic setting: the soft, carpeted park—the people's mattress—became the bedroom and the paved forum became the formal living room (Figures 10 and 11).

But woven into the animosity toward Wall Street among the gathered protestors was a lingering, smoldering dislike for Oakland's police department and BART's security force because of the number of instances over the years where deadly force had been used against young males, primarily African Americans, with limited consequences for the officers involved.

Figure 10. Occupy Wall Street at Oakland City Hall Plaza, November 2011. *Photo by Michael Pyatok*

Figure 11. The lawn's stepped edges became forums for small group discussion. *Photo by Michael Pyatok*

These events spawned demonstrations in front of city hall that were intense and, at times, included a small minority that engaged in disruptive behavior, giving the police an opportunity to apply exceptional force upon all the demonstrators.

Only a little more than a year before OWS began, demonstrations concerning local police actions had occurred in front of city hall (Figure 12). These ended in a melee with tear gas, broken windows, and cracked skulls.

Figure 12. Demonstrators at the Oakland City Hall Plaza in July 2010 protesting the light sentence of the BART police officer who shot Oscar Grant on New Year's Day, 2009. *Photo courtesy of Pyatok Architects*

These earlier local events, in combination with the fact that the gathering place was in front of city hall, at times steered the anger that people felt toward Wall Street and the broader corporate culture of capitalism toward city hall itself. Ironically, this is the one level of government most directly tending to the needs of its citizens and doing so under dire circumstances because of what Wall Street had done to the economy and to the local tax base upon which essential services depend. Equally ironic, all of these events unfolded under the watchful eye of the first woman and first Asian mayor of Oakland, Jean Quan, herself a community organizer in Berkeley during the 1960s.

In summary, in response to the question of why the space in front of the Oakland City Hall became the central place for the East Bay's version of OWS, the following five responses may provide some understanding:

1. Oakland, the largest of the East Bay cities, is the political and administrative center of the East Bay. It is conveniently located with two nearby BART stations and numerous bus lines.

2. Oakland was the home of the Black Panthers and had a long history of political activism. In 1984, about 80 percent of those living in Oakland voted for Jesse Jackson in the Democratic presidential primary.

3. Oakland is home to the largest concentration of working-class families and minorities in the East Bay, and for decades it has been bearing the brunt of corporate capitalism's flight from the US for cheaper labor and less regulated markets elsewhere.

4. Given the paucity of potently symbolic public places in Oakland's downtown, and an absence of such places accompanying the locations of the financial sector, the city hall was the best choice.

5. Finally, the design of Oakland City Hall—as both a park and plaza—contained the physical ingredients to support a longer term occupancy, with places for sleeping and eating and comfortable seating both on and around the lawn; small group gatherings for discussion on the stepped seating along the lawn's edges; large group gatherings at the main forum for fostering public education, strategizing actions, and accommodating speeches by participants, visitors, and supporters. Even spiritual activities by Muslims, Jews, Christians, and Buddhists took advantage of the stepped seating in the semicircular forum.

We could foresee none of these events as the park/plaza's designers. By following our instincts as housing designers, we took into consideration the open space needs for everyday activities and for those special events that take place in domestic settings and made an effort to include communal versions of these at the doorsteps of Oakland City Hall.

West Hollywood Civic Center

The second case study is also a competition I entered for a new civic center in West Hollywood that included a city hall, performing arts auditorium, central library, fire station, and city park. Rich Seyfarth was the collaborating landscape architect. My design placed second, while the winning design was never built, mired in a lawsuit brought by the Sierra Club because it lacked public open spaces equivalent to the park that the civic center was displacing.

In 1987, the city of West Hollywood embarked on a program to build a civic center. At the time, West Hollywood was considered the center of the design and gay-rights communities in Los Angeles, and, with a sizable number of seniors, was one of the few cities in California to have rent control. It now has its own affordable housing trust fund and inclusionary zoning and has adopted one of the first mandatory green building ordinances. In short, the city is proud to be considered one of California's most progressive cities, with a population of only about 35,000 in 1987 and about 38,000 in 2012. In 1987, the city's administrative offices were scattered throughout several private office buildings, and, as a result, West Hollywood suffered from inefficiencies, high rents, and no central location to act as the symbol of the city.

For such a politically engaged citizenry, the choice to sponsor an international two-phase design competition in West Hollywood with anonymous entries seemed contradictory. In such competitions, teams of designers, most of whom do not live in or near the city, invent solutions without any contact with clients, users, or neighbors. With nothing more than a cold listing of space needs and requirements, called a "program," about four hundred design teams set out to assemble solutions that they thought might appeal to the locals. Only after the first phase of judging would the four finalists be revealed to the public. In some ways, something as symbolic as a "civic center" (with a city hall, performing arts center, library, fire station, public garage, and an array of outdoor recreational uses) should actively utilize a participatory design process. Only in this way could there be some assurance that the results would reflect the wishes of the residents regarding a place so loaded with symbolic meaning. The winning solution by Roger Sherman from Cambridge, Massachusetts, soon met resistance by residents who objected to the loss of the West Hollywood Park and to the formal nature of the smaller park that was proposed. In 2002, fifteen years later, Johnson Favaro architects, a local team from Culver City, were selected by the city to orchestrate a successful 1.5-year community process that engaged a broad spectrum of the residents in redesigning their park, including a library and a public parking garage.

Even more challenging than the nonparticipatory approach of an open competition was the fact that the site was already a much-cherished open space among the city's residents. It was, and still is, the West Hollywood Park, near the intersection of Santa Monica and San Vicente Boulevards. It is filled with places that support not only daily recreational needs but also many of the city's festivals and shared events. It has a toddler playground, an older kids' playground, a recreation center, basketball and tennis courts, a baseball field, a heated swimming pool, and, more recently, a state-of-the-art library by Johnson Favaro. It was inevitable that the 1987 competition dictating the location of over two hundred thousand square feet of new buildings would cause controversy. The council was torn between two sites—the West Hollywood Park, which they already owned, and an older shopping center site on Santa Monica Boulevard, which they would have to purchase. They settled on the former as the future site for the new civic center in a 3-2 vote.

From among the four hundred designs submitted by architects from around the world, four were selected to compete in a second phase of refinement. The jurors included Charles Moore, Ricardo Legoretta, Cesar Pelli, Peter Walker, Deborah Sussman, and Robert Harris. The four selected designs originated from Los Angeles; Cambridge, Massachusetts; Eugene, Oregon; and mine from Oakland. The team from Cambridge, selected as the winner at the end of the second phase, faced two years of public debate by citizens who felt the chosen design had an inadequate amount of recreational open space and that the open space provided was laid out as a formal forecourt to the government and cultural facilities, not adequately lending itself to the rich array of recreational uses already there.

Unlike the site for the Oakland City Hall competition, the site for the West Hollywood competition already functioned as an open space that allowed for a rich array of recreational uses. These informal ingredients for recreation and relaxation reflected the spirit of this progressive, people-oriented city government and set the tone for the rest of the civic center. With this mix of uses, often found within residential neighborhoods, it seemed to me that it would be difficult to create a traditional, formal government complex, and I expected a great mix of "populist" design effort. While there was a fair share of such whimsical entries in the competition, there were also a surprising number of formal, government complexes.

I assumed that the buildings should be pushed to the very northern edge of the site, serving merely as background stage sets to maximize the area devoted to a variety of open spaces that would serve everyday recreational activities. These outdoor functions would become the central image of the civic center, not the buildings. As can be seen in the plan (Figure 13), all of the major building ingredients are condensed in the north corner to allow for maximum park space. Only one building, the central fire station, was placed on the south end so that it had easy access to San Vicente Boulevard.

The plan sought to encourage a broad range of everyday activities and relaxation: There was to be a "participatory fountain" equipped with stepped seating in the water (Figure 14), a large multipurpose meadow, barbeque pits, picnic alcoves, and an outdoor amphitheater. The offices of the mayor and city manager were to overlook a twenty-foot wide avenue lined with booths for lobbying, signature gathering, and speech making, aptly called the "Calle de Politica" (Figure 15). In the event of citizen demonstrations, I

Figure 13. The proposed plan for the West Hollywood civic center. *Model by Pyatok Architects*

Figure 14. Peering through San Vicente Portico toward the participatory fountain. *Illustration by Michael Pyatok*

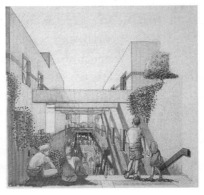

Figure 15. Descending into the Calle de Politica from the third level of the city garage. *Illustration by Michael Pyatok*

envisioned the base of a towering light sculpture in the main plaza to serve as a raised speaker's podium and sound system (Figure 16).

The civic center and large park I proposed for West Hollywood assertively pursued a similar "populist" approach to what was to become later realized at Oakland City Hall and Frank Ogawa Plaza. But the design competition for the civic center had no winners in the end because the West Hollywood citizenry rose up and fought for what mattered to them: a civic

Figure 16. Entry Plaza with the Tower of Light and Achievement to the left. *Illustration by Michael Pyatok*

space supportive of the full range of human activities, from the most common forms of relaxation to the most profound debates about what the responsibilities are of citizens and of a government within a democracy. To those of us who entered this competition, it provided an opportunity to plumb the depths of our own belief systems about the role of government and its place in our lives. For me, it highlighted how important open space design is for the residential projects I have undertaken during the twenty-five years since that time. That brief experience made me a better designer of residential environments, as much as I had hoped my residential sensibilities would have made a better government center.

As for Oakland, my offices are still one block from city hall and its plaza, and my home just ten minutes from there. I can see each day how time transforms the place, and how people can come to it to celebrate moments of sheer bliss and contentment or to express rage and frustration over our society's injustices. This particular public open space seems like the natural place to let it all hang out, just like home. In this manner, a public space became a collectively shared domestic space.

Shaping Public Space, Shaping Our City

Susan Chin

WHO DECIDES HOW our public spaces are used and for what purposes? What is the process for making these decisions? What values guide the process?

The forcible eviction of protestors from Zuccotti Park and from other public spaces in cities throughout the country during the fall of 2011 made these questions become visceral and immediate. However these types of physical struggles over public space—the tear gas, the riot gear, the arrests—are relatively rare. In reality, the process of planning, designing, and regulating public space is much more mundane and less visible, but has far-reaching impacts that affect a wide range of spaces and citizens. Zoning, for example, can be used to transform an industrial district into a neighborhood of high-rise condominiums or to preserve a ribbon of waterfront green space for public use. Tax incentives can be leveraged to spur the development of a sports stadium in downtown Brooklyn or to support environmentally friendly affordable housing in the South Bronx. Every day, in ways large and small, these tools collectively weave the complex tapestry that makes up our city and its public space.

The debate about democratizing public space is an important one, for both the architectural and planning community and the broader public. As more than 50 percent of the world's population live in cities, meeting public space needs is a challenge for every city and its citizens. Meeting the public space needs of nearly 8.3 million New Yorkers and more than 50 million visitors per year requires a clear vision and regulatory framework to properly serve a rapidly evolving and diverse population. And it requires a process that is informed by public participation.

My views on this topic have been informed by my experience as an architect, former government official, and executive director of the Design Trust for Public Space, a nonprofit organization that has been at the forefront of shaping New York City's parks, plazas, streets, buildings, and infrastructure since 1995. I believe in the value of design in shaping successful public spaces and in the key role that the "public'" must and can play in making public space, determining its uses, and keeping it accessible.

The Design Trust has found that the most successful public space projects begin with dedicated partners—community groups, public agencies, and other nonprofit organizations—that are deeply engaged in communities and in the process of placemaking. These key constituents decide together how our public space is created and how it is used—the "heart" of the approach is in working together. Working across disciplines draws out the best design thinking. As a result, Design Trust projects have a strong vision that is derived from stakeholder engagement and in-depth research, design, and planning.

The Design Trust was established in 1995 by Andrea Woodner, founder and board president, to change the city through design and a cross-disciplinary approach to solving public space challenges. Every two years, the Design Trust issues a Request for Proposal for projects that affect how public space is planned, designed, or used. After projects are selected by a jury, the Design Trust issues a call for Fellows to bring on experts to work with stakeholders and to research, analyze, and make recommendations. Stakeholders and the public are continuously involved in the process through surveys, interviews, meetings, design charrettes, workshops, videos, and photographs. The final recommendations serve to influence public opinion and policymakers and oftentimes to catalyze change in underutilized public spaces.

The following three projects highlight various ways of pulling interdisciplinary teams together with experts (architects, landscape architects, urban planners, urban designers, graphic and web designers, policy analysts, photographers, and videographers): engaging stakeholders, involving the community, and working across disciplines. These approaches are replicable on any project and in any city, though each of them has unique characteristics that are defined through the process. These successful public spaces reflect community stewardship, the neighborhood's character, and the city's collective imagination. They are authentic, have a focal point, are accessible to local residents and tourists, and allow the public to socialize and gather for a communal purpose, such as dining or relaxation.[1]

Engaging Stakeholders: Five Borough Farm

Across rooftops and vacant lots, schoolyards and public housing projects, urban agriculture is transforming New York City. This movement creates new opportunities for community development, local food production, environmental stewardship, and public health. However, two barriers prevent government officials from developing a long-range, citywide urban agriculture plan or making large-scale resource commitments: 1) lack of evidence demonstrating urban agriculture's value to the city from a social, health, economic and environmental perspective and from a land use perspective; and 2) the absence of a structure or process to coordinate actions across multiple agencies and engage key stakeholders in decision making.

The Design Trust's Five Borough Farm project, in partnership with Added Value,[2] tackles this issue head-on. This project has documented over six hundred urban agriculture sites throughout the city that perform functions traditional parks cannot. Community groups and dedicated individuals have converted approximately one hundred acres of empty lots, rooftops, and interstitial spaces, such as traffic islands and near railroad easements, into community gathering places and productive growing areas. These spaces provide an opportunity for community cooperation, civic pride, and citizen engagement through gardening and urban agriculture. They also contribute to healthier neighborhoods through environmental benefits (cleaner air), social networks (intergenerational opportunities), lifestyle benefits (reduced

---

1. See, for example, the expanded traffic circle at Columbus Circle at 59th Street with its attractive plantings, lively fountains, and expansive benches; or the David Rubenstein Atrium at Lincoln Center, a privately owned public space, which is a through block having a café, performance space, and discount ticket counter with skylights, living green walls, small fountain, benches, and artwork.
2. The project was headed by Ian Marvy and Design Trust Fellows Nevin Cohen (Urban Food Policy Fellow), Agnieszka Gasparska (Graphic Design Fellow), Rupal Sanghvi (Public Health/Metrics Fellow), and thread collective fellows Gita Nandan and Elliott Maltby (Sustainable Design Fellows).

obesity, fresh food), economic benefits (job creation), and recreational and educational activities.

The urban agriculture sites citywide grow and distribute food, provide value to formerly vacant lots, capture storm water, educate young people, contribute to the health of the community, and much more. Yet, New York City government does not have a citywide urban agriculture policy that would oversee these public spaces holistically or as a system of food production. Most of these growing spaces are on publicly owned land, or under the jurisdiction of a city or state agency (i.e., NYC Department of Parks & Recreation, NYC Housing Preservation and Development, NYC Housing Authority, or the Empire State Development Corporation). Of the 490 sites, nearly 390 community gardens that report growing food are required to have some public hours. These sites represent a type of public space that is part of the community.

Community stakeholder workshops like "The Future of Farming in NYC" organized by the Design Trust also play a key role in developing strategies and making policy recommendations for how public space is used. This workshop brought together a diverse mix of ninety farmers, gardeners, funders, nonprofit advocates, health professionals, and planners to discuss goals and priorities, resources needed to sustain their work and ways to evaluate urban agriculture's benefits. Among the topics for discussion, stakeholders reviewed the pros and cons of increasing land availability, increasing land tenure, and securing farms and gardens from theft and vandalism, which figure prominently in these public spaces. The priorities emerging from the workshop were then incorporated into the Five Borough Farm policy development.

After Local Law 48 of 2011 was enacted to increase transparency in government to the public by creating open data standards, New York City government developed an inventory of vacant land citywide. However, no process was established to determine what city-owned land would be suitable for urban agriculture, or to decide which groups or individuals would be allowed to start a farm or garden. Without a citywide, transparent approach, farmers and gardeners say the current process for making city-owned land available to the public for urban agriculture is unpredictable and unfair. The Design Trust established a citywide Urban Agriculture Task Force to give farmers and gardeners an opportunity to participate in shaping policy and reviewing current practices. Working together with city agencies, the Design Trust will coordinate these key stakeholders to develop criteria for land suitability and a selection process for allowing future farmers and gardeners access to city-owned property.

Involving the Community:
High-Performance Landscape Guidelines

The New York City Department of Parks and Recreation realized that there was no comprehensive guide for designing twenty-first-century parks and sharing best practices on managing soil, water, vegetation resources, and community engagement. Most practices were anecdotal and not systematic. In 2007, the department proposed to partner with the Design Trust[3] to produce a comprehensive primer for creating sustainable parks from design and construction to the maintenance of its twenty-nine thousand acres, and, in three years, developed the award-winning "High Performance Landscape Guidelines for 21st Century Parks." Within these guidelines, community involvement is seen as a key ingredient in creating vibrant public spaces. Public participation is encouraged early and throughout the park design process to promote community ownership of the park, to encourage volunteerism, to incorporate local knowledge that can inspire design innovation, to promote awareness about sustainable design considerations, to encourage a greater diversity of users and flexibility of uses, and to help obtain required approvals from agencies such as the Community Planning Board, the Landmarks Preservation Commission, and the Public Design Commission.

For example, in the renovation of the Pearly Gates playground in the Bronx, the Guidelines focused on encouraging community design and stewardship; promoting efficient use of resources; sourcing renewable materials; capturing and reusing water from fountains and spray features to water trees and newly created planting beds; and incorporating sustainable strategies at all stages of park planning—design, construction, and maintenance. The goal for public spaces such as parks, plazas, and green streets in the coming century is to increase their ability to clean the air, catch storm water and runoff,

---

3. The Design Trust worked with Parks employees and Design Trust fellows Michele Adams (Water Resources Fellow), Steven Caputo (Sustainability Fellow), Jeannette Compton, Tavis Dockwiller, and Andrew Lavallee (Landscape Architecture Fellows).

and cool the heat island effect of New York's concrete and built environment to improve the health of the surrounding community and its residents.

Working Across Disciplines:
TKTS Booth at Father Duffy Square in Times Square

In 1999, the Van Alen Institute, together with the Theatre Development Fund (TDF) and NYC 2000 Millennium Commission, organized a design competition, TKTS2K, to replace the temporary TKTS booth, which since 1973 had sold over 47 million discount theater tickets. The winning concept for the red glass steps enclosing the booth by Australian architects John Choi and Tai Ropiha was selected from 683 competition entries for its artfully simple yet dramatic solution. However, the implementation of this simple concept for a highly complex glass structure on a heavily used public square with cross-jurisdictional, quasi-public management and multiple constituencies required the mandate of the NYC 2000 Millennium Commission and Mayor Bloomberg and strong advocacy by the Times Square Alliance, TDF, and the Coalition for Father Duffy.[4]

The new TKTS booth redefined the concept of public space, blurring the boundaries between park and transportation, amidst the cacophony and gridlock of Times Square. Audiences were invited to coalesce on the amphitheater-style steps to watch the hyperactivity of Times Square that made people, cars, and buses a theatrical spectacle. It created a welcoming nexus for people to linger, not just pass through or stand in line for a ticket. The public critique was crucial to the design of the plaza paving and materials, and enhanced accessibility to the space in the placement of benches, lighting, signage, and artwork. This project was also critical to catalyzing the City's unprecedented initiative to close major streets to vehicular traffic in the "Bowtie" at Broadway and 7th Avenue, one (if not the most) heavily trafficked intersections in the city for use by pedestrians.

---

4. To accomplish this groundbreaking work, a trifecta of nonprofits, Times Square Alliance, TDF, and the Coalition for Father Duffy, led a complex team of architects and engineers—including structural, mechanical, electrical, civil, and geotechnical engineers, lighting designers, glass designers, preservation architects, and construction managers—and coordinated with multiple city agencies, including the NYC Department of Cultural Affairs, NYC Department of Design and Construction, NYC Department of Parks & Recreation, NYC Economic Development Corporation, NYC Department of Transportation, and Metropolitan Transit Authority.

Keep the Public at the Heart of Public Space

Design thinking is the glue that brings many stakeholders together to solve complex problems. Over the last two decades, the renewed interest of architects and planners in improving our shared urban fabric has dramatically transformed the way New Yorkers define and regard public space. The public now recognizes the value that can be created from obsolete industrial structures such as the High Line; traffic circles such as the Grand Army Plaza; and vacant lots that can be turned into community gardens.

As we prepare for a million new New Yorkers in the next twenty years, our public spaces need to serve multiple functions and contribute to our city's sustainability. There is a limited amount of land available for public open space—streets, sidewalks, parks, plazas, and so on. Each of these provides a unique opportunity and civic value, beyond the traditional uses of a park, plaza or other public venue. We need to think creatively to optimize and build in flexibility of uses into the public space that we have.

By using a participatory community process, New York City's government policies informed by cross-disciplinary thinking can create a more sustainable and dynamic city that is accessible to all. This inclusive process reflects the city's collective imagination and design thinking, and provides a space where we can listen and learn from each other and about ourselves, especially when stakeholders have different values. We create a vibrant city together that is ever changing in response to new challenges and ideas.

Public space is the lifeblood of our cities. It anchors our civic and cultural life. It is our collective living room and shared backyard. It directly affects our daily lives, how we feel about ourselves and perceive our city. The social, health, economic, and environmental benefits of high-quality public space to our city have been clearly documented, such as community cohesion, physical and mental well-being, lower crime rates, increased real estate values, and cleaner air to name a few. Above all, public space is a democratic mixing chamber where individuals with extremely diverse backgrounds and beliefs can assemble for a picnic, or even a protest. By actively engaging with our city, its citizens, leaders, and design thinkers, we keep the public at the heart of public space.

Public Space

OPENING STREETS AND SIDEWALKS

Jonathan Marvel

WILLIAM HOLLY WHYTE documented the way New Yorkers use public spaces. He discovered people hanging out on street corners, lingering on linear sidewalk ledges at lunchtime, and shifting a chair inches before sitting down, giving them ownership of that seating element. The result of this study was an appreciation of scale, openness, and moveable furniture in our public spaces. Dan Kiley's Paley Park in Midtown, which accommodates an occupancy of no more than fifty seated people, is the embodiment of all things successful in the post Holly Whyte era of creating a dynamic and popular urban park. Kiley's additional touches of a soothing waterfall and the shade of a grid of honey locust trees, programmed with a small café, made this a model for later parks including the significantly larger Bryant Park, which provides comfortable refuge and programming for one to two thousand occupants.

In the post-9/11 era, these advances in public space design have taken a backseat to issues of public safety and terrorism prevention. New York City's streets and sidewalks have become extra challenged by the need for security devices to protect high-risk terrorist targets—such as transit hubs, financial and corporate headquarters, and city, state, and federal public buildings—and their adjoining public plazas and parks. These new security barriers compromise the flow of foot traffic and can also threaten the sense of openness and accessibility to public buildings and squares. In the case of the privately owned public spaces (POPS), doors, guards, and limited hours discourage the use of many of these areas from uninhibited pedestrian traffic. Often, the public status of these spaces has been so obscured that what remains hardly constitutes an adequate space for the public life.

While these security measures contribute to the fragmentation of public space in New York City, the inherent nature of the city's public space is non-existent, marginalized, compartmentalized, and small-scaled. The battle over the use of Zuccotti Park by the Occupy Wall Street movement called attention to the lack of adequate public spaces for the congregation of hundreds and thousands of protesters, an inherent right as part of the First Amendment. New York City parks are off-limits because they are not designed to withstand the foot traffic and do not have adequate services to support that density over long periods of time. Other pressures on New York's parks such as the support of biological life and recreation appear to necessitate these restrictions on their use, but, in favoring limited use, they do so at the expense of a suitable public forum in New York City. In fact, there is no large open space near the symbolic center of the city, like London's Trafalgar Square or Paris's Arc de Triomphe or Place de Bastille. Instead, the most obvious place, what once was the largest downtown plaza, the World Trade Center public plaza, has been replaced by a tree-gridded garden of remembrance. It could have been both. It could have served as both a memorial of the past as well as a place for future civic life, much like Union Square or the Lincoln Memorial in Washington, DC. These are places that commemorate a tragic moment in our nation's history and are also places to exercise the First Amendment and freedom of speech.

Manhattan lacks a ceremonial celebratory assembly space largely thanks to the development-friendly Commissioners' Plan of 1811. In contrast to the utopian minded boulevards connecting large ceremonial open spaces characterizing the L'Enfant plan commissioned by Washington and Jefferson in 1787 for the young nation, the civic leaders in New York created a model of efficiency for land speculation that maximized the private domain. Ironically, Washington purchased the new hundred square miles of federal capital along the estuary of the Potomac River using third party entities to protect from land speculators. To the north, however, the grid of Manhattan created the capacity to build quickly, maintaining open space for infrastructure, transportation of people and goods, and water reservoirs rather than open space for public recreation, assembly, and memorialization. New York City's "Squares" and "Circles," the oblique public spaces strung along

Broadway—Union Square, Madison Square, Herald Square, Times Square, and Columbus Circle—are open because of the accidental result of the intersection of the diagonal Broadway and the orthogonal east-west avenues.

Union and Madison Squares are largely dedicated to park activities—passive recreation and plantings. The high cost of maintenance of these parks is largely absorbed by neighborhood groups, effectively tying the perpetuation of park space to private rather than public concerns. In this model, public space is dependent on the private wealth of adjoining communities, raising serious questions of public space equity. Private influence not only affects the quality of public space but also can restrict the public's range of uses. The notion that we can have an antinuke rally on the Sheep Meadow in Central Park as it happened in 1980 is no longer possible. Our parks close at 1:00 a.m., and a permit is required for gatherings of twenty-five or more.

So if our parks are no longer appropriate for reasonably unencumbered public consumption, what is? The transformation of Times and Herald Squares from vehicular intersections to pedestrianized corridors—the conversion of streets from car-centric, single-purpose corridors to multipurpose shared streets achieves a balance between cars, people, and cyclists. In Times Square, Broadway is closed for vehicular traffic from 47th to 42nd Streets, allowing people to move freely in an environment once dominated by cars. This street conversion creates spaces for large gatherings year-round and not just one night out of the year. The effort to convert existing streets to public, pedestrianized gathering spaces is becoming the future reality. While parks and existing public squares struggle to accommodate often conflicting demands and concerns, the shared street demonstrates the capacity of infrastructure to accept flexible and multipurpose uses. Unlike parks, the maintenance is minimal, the access is easy, and the opportunity for expansion unlimited if we consider that almost 30 percent of the city's surface area is dedicated to streets and sidewalks. Public streets not only offer ample space for public life but also provide opportunities for program, maintenance, and operational overlaps that can tie the perpetuation of public space to complementary concerns of public utilities and transportation.

The New York City Department of Transportation (DOT) has been pursuing street narrowing options with the addition of dedicated bicycle lanes and sidewalk bulbouts and the introduction of temporary and enlarged traffic islands along segments of Broadway. These efforts have improved ridership as well as lowered traffic incidents for cyclists and pedestrians. Independently, the Brooklyn Greenway is developing public parks along a bike path that circumnavigates the Brooklyn shoreline. One of the very first street closures to create a pedestrian-centric, car-free zone was the Nassau Street closure in Lower Manhattan. While this was controversial, it did introduce a retail corridor in Lower Manhattan where there was very little street life—in an era when there were very few residential units. Pedestrianized streets were subsequently introduced in the South Street Seaport district, and, more recently, the streets around the New York Stock Exchange were closed from ordinary vehicular traffic in the recognition that not all streets must provide the same level of vehicular access.

The current area of experimentation under the auspices of DOT is ongoing in the meat packing district, on Ninth Avenue between Gansevoort and 16th Street. At 14th Street, Ninth Avenue continues straight south, but the vehicular traffic veers east down Hudson Street, leaving a wide avenue-like space without the cars. The long-term intent is to create a culture of the shared street, where people, cars, and cyclists cohabit a zone with minimal curbs and without traffic signals, formal lanes, and crosswalks. The result is predicted to be slower yet constantly-moving traffic, a free flow of pedestrians, and the encouragement to ride a bicycle at a pedestrian-friendly speed. Holly Whyte's barometer for healthy civic activities of cafes, restaurants, vendors, and people lingering on street corners will be promoted and encouraged. In carving out these new spaces for the public, issues of scale and adjacency are of utmost importance. It is not enough to divide the space of the street, making sections for cars, people, and bikes while failing to provide the space for any of these occupants. Shared streets thrive only when they are truly shared and overlaps allowed, taking full advantage of every inch of pavement. The success of such shared street models in promoting public space while calming traffic has been documented from northern Europe to Vancouver. The most well-known example of shifting priority from vehicles to pedestrians is the Dutch *woonerf*, which has reclaimed the street as a place for community living.

Can this new zone also double as a space for public assembly, where spontaneous gathering will not only be permitted but also encouraged? Many of the contributors to this book make points that apply to the shared street concept. Marshall Berman spoke of the agora in Athens, a "big, sloppy space," a place that made you feel at home. (See Marshall Berman's essay in this volume). Can the shared street be today's "sloppy" home for public activities and protests? Jeffrey Hou made it clear that a public space represents "institutionalized insurgency" and should be initiated by people, not institutions. (See Jeffrey Hou's essay in this volume). Will the public continue to take to the streets as the Occupy movement did following their eviction from Zuccotti Park? Paula Z. Segal characterized the form of space as never complete and that it always represents the act of placemaking. (See Paula Z. Segal's essay in this volume). Can this "act of placemaking" be encouraged and nourished in the space of the street? And Jerold Kayden points out that anything private "alters the nature and quality and the status of the space." The collective voice applies directly to a shared street concept: it is owned and used by the public, and it is both a piece of infrastructure maintained by a city agency and the undefined zone of Holly Whyte's chair, where when you adjust it an inch, it is yours.

The status of public space that Kayden is interested in redefining is ownership driven. He goes on to say that the "very identity of the owner becomes outcome determinative." Apply this to the shared street concept where the ownership lines are blurred between pedestrian space and vehicular space. Here, there is flexibility of use and the spontaneous initiated sense of program and event mobility, shifting time from day to night, summer to winter, large crowds to small crowds, but still all within the container of the street. That's why Manhattan has an endless supply of public space—it is there for the taking.

Designed to Be Occupied

Signe Nielsen

AS A LANDSCAPE architect and de-
signer of urban public space, one of my measures of success is the manner in
which people occupy the spaces I design. A significant challenge of creating
public open space is that there is rarely a program or determined list of features that need to be incorporated. Clients, be they public entities, not-for-
profits, or private owners, tend to think of public space either as a valuable
asset or a necessary evil, but rarely is it viewed through the lens of function
and meaning. One of the great freedoms of our profession is that our actual
clients or users are largely unknown. Certainly, one can anticipate specific
activities such as employees entering and exiting an office building, transit
riders rushing headlong through the space, or lunchtime crowds seeking a
few moments of respite from their computer screens. Beyond those obvious
predictions that are based on context, one would hope that a public space
had enduring purpose and value so that it would encourage a much broader
potential spectrum of participants over a sustained period of time.

How do we begin to think about design then in the absence of prescriptive functions? One of the first philosophical decisions is whether to create
a "loose" or a "tight" space. A loose space is one in which the physical elements allow the occupants freedom to meander, appropriate, and personal-
ize. Movable furniture that can be relocated into the sun or shade, put away
from the wind, or reconfigured to suit an individual or a group is the classic
example of personal adaptation in public space. However, portable furnishings have a management burden that few owners are prepared to accept. For
example, tables and chairs that are unattached tend to get rearranged by the

Figure 1. Bryant Park. *Photo by Signe Nielsen*

public in response to the space's microclimate or sociological habits; at the end of the day, these either need to be put back into some order or stored for the next day's deployment. This cycle is repeated day in and day out, which requires a permanent labor force. An alternative is to offer a variety of fixed seating strategically placed to accommodate climatic variations, views, and interactive choices. Clearly many elements must be fixed such as trees, steps, walls, drinking fountains, and bike racks. However, the designer needs to decide from the outset as to the balance among the components. Will the layout largely dictate the types of uses or will the occupants have a significant measure of freedom of choice? Another variation on a loose space is one that accepts a broad spectrum of activities, from small groups to temporal markets to spontaneous or programmed performances. Classic New York examples are the interior of Bryant Park (Figure 1) or the areas flanking the steps to the Metropolitan Museum. A more contemporary example is the North Plaza tree grove at Lincoln Center (Figure 2).

What these three spaces have in common is a geometric arrangement of trees, movable seating, and the ability for people to manipulate their personal space in response to planned or spontaneous activities within the surrounding context. Food kiosks, vendors, and performances are part of the spatial mix, and people may bring their own food, laptops, or other personal

Figure 2. North Plaza grove at Lincoln Center. *Photo by Signe Nielsen*

entertainment devices. But while these additives offer comfort and stimulus, they are not essential to the value of the space. These and similar loose spaces offer opportunities to engage with the unexpected, to be stimulated by multisensory experiences, and to have the freedom to be with other people or the freedom to be alone and anonymous.

A tight space is one with limited points of access and rigidly placed agglomerations of plantings and furnishings that respond more to an imposed order than to the intuitive ways in which people might circulate, gather, or seek solitude. A tight space is essentially obstructed, uncomfortable, and thwarting to human interaction and enjoyment. This design strategy tends to curtail possibilities and render the users a passive audience rather than active players in the theater of public space. While owners and property managers appreciate the predictable and consonant qualities of their outdoor real estate portfolio, potential users are put off by the opacity, inalterability, and prescriptiveness of these spaces. One only needs to read William H. Whyte's seminal work on *The Social Life of Small Urban Spaces* (1980) to be reminded of the plethora of flawed public spaces that proliferated after a 1961 zoning ordinance opened the door to the "bonusable" plaza. Some of the most egregious include sunken plazas such as the original General Motors Plaza (Figure 3), which is Trump Plaza at 59th Street today, and

Figure 3. General Motors Plaza in 1978. *Photo by Signe Nielsen*

Paramount Plaza on Broadway. Set below the sidewalk level, these plazas are visually constrained, intensely shady, and unnecessarily arduous to access, never mind casually traverse. Cut off from the action of the street, people are reluctant to descend into their abyss of darkness.

Grace Plaza (Figure 4), at Sixth Avenue and 43rd Street, is exemplary of how poor siting and bad architectural decisions can permanently compromise the ability of a space to provide public benefit. Soon after its opening, the brilliant architectural critic Ada Louise Huxtable dubbed it the worst public space in New York. Over the years since it was completed in 1971, there have been at least three major renovations, ranging from completely fencing in the plaza to prevent drug dealing to peppering the space with clusters of planters and seating. None of these has been successful, partly because of the plaza's northwesterly orientation, which results in a permanently shaded windswept microclimate, and partly because of the insistence on aligning the "amenities" with the relentless grid pattern in the paving. These tight spaces, regardless of their relative aesthetic merits, are fundamentally over engineered outdoor boxes that fail to invite, welcome, or comfortably sustain people physically, socially, or intellectually.

A third category of public space is what might be generously called minimalist. At first blush, one might think of these plazas as loose because

Figure 4. Grace Plaza's second redesign 2005. *Photo by Signe Nielsen*

they are free of clutter and seem physically capable of becoming flexibly appointed or programmed. On closer inspection, the simplicity is actually an intentional lack of places for people to occupy. These plazas defend themselves by displaying significant works of art such as the Noguchi cube at 140 Broadway (Figure 5), the Dubuffet and Noguchi pieces at Chase Plaza, and a Cook bronze at 345 Park Avenue. Designed during the years when public space was perceived more as a liability than an asset, these plazas avoid the annoyance of "undesirables" by themselves being undesirable.

Students of public space can read these plazas by the ordinance under which they were created. Privately owned public space in New York City is governed by a zoning ordinance that was first created in 1961 and then, in response to a number of abject plaza failures, was revamped in 1975 to embed higher design standards and functional

Figure 5. Noguchi cube at 140 Broadway.
Photo by Signe Nielsen

Figure 6. Pedestrian street in Lower Manhattan. *Photo by Signe Nielsen*

amenities. Most recently, under the leadership of Amanda Burden, the plaza ordinance has been revised again to be much more prescriptive regarding quantities of trees, amount and types of seating, heights of walls and steps, percentage of openness, and the like. The tight and minimalist spaces cited above were designed under the 1961 or 1975 plaza ordinances, which contained few programmatic criteria and left the developer and designer with much more flexibility. The current plaza ordinance is considered by some designers to be overly controlling. A valid question is whether government can effectively legislate "good" design. Do all the requirements and prohibitions result in better spaces for people?

Speaking personally, I try to look beyond the physical analysis of context, circulation, environmental conditions, and regulatory requirements to seek out the "genius loci"—those qualities that will imbue the space with a meaning that will resonate with many people for many years. Observing human behavior and translating this observation into design is a skill that is honed over a lifetime of successes and failures. Some of the best places I have designed engendered uses that I never imagined: a waterfront pier has become a premier wedding photo spot, a widened sidewalk has spawned community gardens, a subway plaza has evolved into a farmers market, and a cobble-lined street has transformed into a vibrant bar scene (Figure 6). What went right?

Before those unwitting successes comes the moment of anxiety when a client or community board sees the design take shape on paper and begins to understand the spatial manifestation of the designer's vision. Questions arise that are frequently based on a negative view of behavior: How will you stop skateboarders? How will you prevent the homeless from taking over the benches? How will you keep the dogs off the plants? How will you keep people from blocking the steps? Designers have two basic choices: succumb to the slippery slope of progressively more robust preventative measures or imbue the design with a resilience that accepts some level of assumed abuse but essentially relies on positive behavior to outweigh misuse. Designing a masterful public space is like raising a child: after the parents have instilled sound values in them, nurtured their minds and souls, and tried to protect them against harm, children grow up and make their way in the world. So too a public space evolves from an incipient idea into built reality through an evolutionary process of questioning, examining, and collaborating. When the space is completed, the designer must let it free to survive the vagaries of weather, human behavior, and management decisions. Successful places need to be instilled with both beauty and practicality and be inherently flexible, regardless of their size, so that multiple activities can occur simultaneously over the course of a day, week, and year. In so doing, I believe, it is possible to create a public space that is as comfortable for the few as it is welcoming to the many.

Perhaps a corollary question is whether a space can be too successful. I would say that there are instances where a place has drawn such large crowds due to its popularity that the result is unintentional physical damage to its more vulnerable components, such as the turf or flower beds. We have seen this time and again in the Sheep Meadow of New York's Central Park after a major outdoor concert or in Madison Square Park after the opening of the Shake Shack, where the sheer number of people compacted the soil or spilled over the pavement causing deterioration of the landscape. More recently at the High Line (Figure 7), people literally come to a standstill at some of

Figure 7. The High Line at the Tenth Avenue overlook. *Photo by Signe Nielsen*

the pinch points along its narrow path. These "victims of their own success" can be managed, though control strategies are often met with resistance by users of the space. For example, the New York City Department of Parks & Recreation has reduced the frequency of free concerts in Central Park, the Madison Square Park Conservancy has converted turf to pavement around the food concession, and the Friends of the High Line has considered limiting the number of people that can access the elevated park.

One cannot reasonably deny that public space has been the source of trepidation in spite of its critical role as a relief valve in dense urban areas. As an undergraduate student in the late 1960s, I marched, occupied, and generally misbehaved in countless public and not-so-public spaces. As a landscape student in the 1970s, I catalogued public spaces for William Whyte's study that led to the plaza rezoning and observed people's distaste or abuse of furnishings that appeared to be designed to survive the next nuclear attack. Not surprisingly, as our city has gotten safer and wealthier over the past few decades, public spaces have become kinder and gentler. Indeed, our city has numerous examples of civic spaces that are responsive to notions of well-being, social interaction, and engagement.

In the end, what distinguishes good public space from hostile or mediocre public space is the fundamental philosophical shift from believing that more people misbehave than act benignly in the public realm. Again, Bryant Park and the Metropolitan are useful laboratories. Bryant Park was a haven for drug dealers and in spite of its prominent location, surrounded by thousands of workers, tourists, and library visitors, was considered so dangerous that the Parks Department threatened to close it. William Whyte was enlisted to contribute his sociological observations as part of the restoration of Bryant Park. His key recommendations were to increase access by removing fences and adding new entrances, to improve sight lines and transparency by removing hedges, and to introduce amenities that would attract the general public. The park's popularity is legendary and is considered a textbook example of thoughtful design and intense programming in combination with good management and private security. The homeless still reside on some of the more remote benches, but the menacing users have sought other ground.

The Metropolitan Museum (Figure 8) embarked on a renovation in the early 1970s and took the daring step of putting out Parisian bistro chairs under the newly planted trees along the wide Fifth Avenue sidewalk. Most

articles at the time ridiculed the movable chairs as something that would last two weeks. In 1974, an article by William Whyte reported that no chairs had been stolen from either the Metropolitan or Paley Park and concluded that "Places that treat people with amenity are usually treated in kind." I am a firm believer in this optimistic view of human behavior as a guide for public space advocacy and design. Design alone cannot increase people's income or heal the sick, but sensitively created spaces can gracefully serve a diversity of people as long as the general public and owners of the spaces perceive the balance to be weighted heavily toward the benign users.

In 2001, the cataclysmic World Trade Center attacks befell our city; this event set in motion a profound confusion about the role and benefit of public space in our society. In the aftermath, which continues today, site-specific rules are hastily taped to planter walls or buried in the fine print of some administrative ordinance, and the public is left to the affront of officers and private security personnel who seem equally confused but nonetheless persistent in their enforcement. Security cameras have sprouted from nearly every vertical pole, photography is randomly forbidden, and bollards and barricades impede our ability to move freely.

Figure 9. Tents in Zuccotti Park. *Photo by Signe Nielsen*

Zuccotti Park fulfills much of the definition of a loose space with its po-
rous edges, pedestrian circulation, gracious canopy of trees, multiple seating
arrangements, and space for vendors and farmers market—although most
likely the Occupy movement selected this space because of its proximity to
the reviled Wall Street, rather than because of its design. I fully support the
inclusive agenda and public presence of Occupy Wall Street, but I drew
the line when Zuccotti Park became an encampment of the few to the exclusion of the many. During the first weeks, protesters would gather over the
course of the day and set up placards, and people would gather in groups
to listen to speakers, share news, and express their various concerns. Those
of us who live or work in the area could still traverse the plaza, albeit with
some maneuvering, but we could still have lunch, sit on the benches, and
enjoy the outdoors. By nightfall, the plaza would shift from being largely
occupied to sparsely populated, and one of its main design features would
reemerge as people cut diagonally through on their way to mass transit.
The plaza's looseness was an asset to all. But then tarps were strung from
the trees and soon after there were tents (Figure 9); the police presence
grew exponentially around the perimeter as the media frenzy drew more
attention to the ongoing demonstration. The officers and their vehicles
became a phalanx around the perimeter and largely stood there not know-

Figure 10. Tents in Freedom Plaza. *Photo by Signe Nielsen*

ing what to do in the absence of violence or illicit activity. The general public was relegated to walk along the periphery until the barricades made that impossible and forced pedestrians to walk elsewhere. As someone who considers herself firmly in the 99%, I did not challenge the protesters to move out of the way for my convenience; I was neither afraid nor put off by the media's sensationalism of misbehavior, but after a few weeks of cheek-by-jowl tents, I began to question how long the occupation would preclude the general use of the plaza. The balance had shifted. However, it did not shift as it did in Bryant Park, where violent or threatening behavior resulted in exclusion; it shifted because the presence of tents and occupants' accoutrements made it physically impossible to even enter the space or traverse its sidewalks. In this regard, it is interesting that the Occupy movement in Washington, DC, has been allowed to set up camp on a portion of Freedom Plaza (Figure 10): orderly barricades define the occupied portion, while the remainder of the space remains open and accessible to the general public.

The Occupy movement raises many important questions about the use of privately owned public spaces. Would the eviction of protesters have happened if the demonstrations had taken place in a public park rather than a privately owned public space? I don't know. Each city, whether it be Los Angeles, Washington DC, Oakland, or New York, has handled the protest

in different ways depending on local regulations and site-specific management rules. Was there a predominance of people behaving badly or homeless
individuals seeking free food within the park? I doubt it. How long should
a group of individuals be allowed to preclude any use of a public space by
other individuals of equal rights? This remains an open question to me. Is
Zuccotti Park a "victim of its own success"? In many ways it is. Its location
and adaptability have fostered the right of people to democratically express
their opinions and protest injustices in public space. This ability for free and
fearless protest is indeed another measure of the success of public space.

As designers of public space, we need to be advocates and educators
as much as we need to be a creative force. But we also need to recognize
that the creation of truly open public space cannot solve other failures of
our society. We cannot design away substance abuse, homelessness, and
unemployment. We must eschew lockable gates, barriers, and physical im-
pediments to social interaction. We should not be afraid of open space by
filling it up with eye-candy clutter. We need to push for clarity from our
clients and reviewing bodies to ensure that rules (fewer rules preferred) are
democratically written and equitably enforced, and we need to remember
that throughout history, public space in great cities has been a source of
solace, celebration, and a platform for societal discourse—a mirror of our
collective consciousness.

Reference

Whyte, W. 1980. *The Social Life of Small Urban Spaces*. New York: The Project for
    Public Spaces, Inc.

POPS, Out of the Shadows

A DESIGNER'S PERSPECTIVE

Thomas Balsley

THE OCCUPY WALL STREET movement made Zuccotti Park famous, and in doing so it had an inadvertent effect on the public's awareness of our small urban parks. Particularly at the forefront of public consciousness are the privately owned spaces like Zuccotti Park that proliferate in Manhattan's public realm and have sprung up in other US cities as well. In New York City they are known as privately owned public spaces (POPS), and in San Francisco as privately owned public open spaces (POPOS). Though each is small in size, taken together New York City's POPS total ninety acres of precious land in the densest residential and commercial areas of Manhattan and make up a virtual "shadow park system" for the city. There are other parks that are in fact public but are run by conservancies, friends, authorities, etc. (think Battery Park City parks, Bryant Park, and the High Line), which makes them hybrids. They feel public but their management, maintenance, and programming are put into the hands of private or nonprofit organizations. Together, the hybrids and the POPS represent Manhattan's most heavily used public spaces.

Though POPS do not have the name recognition associated with the hybrids (except for Zuccotti Park now), they play an incredibly profound role in the quality of New York's urban life. Because they are scattered throughout the densest portions of Manhattan, they can usually be found within two or three blocks of where New Yorkers live or work, providing a serendipitous attraction that has the potential to touch their daily lives very differently than the occasional trip to Central Park or a waterfront park. Their form and dynamic are quite unique and new to the conventional typology of urban parks. Thanks to the Zuccotti Park occupation, the elevated public awareness of these spaces has raised questions of ownership and management, use and access, and program and purpose that have crossed over into the mainstream psyche, moving beyond the limited interest of urbanists and developers and into a broader and more inclusive public discourse.

Why are public spaces so important to our society? Most people generally agree that parks are important, but only recently have metrics come forth that begin to measure their contribution to the environmental, social, and economic sustainability of cities. We are coming closer to the day when the public health and welfare benefits offered by parks will have greater influence over municipal budgets.

Besides their emerging metrics, the consistent and compelling argument for our urban parks is that they reflect who we are as a society, as well as the quality of life we promise our citizens. In more ways than almost any other civic impression, parks and plazas provide a transparent display of our democratic principles (freedom of assembly, freedom of speech, equal rights, etc.) at work for all to see; and in so doing, they sometimes reveal our social ills and conflicting principles, as we have seen at the Occupy Wall Street movement in New York City's Zuccotti Park. The highly regarded urbanist and social observer William Whyte would have reminded us that it is these messy moments at the urban core that mark the existence of a vibrant, livable city.

Typology of Parks

Socially sustainable cities depend on a robust and diverse inventory of public open spaces. Setting aside for the moment the streets, indoor spaces, and natural areas, this park inventory should vary in size, character, and purpose to best serve the city's diverse population and its visitors. I will mention a few types here that, by comparison, help to put the small public spaces and POPS into context, especially with respect to performance expectations. High-profile parks like New York City's Central Park or Vancouver's Stanley Park or Chicago's Grant Park are, for the most part, destination parks: spots for the city's population to plan a visit to, except for the select few fortunate enough to live or work nearby. For this reason it is possible that the ubiquitous small social spaces and neighborhood parks actually have a more profound effect on our daily lives.

Chelsea Waterside Park, New York City. *Photo by Michael Koontz*

Large civic parks are typically located near the urban core and, as such, provide the common ground on which civic life unfolds as well as a venue for festivals, celebrations, performances, and displays of civic pride. Contemporary urban lifestyles and a resurgence of downtown living have led the way for a change from the overly formalized spaces of the past to ones teeming with daily life—filled with cafés, play areas, interactive fountains, and even dog runs—yet flexible enough to host thousands. New York City's Bryant Park and Discovery Green in Houston are excellent examples of these emerging hybrid spaces.

Not as well known are the community and neighborhood parks found throughout all corners of the city. Though their sizes vary, their purpose strikes a balance between active and passive interests. Tennis, basketball, and handball courts, ball fields, picnic areas, playgrounds, dog runs, and gardens are but a few of the attractions that can be shared by individuals or groups on any given day in these important parks. Most of these are mapped public parks and are beneficiaries of early city making or more recent visionary urban planning that placed high priority on strategically distributed open space within our communities. Chelsea Waterside Park is the by-product of an extraordinary process of community advocacy planning that carved a new neighborhood park out of the development and realignment of a state highway.

Main Street Garden Park, Dallas. *Photo by Craig D. Blackmon*

Riverside Park South, New York City. *Photo by John Donnelly*

Paley Park, New
York City. *Photo by
Milan Riva*

Another example of new park making can be found in the heart of down-town Dallas where an underutilized block of vacant buildings and parking garages was acquired by the city to serve the influx of residents, students, and faculty at this downtown commercial and retail core. The result, Main Street Garden Park, boasts pavilions, café terraces, play areas, dog runs, and a large, open lawn for yoga, summer movies, or just kicking a ball.

In response to continuing urban growth, many recent parks have re-sulted from public/private partnerships in which mutually beneficial goals are met. Mapped as a twenty-six acre public park, New York City's Riverside Park South emerged from a unique coalition of community groups, civic organizations, and developers that was formed to rezone sixty-five acres of abandoned rail yards along the Hudson River. Similarly, the High Line is a new public park that started as a grassroots movement and slowly attracted broad public and nonprofit sponsorship.

With different results, development approvals and zoning incentives have coincided with public benefit to produce numerous privately owned public spaces in cities across the country. The public's awareness and under-standing of these strangely named spaces is vague at best. As is one of their goals, they have been embedded into our daily lives to look and feel like the public parks and plazas they emulate; so it is not surprising that there has been so much confusion and outrage over the jurisdictional constraints that have come to light with the Occupy Wall Street movement's encampment at Zuccotti Park. Some of these privately owned spaces—like the highly acclaimed parks at Battery Park City that were incorporated into the urban design plan by the Battery Park City Authority—operate with their own maintenance and security departments. On a smaller but no less successful scale, the privately owned Post Office Square in Boston has proven to be a worthy precedent for such initiatives. This urban park jewel was chipped out of a block of parking garages by the surrounding commercial property owners and then ingeniously placed over a new sunken garage whose revenue stream has financed the construction and maintenance ever since. The rooftop at 343 Samsone Street in San Francisco is another fine example of a successful POPOS.

New York City's Bonus Plazas or POPS

A particularly interesting breed of this privately owned public space model is New York City's POPS, of which Zuccotti Park is one. Over three hundred of these unique spaces can be found in residential and commercial districts throughout Manhattan. Inspired by the piazzas and plazas of European cities, and in recognition of New York City's dire need for new open space in its densest locations, a zoning resolution in the 1960s provided property owners in select neighborhoods with a compelling offer: receive a floor area bonus (worth incalculable value) to your planned development in exchange for financing, building, and maintaining an on-site public plaza. It should be noted that not only was the floor area bonus attractive, but the value of the higher floors would also increase since it is all about views. If done well, the open space would also have the potential to provide the building with a valuable verdant foreground setting not usually found in the historical street-to-wall buildings.

Unfortunately, unforeseen problems resulted. Developers who received the bonuses sold to co-op owners who, rather than benefitting from the bonus, were saddled with the responsibilities that came with it, and began to look at the public plazas as their front doors rather than spaces meant to invite public use and enjoyment. Of course this condition was exacerbated by the social upheaval and urban deterioration of the 1960s and 1970s, as the general public stigmatized public plazas as magnets for the least desirable aspects of public use. When the spaces were not physically close enough to the lobby to enhance the entrance, the plazas were often left in poor condition, with spikes on the required seating, or even illegally closed. Many of the early spaces from the 1960s and 1970s were developed under weak guidelines with respect to access, amenities, and location. The early guidelines never addressed the quantity or the quality of seating, or trees and planting. They even allowed bonus spaces to be one story above or below grade, effectively hiding themselves from the public they were meant to attract and serve.

Another challenge to the success of these spaces has been their location in the urban context. In almost all cases, their location is a by-product of the mysterious real estate assemblages of development parcels, not of sound urban planning processes. For example, why would we need a plaza located at mid-block on a residential street when there is a retail node or subway at the corner where it would be better suited? Because that is where the assemblages happened to be and the plaza cannot be "transferred." Location represents a design challenge for many of these POPS and for those who are trying to design them in ways that live up to the neighborhood's expectations. Only so much design genius can overcome the age-old problem of location, location, location. Manhattan's vest-pocket parks like Paley Plaza or Greenacre Park were heralded as prototypes for a busy dense city but the philanthropic private sector never followed suit. Both are located at mid-block in commercial districts and are successful, but it would be hard to justify so many hard-paved bonus plazas in the middle of quiet residential streets. Inspired by the Greenacre Park model, we have recently begun treating these spaces as pocket parks—sanctuaries of greenery and quiet that have real appeal to the neighborhoods they serve.

As an aside, one of the most successful plazas that I have ever encountered was in San Francisco, where, in a tiny triangle on Market Street, long pew-like benches filled with people faced the busy sidewalk. That's all! Here the designer seems to have recognized the power of this unique stage-like location with its ongoing performance of street life and to have chosen to celebrate and not compete with it.

The reasons and the challenges cited above have left scores of barren or underperforming POPS throughout the city as undeniable evidence of the incentive zoning's weaknesses. On the other hand, most POPS have met their broad goals and many others have met or exceeded the public's highest expectations, combining all of the ingredients of a successful urban open space formula. It is here that we can witness the powerful contribution of these vibrant spaces to the quality of life in many Manhattan neighborhoods. This is social sustainability in its most focused and recognizable state. It is the social interaction that is fostered in these small spaces—close encounters—that New Yorkers crave. Their dynamic sometimes reminds me of a party whose room at first seems a bit too small, too crowded; but it is the energy from that friction that is seductive and attracts a new wave of New Yorkers from around the world every year.

Case Studies of Successful POPS Design Strategies

When effective urban design research and inclusive dialogue are applied, designers can creatively convert some of the "shortcomings" of location and size into assets. One example of this is the highly acclaimed Capitol Plaza in New York, situated between 26th and 27th Streets, just east of 6th Avenue. In spite of the successfully retooled Madison Square Park's plan one block away, this forty-foot-wide mid-block plaza is packed with people through-

Capitol Plaza, New York City. *Photo by Bruce Katz*

325 5th Avenue, New York City. *Photo by Shigeo Kawasaki*

out the year. Its design has tapped into the quirky neighborhood of creative class, hip-hop fashion retailers, and young high-end residents. On any given day shoppers dragging black plastic bags are commingling with bike messengers, website designers in conferences, and acting students in mock rehearsals. Why are they there? Because the design and social furnishing of the space more closely reflect their contemporary urban lifestyles. The single rows of benches along the promenades of Madison Square Park do not foster the social experience that attracted this particular breed to the city.

In a neighborhood with a dearth of any parks or plazas, 325 5th Avenue Plaza on 33rd Street has emerged as the place to be. The incentive zoning language was very specific in its requirement that the bonus plazas be exposed to direct sunlight. Dark, northern orientations were forbidden unless reasonable hardship could be demonstrated. A narrow, north-facing plaza, 325 5th Avenue received City Planning Department approval by demonstrating such a hardship. The plaza's success can be attributed to an innovative and mitigating design approach to lighting, color, and public seating. Colorful murals one hundred feet long frame the space, innovative LED lighting is integrated into pavements and walls, and a custom-designed array of fifty-foot-long banquette lounge benches, extended urban picnic

Silver Park, New York City. *Photo by Michael Koontz*

tables, and raised bar tables with swivel seats have all worked together to attract crowds of residents, workers, and tourists.

Occasionally we find POPS that are of a generous size, such as the three-quarter-acre Silver Park on West 42nd Street between 11th and 12th Avenues. Located in the emerging West 42nd Street residential neighborhood, which is otherwise devoid of parks, this successful space has been designed as a community park-like setting instead of a street plaza, with a tot play area, a dog run, a café, and seating surrounding an open, flexible lawn. It has attracted the full embrace of the neighborhood.

As encouraging as these examples are of the new breed of POPS being developed, we are still left with the task of what to do about those barren, lifeless plaza failures that can be found throughout Manhattan and other US urban areas. The owners and developers of these spaces have received their bonus, and it seems that the public interests have lost their leverage in the bargain. Many see these spaces as "the glass half empty," or worse, as proof that the public was shortchanged. Yet even if the success rate was only fifty percent, Manhattan got forty-five acres of new open space. No other city could have found the finances or political will to wrench these properties from private ownership and into the public realm.

The public awareness and discourse that have come out of the Occupy Wall Street movement and Zuccotti Park events can and will be marshalled to demand that these many acres of failed spaces begin to finally deliver on their promise. How? Here is one way: most of the POPS were built over parking garages, which require waterproofing, which in turn has a lifespan. When these membranes begin to leak, the owners have no alternative but to remove the surface plaza in its entirety, at which time we have the chance to get it right. By using the more rigid current guidelines of the Department of City Planning, heightened regulatory oversight, and public scrutiny, the future designers will have all of the tools that have proven necessary to create vibrant public spaces. Where some see hopelessness, I see an extraordinary "land bank" waiting for a second chance. Remember, these "bonus" spaces are here in perpetuity. Even those spaces with the most daunting challenges like the elevated 55 Water Street in downtown Manhattan can be brought online with innovative design, public support, and enlightened ownership.

Equally exciting is the possibility of a completely new vision for the role some of these spaces can play in our ever-evolving contemporary culture of open space. Conventional expectations can be retooled—why not enlist those technological advances that have physically separated us into new forms of social connections, culture, and education? For example, while New York City continues to struggle through the democratic and bureaucratic challenges of simply providing public restrooms in our public streets (instead of at every Starbucks), why not locate them in some of those underperforming POPS?

Dramatic transformations such as these are blossoming in all types of parks across the United States. Skyline Park in Denver, Perk Park in Cleveland, and Union Square in San Francisco are just a few recent examples. Just as they have offered a bright future for those downtowns, many POPS in New York City are getting a second life. This includes Zuccotti Park, which was made over in 2006 by an enlightened consortium of downtown interests including its owner.

In a similar example, the redesign of a barren plaza at the corner of 57th Street and 9th Avenue into Balsley Park has helped transform the West 57th Street neighborhood character and sense of pride. From the moment it was built, this space (originally called Sheffield Plaza) was destined to fail.

Before redesign: Balsey Park, New York City. *Photo by Steven Tupu*

After redesign: Balsey Park, New York City. *Photo by Michael Koontz*

The space was not contiguous with the "bonus" building (out of sight/out of mind) and took the form of an open paved plaza with an amphitheater designed to host a local theater group who disbanded shortly after. The plaza was left looking empty and soon became home to the local pigeons and the few whose illegal businesses depended on such conditions. After fifteen years of this blight came a rare agreement between the neighborhood and an enlightened owner to start over. The designer was able to build a broad consensus on a new park-like character whose programmatic components would build a diverse constituency and ensure the park's long-term success. The new space has become the community common, has raised real estate values, and changed the image of West 57th Street in the minds of New Yorkers.

A key strategy in the Balsley Park transformation was to provide a nighttime closing component that would allay the concerns of a neighborhood that had seen the worst and was skeptical of late-hour activities. Generally POPS are required to remain open twenty-four hours so that nocturnal New Yorkers (and there are many in the "city that doesn't sleep") have access to the same benefits as their daytime counterparts. It is interesting to note the irony here that most New York *public* parks have nighttime closing hours. Balsley Park received approval for nighttime closing based on a hardship application that demonstrated its past history with nighttime crime and vandalism, but only with the promise of maintaining full openness during its daytime use. An effective folding gate system was designed to meet both goals: during the park's open hours the folding fence panels tuck away, undetected into their cabinets, while at night they are secured to prevent entry. In other nighttime closing hardship requests, owners have been convinced to accept low bollards and forty-two-foot-high removable panels as adequate deterrence from entry. This approach preserves the open, seamless relationship with the sidewalk during the day that successful plazas need.

Ironically, had Zuccotti Park been protected with a similar system, the Occupy Wall Street movement would not have considered building an encampment there or would have sought it elsewhere. But where? Yes, it was a convenient location given the unique nature of this particular protest and occupation, but it would certainly not be adequate in size nor would it be a strategic *civic* location for any number of other general public demonstrations or events. This brings me to the final question for New York. Trafalgar Square in London and the National Mall in Washington, DC, are spaces that have always been understood as arenas for political expression. Most world-class cities have one or more. How extraordinary is it then that New York, the self-proclaimed Greatest City in the World, the center for democracy and freedom of speech, has no such place? The fact that a tiny POPS park was made to act in lieu of a dedicated civic forum for popular protest should serve as a wake-up call for New Yorkers and their government to create a twenty-first-century innovative space to do what POPS cannot.

Developing the Public Realm

A CONVERSATION WITH JONATHAN ROSE

Ron Shiffman

JONATHAN ROSE COMPANIES, founded in 1989 by Jonathan Rose, is a for-profit social enterprise whose mission is to repair the fabric of communities. This unique development firm integrates policy, planning, and real estate development with values of social, economic, and environmental sustainability, creating a new model for for-profit enterprises. Their projects encompass planning, affordable development, policy, real estate investment, and civic development, and their works are scattered around the world. In February 2012, Ron Shiffman sat down with Jonathan Rose to talk about his perspective, as a progressive developer, on the issues of public space, design, and democracy raised by Occupy Wall Street.

Ron Shiffman (RS): Given your company's emphasis on promoting the public good through thoughtful design and development, do you often incorporate open space into your projects?

Jonathan Rose (JR): All of our projects have some element of open or public space. I have a theory about open space, developed from looking at the way communities developed around open space and throughout history. Here is the common pattern I found: all communities, all settlements, start with the most private space and progress to semiprivate, to semipublic, etc. There is a continuum and a progression. For example, there is the very traditional model of the courtyard house, with private spaces such as bedrooms surrounding a courtyard that is communal to the family. Then, there is the rooftop or alley that is a semipublic space, followed by the most public, which is often a town square. Interestingly, the public space is where both commerce and spirituality happen. It's where the church or the kiva—the center of spirituality—is, but it's also where the market is located. We try to mimic this in our buildings. The Via Verde project's roof system mirrors this progression from private to public within the building. The more private spaces are for reflective activities and the more public spaces are for growing food, for example, and the building ends with an amphitheater at the bottom in the courtyard.

In another project we finished recently in Albuquerque, New Mexico—which has a population mix that ranges from market-rate unit dwellers to affordable housing renters to a special-needs population of homeless individuals with behavioral disabilities—we held a competition with local Native American artists to create a center of contemplation in the common space. The winning design features a totem pole at the center of a spiraling garden. We often put spaces of reflection and contemplation to guide the space.

RS: I remember that after 9/11 you put together a proposal for the site that included this sort of open space, combining spirituality and the market with other activities.

JR: My idea for the World Trade Center site was that it began with most public and active spaces and then became more intimate, spiritual, and quiet as you moved inwards. In the very heart of it, there would be a church of all faiths, or institutions of many faiths to create a center of commonality.

RS: There is a long history of citizens using public spaces as places for discussion or debate. However, this idea of the "citizen" was initially very narrow and exclusive. Over time, we've expanded the notion of who has the right to occupy those spaces. In light of recent events, to what extent do you see the spaces you create as being open to or conducive to social or political inclusion? Open to discussion and debate, and even protest?

JR: The spaces I've described are internal to the projects, for security reasons and because it's what the users or residents have asked for. There is a clear demarcation between what's inside and what's outside. Building the "outside" social realm is something we've done much more outside of New York City, in other places in the United States. For example, we created a twenty-seven-acre urban infill village in Denver, Colorado, called Highland Garden Village where all the public space is open and accessible whether you are a resident or not. It has a public town square, parks, and gardens—a wide range of public spaces that are truly public. Here's what's interesting about this story: when we finished the residential and public portion of the project, we began to seek an affordable supermarket for the commercial portion. The only affordable supermarket we could attract to the area at that time was Walmart's small neighborhood market model. The unions started protesting on our property, and were there for a while. The Walmart did not end up happening.

RS: What if the protesters had stayed longer, as they did recently in Zuccotti Park?

JR: They were there a while, but they didn't stay overnight. Those public spaces are actually managed by the homeowners' association, not by us. Those homeowners actually live there—they walk their dogs there, their children play there. It's their space. I think there's a point at which they would have asked to have their space back. As the developers, it wasn't our place to say yes or no. It was the community's; but that's my guess as to what would have happened.

RS: In Zuccotti Park, people are exercising their right to petition government. From your perspective as one of the most progressive developers in the field, what do you think should be the roles of the public and private sectors in the development of public spaces? There is always a critical tension between the right to express oneself, the right to make others uncomfortable, and the right to be comfortable. How do we balance the rights of free speech with the right to be comfortable, safe, and secure?

JR: In London there is the tradition of Speakers' Corner, a place where people can go and speak their minds. It is interesting to me that Occupy London did not happen at Speakers' Corner; they chose to protest at St. Paul's church (though there may have been a legal reason for that). There was also the instance of people living in tents in Jerusalem to protest the lack of affordable housing in the summer of 2011. I think it is a public function—

a public responsibility—to provide multiple layers of public space to enable the multiple layers of democracy to take place.

Just as there is a progression from private space to the most public space, perhaps democracy also needs such a progression. There is a broad spectrum of ways democracy gets played out, and part of that is the people's voice and collective action. Our generational legacy is the civil rights marches and the antiwar marches in the 1960s; they have become part of the political DNA of our generation. We needed a place for these things to happen. The physical infrastructure of a democratic society must enable democracy to exist.

RS: I went to the March on Washington in 1963. The energy was palpable; people were pouring into the Mall like I'd never seen before. It changed my life.

JR: In that time, these were extraordinary events that lasted a day or lasted a weekend. Today, we are looking at events that last for months. What was so interesting to me about Occupy is the way it worked itself into the national and international consciousness. It takes a lot of work to organize a march on Washington; that itself is a barrier and an organizational strain. The amazing thing about Occupy Wall Street was that it was an emergent phenomenon, which took more time to develop. It changed the dialogue in its persistence, and the way it was self-organized. So the challenge is how to allow that persistence to unfold when it needs to, but prevent someone's neighborhood from being occupied permanently.

RS: Occupy Wall Street intentionally chose Zuccotti Park; it is interesting that they knew they wanted a small space, and the one place they could stay was a privately owned space. Why do you think we don't have something comparable to Tahrir Square in New York City?

JR: To protest in a space that has impact, it has to be visible and accessible, and it also has to be small enough to fill.

RS: There is something called the "public forum doctrine." If you were to make a recommendation to a planning group, what would you advise are the design elements of successful public spaces? How do you encourage public debate and protest, but prevent violence and abuse?

JR: I believe in the public right of assembly, and that cities need to accommodate for that and provide that. We need to design spaces for assembly—the necessary civic infrastructure. Around the world, I see a lot of these "fake amphitheaters" that are never used. They are designed for assembly and could be quite useful for public performance; however, the hardware of the space needs the software of the community in order to work. It needs to be mass-transit accessible, easy, and affordable to reach; and there needs to be a relative sense of enclosure and intimacy. Tiananmen Square, for example, would not work for a small protest of one thousand people. They would get lost there.

I also think we need regulations, because there can be competing yet equally legitimate uses for public space—say, separate protests for separate issues. How do we mitigate those interests? Simply designing a space is not enough.

RS: After 9/11, a group of New Yorkers went to Europe to look at public spaces. In Barcelona, the planners and designers there kept referring to the need to create public space for social inclusion, where groups from different socioeconomic strata would gather. What is your advice for the design, maintenance, and operation of those spaces of intersection?

JR: There is an aspect of social inclusion that is happening primarily in the economy, with concepts such as collaborative space, collaborative ownership, and collaborative or shared use (such as Zip Car). These models allow many more points of entry into social and economic participation. This is the "shared ownership" or "collaborative consumption" movement that has evolved out of the old farmers market model, which has always been a great gateway into small entrepreneurship. All over the world there are examples of these of "pop-up markets" that are basically made out of plywood and could be there for a season or for a day, whether there is something to sell or whether there isn't. Earlier I talked about how the markets, the commercial town centers, were also the centers of spirituality. People need to develop the habit of going somewhere, and not all activities are 365-days-a-year activity. Markets are used daily and yearly, even though what is sold or what happens there changes. Creating spaces that are economically inclusive allow for multiple uses and emergent entrepreneurship.

RS: How do you go from a marketplace of goods to a marketplace of ideas?

JR: These are cultural questions. One has to foster a culture of the marketplace of ideas. Our press culture has to be a true marketplace of ideas. There are many ways that cultural habits take hold…Sometimes they are seeded, and sometimes a powerful person promotes them. But there are also ideas that just emerge.

RS: I do think Occupy Wall Street has changed the nature of the discourse, changed the questions that are asked and the ideas that are produced…Occupy Wall Street was triggered by virtual space, but was acted out in actual space. We see a mirroring between virtual space and physical space, and we also see a new relationship between the virtual and the real.

JR: I may be old fashioned, but I do believe we operate differently in virtual space than in physical space…In our brains, we have mirror neurons, which is why we intuitively mirror each other's behavior…We see this in other primates, we see this in babies, in physical behavior and in speech. It is actually a way of showing empathy. This behavior is thought to be the root of altruism, and has developed as an evolutionary benefit. In prehistoric times, those who were part of a community survived better than those who were not. Now we have this whole neural system that is designed for this attunement to others and for compassion. These neural connections do not happen over the Internet as well, so cyberspace does not fully mirror the empathic side of our human nature. We have not learned how to create an embodied sense of community electronically.

Another issue we have learned is that attitudes follow behavior, rather than behavior following attitudes. For example, the physical act of recycling makes you more likely to recycle. Behavior is an embodied experience. And so we need to encourage the physical gathering of communities, as support for communal activities is more likely to grow from the communal experience…A danger is a society where the cyber is out of balance with the physical.

RS: Do you think it's possible for the public sector to provide for the public infrastructure and public space we've been talking about? We have to rethink the ways we finance things. Instead of making it the developer's responsibility to provide waterfront access, or affordable housing, what if we required the developer to build these things but financed them publicly and taxed them back? Now, we barter our public goods, rather than tax them and spend the money properly.

JR: We need the public to develop a cohesive, planned public space system rather than a haphazard one. The intention for its use has to come first from the public realm. The public has to own the responsibility of the public realm. I don't think this is the responsibility of private developers. Once the intention is there, we can figure out how to finance it; and I believe there are multiple solutions, which can include the private sector, but the focus should be to carry out the public plan.

RS: I've branded you as a developer in this discussion, but really you do a lot more. Have these questions about the design of public space affected projects you're looking at elsewhere, or shaped the way you're approaching your current projects?

JR: Let me ask you this: Where did the prophets go in biblical times? The market. They went to the market because the public had to be there to hear them. You also spoke of the Internet…but I maintain there still needs to be a physical space to be heard. On the other hand, let's say we had a really progressive public, and they set up an "occupy park" with spots for your tent, facilities, running water…

RS: No one would go there to protest.

JR: Exactly. The challenge is that if you overplan the space and the process, it loses its effectiveness. This is the balance we attempt to reach. In the end, the goal is for civil society to be civilized.

Programming Public Space

A CONVERSATION WITH CARLTON BROWN

Ron Shiffman with Anastassia Fisyak

Ron Shiffman (RS): As the principal and founder of New Spectrum, could you please describe its mission and some activities that New Spectrum has engaged in?

Carlton Brown (CB): We started our firm in 1987–88, a while ago. New Spectrum's vision came out of my experience as someone coming of age in the late 1950s and early 1960s. My parents moved to Mississippi to work in the civil rights movement in 1967, after Emmett Till was brutally murdered. I grew up in a household that instilled in my sister and me that if there was something broken, you shouldn't complain about it, you should fix it. That became my framework for the business.

I studied architecture and urban planning. I worked for an architect for a while and then worked for AT&T's real estate group. That is when New Spectrum started doing business. I think it was what I always really wanted to do. As a mature adult, one of the challenges I saw was that there were a lot of great plans and discussions, but I really wanted to be a doer, I wanted to be a fixer. We opened our business because we saw a lot of things in my community that were broken. There were a lot of people sitting on the sidelines talking about how broken things were, how hopeless it was, and how nothing could be done.

Our business started with a sense of optimism. Poor communities, black and brown communities, could actually be fixed. Clearly, there are structural challenges to that. The whole system is broken. But in the context of a broken system and structural challenges, there are things you can do to make a better life for people, to use and share resources more equitably. We started with the notion of creating something that was not second-class for poor communities. From my perception, people too frequently thought that because communities were poor, if you just gave them a little ol' something, they will be okay. That never really seemed to work.

I finished college in 1973. While I was in college, model-city programs were being undertaken all over the country. I remember working as an intern with an architect in Newark, who was involved with these projects. By the time I opened my business, the place was a complete wreck. It was brand new in 1969, and by 1988 it was a place no one wanted to live in. A lot of money was spent to create something that had no human benefit at all. When we started our business, we said, yes, we want to build buildings, but what we really want to do is create communities that are healthier for people, to develop something more than just bricks and mortar.

RS: There is a lot going on in the streets of New York, Oakland, and in other parts of the country. People have begun to occupy public spaces and talk about the needs of the 99%. From your perspective and the work you've done, how are you addressing the needs of the 99%?

CB: Since the beginning, every project we have done, with the exception of one at Battery Park City, has focused on the needs of the 99%. When I focus on the 99% conceptually, I start with a different notion. The 1% believe that ultimately there are not enough resources to go around, and because of that, if I'm part of that 1%, the only way I can really assure that I thrive is by taking my share. We start from a different premise, that there are enough resources to go around. What happens with the 99% is they get sliced and diced by race, ethnicity, gender, orientation, nation, region, and religion until they don't know that their class interests are the same. The 99% is sliced into all these little segments. They are placed into their own individual *Bantustans* where they say "this is mine." The notion of saying "this is ours" is the big challenge. Our work is always trying to talk about "this is ours" as opposed to "this is mine." When you start to talk about shared resources instead of "this is mine" and "this is yours" is when you start talking about the public realm. One of the challenges with advanced capitalist societies is that you do not talk about "ours." It's self-defeating for the 99% because it keeps us from talking about what we can do collectively.

For instance, we engaged in mixed-income housing long before the development community was asked to or required to. We were building sustainable housing long before anyone talked about sustainable housing. For the 99% that have fewer resources, compromised immune systems, and no health care, building homes with better indoor air quality should be required. It is a responsibility. Building homes that use less energy should just be baseline. We always believed in a sustainability baseline because we were building in communities that had fewer resources. You had to do it that way. That's what we talk about now, but in 1988, people were not talking about it, except for the Pratt Center.

RS: I want to discuss the points you just made. Let me start with the first one, with what you refer to as slicing. Many in power engage in a divide and conquer mentality. Therefore, there is a need for different groups to get together to demand their fair share and to exert their rights. In a conversation I had with Maya Wiley around this issue, we talked about the need to achieve a level of social cohesion within a community in order to achieve the goal of social inclusion. You have to build confidence within the group, and only then will people feel comfortable to work collectively with others. Some of us believe there is a need for places for that to occur, that it just doesn't occur without the space for people to interact. Roland Anglin, another contributor to this volume, points out that communities of color that have integrated and moved out of the center of the city often see their power base dissipated as there is no place in the suburbs for organization to take place. Mindy Fullilove also addresses the role that place has played in the African American struggle. To what extent has the work you've done addressed the provision of those kinds of spaces?

CB: I believe these kinds of spaces are something I call the "neutral zone." They're places where people, whether they are similar or different, can go and feel comfortable in engaging each other. Those neutral zones naturally occur. On any Saturday, you can go out to Prospect Park and you will see people playing soccer. They won't speak the same language, they won't look alike, they are of different nationalities, different races, different sexual orientations, and they'll play pick-up soccer. Sports are one of those places where that happens naturally. For me, the challenge is, what is it about those spaces that allows people to create neutral ground and engage with each other? What is it that is so different? I don't know. What we try to do, since we don't know what that is, is to create spaces in the communities and developments that we are building for those activities to naturally occur. Some social psychologists can probably tell you exactly why that happens in those kinds of spaces, but that's not my role.

What we have tried to do, and what I'm trying to work on with my colleague, Bruce Lincoln, is to create those types of spaces, both physical and virtual. For instance, in the Kalahari, a development Full Spectrum undertook in Harlem, we created a space called Street Squash. When we went there to build, there was a little league baseball team, the South Harlem Reds, that used that lot. They hung a sheet out on a building—"Full Spectrum is the devil incarnate"—so we went to talk to them. Ostensibly, they were concerned that they would not have a place to play. Part of the deal was to build another baseball field in Marcus Garvey Park, but more important than that, we tried to bring in another athletic organization that does something more than just play baseball or basketball. Ultimately, we found a group called Street Squash that works with kids who are the 99% from public housing and public schools. In New York, on average, if you live in public housing, someone has written your history and your future all in one sentence—you are nothing and you will be nothing. That is the expectation people bring to kids in public housing. The squash program changes that whole set of expectations because squash is a unique program sport that crosses class and race lines and takes the kids to places they didn't even know existed. When you live in Grant Homes in Harlem, you don't know what squash is, what a prep school is. You don't know what Brown or Wesleyan is. They take these kids, they teach them squash, they play with prep school leagues, then they take them up to universities. They open boundaries for them.

Since the program has been around, nearly 100 percent of the kids have graduated high school and have gone on to colleges. Some of them are in community colleges, some are at Yale, Princeton, Brown, Stanford, and Cal State. That's good, but what is really wonderful is that you go back around Christmas or summer holidays and all those kids are back and are teaching other kids. Athletics, as a neutral ground, can be something that empowers people. It brings people together and gives them the opportunity to change their prospects.

RS: One of the most beautiful things that takes place in the fall and spring is when you go to the "parade grounds" that adjoin Prospect Park, and youngsters are playing soccer from sunrise to sunset. It is a mirror of the United Nations.

CB: It is.

RS: Every kid out there…

CB: …from every portion of the planet.

RS: These relationships grow out of the effective use of places. You have a range of places where people can interact—public schools, parks that are set aside for those opportunities—but where are the spaces where people can get together to either play chess or skateboard, but also to sit down and talk about life or politics? When I grew up in New York and first started to work in Bed Stuy in the mid-1960s, people would sit in front of the barber shop and talk, they would get together on corners and talk, there were even soap boxes to be found on many a street corner.

CB: When I moved to New York in 1977, there were still a lot of places like that.

RS: You would go to 125th Street and Lenox…

CB: …before they tore down the bookstore there and built the state office building…

RS: Are we losing those spaces? Do you think about them when you plan a community in Mississippi or when you're doing your work abroad?

CB: To answer the first part of the question, yes, we're clearly losing those spaces. In a lot of cases, we've lost those spaces to the real estate industry. Someone wants to build on every open square foot in New York. But this is not endemic to New York; these kinds of spaces have been lost all over. My perception is that it is not just because of real estate development; it has to do with the people that use those spaces. One reason spaces aren't used that way is that people have lost that personal engagement. You can get a group of kids together and they will stare at the screen with a controller in hand, they will scream at the screen, they will have a great time, but they are not talking to each other. The way we engage with each other has changed.

We have to think about space to increase public engagement. We have to start thinking about how we can create physical spaces for that to happen and we have to do some programming for it to happen. We can get folks to sit in a meeting, but they text and check emails—we've been programmed to multitask, to do other things, to lose focus. If you're going to provide the physical space you have to have a program to get people to be there and to be engaged.

The second thing is that the world has changed in the way we talk about social groups. There was a time when we were connected physically in our social groups. We saw them, we spoke to them, we wrote to them, we got together. The notion of the social group is so different now because so much of it is virtual. Everybody you're friends with on Facebook is not really your friend, everybody on Foursquare you don't really know, everyone you tweet with isn't someone you have a real connection to, but, in terms of the number of people you come into contact with, it is a lot more than before. In the past, the constraints were largely physical, you needed to be in the same physical space. Now, you don't really have that constraint. The question is how can you take and create space, virtual space, and the opportunity for real meaningful interaction. The answer is the same thing as it is for creating real physical space. You have to program it effectively.

Programming is deprogramming us from what we have recently become accustomed to. For instance, in the space we're working on called "My Image Studio," we are providing spaces where all sorts of things will occur—with space for discussions, a café, and a bar. We plan to video the events, and distribute them virtually through new media and old media. We want to reach out to people, to engage them in a physical space where they can get together regularly, and to do it in a media rich environment in order to deprogram people from the other media-rich stuff they were going to do, and then create content around it.

RS: I find it interesting that you're developing a space that brings people together because what happened with Occupy was that it happened first in virtual space and then in physical space. People needed to see each other's faces and touch each other.

CB: I believe we need to do that, that is something we need as humans. Occupy is a great example, because, you're right, it started with the tweeting. If you think of some of the upheavals in the Middle East and North Africa in the last two years, so much of it started like that.

I wonder if that is a generation thing. I know for me it's different. My children are twenty-seven and twenty-nine; I would like to ask them if it's different. Ana, is it different for you and your colleagues?

Anastassia Fisyak (AF): I feel that as far as Occupy and social media were concerned, it served as a way to get people on the street—to mobilize people. It's a question not only of generation but also of culture. For example, the role of social media is different between the United States and the Middle East. For one of my fellow students from Iran,[1] Facebook is never a form of personal discussion; it's a form of political discussion. The conceptualization of that infrastructure is different. Not so much individual reporting of day-to-day activities, but an engagement.

RS: What I have observed in many of my students is that if they need to do work, they won't go home, but they'll go to a coffee shop with a Wi-Fi connection where there are other people doing their own work. At play is a human instinct, the need to be around other people. You learn from people's body movements and expressions and not only from their words. You want to see their eyes, their hands, their body motions, because that too is a form of communication. There is a unique linkage between the virtual and the real. Both are needed to gain a better understanding of issues, for political organizing, for education, for building solidarity. One needs real space to break down barriers and create a more equitable society.

AF: But the thing is, in a coffee shop you have your computer in front of you. The cultural notion of what a coffee shop used to be in nineteenth-century France, for example, was a place for discourse.

---

1. See Sadra Shahab and Shirin Barghi's essay in this volume.

RS: But they had newspapers in front of them and smoke screens protecting them from interacting with others.

CB: I'm happy to have people with computers there, but it is still possible to create a culture of place. For instance, if you go to Jackson Square, New Orleans, you know there are certain things that will happen there, it's been happening for generations because that is the culture of place that emerged there. But can't we create the culture of place that we make specifically for interaction?

RS: We can, that's the question. Are you doing that in addition to the space in Harlem? A lot of what I am discovering by reading the other articles is that we're rapidly privatizing open space in this country—not only private space, but by our regulatory powers, we are privatizing public spaces, too. The young people you were talking about in public housing can't congregate in front of their own houses without being stopped and frisked. The only way they're safe is if they're in front of a screen.

CB: I haven't thought about that, but that's an unfortunate fact.

RS: How do we take back those spaces? How do we allow those kids to gather there? Many developers are building malls that are replacing our streets. They have their own police force, they have their own rules and regulations, you can't distribute literature in them because they're not public forums anymore. The *New York Times* recently ran an op-ed[2] piece that pointed out that 10 percent of the housing units in the United States now are in gated communities. How do we begin to create spaces that can once again function as a public forum?

CB: Every time I see a gated community, it looks like South Africa. South Africa is one giant gated community for the middle class and the wealthy. I'm talking barbed wire, electric wire, razor wire. Is that really how people want to live? In these sort of prisons?

Jackson, Mississippi, is where Full Spectrum is engaged. Jackson is a place in America with lurid classism and racism. The population of Jackson

---

2. See Benjamin 2012.

in the last two censuses shrank from 200,000 to about 180,000 people; the metropolitan area has grown from 350,000 people to just under 600,000 people. The wealth of the Standard Metropolitan Statistical Area (SMSA) has grown tremendously. When you look at the SMSA in terms of wealth and education, they're 30 to 40 percent over the median for the country. When you look at the city of Jackson it is significantly under the median, probably 25 percent under the median. When you get outside of Jackson, that's when you find the middle class and it doesn't matter if they're black or Latino. Jackson has become this sort of poor community where there's been tremendous job growth, even through the recession. According to the Brookings Institute, from the start of the recession through 2011, Jackson was in the top three cities for job growth.

RS: Were those jobs accessible to residents of the inner city?

CB: Absolutely not. In no way, shape, or form.

RS: Were these job located in the center?

CB: All were located in the city. The largest employer in the state, the Mississippi State Medical School, is in Jackson. There are two other teaching hospitals and eight hospitals all together. The Mississippi State Medical School is larger than any of the auto plants that have moved to Mississippi to put people to work at nonunion "I'm almost making a living" wages. The people benefiting from the job growth are largely in the medical and law professions.

Three years ago two of the highest-billing law firms were located in Jackson because of lenient tort laws. Jackson has become two worlds; and suddenly there's a clash between classes, and they can't figure out how to deal with it. Our project there is trying to address that divide. When you look at the institutions that drive the city, they are the legal, medical, and academic professions. The common denominator is that they're looking for young, thirty-five-year old, well-educated professionals. The last place on earth those people want to live is in the suburbs of Jackson. The institutions that have driven the economy have to pay people more to come here because the professionals they want to recruit don't want to come. The cost of living is lower, but so is the quality of life. If they come, they stay for two, three, four years, and then they leave because they're looking for a more urban experience.

RS: There's no quality of life.

CB: Precisely. And they're looking for the public realm. The city, county, state governments and the chamber of commerce got together and issued an RFP [request for proposal] to develop a block in the middle of nothing, a deserted warehouse district at the edge of downtown, which is the oldest part of town overlooking the river. Full Spectrum submitted a proposal to do a master plan for the entire fourteen-block area, and we looked at how to reintegrate it back into the rest of city and how to create public space there. Originally, when Jackson was planned in 1822, it was planned very much like Savannah around a public square. That plan never got executed. There were two public plazas: one where the governor's mansion stands and another where city hall is located. Both were built with slave labor. It was a different place then. One of things we've tried to do is create the public realm again. We're not creating squares like Savannah, but we're creating broad avenues, and we are going to use those streets to harvest rainwater for use in the central chilled water plant. We're developing mixed-income communities. There are large plazas with programmed space around buildings. The blocks are three hundred by three hundred and they're built with buildings around the edge and down the street. There are open, U-shaped plazas with stores wrapped around them. The public plaza has space that can be programmed. That's our first phase.

RS: Are there spaces that can be unprogrammed?

CB: Space can be programmed and unprogrammed. It invites spontaneity, there are no rules, but to get people into the habit of coming out again we've decided to program the space. There's a large historical black university there, Jackson State. There's Belhaven University, Millsaps College, and Tougaloo. We've gone to those schools and got them to collaborate on programming. What does that do? It crosses lines of class and race because all those schools are as different from each other as you can imagine. Belhaven is a conservative Christian school. Millsaps bills itself as the Wesleyan of the South. Jackson is historically a black university. Tougaloo has always billed itself as the Brandeis of the South, as progressive radical thinkers—and pretty much they were—but all these institutions have never had any engagement with each other either at the faculty or at the student level. We thought programming space collaboratively with those institutions would be a way to start to tear down the lines of class and race that have been rigidly drawn through that city. Programming a space is important. The virtual programming of the space is as important as the physical portion. In addition, having opportunities for unprogrammed activities to occur is also critical.

Another thing we're trying to do is integrate low-cost broadband into all of the spaces we develop. The truth of the matter is, everyone has cellphones, but what they don't have in poor communities is broadband. So far we've been able to provide free broadband in public spaces. It's not totally free. I'm really taking the saved energy costs and paying for broadband, and giving it to people for free. But it's not really free.

I went to see a site in rural Kenya, where they built a community computer telecom center with ten computers. The people there have been able to have better access to weather [reports] and to markets to sell the food they grow; but, more importantly, young Kenyans are making content for the Internet and they're one of the largest providers of original content sold on the Internet. This is in a rural community where no one taught them do anything, they just made the resources available. It's a demonstration of what broadband access can do even in a rural sub-Saharan area.

RS: You talk about the linkage between virtual and real space, about how the virtual can become a place for building community, for health benefits, and for a variety of other goods. A number of years ago, when we were in New Orleans together, people talked about neutral ground. Those are the places that belong to everybody, but what we're beginning to see is that those places either do not exist or are being privatized. What do you think the future possibility is of using both broadband and development to make sure there are places where people can express themselves? If we can't provide either through virtual or real spaces for people to come together, our democracy will be challenged.

CB: Let me say this, the future could be dim. When people say they want to be a developer, what they're really saying is they want to be Donald Trump and build towers for the high and mighty and they want to be personally wealthy and have power. That is as demented as someone saying, I want to be a doctor so I can get a private plane, as opposed to I want to be a doctor so I can heal people. The appropriate role of the practitioner as a developer is really to heal the built fabric. If you think about it in terms of Maslow's hierarchy of needs, the built fabric is the little piece at the very bottom of the pyramid. The appropriate role of development people is to build something that creates human benefit at the base of that pyramid, and that also creates communities that move us to a more aspirational level at the top of the pyramid. That is the appropriate role for developers right now.

Reference

Benjamin, R. 2012. "The Gated Community Mentality." *New York Times*, March 29.

A Call for Actions

Ronald Shiffman and Jeffrey Hou

IN FALL 2011, as the Occupy protests spread across North America and other parts of the world, the movement called attention to several important shifts in our society. First, it brought to light that, more than ever, the hegemony of global financial/political institutions dictates the economic and social life of individuals and communities and perpetuates inequality around the world. Second, as an outcome of the protests, the movement revealed the increasing curtailment of the public realm that is fundamental to the freedom of expression meant to bring accountability to our political systems.

As protest sites were barricaded and protestors harassed and attacked, our democracy came in question. The kind of oppression often associated with police states and totalitarian regimes appeared eerily in front of our eyes, if not felt physically on our limbs. The growing measures of hyper-security against terrorism and unwanted elements over the decades in cities across North America were turned against peaceful protestors and citizens. In the face of increasing regulation, privatization, and concern for security, public space as a forum for political expression and dialogue seemed like a far-flung idea from a bygone era.

The reader by this point will have been exposed to a variety of perspectives on the important role that public space plays in preserving and enhancing our democratic principles. Hopefully, the idea that constant vigilance is needed to protect our democratic and inalienable rights has emerged. Without those rights, we surrender control of our democratic way of life to those who can buy, regulate, and police our use of space—and in the process, they control our ability to educate, organize, and exercise our right to free and informed speech. In essence, if we continue to allow the financially powerful and the corporate elite to take control, our government by the people will erode into an oligarchy where the 1% controls the 99%, where disparities are unchallenged and where our freedoms are eroded.

This is not a debate about capitalism, socialism, or communism, it is a debate about democracy and a political system. It is also an issue and a struggle that architects, landscape architects, designers, and planners must participate in. In this book, we have listened to how professionals and scholars view public space—their theories, their fears, and their aspirations—and read their ideas about how to maintain, preserve, and enhance the public access, public control, and ownership of these critically important spaces. However, discourse and discussion can only go so far. It's time to translate ideas into action.

The barricades against the Occupy protests signaled a wake-up call to professionals concerning their role in society. It reminds us of our ethical responsibility to protect not only public health, safety, and welfare but also social equality and the rights of citizens and communities. The Occupy movement reminds us that change must begin with ourselves as individuals, joining with our neighbors, colleagues, and others who also cherish the idea of a free and accountable democracy. It was with this in mind that Architects/Designers/Planners for Social Responsibility (ADPSR) released a statement of support for the Occupy movement in December 2011.

As designers and planners who create places, what can we do to protect and promote the public realm? How can we help bring about a more just and egalitarian society? The ADPSR statement can guide not only our professional community, but also those who engage us to shape the built environment. Every community should undertake a scan of public space in their community and determine if it is appropriate and adequate to meet their needs and also determine if it is equitably distributed and accessible. Policies of making and regulating public space should be discussed, and we should determine if privatization is a practice in our community and to what extent is it a positive or negative force. If it is positive, we can develop strategies to keep it that way, and if it is negative, we must find ways to change it. We need to be vigilant to assure that both the availability of public space and the policies that govern its use in no way impede the right to assemble.

Rules need to be assessed in terms of social inclusion. Vibrant cities are naturally pluralistic, allowing members of minorities to maintain their traditional cultures and unique points of view. Imposed monolithic rules destroy the healthy diversity of social and political ecologies. Let us be alert to signs of forced conformity and proactively work to encourage diversity.

Let us remove any barriers in public spaces that exclude participation because of class, race, ethnicity, and gender. Let us find ways to allow our differences—be they political, social, or economic—to be debated in a civil and respectful manner that allows dissent to rear its head when necessary. Let us collectively think about the function of public space as well as the design of public space. Let us organize forums to discuss and debate controversial issues. Let us link these discussions to the issues indigenous to the area in which we live or work. Let us begin to occupy spaces that are public, or need to be public, which allow us to express ideas and pursue the policies important to our communities. Let us open spaces to confront publicly the inequities in our society that threaten future generations and their ability to live a healthy and sustainable life. Let us occupy these public places because our democracy depends on our willingness to engage. Let us make sure public places exist that allow ideas to be nurtured, discussed, refined, and animated.

Importantly, let us also learn to occupy the voting booth, to develop a way to enable our concerns, our ideas, and our energies to translate into political power so that we can begin the arduous task of redressing the disparities that we have allowed and begin to protect and refine our democracy.

We conclude this book with a call for actions, asking design and planning professionals, in particular, to not only to support the Occupy movement and its goal of economic and social democracy, but to also act as engaged citizens through participation and leadership in their neighborhoods, communities, and professional forums. Citizen-initiated movements—large, small, global, and local—are essential for any society to self-correct its direction. We share the following ADPSR statement with you, not to end this book, but to open a new page for visionary initiatives.

ADPSR Statement of Support for the Occupy Movement

December 15, 2011

Since September 2011, the Occupy Movement has sprung up in cities and university campuses around the world, calling attention to the economic inequality and injustice under the current global financial system and institutions. In keeping with its mission of working for peace, environmental protection, ecological building, social justice, and the development of healthy communities, Architects/Designers/Planners for Social Responsibility (ADPSR) stands in support of the goal and cause of the Occupy Movement. Specifically:

1. We support the right of citizens to peaceful protests and freedom of expression.
2. We support the principle of nonviolent actions for social change.
3. We support the use of public space for political expressions and dialogues.
4. We stand in solidarity with communities and activist organizations around the world seeking democracy and economic, environmental and social justice.
5. We call architects, designers, landscape architects, and planners to support the Occupy Movement through individual and collective actions.

We believe that public space is fundamental to our democracy. Public space should serve not only as a place for social gathering and recreation but also as a space for active political expressions and dialogues. Article 20 of the Universal Declaration of Human Rights supports the right of every individual to freedom of peaceful assembly and association. The First Amendment to the US Constitution also guarantees the right of people to peacefully assemble. With citizens engaged in peaceful protests being evicted from public space in cities around the United States and students and faculty being intimidated and attacked by campus police, we call for actions and measures to safeguard the function of public space for peaceful assembly and political expressions.

Contributors

Roland V. Anglin is director of Rutgers University's Joseph C. Cornwall Center for Metropolitan Studies. Dr. Anglin previously served the Edward J. Bloustein School of Planning and Public Policy at Rutgers–New Brunswick, where he was Faculty Fellow since 2000. He is the coeditor of *Resilience and Opportunity: Lessons from the U.S. Gulf Coast after Katrina and Rita* (2011) and *Katrina's Imprint: Race and Vulnerability in America* (2010), and the author of *Promoting Sustainable Local and Community Economic Development* (2010).

Caron Atlas works to support and stimulate arts and culture as an integral part of social justice. She directs the Arts & Democracy Project, codirects the Naturally Occurring Cultural District Working Group (NOCD-NY), teaches at New York University and Pratt Institute, and is a member of the New York City Steering Committee for Participatory Budgeting.

Thomas Balsley, FASLA, is the principal designer of Thomas Balsley Associates, best known for its practice of landscape urbanism within public parks. Among a number of local and international works, his notable projects include Leeum Museum in Seoul; Gate City Park in Tokyo; Pacific Design Center in Los Angeles; and Gantry Park, Riverside Park South, and Chelsea Waterside Park in New York City.

Terri Baltimore is vice president of Neighborhood Development at the Hill House Association in Pittsburgh, Pennsylvania. She oversees the agency's arts programs and manages its interests in a variety of community settings.

She also directs the Hill House Community Collaborative, a program that assists women with substance abuse issues and their children. Baltimore is a member of the Hill neighborhood's network of green organizations working on environmental initiatives.

Shirin Barghi is an Iranian journalist, photographer, and soon-to-be graduate of New York University. She has more than three years of journalism experience in Tehran, where she studied and worked before moving to New York City in 2010. She is currently working on her master's thesis on journalism education in post-revolutionary Iran.

Rick Bell, FAIA, is executive director of the New York Chapter of the American Institute of Architects (AIA). He was instrumental in the creation of AIA's New York New Visions design and planning coalition, which has helped to catalyze and critique the redevelopment of Lower Manhattan. A registered architect and a fellow of the AIA since 2000, Bell currently heads the AIA national staff association, CACE, and represents it on the AIA national board.

Marshall Berman is distinguished professor of political science at the City College of New York. He is a member of the editorial board of *Dissent* and has written in the *New York Times*, *Village Voice*, *Dissent*, *The Nation*, and *New Left Review*, among other publications. His books include *The Politics of Authenticity: Radical Individualism and the Emergence of Modern Society* (2009), *On the Town: One Hundred Years of Spectacle in Times Square* (2009), and the groundbreaking *All That Is Solid Melts Into Air: The Experience of Modernity* (1988).

Julian Brash is assistant professor of cultural anthropology, geography, and interdisciplinary urban studies at Montclair State University. His research focuses on urban neoliberalism, political economy, and the politics of space and place. He is the author of *Bloomberg's New York: Class and Governance in the Luxury City* (2011). His work has been published in *Urban Anthropology*, *Critique of Anthropology*, *Social Text*, and *Antipode*.

Wendy E. Brawer is a designer, social innovator, consultant, and public educator. Based in New York and focused on sustainable design since 1989, Brawer has led the development of the nonprofit Green Map System, now active in over seven hundred diverse cities in fifty-five countries. She was most recently included among the 50 Visionaries Changing Your World by *UTNE Reader*.

Paul Broches, FAIA, is a partner of Mitchell-Giurgola, an architectural firm in New York that focuses on minimizing the use of nonrenewable energy sources, reducing pollution, and conserving energy expenditures. He is active on AIA's Committee on Architecture for Education and Committee on Urban Design, as well as a member of the Board of Advisors of Architects/Designers/Planners for Social Responsibility (ADPSR).

Carlton Brown is the chief operating officer of Full Spectrum, New York, which he cofounded in 1983. Brown's vision for Full Spectrum has led to the firm's recognition as a national leader in the development of affordable green and smart buildings in emerging urban markets. Mr. Brown has served on several boards including the New York Chapter, AIA; the Business Resource & Investment Service Center of the Upper Manhattan Empowerment Zone; BEN Asset Group; and is the current board chair of 651 Arts. In September 2006, Mr. Brown was the only developer appointed to New York City Mayor Bloomberg's Sustainability Advisory Board.

Lance Jay Brown, FAIA, DPACSA, is the principal of Lance Jay Brown Architecture + Urban Design in New York City, fellow of the Institute for Urban Design, ACSA Distinguished Professor at the Spitzer School of Architecture, CCNY, and president-elect-2014 of the American Institute of Architects, New York Chapter. He is coauthor of *Urban Design for an Urban Century* (2010) and *Planning and Design Workbook for Community Participation* (1970), and a recipient of the AIA/ACSA Topaz Medallion for Excellence in Architectural Education. He has served as director of the School of Architecture at CCNY, director of the City College Architectural Center, and assistant director for programs at the National Endowment for the Arts.

David Burney is the first architect to hold the title of commissioner of the New York City Department of Design and Construction (DDC). At Mayor Bloomberg's direction, Burney launched a Design and Construction Excellence Initiative with the goal of raising the quality of design and construction of public works throughout New York City. Prior to joining DDC, Burney was director of design and capital improvement at the New York City Housing Authority.

Brennan S. Cavanaugh is a photographer and member of the Occupy Wall Street Sustainability Working Group and the Occupy Wall Street Photo Team. He is also a member of the direct action environmental group Time's Up! and bikes to raise awareness of how we can live causing less damage to our environment.

Susan Chin, FAIA, is executive director of the Design Trust for Public Space. Prior to this, she served as the assistant commissioner of Capital Projects at the New York City Department of Cultural Affairs for twenty-three years. She is an American Institute of Architects Public Architects award recipient, and chair of the AIA Gold Medal Award advisory committee. She is the current vice president of the American Institute of Architects (AIA) and a former president of the AIA New York Chapter.

Alexander Cooper, FAIA, is a founding partner of the New York City architecture and design firm Cooper, Robertson & Partners. Cooper's major urban design and planning projects include Battery Park City, New York City's Hudson Yards Redevelopment Project, the expansion of the Museum of Modern Art, the International Trade Center, and Yale University's Framework for Campus Planning. He has designed numerous prominent buildings and is the architect of Zuccotti Park in New York City.

Arthur Eisenberg is the legal director of the New York Civil Liberties Union, where he has worked for more than thirty-five years. During this time, he has been involved in more than twenty cases that were presented to the United States Supreme Court. He has litigated extensively around issues of free speech and voting rights and, in recent years, has been increasingly involved in litigation concerning national security and civil liberties. Eisenberg is the coauthor of *The Rights of Candidates and Voters* (1980).

Lynne Elizabeth is founder and director of New Village Press and past president of Architects/Designers/Planners for Social Responsibility (ADPSR). Prior to this, she was founder and director of the Eos Institute, an education center for the study of sustainable community development. She is coeditor of *What We See: Advancing the Observations of Jane Jacobs* (2010), *Works of Heart: Building Village through the Arts* (2006), and *Alternative Construction: Contemporary Natural Building Methods* (2000).

Anastassia Fisyak is an urban planner, cartographer, editor, curator, and designer receiving a master's degree in city and regional planning from the Pratt Institute. She is the coeditor of *MultipliCITY*, serves as an APA student representative, and held an urban planning fellowship at the Pratt Center for Community Development.

Karen A. Franck is professor and director of the PhD program in urban systems in the College of Architecture and Design at the New Jersey Institute of Technology. She continues to pursue a longtime interest in the design and use of public space. With Quentin Stevens, she coedited *Loose Space: Possibility and Diversity in Urban Life* (2007). She is currently writing a book with Quentin about public memorials, *Spaces of Engagement* (2013).

Michael Freedman-Schnapp is New York City Council Member Brad Lander's director of policy. He previously served as senior policy associate for the New York Industrial Retention Network and a planner for the Center for Court Innovation. He has written about the Bloomberg administration's downzonings, New York's food manufacturing sector, and the intersection between electoral politics and community development. He holds a master's in urban planning from NYU's Wagner School for Public Service.

Mindy Thompson Fullilove, MD, is professor of clinical sociomedical sciences, Mailman School of Public Health, and professor of clinical psychiatry, College of Physicians and Surgeons, at Columbia University. Her research examines the mental health effects of environmental processes such as violence, segregation, and urban renewal. She is the coauthor of *Collective Consciousness and Its Discontents* (2008) and *Homeboy Came to Orange: A Story of People's Power* (2008), and the author of *Root Shock: How Tearing Up City Neighborhoods Hurts America and What We Can Do About It* (2005). Her forthcoming book, *Urban Alchemy*, will be released in 2013.

Gan Golan is a *New York Times* bestselling writer and illustrator. He is the coauthor of *Goodnight Bush* (2008) and *The Adventures of Unemployed Man* (2010), both with Erich Origen, and he spent many years as a grassroots community organizer and activist. He studied economic geography at the University of California at Berkeley before earning a master's degree in urban planning and international development at the Massachusetts Institute of Technology. As a visual artist, he has created artwork for a number of well-known musicians including Erykah Badu, Henry Rollins, Willie Nelson, Ben Harper, and Nick Cave, for which he has won several national awards.

Jeffrey Hou, ASLA, is associate professor of landscape architecture at the University of Washington. Hou's research, teaching, and practice focus on engaging marginalized communities and citizens through community design, design activism, and cross-cultural learning. He is a recipient of 2011 CELA Award for Excellence in Service-Learning Education and the 2010 Great Places Book Award. Hou is the editor of *Insurgent Public Space: Guerrilla Urbanism and the Remaking of Contemporary Cities* (2010) and coauthor of *Greening Cities, Growing Communities: Learning from Urban Community Gardens in Seattle* (2009).

Te-Sheng Huang, a licensed architect from Taiwan, is currently enrolled in the Urban Systems Program at the New Jersey Institute of Technology. His dissertation topic is the design and management of New York's interior, privately owned public spaces.

Lisa Keller is associate professor of history at Purchase College, State University of New York. Her research focuses on transatlantic, women's, and urban history. She is the author of *Triumph of Order: Democracy and Public Space in New York and London* (2010) and the executive editor of the *Encyclopedia of New York City: Second Edition* (2010).

Michael Kimmelman is the chief art critic of the *New York Times* and a contributor to the *New York Review of Books*. He was a finalist for the Pulitzer Prize in 2000 and is the author of *The Accidental Masterpiece: On the Art of Life and Vice Versa* (2006) and *Portraits: Talking with Artists at the Met, the Modern, the Louvre and Elsewhere* (1999), which was named as a notable book of the year by the *New York Times* and *Washington Post*. He has written on public housing, community development, and social responsibility and has hosted various television shows about the arts.

Brad Lander was elected to the New York City Council in 2009, where he chairs the Subcommittee on Landmarks, Public Siting & Maritime Uses, and is a founding cochair of the Progressive Caucus. Before his election, Lander led the Pratt Center for Community Development and the Fifth

Avenue Committee. He holds a master's degree in city and regional planning from the Pratt Institute and a master's degree in social anthropology from University College London.

Peter Marcuse, a planner and lawyer, is professor emeritus of urban planning at Columbia University. Among other publications, he is coeditor of *Cities for People, Not for Profit: Critical Urban Theory and the Right to the City* (2011) and author of *Searching for the Just City* (2011). He has taught in several countries and written extensively in both professional journals and the popular press. His fields of research include city planning, housing, the use of public space, rights to the city, globalization, and urban history, with a particular focus on New York City.

Jonathan Marvel, FAIA, is a principal at Rogers Marvel Architects. He is a registered architect in New York and NCARB. Marvel has taught design studios for fifteen years at Columbia, Harvard, and currently teaches at Parsons New School for Design. He is a former board member of the New York Chapter of the AIA and currently serves on the preservation committee of the Municipal Art Society and on the streetscape committee for the New York City Design Commission.

Signe Nielsen, FASLA, is the principal of Mathews Nielsen Landscape Architects and has been practicing as a landscape architect for more than thirty-five years. Nielsen is a fellow of the American Society of Landscape Architects and for thirty years has been a professor in both the graduate and undergraduate Schools of Architecture at the Pratt Institute. Her design work has received more than sixty major national and international awards and exhibits of her work have been shown in New York City, Washington DC, and Chicago. Since 2003, Nielsen has been a member of the New York City Public Design Commission and currently serves as its president.

Michael Pyatok, FAIA, is the principal of Pyatok Architects, Inc. Pyatok has served as a professor of architecture and design at the University of Washington, Harvard University, and Arizona State University. Since starting his practice in 1984, he has designed more than thirty-five thousand units of affordable housing in California, Washington, and Arizona, as well as master planning communities in Hawaii, the Philippines, and Malaysia.

Michael Rios is associate professor in the Department of Environmental Design at the University of California at Davis. He has contributed numerous publications on the topics of placemaking, marginality, and the ethics of practice, including *Diálogos: Placemaking in Latino Communities* (2012), coedited with Leonardo Vazquez. Rios has published articles in the *Journal of Architectural Education, Landscape Journal, Berkeley Planning Journal*, and *Journal of Urban Design*.

Jonathan Rose is president and founder of Jonathan Rose Companies, a multidisciplinary real estate development, planning, consulting, and investment firm, which has established itself as a leading green urban solutions provider. He is a trustee of several organizations including the Urban Land Institute and the Natural Resources Defense Council, and vice chair of Enterprise Community Partners. Mr. Rose is a frequent speaker and writer. His work has received widespread media attention from CNN to the *New York Times* and was profiled in *e² design*, a PBS series on sustainable development.

Janette Sadik-Khan is commissioner of the New York City Department of Transportation. For her efforts at improving traffic flow, fostering sustainable transportation, and increasing New Yorkers' access to open public spaces, she was awarded the 2011 Jane Jacobs Medal for New Ideas and Activism by the Rockefeller Foundation. She is also president of the National Association of City Transportation Officials, chair of the Transportation Research Board's Committee on Transportation Issues in Major U.S. Cities, and was appointed to the Energy Secretary's Energy Efficiency and Renewable Energy Advisory Committee.

Saskia Sassen is Robert S. Lynd professor of sociology and cochairs the Committee on Global Thought at Columbia University. She also serves on several editorial boards and is an adviser to several international bodies. Her research and writing focus is on globalization, immigration, global cities, and changes within the liberal state. Her publications include *Cities in a World Economy* (4th ed. 2011), *Territory, Authority, Rights: From Medieval to Global Assemblage* (2008), and *A Sociology of Globalization* (2007).

Paula Z. Segal is an urban lawyer, advocate, and founder of 596 Acres, a public education project aimed at making communities aware of the land resources around them. She is a member of the National Lawyers Guild

NYC Chapter, a founding member of the New York City NLG Street Law Team, and part of the Brooklyn Food Coalition Policy Working Group.

Sadra Shahab is an Iranian urban planner and civil rights activist based in New York City. A cofounder of the group "Where Is My Vote—NY," he organized protests and events in support of the social uprising in the wake of the 2009 presidential elections in Iran. He is currently working on his thesis on urban land evaluation models at Pratt Institute's Programs for Sustainable Planning and Development.

Benjamin Shepard is an assistant professor of human service at New York School of Technology/City University of New York. He is the author or editor of six books including *The Beach Beneath the Streets: Exclusion, Control, and Play in Public Space* (with Gregory Smithsimon, 2011), *From ACT UP to the WTO: Urban Protest and Community Building in the Era of Globalization* (coedited with Ron Hayduck, 2002), and *White Nights and Ascending Shadows: An Oral History of the San Francisco AIDS Epidemic* (1997). He has done organizing work with ACT UP, SexPanic!, Reclaim the Streets New York, Times UP, CIRCA, CitiWide Harm Reduction, Housing Works, and the More Gardens Coalition.

Ron Shiffman, FAICP, Hon. AIA, is director emeritus of the Pratt Center for Community Development and a professor at Pratt Institute's Graduate Center for Planning and the Environment. He served as a member of the New York City Planning Commission from 1990 to 1996 and worked with the Central Brooklyn Coordinating Council and senator Robert F. Kennedy's office to launch the Bedford Stuyvesant Restoration Corporation, one of the first community development corporations in the country. He is the recipient of ADPSR's 1998 Lewis Mumford Award in Development.

Gregory Smithsimon is assistant professor of sociology at Brooklyn College, the City University of New York. His works include *September 12: Community and Neighborhood Recovery at Ground Zero* (2011) and *The Beach Beneath the Streets: Exclusion, Control, and Play in Public Space* (with Benjamin Shepard, 2011). His research focuses on how the design of urban spaces affects social relations and fosters inclusion or exclusion, segregation or integration, and social life or social isolation.

Michael Sorkin is distinguished professor of architecture and director of the Graduate Program in Urban Design at the City College of New York. He lectures widely and is the author of several hundred articles on architectural and urban subjects. For ten years, he was the architectural critic of the *Village Voice* and is currently contributing editor for *Architectural Record*. His books include *All Over the Map: Writing on Buildings and Cities* (2011), *Twenty Minutes in Manhattan* (2009), and the bestselling *Variations on a Theme Park* (1992).

Nikki Stern has contributed to a number of publications, including the *New York Times, Newsweek, USA Today, American Humanist Magazine*, and several online magazines. She wrote *Hope in Small Doses* (2012) and *Because I Say So: The Dangerous Appeal of Moral Authority* (2010). She has served as executive director of Families of September 11 and was a member of New York New Visions and several memorial-related committees of the Lower Manhattan Development Authority.

Anusha Venkataraman is currently the acting director of the Green Light District initiative at El Puente in Brooklyn, New York. From 2005 to 2008, she was the youth and outreach director at the Steel Yard, an industrial arts community center in Providence, Rhode Island. She edited *Intractable Democracy: Fifty Years of Community-Based Planning* (2010). She holds a master's degree in city and regional planning from the Pratt Institute.

Maya Wiley is the founder and executive director of the Center for Social Inclusion. A civil rights attorney and policy advocate, Wiley was a senior advisor on race and poverty to the director of US Programs of the Open Society Institute. She has worked for the American Civil Liberties Union National Legal Department, the NAACP Legal Defense and Educational Fund, Human Rights Watch, and the Council on Foreign Relations, among others. She currently serves on the Tides Network Board. Wiley was a contributing author to the National Urban League's *The State of Black America 2006*.

Page references followed by *fig* indicate a
photograph or illustrated figure.

"act of placemaking," 338
ACT UP, 29
Adbusters poster (Wall Street Bull), 147
Added Value, 329
ADPSR Statement of Support for the Occupy
  Movement, 384, 385, 386
African American community (Pittsburgh):
  Black Males Solidarity Day and, 104;
  description of the, 100–101; Occupy Pittsburgh participation by, 99–111; urban re-
  newal proposal protested by, 101*fig*–102*fig*
African Americans: development of post-
  World War II communities of, 128; historical black universities serving, 380–381;
  Occupy Pittsburgh participation, 99–111;
  second-line jazz funerals of New Orleans
  communities of, 154. *See also* marginalized
  populations; people of color
agora (outdoor space): ancient Greek concept
  of public space in, 198, 237, 266; Antigone's
  understanding of democratic, 189–190;
  OWS community application of, 221–222,
  266; as a place that makes you feel at home,
  337–338; women excluded from ancient
  Greek, 199; Zuccotti Park as NYC, 21
ahimsa (no harm to any), 173
AIA New York Risk and Reconstruction Committee, 225
Alcatraz Occupation (1969), 255
Al Farooq Junction (was Pearl Square) [Bah-
  rain], 7
Alinsky, S., 124
Al Jazeera English (AJE), 7, 9
The American Crisis (Paine), 234
American Institute of Architects (AIA), 223
American Recovery Act, 226, 228
American Revolution, 234–235
ancient Greece: *agora* concept of public
  space in, 198, 237, 266, 337–338; *Antigone*
  (Sophocles) of, 198–199; birthplace of democracy in, 197–198; "Old Oligarch" of,
  198, 199; paradox of public space in Athens,
  199–200; "Pericles's Funeral Oration"
  (431 BC) of, 199; Socrates's execution in,
  200–201, 204
Anonymous, 259
Antigone (Sophocles), 198–199
Arab League (Cairo), 4
Arab Spring: Egyptian social revolution (2011),
  3, 4–6, 149, 206, 245, 256; social and political claims of, 68; tweeting role in upheavals
  of, 377
architects: ADPSR Statement of Support for
  the Occupy Movement, 384, 385, 386;
  approach to making or remaking public
  space, 308; designing civic places, 312–313;

designing infrastructure supporting public
  space, 220, 222–223, 224–226, 301; how
  public space is determined by, 299–308;
  OWS as call for action by, 383–385; perspectives on POPS by, 351–363; responsibilities for developing the public realm,
  364–370; responsibilities for programming
  public space, 371–382; schooling of design
  professionals, 310–312
Architects/Designers/Planners for Social Responsibility (ADPSR), 383, 386
architectural designs: Boston City Hall and
  Boston City Hall Plaza, 312*fig*; for civic
  places, 312–313; creating a "loose" or
  "tight" space, 339–340; designing for occupation, 339–350; focusing on the needs
  of the 99% instead of the 1%, 372–373;
  Jonathan Rose on public space, democracy,
  and, 364–370; Oakland City Hall and Frank
  H. Ogawa Plaza, 309–310, 313–322, 326;
  West Hollywood Civic Center, 309–310,
  322–326*fig. See also* urban infrastructure
Art Is My Occupation, 147
arts: how space is defined by, 73; Noguchi
  cube, 343*fig*; NYC's restriction of art vendors in public parks, 285–286; radical imagination expressed through, 146–155; spaces
  of intervention created by, 147–152
Arts & Culture: as Occupy working group, 73
Arts & Democracy Project, 152
assembly. *See* right to free assembly
Athens: *agora* in ancient, 198, 237, 266, 337–
  338; public space in ancient, 199–200, 206;
  Socrates's execution in ancient, 200–201, 204
Austin City Hall/Occupy Wall Street, 313*fig*

Balsley Park (NYC), 361–363
Baltimore, T., 99, 110
Bangladeshi community (NYC), 290–291
Barcelona (Spain): Plaça de Catalunya occupa-
  tion in, 3, 5*fig*, 7, 9, 11, 12; Real Democracy
  NOW (or the Indignants) movement in, 7;
  "spaces of social inclusion" concept found
  in, 114
Battery Park City, 356
Battery Park (NYC), 285
*The Beach Beneath the Streets: Contesting New
  York City's Public Spaces* (Smithsimon), 24

397

Bell, R., 214, 217, 218, 219, 221, 223, 225, 226, 227, 228, 230, 232, 233, 234, 235
Bell, T., 215, 216, 220, 222, 224, 231
Berman, M., 197, 275, 337, 338
Beyond War (later Search for Common Ground), 174
bicycles near Moynihan Station, 228*fig*
Bill of Rights: ancient Greece beginnings of the, 201; First Amendment, 74–76, 80–84, 194–195, 233; formalizing the right to free assembly, 247–248, 250, 283–284, 300; ratification of the, 235. *See also* OWS constitutional issues
biopower (or biopolitics): description of, 157; examining inequalities of NYC neighborhoods to see, 157–159; Hitler's Telegram 71 order as example of, 159
Black Males Solidarity Day, 104
Blackness and the Politics of Memory (Regis), 154
"Bloody Sunday" demonstration (London), 191–192
Bloomberg, M.: Athenian Oath quoted by, 229; "filth" rhetoric against OWS by, 42, 61, 62, 65, 66; Ground Zero plans to present to, 180; OWS constitutional issues and position of, 79–80; OWS negotiation offers by, 43; PlaNYC (2007) launched by, 293–294; TKTS2K design competition requiring mandate of, 332
Blue House (Hong Kong), 96
"bonus" open space. *See* POPS (privately owned public space)
Book of Kings, 201–202
Boston City Hall, 312*fig*
Boston City Hall Plaza, 312*fig*
Bramante, 244
Brandt, D. H., 247–249
Brash, J., 61, 63
Brawer-Cavanaugh interview, 49–59
Brentwood Academy case (US), 79, 80, 81–82
Broches, P., 299, 300, 301, 303, 306, 307
Brookfield Properties: criticism of, 24–25; evacuation cancelled by, 8; policy of searching OWS activists by, 83, 84–85; public space requirement made of, 12–13, 25n.1; reopening Zuccotti Park in 2006, 77; Zuccotti Park activities evicted by, 24, 26–28. *See also* Zuccotti Park (NYC)
Brooklyn Bridge, 254–255
Brooklyn Bridge Park (NYC), 285–286
Brotha Ash Productions, 105
Brown, C., 371–382
Brown-Shiffman-Fisyak interview, 371–382
Bryant Park (NYC), 239, 334, 340*fig*, 346, 349, 353
Buckley, C., 8, 15
"bundle of rights" notion, 280
Burbank, C., 171–172, 177

Carr, S., 241, 242
Cavanaugh-Brawer interview, 49–59
Cavanaugh, B. S., 49–59
Center for Architecture of the American Institute of Architects, 215, 216, 225
Center for Constitutional Rights, 115
Center for Social Inclusion (CSI): description and mission of the, 112; global discourse influencing name of, 114; model of community economic development used by, 121–122
Central Park (NYC): designed with monumental civic scale, 248; long-standing policy to deny permits for meetings in, 196; opening (1857) of, 224; reduced frequency of free concerts held in, 346; restricting spaces for art vendors in, 285; Sheep Meadow of, 336, 345; Vietnam War protest demonstrations held in, 309
change agents. *See* public sector change agents
Chelsea Waterside Park (NYC), 353*fig*
cities: building human-scale, 248; evidence of public space in Catal Huyuk (Anatolia), 237–238; Hippodamas model of planned, 199; Jane Jacobs on people creating, 229; openhearted, 170–177; public space in ancient Athens, 199–201, 204, 206; "right to the city," 46–47; shaping public space to shape our, 93–94, 327–333; state of exception restricting public rights in, 133–135; tactics for forming bonds as neighbors within, 160–168. *See also* inner cities; neighborhoods; New York City
citizenry: building Giant Stew of transformation of cities, 170–171; building respect and building community, 171–173; cities that provide space to heal for, 175–177; community policing versus informal behavior management by, 300; POPS and loss of civic capacity and access by, 248–249, 335–338, 351–352, 361; popular participation required for democracy, 188; sitting face-to-face with the Other, 174–175; social agency of, 259; wisdom of loving your city, 173–174. *See also* demonstrations; political protests/expression; resistance; social movements
City Planning According to Artistic Principles (Sitte), 241
City of Quartz: Excavating the Future in Los Angeles (Davis), 246
civic space: Boston City Hall and Boston City Hall Plaza, 312*fig*; description and functions of, 312–313, 335; National Mall (Washington, DC) dedicated to political expression, 363; Oakland City Hall and Frank H. Ogawa plaza space, 309–310, 313–322, 326; Trafalgar Square (London) dedicated to political expression, 190, 191, 192, 335, 363;

West Hollywood Civic Center, 309–310, 322–326*fig. See also* political protests/ expression

Civic Valentines (Di Cicco), 173

civil disobedience, 172–173, 249

civil rights movement, 128, 371

communities of color: CSI's model of community economic development for, 121–122; CSI's work to provide Internet to, 116; "cultural commodities" provided by small businesses in, 120; Occupy movement as historical moment for, 126; Occupy Pittsburgh movement, 99–111; OWS activities and participation by, 116–124; post-World War II urban migration and segregation of, 127–128; racial balance of NYC, 120; regional equity movement and, 130–132. *See also* people of color

community/communities: building Harlem (NYC), 374–375, 378; building respect and building, 171–173; contemporary challenges facing, 128–130; gated, 378; how nonprofit organizations transform public space in, 95–97; InterOccupy Arts Calls' work in building, 147; involving as public sector change agent, 331–332; NYC Bangladeshi, 290–291; NYPD spying scandal on Muslim, 258; Ocean Hill-Brownsville school center (Brooklyn) for, 304–305*fig*; post-World War II migration by people of color and impact on, 127–128; public housing, 374; regional equity movement and, 130–132

community policing: Consortium for Police Leadership in Equity promoting, 172; negotiation and future of protest in public space role of, 42–47; Occupy Salt Lake City and respectful, 171–172; when "citizens" are more effective than, 300. *See also* New York City Police Department (NYPD); OWS constitutional issues

Companion to Urban Design (Day), 93

Consortium for Police Leadership in Equity, 172

constitutional issues. *See* OWS constitutional issues

COOLS (Cultural Occupation of Liberty Square) [NYC], 28–30

Cooper, Robertson & Partners, 209, 212

creative expression: creating spaces of imagination, 154–155; creating spaces of intersection, 152–154; creating spaces of intervention, 147–152; how the Occupy movement has unleashed, 146–147

crime: NYC (1850 to 1900) policies for preventing, 189–190; POPS nighttime park closing permission due to, 363; school becoming center of community and reducing, 305

criminalization/racial profiling, 115–116

Critical Mass bike ride (NYC) [September 2011], 21

Critical Mass! movement, 21, 31

Cruz, T., 147, 227

Darden, J., 103–104

Dattner, R., 246–247

Davis, M., 134, 246

The Death and Life of Great American Cities (Jacobs), 229, 241

de Certeau, M., 159, 160, 166

democracy: adopted by Occupy Wall Street, 230; *agora* concept of, 21, 189–190, 199, 221–222, 226, 237; creating governing places for, 277–292; creating people-driven city strategy within a, 160–168; democratic expression in public space, 288–291; Greek origins of, 197–201; how biopower (or biopolitics) diminishes, 157–159; how the OWS revealed contradictions in American, 277; Jonathan Rose on public space, design, and, 364–370; making self-governance possible goal of, 159–160; only as strong as the people who use it, 31; OWS as a debate about a political system and, 384; OWS protected activities legacy for, 44–47, 277–278, 302; physical space required for, 70; popular participation on all levels required for, 188; "practicing of place" as means toward, 138–139; public space as being an enabler of, 42, 275–276; spaces of imagination and dynamic process of, 154–155. *See also* negotiation

democratic tactics: democratic expression in public space, 288–291; democratizing public space, 327–333; draw pictures with arrows, 166–168; go there and put a sign on it (govern your own city), 160–165*fig*; use maps as megaphones or spatially organized social networking, 165–166

demonstrations: against the Vietnam War, 309; "Bloody Sunday" (London), 191–192; crackdown against Iranian Azadi Square, 256; disallowed in Central Park, 196; "Dod Street trick" promoted by George Bernard Shaw, 191, 192; examining New York and London's policies on public, 188–196; Green Scroll march (2009), 254; The Line practice of, 150*fig*–153*fig*; London's Trafalgar Square site for public, 190, 191, 192; New Orleans second-line jazz funerals, 154; Oakland Occupy, 320–321*fig*; Poor People's March (1968), 309; resistance to free use of public space for, 274; tightening of permission since 9/11, 195; Wobbly demonstrations (NYC), 193–194. *See also* citizenry; political protests/expression; resistance design. *See* architectural designs; urban infra-structure

Design Trust for Public Space, 328–331

dialogue. *See* OWS dialogue

Diggers (St. George's Hill, England) [1649], 32

Dixon, D., 245–246

DNAinfo.com, 9

"Dod Street trick," 191, 192

Douglas, M., 62–63, 64, 65, 66

Draft Riots (NYC) [1863], 192

DSGN AGNC, 166

Duarte Square (NYC), 225*fig*

ecoCultural.info, 49

Egypt: successful revolution (2011) in, 256; Tahrir Square demonstrations in Cairo, 3, 4–6, 9, 11, 149, 206, 245, 260

Eisenberg, A., 74, 280

Elizabeth, L., 170

The Empire City: A Novel of New York City (Goodman), 232

Enlightenment, 204–205

Evans v. Newton (US), 80–81

Everyday Urbanism (Crawford), 93

Facebook: artificial social groups on, 376; Critical Mass bike ride (NYC) [September 2011] posted on, 21; Occupy Art: The People's Movement in Visual page on, 147; Zuccotti Park occupation news reports posted on, 23. *See also* social networking; virtual space

Fathi, Y., 9, 11

Federal Hall occupiers, 305–306*fig*

57th Street and 9th Avenue (NYC), 361–363

"filth" rhetoric (NYC's OWS), 61–66

Final Environmental Impact Statement (NYC), 222

firmitatis concept, 219

First Amendment: applications to privately owned facilities, 74–75; *Brentwood* and *Evans* cases application to, 79, 80–82; Gitlow decision (1925) applying free speech to states, 194–195; OWS protest restrictions in context of, 74; "public forum" doctrine of, 82–83; ratification of, 233; setting minimum threshold for free speech, 274; state action doctrine and the, 75–76; symbolic speech protected by, 83–84. *See also* freedom of speech

Fisyak-Brown-Shiffman interview, 371–382

596 Acres: collective action goal of, 166; fence pansies used as canaries of community-controlled space, 164*n*; photos of tactics used by, 160*fig*–161*fig*, 164*fig*, 165*fig*; using signs to promote self-governance, 160–165

Five Borough Farm project, 329–331

"Foreclosure" (song sheet), 148*fig*

Foucault, M., 157, 159

France: Arc de Triomphe (Paris) in, 335; Paris Commune (1871) of, 28; Place de Bastille (Paris) in, 335; Place de Vosges (Paris) in, 239, 302; student uprising in Paris (1968), 126

Francis, M., 241, 242

Franck, K. A., 3, 4*fig*, 93

Frank H. Ogawa Plaza (Oakland City Hall), 309–310, 313–322

free assembly. *See* right to free assembly

Freedman-Schnapp, M., 277, 289

Freedom Corner (Pittsburgh), 100, 102–110

Freedom of Expression National Monument, 151*fig*–152

Freedom Plaza (Washington, DC), 349*fig*

freedom of speech: comparing UK and U.S. tolerance for, 187–188; consequences of unfettered, 189; democratic expression in public space, 288–291; examining New York and London policies regarding, 188–196; First Amendment setting minimum threshold for, 274; Gitlow decision (1925) and state rights to, 194–195; shaped by design, 235; tradition of public space and, 215–216. *See also* First Amendment

Fullilove, M. T., 99, 102, 106, 108, 110, 128

Fulton Street Transit Hub construction, 223*fig*

"The Future of Farming in NYC" workshop, 330

Gamaliel Foundation, 130

Gandhi, M., 172–173, 177, 249

Garvin, A., 229, 278

gay Americans, 125

General Motors Plaza (NYC), 341–342*fig*

Gindroz, R., 244–245

Gitlow decision (1925), 194–195

Global Revolution media, 22–23

Global Street notion, 68–69

Golan, G., 70, 148–149

Gospel of Matthew, 202–203

Grace Plaza (NYC), 342, 343*fig*

Gramercy Park (NYC), 302

Grand Concourse (Bronx), 239

Great Britain: common law of, 187; common urban form of public open space in modern, 273–274; comparing public spaces tolerance of U.S. and, 187–196; Countryside Agency (or Countryside Council for Wales) in, 271; enclosure movement in, 273; Occupy London, 366; walking paths throughout, 271–273. *See also* London (1850-1900)

"The Great Gathering of Armies" (*The Iliad*), 197

Greenacre Park (NYC), 357

Green Map System, 49

Green movement (Iran), 254, 256–257

Green Scroll march (2009), 254

Ground Zero: death in public place of, 178–179; discussions on qualities of public space of, 223; importance of infrastructure of memorial at, 222–223; Jonathan Rose's proposal for memorial site of, 365; life-affirming responses to 9/11 memorial at, 181–183; planning sessions and debates over what to do with, 179–181; witnessing the devastation at, 178. *See also* September 11, 2001 attacks; World Trade Center (WTC)

Harlem (NYC), 374–375, 378
Hayden, T., 291–292
Highlander Folk School (Tennessee), 124
Highland Garden Village (Denver), 366
High Line (NYC): creative community organizing work by, 151–152; crowded and "victim of its own success," 345–346; flyer on the, 150*fig*; people gathering on the, 226*fig*, 345*fig*; public recognition of successful transformation of, 333; restricting spaces for art vendors in, 285; second parade of, 153*fig*
"High Performance Landscape Guidelines for 21st Century Parks" (NYC DPR), 331–332
Hip Hop Occupies' Rise & Decolonize events, 146
Hippodamas of Miletus, 199
historical black universities, 380–381
Hitler's Telegram 71 order, 159
Homeland Security, 176, 259–260, 274–275, 334–335, 347
Hong Kong, 90*fig*, 96
Horizontalism (Sitrin), 22
Hou, J., 3, 89, 90, 95, 138, 275, 338, 383
How the Greeks Built Cities (Wycherly), 237
HSBC Headquarters (Hong Kong), 90*fig*
Huang, T.-S., 3, 4*fig*, 11
human rights, 204–205
Hunken, M., 28, 31
Hyde Park (London), 284, 302, 308

The Iliad (Homer), 197
The Image of the City (Lynch), 241
Independence Park (Philadelphia), 250*fig*–251*fig*
Indignants. *See* Real Democracy NOW (or the Indignants) (or Los Indignados) [Spain]
infrastructure. *See* urban infrastructure
inner cities: contemporary challenges facing, 128–130; CSI's model of community economic development for, 121–122; invisibility in the image of, 135–136; negotiative spaces of marginalized places in, 136–138; placemaking in, 138–139; post-World War II migration to, 127–128; property tax inequalities impacting, 130; regional equity movement to improve, 130–132. *See also* cities; urban renewal

Institute for Applied Autonomy, 165
institutional public space, description of, 91
insurgent public space, 91–93, 275
Insurgent Public Space (Hou), 91
"International Mother Language Monument" vote (NYC), 291
International Workers of the World (Spokane), 46
Internet filtering mechanisms, 259
InterOccupy Arts Calls, 147
Iran: crackdown against Azadi Square demonstrators in, 256; Green movement in, 254, 256–257; state control of public space in, 257–258, 260
Iranian Revolution (1979), 257
Iran-Iraq War (1980-1988), 255

Jackson (Mississippi), 378–380
Jackson Square (New Orleans), 378
Jacobs, J., 37, 38, 40, 173, 229, 241
Jerusalem tent city protest (2011), 366
Jesus Christ, 202–203
Jonathan Rose Companies, 364
Justiceville (1985 homeless encampment), 151

Kayden, J. S., 8, 9, 13, 241, 338
King, M. L., Jr., 103, 119, 177, 204, 249

Latinos: criticism regarding nonunion jobs taken by, 118; development of post-World War II communities of, 128; social movements based on redressing marginalization of, 125; Zuccotti Park occupation participation by, 117–124. *See also* marginalized populations; people of color
Lee-Pyatok-LaRocca, 314
Lee, Y. H., 309, 313
L'Enfant plan (Washington, DC), 335
Liberty Plaza Park (now Zuccotti Park) [NYC]: cleanup and redesign following 9/11, 207–208; damaged by terrorist attack of 9/11 and reopened as Zuccotti Park, 8, 77, 207–213, 281–282; NYC's commitment to public space creating, 37–38. *See also* Zuccotti Park (NYC)
Libeskind, D., 222
libraries: NYC public space in form of, 287–288; Occupy Zuccotti Park Information Center and, 9, 10*fig*, 13, 14, 73, 228*fig*
Life Between Buildings: Using Public Space (Gehl), 241
Lincoln Center (NYC), 340–341*fig*
The Line. *See* High Line (NYC)
Listening to the City events, 221
Local Law 48 (NYC), 330
Loma Prieta earthquake (1989), 313
London (1850-1900): "Bloody Sunday" demonstration in, 191–192; comparing demon-

stration controls in New York and, 190–192; comparing public speech/demonstrations policies of New York and, 188–196; "Dod Street trick", in, 191, 192; Hyde Park, 284, 302, 308; population (mid-eighteenth century to 1900) of, 189; Speaker's Corner emergence in, 191, 284, 308, 366; Trafalgar Square site of public demonstrations in, 190, 191, 192, 335, 363. *See also* Great Britain

Loose Space (Franck and Stevens), 93

Los Angeles Poverty Department (LAPD), 150, 151–152

Los Angeles protest locations, 208*fig*, 210*fig*, 234*fig*

Lower Manhattan Construction Command Center (LMCCC), 8

Lower Manhattan Development Authority (LMDC), 180

Low, S. M., 93, 241

Madison Square Park Conservancy, 346

Madison Square Park (NYC), 336, 345

Main Street Garden Park (Dallas), 352*fig*

The Mall (Washington, DC), 302–303, 363, 367

Mandela, N., 177

March on Washington (1963), 367

Marcuse, P., 242, 274

Marcus Garvey Park (NYC), 374

marginalized populations: CSI's model of community economic development for, 121–122; CSI's work to provide Internet to, 116; "cultural commodities" provided by small businesses serving, 120; cultural and political identities by claiming rights, 138–139; Occupy movement as historical moment for, 126; Occupy Pittsburgh movement by, 99–111; OWS activities and participation by, 116–124; perceived sense of belonging by, 137; post-World War II urban migration and segregation of, 127–128; public housing communities and, 374; racial profiling/criminalization of, 115–116; regional equity movement and, 130–132. *See also* African Americans; Latinos

Maslow's hierarchy of needs, 382

media coverage: Global Revolution media filming the first days of OWS, 22–23; of "Million Hoodies" demo (NYC), 31–32; OWS Media Center/Team, 51; public space occupation and, 9; *Saturday Night Live* (SNL) satire on Bloomberg and OWS, 61, 62, 65; of Zuccotti Park evictions, 27. *See also* social networking

Mellon Bank (Pittsburgh), 99–100

Metropolitan Museum (NYC), 340, 346–347*fig*

Middle East: Arab Spring social and political claims in the, 68; Egyptian social revolution (2011) in, 3, 4–6, 149, 206, 245, 256; Iranian

power struggle over public space, 255–258, 260; tweeting role in upheavals in, 377

"Million Hoodies" demo (NYC), 31–32

minority populations. *See* people of color

Mississippi State Medical School, 379

Mitchell, D., 17, 93–94, 134

Mitchell, T., 7, 9, 11

Moholy-Nagy, S., 237–238

Montesquieu, 204

moral ambiguity issue, 62–66

Moynihan, C., 8, 44

Mubarak, H., 3, 4

Muslim community/NYPD spying scandal, 258

NAACP, 103

National Mall (Washington, DC), 302–303, 363, 367

Native Americans, 125, 255

negotiation: of the future of protest in public space, 43–47; placemaking creating negotiative spaces of marginalized places, 136–138; public space and the inevitability of, 42–43; Zuccotti Park occupation and evolution of, 12–17, 34, 42–47. *See also* democracy

neighborhoods: comparing inequalities of NYC, 157–159; democratic goal of self-governance by, 159–160; Harlem (NYC), 374–375, 378; nighttime park closing requirements to protect, 363; primary school in Ocean Hill-Brownsville (Brooklyn) as center of, 304–305*fig*; tactics for forming bonds as, 160–168. *See also* cities

Nepantla (Mayan concept of space), 152

neutral zone space, 373–376, 381

New City Spaces (Gehl and Gemzøe), 241

New Left, 291–292

New Orleans second-line jazz funerals, 154

New Spectrum, 371

New Urbanism, 136

New York City (1850 to 1900): Commissioners Plan (The Grid) policies of, 193; comparing demonstration controls in London and, 190–192; crime prevention policies of, 189–190; Draft Riots (1863) in, 192; emergence of political gathering sites in, 193; Orange Day marches (1871) in, 192; population of, 189; regulation of street procession and assemblies (1872) in, 192; Wobblies fueling the labor movement in, 193–194

New York City 2000 Millennium Commission, 332

New York City: debate about democratizing public space in, 327–333; map showing vacant public land being warehoused in, 163*fig*; New York City Master Plan (1811) for, 306, 335; participatory budgeting process in, 288–291; "The Sidewalks of New York" (Sorkin) on public rights in, 143–145. *See also* cities; parks; plazas; POPS (privately owned public space); Zuccotti Park occupation

New York City Department of Parks & Recreation (DPR), 285, 331

New York City Department of Transportation (DOT), 241, 252, 293, 294, 295, 336–337

New York City Fire Department, 55

New York City Master Plan (1811), 306, 335

New York City Planning Commission, 270, 283, 335

New York City Planning Department: developer's chafing against zoning laws enforced by, 35–36; diminished public space permitted (1960s) by, 36–37*fig*; history of, 38–39, 39–42, 267–269; issues raised by the Zuccotti Park occupation for, 267–270; Local Law 48 (2011) to increase transparency in, 330–331. *See also* zoning codes

New York City Police Department (NYPD): clashes between OWS occupants with, 8, 24, 26–28, 30–31, 49–50, 50*fig*, 52, 78, 256, 258–260; how the OWS was compromised by the, 258–260; "Million Hoodies" demo (NYC) response by, 31–32; spying scandal on Muslim communities and organizations, 258; zero-tolerance policing and tactics (2000-present) of the, 39–40. *See also* community policing

New York Civil Liberties Union (NYCLU), 44, 46–47, 74n.1

New York Times, 27, 291

Nielsen, S., 339, 340, 341, 342, 343, 344, 345, 347, 348, 349

Noguchi cube, 343*fig*

North Plaza grove (Lincoln Center) [NYC], 340–341*fig*

Oakland (California), 319–322

Oakland City Hall (1917), 314*fig*

Oakland City Hall (1999), 315*fig*

Oakland City Hall Plaza: demonstrations and police action in, 320–321*fig*; design features of, 313–319; how it continues to transform, 326; Occupy Oakland in the, 69, 319–322; prize winning award of, 309, 310; reasons why the Occupy Oakland site was, 321–322

occupation: defined as a gathering threatening social order, 300; designing for, 339–350; as form of resistance, 255; as top-down hegemonic force of action, 255. *See also* OWS (Occupy Wall Street); public space occupations; territory

Occupied Real Estate office (NYC), 150

Occupy Art: The People's Movement in Visual's Facebook page, 147

Occupy Austin: Austin City Hall site, 313*fig*

Occupy Boston, 233

Occupy Broadway, 146

Occupy Broadway (December, 2011), 28

Occupy Dance's Ballet Barre on the Barricades,

146–147

Occupy the Empty Space (theater event, NCY), 28, 31

Occupy Farms, 29

Occupy Halloween, 146

Occupy the Hood, 112–113

Occupy London, 366

Occupy Los Angeles, 208*fig*, 210*fig*, 233–234*fig*

Occupy Oakland, 69

Occupy Philadelphia, 227, 227*fig*, 233

Occupy Pittsburgh: beginnings of the, 99–100*fig*; geography and rallying point of, 100, 102–104; legacy and reflections on the, 104–106, 108–111. *See also* Pittsburgh (Pennsylvania)

"Occupy with the Provision of Public Space: The City's Responsibilities" (Marcuse), 242

Occupy Salt Lake City: Pioneer Park site, 171–172

Occupy Sound, 146

Occupy Times Square March (2011), 53*fig*

Occupy Wall Street Homeless Youth Caucus, 27

Occupy Wall Street Photo Team, 49

Occupy Wall Street Sustainability Working Group, 4, 49, 54–58*fig*

Occupy Washington, DC, 233*fig*

Ocean Hill-Brownsville primary school (Brooklyn), 304–305*fig*

"Office of the People" space, 70–72

Ogawa, F. H., 314–415

Oklahoma City bombing (1995), 274

"Old Oligarch" (ancient Greek), 198

Olin, L., 249–252

On the Plaza; The Political of Public Space and Culture (Low), 241

openhearted cities: benefits and advantages provided by, 170–177; Beyond War (later Search for Common Ground) contributing to, 174–175

Orange Day marches (NYC, 1871), 192

Organizing for Occupation (O4O), 149–150

the Other: meeting face-to-face with, 174–175; neutral zone space for interacting with, 373–376, 381

ownership: beliefs of the 1% on limited resources and, 372–373; occupants in public space empowered by, 305; pubic space with "shared," 368; U.S. history of land, 273. *See also* POPS (privately owned public space)

OWS community attributes: the base, 219; common definition of occupy, 216–217; connection points of infrastructure, 225–226; demonstration of common sense, 234–235; design matters, 220; free speech in public space, 215–216; functionality, 219–220; the future is now attitude, 224–225; importance of details in design, 231; importance of infrastructure, 222–223; logic and proportion lessons, 229–230;

people and the *agora*, 221–222, 266; people and public space, 229; political expression of all occupied cities, 233–234; rules about public space, 217*fig*–218; stimulus and occupy, 226–227; as sum of its parts, 232; up against the wall, 223–224; validating role of architects in society, 227–229; Vitruvius rules and community, 218
OWS constitutional issues: *Brentwood Academy* case applied to, 79, 80, 81–82; *Evans v. Newton* (1966) case applied to, 80–81; examining Zuccotti Park occupation in context of democratic governance and, 265–270; First Amendment applications to privately owned facility, 74–75; policy of searching OWS activists for sleeping bags as, 83, 84–85; on protest restrictions and First Amendment standards, 74; regarding restriction of NYC public access, 44–45, 79–80, 85–86; state action doctrine and Zuccotti Park administration, 75–76, 78–82; U.S. "public forum" doctrine, 82–83. *See also* Bill of Rights; community policing
OWS dialogue: on community identity provided by businesses, 120; on constant need to reevaluate spaces, 124; on creating space for political conversation, 122–124; on CSI's approach to, 113–114, 116–117, 121–122; on OWS constitutional issues, 119; phraseology and language used for, 112–113; on psychological aspect of space, 115–116; on racial and inclusion aspects of OWS movement, 117–118, 119–120; on "spaces of social inclusion," 114–115; on Zuccotti Park lessons, 118–119
OWS negotiations: constitutional issues of, 74–86; Zuccotti Park occupation and evolution of, 12–17, 34, 42–47
OWS (Occupy Wall Street): as call for action, 383–385; common characteristics of sites selected for, 208*fig*–213; examined in terms of radical imagination, 146–155; first days of, 21–25; limited participation by people of color, 116–124, 125–132; phraseology and language of, 112–124; protected activities legacy of the, 44–47, 277–278, 302; renegotiating public rights and redefining public space, 254–256, 258, 260; revealing the lack of adequate public space, 248–249, 335–338, 351–352, 361; similarity between Times Up! and, 52; Tahrir Square activists sending open letter of support to, 25. *See also* occupation; public space occupations; Zuccotti Park occupation
OWS sanitation issues: "filth" rhetoric creating moral ambiguity, 42, 61–66; NCY's resistance to providing toilets and water, 53–54; occupiers cleaning the park, 54*fig*

Paine, T., 234–235
Paley Park (NYC), 334, 347, 355*fig*, 357
Palmer and Hornbostel, 313
Panic of 1857, 224
Parabola (Jane Jacob interview), 173
park closing requirements, 363
Park Place Gallery (NYC), 231
parks: Balsley Park (NYC), 361–363; Battery Park (NYC), 285; Brooklyn Bridge Park (NYC), 285–286; Bryant Park (NYC), 239, 334, 340*fig*, 346, 349, 353; Capitol Plaza (NYC), 358*fig*–359; Central Park (NYC), 196, 224, 248, 285, 309, 336, 345, 346; Chelsea Waterside Park (NYC), 353*fig*; Gramercy Park (NYC), 302; Greenacre Park (NYC), 357; High Line (NYC), 150*fig*, 151–153*fig*, 226*fig*, 333, 345–346, 345*fig*; "High Performance Landscape Guidelines for 21st Century Parks" (NYC DPR), 331–332; Hyde Park (London), 284, 302; as inadequate public space in NYC, 335; Madison Square Park (NYC), 336, 345; Main Street Garden Park (Dallas), 352*fig*; Marcus Garvey Park (NYC), 374; nighttime closing of public NYC, 363; NYC Master Plan (1811) on, 306, 335; NYC's restriction of art vendors in, 285–286; Oakland City Hall and Frank H. Ogawa Plaza and, 309–310, 313–322; Paley Park (NYC), 334, 347, 355*fig*, 357; Pearly Gates (Bronx), 331–332; as public space, 284–286; Silver Park (NYC), 360*fig*; TKTS2K design competition overlapping transportation and, 332; transformations across the U.S. of POPS, 361; typology of, 352–356. *See also* New York City; plazas; POPS (privately owned public space); Union Square (NYC)
Parque Central (Cuba), 303*fig*–304*fig*
Participatory Democracy: The Dream of Port Huron (Hayden), 291
Paternoster Square (NYC), 244
Paul, Saint, 203
Pearl Square (Bahrain): demonstrators' manner of living during occupation of, 11; examining the public space occupation in, 3; February (2011) demonstrations in, 6–7; map of, 5*fig*; media coverage during occupation of, 9; physical description of, 6; renamed Al Farooq Junction, 7
Pearly Gates (Bronx), 331–332
pedestrians: the Dutch *woonerf* for, 337; Great Britain's walking paths, 271–273; how POPS discourages traffic by, 334–335; NYC CityBenches program for, 296; NYC DOT's promotion of bicycle and sidewalks for, 336–337; NYC DOT's Weekend Walks program and Summer Streets for, 296; opening streets and sidewalks for, 294, 296, 334–338; pedestrian street in Lower Manhattan, 344*fig*; Times Square (NYC), 294

The Peloponnesian Wars (Thucydides), 199
people of color: historical black universities serving, 380–381; Occupy Pittsburgh movement participation by, 99–111; OWS limited participation by, 116–124, 125–132; racial balance of NYC, 120; racial profiling and criminalization of, 115–116; social movements based on redressing marginalization of, 125. *See also* African Americans; communities of color; Latinos
Pericles, 199, 200, 202, 206
"Pericles's Funeral Oration" (431 BC), 199
Perk Park (Cleveland), 361
The Persian Letters (Montesquieu), 204
Philadelphia: Independence Park in, 250*fig*–251*fig*; Occupy Philadelphia in, 227, 227*fig*, 233
physical space: claiming territorial, 67–69; how Arts & Culture define the, 73; interaction between social/political space and, 113–114; occupying infrastructure of, 71–72; OWS creation of "Office of the People," 70–72; required for democracy, 70; stories told by, 72–73; virtual versus, 369, 376, 377, 381
Pienza (Italy), 238*fig*, 239
Pittsburgh (Pennsylvania): African American community of, 100–101; description of the, 100; Freedom Corner of, 100, 102–103, 106–108; Hill District Community Development Corporation of, 107; ONE HILL demonstrations in, 110; proposal for urban renewal in, 101*fig*–102*fig*; proposed locations for truth and reconciliation park in, 108–110. *See also* Occupy Pittsburgh
Plaça de Catalunya (Barcelona): demonstrators' manner of living during occupation of, 9; examining the public space occupation in, 3; handmade signs and posters used by occupiers of, 9; libraries and information desks during occupation, 9; map of, 5*fig*; physical description and functions of, 7; Real Democracy NOW demonstrations in, 7; relationship between demonstrators and passerbys in, 11, 12
place: "act of placemaking," 338; building democracy by creating governing, 277–292; cultural and political identities by claiming rights and, 138–139; invisibility in image of city, 135–136; negotiative spaces of marginalized, 136–138; new political subjectivities formed in, 139. *See also* space
Place de Vosges (Paris), 239, 302
placemaking, 137–139
Places Magazine, 244
PlaNYC (2007), 293–294
Plato, 199, 200
plazas: General Motors Plaza (NYC), 341–342*fig*; Grace Plaza (NYC), 342, 343*fig*; NYC Department of Transportation (DOT) programs for, 295; NYC's POPS or bonus, 356–358, 363; Oakland City Hall and Frank H. Ogawa Plaza space, 309–310, 313–322; public space of, 286–287. *See also* New York City; parks; POPS (privately owned public space)
police. *See* community policing; New York City Police Department (NYPD)
political power: biopower or biopolitics concept of, 157–159; divide and conquer mentality and slicing, 373; Global Street representing those without formal, 68–69; how technology has expanded power struggle over territory, 259–260; "illusion of transparency" masking, 136
political protests/expression: centrality of urban space to, 65; dissent in public space form of, 17–18; efforts by urban elites to repress, 64–66; evolution and negotiation during Zuccotti Park, 12–17, 34, 42–47; Gandhi's civil disobedience commitment to *ahimsa*, 172–173, 249; Global Street notion of, 68–69; lack of dedicated space in NYC for, 363; moral ambiguity created to repress, 62–66; OWS as politics out of place, 65; public space as the space for negotiating, 34; role of tweeting in, 377; significance of occupying territory during, 68; similarities in public space occupations by, 9–12; symbolism of public space, 32–33; US phenomenon of legal management of, 17–18. *See also* citizenry; civic space; demonstrations; social movements
The Politics of Authenticity (Berman), 205n.2
pollution beliefs, 62–64
Poor People's March (1968), 309
POPS design strategies case studies: across the US, 361; Capitol Plaza (NYC), 358*fig*–359; 57th Street and 9th Avenue into Balsley Park (NYC), 361–363; Silver Park (NYC), 360*fig*; 325 5th Avenue (NYC), 359*fig*–360
POPS (privately owned public space): Battery Park City, 356; "bundle of rights" association with, 280; challenge of elevated 55 Water Street (NYC), 361; Chelsea Waterside Park (NYC), 353*fig*; failure as adequate substitute for true public realm, 91; Greenacre Park (NYC), 357; how pedestrian traffic is discouraged in, 334–335; Main Street Garden Park (Dallas), 352*fig*; NYC regulations governing pre-2007, 279; NYC's bonus plazas or, 356–358; NYC Zoning Resolution (1961) on, 281, 282; NYC Zoning Resolution governing th edesign of, 17; OWS revealing loss of civic capacity in, 248–249, 335–338, 351–352, 361; Paley Park (NYC), 334, 347, 355*fig*, 357; as part of entrenched political and institutional crisis, 97; public benefits of the new open

space of, 358–363; question of what to do about failed, 360; as real-estate-led urban development tool, 278; revealing the prevalence of NYC, 166–168; Riverside Park South (NYC), 353*fig*, 355; taken as right by OWS, 139; typology of, 352–356; Zuccotti Park (NYC) as, 52–53, 59, 139, 248–249, 278–283, 361. *See also* New York City; ownership; parks; plazas; public space

Port Huron Statement, 291

poverty rates, 129, 130–132

power. *See* political power

The Practice of Everyday Life (de Certeau), 159, 166

Privately Owned Public Space: The New York Experience (Kayden), 241

privatized spaces: end of hubris and suburbanized (2000-present), 39–40, 42; gentrification and filtering (1975-2000) of, 38–39; history of social unrest (1961-1975) in, 35–38; OWS constitutional issue of public right to access, 44–45, 79–80, 85–86

protests. *See* political protests

the public: distinction between space and, 90–91; kept at the heart of public space, 333; making space and making, 94–97; open space benefits of POPS to, 358–363; OWS legacy of protected activities guaranteed to, 44–47, 277–278, 302; OWS and right to access privatized space by, 44–45, 79–80, 85–86; rights to public space by, 43–44

public forum doctrine, 119, 367

public housing communities, 374

public rights: civil rights movement's goals for, 128; collective efforts to redefine public space and renegotiate, 254–260; cultural and political identities by claiming, 138–139; post-9/11 security violations of, 176, 259–260, 274–275, 334–335, 347; to public space, 43–44; "right to the city," 46–47; right to free assembly as, 247–248, 250, 283–284, 300; "The Sidewalks of New York" (Sorkin) on, 143–145; state of exception restricting, 133–135

public sector change agents: architects as, 220, 222–223, 224–226, 299–308; creating governing places for democracy, 277–292; designing for occupation, 339–350; design thinking as heart of, 333; Design Trust for Public Space work as, 328–331; Five Borough Farm and engaging stakeholders as, 329–331; High Performance Landscape Guidelines for 21st Century Parks involving community as, 331–332; need for reviewing public space regulations, 275–276; NYC CityBenchens program, 296; NYC DOT's plaza programs, 295; NYC DOT's Weekend Walks program and Summer Streets for, 296; NYC Planning Commission as, 270; opening streets and sidewalks, 334–338;

PlaNYC launched by Bloomberg, 293–294; reclaiming New Lots Triangle (East New York), 295; responsibilities for developing the public realm, 364–370; responsibilities for programming the public space, 371–382; TKTS2K design competition for involving, 332; transforming Times Square, 294–295. *See also* stakeholders

public space: combining domestic and civic, 309–326; connection between human rights and, 204–205; cultural and civic importance of, 245, 283–284; democracy and role of, 42, 275–276, 288–291, 327–333, 364–370; examining the romance of, 197–206; how urbanism practice maintains illusion of, 135–139; insurgent, 91–93, 275; "neutral zone," 373–376; OWS revealing the lack of adequate, 27–28, 248–249, 335–338, 351–352, 361, 372–373; responsibilities for developing and programming, 364–370, 371–382; security concerns as limiting use of, 176, 259–260, 274–275, 334–335, 347; as the space where social conflicts are negotiated, 12–17, 32–33, 34, 42–47; typology and definitions of, 241–243. *See also* POPS (privately owned public space); regulatory restrictions; space

Public Space (Carr, Francis, Rivlin, and Stone), 241, 242

public space history: the American experience with public landscape, 243; ancient Greece and development of public space, 197–201, 237; Book of Kings's on Jerusalem's public space, 201–202; commentaries on the ongoing evolution of, 243–252; comparing NYC and London's (1850 to 1900), 188–194; evidence of public space in Catal Huyuk (Anatolia), 237–238; examining the historical development of public space, 236–252; Gitlow decision (1925) and state rights to free speech, 194–195; in medieval Sienna (Italy), 238–239; New Testament on the synagogue as public space, 202–203; in NYC, 188–194, 239–240; in Pienza (Italy), 238*fig*, 239; shifting uses of NYC public space in 1980s, 195–196; tradition of public space, 215–216; typology and definitions developed during, 241–243

public space occupations: Alcatraz Occupation (1969), 255; dissent through, 17–18; evolution and negotiation of, 12–17, 34, 42–47; examining widespread 2011, 3; Global Street notion of, 68–69; as infrastructure, 71–72; Jerusalem tent city protest (2011), 366; media coverage of, 9; Plaça de Catalunya (Barcelona), 3, 5*fig*, 7, 9, 11, 12; political significance of, 68; similarities of all political protests engaged in, 9–12; Tahrir Square demonstrations and, 3, 4–6, 149, 206, 245; Tiananmen Square (China), 245, 260,

274, 303; understanding the symbolism of, 32–33. *See also* occupation; OWS (Occupy Wall Street)

public speech: comparing UK and US tolerance for, 187–188; consequences of unfettered, 189; democratic expression in public space, 288–291; examining New York and London policies regarding, 188–196; First Amendment setting minimum threshold for, 274; Gitlow decision (1925) and state rights to, 194–195; shaped by design, 235; tradition of public space and, 215–216

Puig i Cadafalch, J., 7

Purity and Danger: An Analysis of the Concept of Pollution and Taboo (Douglas), 62–63

Pyatok, M., 309, 316, 318, 320*fig*, 325, 326

race/ethnic populations. *See* marginalized populations

racial profiling/criminalization, 115–116

radical imagination: examining the OWS in terms of, 146–147; OWS's collective rage and, 232; spaces of imagination expressing, 154–155; spaces of intersection expressing, 152–154; spaces of intervention expressing, 147–152

Real Democracy NOW (or the Indignants) (or Los Indignados) [Spain], 7, 68

rebuilding strategies: Freedom Corner Monument created as, 106–108; post-OWS and challenges of, 155; protected activities legacy of OWS and, 44–47, 277–278, 302; role of architects in rebuilding public space, 308. *See also* urban renewal

regional equity movement, 130–132

Regis, H., 152, 154

regulatory restrictions: *Brentwood Academy* (US) case on, 79, 80, 81–82; comparing history of New York and London's, 187–196; *Evans v. Newton* (US) on, 80–81; examining First Amendment in context of OWS, 74; need to review public space limitations placed by, 275–276; to privately owned facilities, 74–75; security concerns limiting public space use, 176, 259–260, 274–275, 334–335, 347; US "public forum" doctrine of, 82–83; Zuccotti Park (NYC), First Amendment, and, 8, 76, 77–80. *See also* public space; state of exception

Republic (Socrates), 200

resistance: Iranian Green movement, 255, 256–257; occupation as form of, 255; redefining public space as form of, 260; Tahrir Square demonstrators exercising in, 3, 4–6, 149, 206, 245, 260. *See also* citizenry; demonstrations

"right to the city" concept, 46–47

right to free assembly: formalization of, 247–248, 250, 283–284, 300; OWS legacy for, 44–47, 277–278, 302

Rios, M., 95, 133

Rising Currents exhibition (Museum of Modern Arts), 225

Riverside Park South (NYC), 353*fig*, 355

Rivlin, L. G., 241, 242

Rockefeller Center (NYC), 240, 278

Rose, J., 364–370

Rose-Shiffman interview, 364–370

Sadik-Kahn, J., 241, 293

St. Paul's Cathedral (NYC), 244

San Francisco's El Plan Popular (or People's Plan), 138

sanitation. *See* OWS sanitation issues

Sassen, S., 67

Saturday Night Live (SNL), 61, 62, 66

schools: demonstrations in support of, 308; Ocean Hill-Brownsville primary school (Brooklyn), 304–305*fig*

Seattle: Good Neighbors Agreement in, 138; Growing Vine Street project of, 94–95; Pro Parks Levy (2000) passed by, 95

Seattle Department of Neighborhoods, 94

Seattle Neighborhood Matching Fund, 94

security issues: public rights and space are impacted by, 176, 259–260, 274–275, 334–335, 347; rise of security industry following 9/11, 134

September 11, 2001 attacks: death in public places during, 178–179, 347; Liberty Plaza Park destruction during, 207, 281; responses to Ground Zero memorial of, 181–183; state security violating public rights since the, 134, 176, 259–260, 274–275, 334–335, 347; tightening of demonstration permission since, 195; Zuccotti Park following the, 8, 77, 207–213. *See also* Ground Zero; terrorist acts; United States

Sheep Meadow (Central Park) [NYC], 336, 345

Shepard, B. H., 21, 35

Shiffman-Brown-Fisyak interview, 371–382

Shiffman, R., 112, 364, 383

Shiffman-Rose interview, 364–370

Shiffman-Wiley interview, 112–124

"The Sidewalks of New York" (Sorkin), 143–145

Sienna (Italy), 238–239

Sitte, C., 240, 241

Skyline Park (Denver), 361

Smithsimon, G., 24, 34, 35, 40, 41, 43

social capital, 128

social conflicts: history of privatized spaces (1961–1975) and, 35–38; public space as the space for negotiating, 12–17, 34, 42–47

social inclusion: Barcelona's concept of, 114; collaborative space providing, 368; global discourse on, 114–115; post-9/11 search for public space design with, 368

The Social Life of Small Public Spaces (Whyte), 41

social movements: benefits of loving my city

attitude by, 173–174; civil rights, 128, 371; Critical Mass!, 21, 31; history of, 126; how public space has appeared at forefront of, 260; how society can be change through citizen-initiated, 385; regional equity movement, 130–132; social capital used to create, 128; Tea Party, 132; understanding that public space is central to, 32–33. *See also* citizenry; political protests/expression

social networking: role of tweeting in political upheavals, 377; sharing artistic expression of occupation through, 147; spatially organized, 165–166. *See also* Facebook; Media coverage

Socrates, 199, 200–201, 204

Solomon, King, 201–202

Sophocles, 198

space: combining domestic and civic, 309–326; creating a "loose" or "tight," 339–340; distinction between the public and, 90–91, 93–94; how actions, art, and culture transform, 73, 93–94, 146–155; "illusion of transparency" masking political power in, 136; interactions between social, political, and physical, 113–114; making public and making, 94–97; "neutral zone," 373–376, 381; stories told by physical, 72–73; virtual, 369, 376, 377, 381. *See also* place; public space

Spain: Plaça de Catalunya (Barcelona) occupation in, 3, 5*fig*, 7, 9, 11, 12; Real Democracy NOW (or the Indignants) movement in, 7; "spaces of social inclusion" concept found in Barcelona, 114

spatially organized social networking, 165–166

Speaker's Corner (London), 191, 284, 308, 366

squatting strategy (NYC), 152

SS *Normandie* sinking (1942), 232

stakeholders: design thinking for collaborative problem solving by, 333; "High Performance Landscape Guidelines" for involving community, 331–332; how the Five Borough Farm project engaged, 329–331. *See also* public sector change agents

Standard Metropolitan Statistical Area (SMSA), 379

state: community policing by the, 42–47, 171–172, 300; relationship between law and violence in context of the, 133; suspension of laws and rights by the, 133–135

state action doctrine (US), 75–76, 78–82

state of exception, 133–135. *See also* regulatory restrictions

Stone, A. M., 241, 242

stories: how Arts & Culture is heart of change, 73; OWS library and Information Center to keep the, 9, 10*fig*, 13, 14, 73; told by physical spaces, 72–73

Students for a Democratic Society (SDS), 126, 250, 291

student uprising (Paris, 1968), 126

Studio Daniel Libeskind, 222

sustainability: OWS Sustainability Working Group promoting, 54–58*fig*; Zuccotti Park occupation activities to support, 53–54*fig*, 55–56*fig*

symbolism of public space protests, 32–33

"Tactical Cartographies" (Institute for Applied Autonomy), 165

Tafel Hall (Center for Architecture), 216, 217

Tahrir Square occupation (Cairo): art used to aminate the, 149; cultural importance of, 245; demonstrators' manner of living during, 9, 11; examining the public space occupation in, 3, 4–5; map of, 5*fig*; media coverage during, 9; numerous public demonstrations held in, 5–6; open letter of support sent to OWS from, 25; social movement and uprising role of, 260; women protesting in, 206

Tea Party movement, 132

Tel Aviv's ten city, 68

Ten Books of Architecture (Vitruvius), 217–218

territory: diverse and complex meanings of, 68; Global Street notion of occupying, 68–69; how technology has expanded the power struggle over, 259–260; nationalizing dynamics of claiming, 67; occupation as top-down hegemonic force of action using, 255; political significance of occupying, 68; "territoriality" in human nature, 256. *See also* occupation

terrorist acts: Oklahoma City bombing (1995), 274; security issues raised due to, 176, 259–260, 274–275, 334–335, 347. *See also* September 11, 2001 attack

Theatre Development Fund (TDF), 332

Thoreau, H. D., 249

Thucydides, 199

Tiananmen Square (China), 245, 260, 274, 303

Times Square (NYC), 294, 306, 332, 336

Times Up! (NYC): bike-powered generators of, 27; canceled theater event planned by, 28; description of, 49; Peace Ride of, 28; public space mission of, 52; similarity between Occupy movement and, 52

TKTS2K design competition (NYC), 332

Townscape (Cullen), 241

Town and Square: From the Agora to the Village Green (Zucker), 241

Trafalgar Square (London), 190, 191, 192, 335, 363

traffic: NYC public space impacted by, 240–241; Sitte's comment on loss of space to, 240

Trans-Asia Sisters Association Taiwan, 96

transportation: designs to encourage walking, 271–273, 294, 296; loss of space due to traffic, 240–241; TKTS2K design competition

overlapping parks and, 332
Trinity Church (NYC), 22

Udin, S., 101, 102–103, 106, 107, 108
Un barrage contre le Pacifique (Duras), 225
Union Square (NYC): aerial view of, 307*fig*;
   art vendors restricted in, 285; historic place
   for political gatherings, 193, 194, 214, 248,
   306–307; "Million Hoodies" demo in, 31–
   32; park activities of, 336; random arrests
   (September 24, 2011) at, 50*fig*; shifting use
   of public space of, 195; as transformational
   crossroads, 154. *See also* parks
Union Square (San Francisco), 361
"Unitary Urbanism" (Kotanyi and Vaneigem),
   160
United Kingdom. *See* Great Britain
United States: codified law of the, 187; comparing public spaces tolerance of Great
   Britain and the, 187–196; First Amendment of the, 74–76, 79, 80–83; history of
   land ownership in the, 273; management
   of public dissent in the, 17–18; OWS and
   constitutional issues of the, 74–86; OWS
   exposing income inequality in the, 25, 74;
   "public forum" doctrine of the, 82–83; state
   action doctrine of the, 75–76; state of exception in the, 133–135. *See also* September 11,
   2001 attacks
Unity Council (Oakland), 95, 96
universal human rights, 204; declaration of, 387
University of California at Berkeley's Haas
   Center for Diversity and Inclusion, 124
urban infrastructure: designed to be occupied,
   339–350; divider of public space function of,
   225–226; how gatherings can be facilitated
   by, 301; how our future is determined by,
   224–225; importance of design to, 220;
   Oakland City Hall and Frank H. Ogawa
   plaza space, 309, 313–322; Occupation and
   importance of, 222–223; West Hollywood
   Civic Center, 322–326*fig*. *See also* architectural designs
Urban Justice Center, 289
Urban Parks and Open Space (Garvin), 229
urban planning: creating negotiative spaces
   of marginalized places, 136–138; emplacing practice of, 138–139; examining how it
   maintains illusion of public space, 135–139;
   how public space is determined by, 299–308;
   for occupation, 339–350; OWS as call for
   action by, 383–385; perspectives on POPS,
   351–363; promoting invisibility in image of
   the city, 135–136
urban renewal: Bryant Park's (NYC) restoration,
   346; CSI's model of community economic
   development for, 121–122; designing and
   redesigning for occupation and, 339–350;
   Metropolitan Museum's restoration,

346–347*fig*; Occupy Pittsburgh movement
   focused on, 99–111. *See also* inner cities;
   rebuilding strategies
US Steel, 8, 37
utilitatis concept, 219–220

Van Alen Institute, 332
Vietnam War demonstrations, 309
Village of Arts and Humanity (Philadelphia),
   95–96
violence: of Draft Riots (1863) in NYC, 192;
   of Orange Day marches (1871) in NYC,
   192; right to assembly without, 247–248,
   250, 283–284, 300
virtual space: behaviors in, 369, 376; community benefits from, 381; role of tweeting in
   political upheavals, 377. *See also* Facebook
Vitruvius, 217–218, 230

Walker, P., 223, 324
Walker v. Birmingham (US), 119
walking/walkers: the Dutch *woonerf* transition
   to, 337; Great Britain's paths for, 271–273;
   how POPS discourages, 334–335; NYC
   CityBenches program for, 296; NYC DOT's
   promotion of bicycle and sidewalks, 336–
   337; NYC DOT's Weekend Walks program
   and Summer Streets to encourage, 296;
   opening streets and sidewalks for, 294, 296,
   334–338; Times Square (NYC), 294
Walk the Talk (performance), 150–151
Wall Street (NYC), 8
wall (*weall*), 223–224
Washington D.C.: L'Enfant plan commissioned by Washington and Jefferson for,
   335; memorials which are also civic space
   in, 335; National Mall in, 302–303, 363,
   367; Occupy camp on Freedom Plaza,
   349*fig*; protest locations in, 209*fig*, 211*fig*;
   public space restrictions in, 245; Vietnam
   War demonstrations in, 309
Washington Square Park (NYC), 214, 217
Weekend Walks program (NYC DOT), 296
West Hollywood Civic Center: descending
   into the Calle de Politica, 325*fig*; design
   contest and planning for, 309, 310, 322–326;
   entry plaza with the Tower of Light and
   Achievement, 326*fig*; peering through San
   Vicente Portico, 325*fig*; previous recreational uses as open space, 324; proposed
   plan for the, 325*fig*
#whOWNSpace (Who Owns Space), 44, 166,
   167*fig*, 168
Whyte, W. H., 38, 40, 43–44, 281, 334, 337,
   338, 341, 346
Wiley, M., 112–124, 373
Wiley-Shiffman interview, 112–124
Wilson, K., 152–153
women: Antigone's understanding of demo-

cratic agora, 189–190; conversation invented by, 205; excluded from the agora in ancient Greece, 199; NYC voters among Bangladeshi, 290; protesting in Cairo, 206; social movements based on redressing marginalization of, 125

Woobly demonstrations (NYC), 193–194

woonerf (Netherlands), 337

World Trade Center (WTC): cold impersonality of the, 179; Jonathan Rose's proposal for memorial site of, 365; life and death in public place of, 178–179, 347. *See also* Ground Zero

Wylie Avenue Days (documentary), 104

Yagopartal, 9, 11

Yeats, W. B., 29

Yellow Cab Company, 240

Yoyogi Park (Tokyo), 89, 90*fig*

Zócola (Mexico City), 303

zoning codes: developer's chafing against NYC's, 35–36; governing the design of POPS, 167; how they shape public space, 327; NYCPD public space requirements, 8, 12–13, 25n.1, 35–39, 44–47, 76, 77–80, 85–86, 278–283; NYC's creation of privatized spaces using, 35–39; NYC's public space requirement, 12–13, 25n.1, 46–47; NYC Zoning Resolution (1961), 281, 282; regarding property owner's deviation of NYC public access, 44–45, 79–80, 85–86. *See also* New York City Planning Department

Zuccotti, J., 209

Zuccotti Park (NYC): aerial maps of protest locations of, 208*fig*, 210*fig*; as agora of life of the city, 21; annual 9/11 anniversary commemorations hosted at, 181; behavior not permitted in, 77–78; chosen as the original site of Occupy Wall Street movement, 7–8, 367; continued use by public during occupation, 41*fig*; creation of, 37–38; damaged on September 11, 2001 and reopened in 2006, 8, 77, 207–213, 281–282; examining the public space occupation in, 3; Fulton Street Transit Hub construction near, 223*fig*; "held in trust for the use of the public" status of, 75, 76; legal management of political dissent in, 17–18; New York City Planning Commission regulatory control of, 8, 76, 77–78, 278–283; OWS transforming it into insurgent space, 92*fig*–93, 209, 211; photographed before and after OWS occupation, 212*fig*, 301*fig*; physical description of, 8; as POPS, 52–53, 59, 139, 248–249, 278–283, 361; post-OWS regulatory outcome for, 45–46; requests for public access to, 44–45,

79–80, 85–86; state action doctrine and circumstances of administration of, 75–76, 78–82. *See also* Brookfield Properties; Liberty Plaza Park (now Zuccotti Park) [NYC]

Zuccotti Park occupation: anniversaries (2012) of the, 28–31; Bloomberg's focus on sanitation of, 42, 61, 62, 65, 66; Breenan Cavanaugh interview on, 49–60; camping prior to ban enforced at, 11*fig*; clashes between police and activists during, 8, 24, 26–28, 30–31, 49–50, 52, 256; confrontation on Broadway over, 216*fig*; constitutional issues raised by, 74–86; continued public use during, 41*fig*; day after the raid during, 59*fig*; demonstrators' manner of living in, 9, 13–17, 23, 43*fig*, 49–59*fig*; drumming during the, 15*fig*; evictions (November 15) of the, 8, 26–28; evolution and negotiation during, 12–17, 34, 42–47; examined in context of democratic governance and constitutional issues, 265–270; first days of, 21–25; General Assembly (GA) role during, 55–58*fig*; generating electricity during, 15*fig*; handmade signs and posters used by occupiers of, 9, 23, 49–50*fig*, 51*fig*, 52*fig*, 57*fig*, 58*fig*, 59*fig*; J. Seward Johnson statue with mask during, 9, 10*fig*; keeping the public from using park, 348–349; the Library and Information Center set up during, 9, 10*fig*, 13, 14, 73, 228*fig*; loudspeakers and bullhorns banned during, 9; maps of, 5*fig*, 14*fig*; message sent by participants of, 266; mobilization through, 97; painting during, 12*fig*; people of color participating in, 117–124; photographed before and after, 212*fig*, 301*fig*; policy of searching OWS activists for sleeping bags during, 83, 84–85; POPS aspect of, 52–53, 59, 139; practicality as OWS site, 267; public forum doctrine and, 119, 367; radical imagination perspective of, 146–155; relationship between demonstrators and passerbys during, 11–12, 16; returning to, 231*fig*; revealing loss of civic capacity in privatized public space, 248–249, 335–338, 351–352, 361; sanitation issues during, 53–54*fig*, 55–56*fig*, 61–62; *Saturday Night Live* (SNL) satire on Bloomberg and, 61, 62, 65; Sign Field in first weeks of, 57*fig*; tents used during, 348*fig*; videography (March 21, 2012) of the, 31–32. *See also* New York City; OWS (Occupy Wall Street)

Zucker, P., 241

Zukin, S., 93